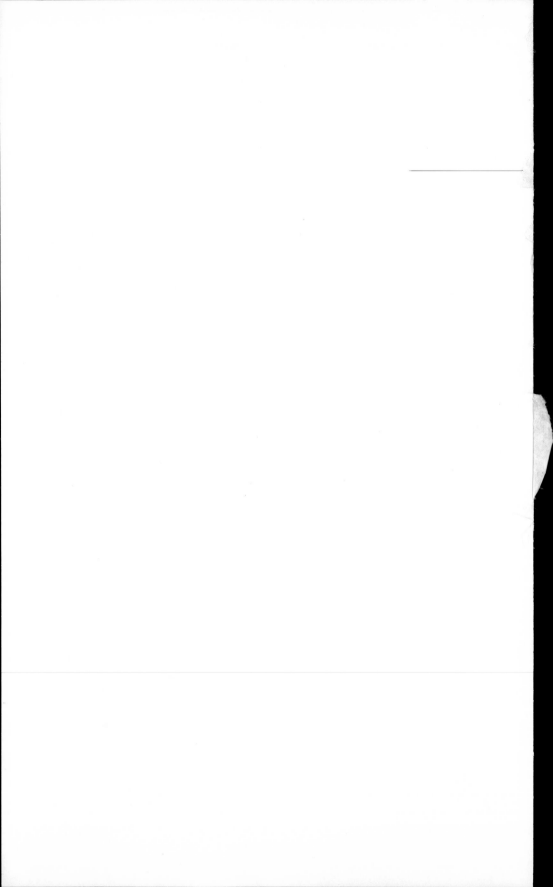

Hermeneutics of Holiness

Hermeneutics of Holiness

Ancient Jewish and Christian Notions
of Sexuality and Religious Community

NAOMI KOLTUN-FROMM

OXFORD
UNIVERSITY PRESS

2010

OXFORD
UNIVERSITY PRESS

Oxford University Press, Inc., publishes works that further
Oxford University's objective of excellence
in research, scholarship, and education.

Oxford   New York
Auckland   Cape Town   Dar es Salaam   Hong Kong   Karachi
Kuala Lumpur   Madrid   Melbourne   Mexico City   Nairobi
New Delhi   Shanghai   Taipei   Toronto

With offices in
Argentina   Austria   Brazil   Chile   Czech Republic   France   Greece
Guatemala   Hungary   Italy   Japan   Poland   Portugal   Singapore
South Korea   Switzerland   Thailand   Turkey   Ukraine   Vietnam

Published by Oxford University Press, Inc.
198 Madison Avenue, New York, New York 10016

www.oup.com

Oxford is a registered trademark of Oxford University Press

Library of Congress Cataloging-in-Publication Data
Koltun-Fromm, Naomi, 1964–
Hermeneutics of holiness : ancient Jewish and Christian notions of
sexuality and religious community / by Naomi Koltun-Fromm.
   p. cm.
ISBN 978-0-19-973648-5
1. Sex—Biblical teaching. 2. Communities—Biblical teaching.
3. Holiness—Biblical teaching. 4. Bible—Extra-canonical parallels.
I. Title.
BS680.S5K65   2010
241′.660915—dc22   2009030183

9 8 7 6 5 4 3 2 1

Printed in the United States of America
on acid-free paper

for Ken, Ariel, Talia, and Isaiah

Acknowledgments

This book started as an idea in the summer of 2000; a summer that I
spent in Berlin not learning any German. Sitting in the Staatsbibliothek in Berlin, not understanding a word of the conversations
flowing around me allowed me to focus my thoughts on holiness. I
thank the staff of the Staatsbibliothek for giving me that space. That
same summer, at a meeting of the European Association of Biblical
Studies in Utrecht, my idea to trace biblical notions of holy-peoplehood gained more clarity and support from the colleagues I met there
(Gary Porton, Lieve Teugels, Joshua Levenson, and Marcel Poorthuis,
to name just a few.) The summer was followed by an exceptional
sabbatical year during which my family and I were hosted by Wolfson
College, Oxford University, and the Oxford Centre for Hebrew and
Jewish Studies, Yarnton Manor. (I was also supported financially by
Haverford College and by a fellowship from The Foundation for
Jewish Culture that year.) In the various and numerous libraries of
Oxford I read copious books on biblical holiness and purity; and by
the end of the year I had a better sense of both. Martin Goodman,
Sebastian Brock, and Alison Salveson generously offered their time
and conversation to me. Martin graciously allowed me to participate
in his graduate seminar and often took me to lunch in the Common
Room, providing both spiritual and physical sustenance. The communities of scholars and families that we met up with and participated in
provided the needed intellectual atmosphere for pursuing

research in an engaging environment. To all our friends in Oxford, thank you for being there!

The following year I returned to Haverford College and to a fellowship at the University of Pennsylvania Center for Advanced Judaic Studies. At the Center I was able to write the first version of what became chapter 6 in this book. Again, the stimulating and engaging atmosphere of the Center, and the colleagues I met that year (Natalie Dohrman, Dalit Ram Shiloni, and Tamar Kadari, to name a few), gave me the collegial support to push forward and produce. Thank you David Ruderman, David Stern, and the staff of the Center for supporting such a wonderful group that year.

Over the next several years I progressed from holiness in the Bible, to the Second Temple Literature, to the early Christian literature, Syriac literature, Aphrahat, and finally the Rabbis. I thank all of my colleagues at Haverford for their enduring support and encouragement. The members of the Department of Religion, but especially David Dawson and Anne McGuire, read various chapters over the years and simply lent their collegial support. Over these same years numerous students have read various drafts and helped me pull things together, especially the students in my seminar on holiness.

My first readers at the University of Pennsylvania Press helped me transform this manuscript from a draft to a book, even if our visions of the final edition eventually differed. I thank you. My readers at Oxford University Press were amazing: pushing me to see things I had not seen before, and allowing me to let go of the unnecessary. Eliezer Diamond not only read an early draft of chapter 7, but at the behest of Oxford read and commented on the whole manuscript, and chapter 7 yet again. Thank you for all your continued and enduring support and encouragement. I want to give a special thanks to my other, anonymous, reader, who read so thoroughly the first time, and then agreed to do it again, you are tremendous!

I returned to Yarnton in the summer of 2008 to participate in an NEH institute. But during my free time I was able to pursue and (mostly) complete the revisions of this manuscript, so once again I thank the people of Yarnton Manor for giving me space to write surrounded by their beautiful landscape.

Many other colleagues answered queries, read passages and even whole chapters over the last decade. Forgive me if I have forgotten anyone: Ellen Birnbaum, David Brodsky, Georgia Frank, Paula Fredriksen, Christine Hayes, Martha Himmelfarb, Marc Hirshman, Jonathan Klawans, Vasiliki Lamberis, Deborah Roberts, Christine Shepardson, Benjamin Sommer, Lucas Van Rompay, and Andrea Weiss. No book is complete without the expert guidance of one's editors: Thank you to Cynthia Read, Linda Donnelly, and their staff at Oxford University Press. I thank my father, who came out of retirement to do some last minute proofreading, as well. Last but not least, I must thank my family, my husband Ken, my children Ariel, Talia, and Isaiah, who have put up with me and this book for way too long. I dedicate this book to them. It's done!

Contents

Abbreviations

AJT	*Acts of Judah Thomas*
ANF	*Ante-Nicene Fathers*
ARN	*Avot de Rabbi Nathan*
BDB	F. Brown, S. R. Drivers, C. A. Briggs, eds. *A Hebrew and English Lexicon of the Old Testament*
BT	Babylonian Talmud
CSCO	Corpus Scriptorum Christianorum Orientalium
FOTC	Fathers of the Church series, Catholic University
LXX	Septuagint
MT	Massoretic text
NJB	New Jerusalem Bible
NJPS	Tanakh and the Holy Scriptures: The New Jewish Publication Society Translation
NPNF	*The Nicene and Post-Nicene Fathers of the Christian Church*
NRSV	New Revised Standard Version Bible translation
OJSB	Oxford Jewish Study Bible
PT	Palestinian Talmud
RSV	Revised Standard Version Bible translation
TDOT	Theological Dictionary of the Old Testament

A Note on Translation

To make this book an easier read for the nonspecialist, I have elimi-
nated almost all of the Hebrew, Greek, and Syriac texts. I have
attempted to transliterate where necessary in the most phonetic ways
possible, not following any standard transliteration system, with a few
minor exceptions. In Hebrew and Syriac I have doubled some letters
where a hard sound warrants it. In Hebrew and Syriac I have added
diacritics to differentiate the *hey* (h) from the *ḥet* (ḥ) and in Syriac further the *semkat* (s) from the *ṣadhe* (ṣ) and the *ṭet* (ṭ) from the *tau* (t). In
Hebrew I differentiate between the *alef* (') and the *ayin* ('). In Greek I
differentiate between an *omicron* (o) and an *omega* (ô) and an *epsilon* (e)
and an *eta* (ê).

Hermeneutics of Holiness

Introduction

In mid-fourth-century Persian Mesopotamia, a Syriac Christian named Aphrahat writes the following:

I write you my beloved concerning virginity and holiness [qaddishuta] because I have heard from a Jewish man that insulted one of the brothers, members of our congregation, by saying to him: You are impure [tam'in] you who do not marry women; but we are holy [qaddishin] and better, [we] who procreate and increase progeny in the world.[1]

With this short notice, Aphrahat underscores a major polemical confrontation of his time: the debate over "holiness" and its relationship to sexual practices. Is holiness attained by a life of marriage and procreation (as the Jews in this text maintain) or, instead, by its opposite—a life of sexual asceticism and abstinence (as Aphrahat claims)? These are two very distant worlds, yet both assert holiness. Who is right? How is human holiness manifested on earth? The answer is important because the holy are those who will live forever in God's midst, a position for which both Jews and Christians vied. Yet, the quest of the present book is not, of course, to pinpoint an answer to this age-old question of holiness, one that will continue to follow us into the distant future. Instead the book's goal is to reveal this ancient nexus of holiness and sexuality and to explore its roots in the biblical texts, as well as its manifestations throughout ancient and late-ancient Judaism and early Syriac Christianity.[2] In particular the

book examines the biblical exegetical underpinnings of Aphrahat's hermeneutic of holiness (which explicitly links holiness with celibacy, but does not
relegate marriage to impurity) and places it within his fourth-century Aramaic
milieu by way of comparison to the rabbinic culture that flourished simultaneously in the same Persian-Mesopotamian context, as well as to the post-biblical literature that preceded them both.[3]

Interestingly, Aphrahat and the early Rabbis understand the nature of
holiness in a similar way and both build their hermeneutics of holiness and
sexuality on related exegetical traditions and interpretive methods. Yet the two
groups arrive at very different practical conclusions for how holiness itself
should be achieved. I contend that the polemic discourse of these two groups
is but a manifestation of these developing communities' essential need for
self-definition, both internally and against the other, as well as in relationship
to God. In the end, Aphrahat's links between virginity, celibacy, and biblically
inspired holiness become his hermeneutic of holiness—it is how he rationalizes and physically demonstrates his elevated relationship to God (and hence
salvation) in distinctly physical human terms. Although posited here in opposition to Jewish constructs of holiness and their resultant practices, it resonates
deeply within early rabbinic thought as well. Sexual asceticism, the direct result
of Aphrahat's interpretive move, manifests itself as sexual restraint, if not full
abstinence, among certain layers of rabbinic tradition. Moreover, these practices embody or further demonstrate a practitioner's more intense relationship
to God, for both Aphrahat and the Rabbis.

This book suggests that sexual practices among Jews and Christians, particularly ascetic sexual practices, are rooted in the history of biblical exegesis
and tradition as much as in any other late-ancient phenomena. Moreover,
the book posits that holiness as sexual practice helped these groups demarcate
borders between communities. Hence, this book establishes the importance
of biblical interpretation for late-ancient Jewish and Christian practices,
the centrality of holiness as a category for self-definition, and fourth-century
asceticism's relationship to biblical texts and interpretive history.

In order to understand the process of biblical interpretation and the study
laid out here, it is necessary to define several key terms and issues, as follows.

Hermeneutics

While I admit to having chosen *hermeneutics* in part because of its appealing allit-
erative effects alongside *holiness* in the book's title and, in so doing, to slightly
stretching the term's usual semantic range, my deeper logic for selecting the

term follows. "Hermeneutics" is usually understood to be the study of the methodologies used in biblical exegesis and interpretation. I use it here more as a lens through which to view the variety of understandings of holiness itself. Phyllis Trible explains, in *God and the Rhetoric of Sexuality*, that her "topical clue" is "the image of God" and that her "hermeneutical clue" is "feminism as a critique of culture."[4] In a similar vein, I would like to claim for my subjects that their topic is holiness, and their "hermeneutic" is sexuality. That is, I, as a scholar, am interested here in those biblical texts (and the biblical exegesis built upon them) in which holiness is described as somehow connected to human sexuality. Hence, when I write of different "hermeneutics" of holiness, I am thinking of the different ways in which my subjects have constructed their notions of holiness, how these notions both exist in and are linked exegetically to the biblical texts, and how these notions manifest themselves in sexual practices.

Holiness

Biblical scholars and academic theorists of religion have attempted to define holiness with varying results. In the early twentieth century, Rudolf Otto, perhaps reacting to social-scientific constructions of religion as human creations, focused on the intangible yet ineffable nature of the holy and therefore defined holiness as the numinous and awesome part of God that no human could possibly understand or achieve, for it belongs solely to God and is in fact what differentiates the divine from the mundane. It is the element of God that most attracts humans, but it is also the reason they cannot know God fully. Moreover, for Otto, it has no physical manifestation and it was shared with only one human in history, Jesus. It is through Jesus that true Christians will become holy ones of God in the next world. But this world retains no physical manifestations of the holy.[5] Building on Otto, but acknowledging certain positions in the scientific study of religion, Mircea Eliade perceived God's holiness in the world around him and in the humans that populate that world. Humans and the divine work together to create and maintain holiness in this world. Places can be holy (as portals to the divine), objects can be imbued with holiness, and people who pursue God can become holy as well.[6] Holiness for Eliade is not just an otherworldly substance that remains elusive to most humans, but is a tangible characteristic of this world. It is God's gift to the world, but it requires constant maintenance by humans. Thus, Eliade and Otto each focused on different elements of holiness as they see it manifested in the world, yet its ultimate source remains God or the divine, however understood. The holy, as a manifestation of God, is transcendent for Eliade and Otto. It cannot be in and of itself a human construct.

Note that I will use the English terms *holy* and *sacred* interchangeably, as they both equally translate the Hebrew root קְדֹשׁ (QDS), which is the focus of this study. Yet I acknowledge that the terms have been distinguished from each other. According to Williard G. Oxtoby, *holy* in general refers to God and the things that God consecrates, while *sacred* is used to describe special or venerated objects. Our bible, for instance, is "holy" while other cultures have "sacred" literature. The key is in the source of the "holiness." That which humans revere as holy is only sacred, unless also consecrated by God.[7] This differentiation between "God-made" and "human-made" holiness proves useful to my discussion, for both types appear within the biblical constructs. While holiness clearly is fundamentally a divine characteristic, other things, places, and people come to be holy (i.e., to participate in the divine) as well. So, for instance, God is holy and therefore can consecrate things to himself: land, sanctuary, or priests. But humans, too, can consecrate items to God (sacrifices, offerings) and sometimes even themselves (the case of the *nazir* is interesting here, as it is a temporary holiness). So while acknowledging the difference between the divine (holy) and the human (profane), the biblical worldview allows for an in-between space in which humans can participate in that divinity either by appointment (e.g., the priest) or by ritualized action (e.g., the *nazir*).[8] This book is an exploration of how Jews and Christians reconstructed that in-between space in their own time and place in the first centuries of the Common Era. While I may describe one group's holiness as "ascribed" (i.e., given at birth) and another as "achieved" (i.e., acquired through ritualized behavior), my subjects most likely saw them as manifestations of the same thing: holiness.

Holiness, then, for late-ancient Jews and Christians, is, on the one hand, the most valued attribute of the God of the Hebrew Scriptures. Yet, on the other hand, sharing in that divine attribute marks a person or community as belonging to God and, hence, as being elevated above other human beings. Moreover, this special relationship with God in this world positions one for privileged placement in the next: salvation. Holiness is a manifestation of power—whether physically in this world or existentially in the next. According to the biblical text, God chose Israel from among all the nations to be that special people—the holy nation of God. In so doing God promised to protect Israel from its enemies. But who in the first, second, third, or fourth century CE could claim exclusive lineage from Ancient and Holy Israel, and therefore be that community with sole access to divine protection? Furthermore, how did they prove it? From the beginnings of the Second Judean Commonwealth[9], various groups competed for that very title. Second Commonwealth Jews, as well as

Jews and Christians in the early centuries of the Common Era, developed their respective communal religious identities out of a shared notion of exclusive access to God. If one community had divine access, the other surely could not. But how could one tell who was holy in this world and hence saved in the next? Retaining or gaining that title, as a community, remained of paramount importance to fourth-century Christians and Jews as it did for their ancestors. In these centuries, the groups who eventually became "Christian" and "Jewish" struggled to separate themselves from each other. Holiness loomed as a fulcrum of difference at the center of these struggles. The community that could prove its exclusive claim to holiness prevailed.

Holiness, Sexuality, and Purity

As we have seen, Aphrahat achieves his holiness through his sexual practices, calling his practice of sexual renunciation "holiness" in his native Syriac (*qaddishuta*). Aphrahat also uses Scripture to forge the link between holiness and sexual practices; yet he is not the first to do so. Even before the Hebrew biblical canon could be constructed as "secured,"[10] biblical exegetes mined its narratives, poetry, prophecies, and law codes for usable prooftexts of holiness. They too often discovered, uncovered, or created a connection between specific sexual practices and individual or community holiness. Here unfolds, then, a history of holiness—specifically of holy people (not places or things), that proves to be dependent on human sexuality—from its biblical beginnings. Aphrahat's hermeneutic of holiness and sexual practices, as well as the chronologically and geographically parallel rabbinic traditions on holiness and sexual practices, are case studies of this long and complex development.

The quotation at the opening of this chapter shows that, for Aphrahat, holiness is linked to celibacy through some notion of purity; in other words, for him, chastity, purity, and holiness fall under a single religious rubric. Yet, while it is impossible to discuss holiness without reference to purity, they are not one and the same. In the biblical context, one pursues purity in order to protect or achieve holiness. But purity can be procured without any attainment of holiness. Holiness ultimately comes from God. It is God's to give or take away, and therefore it remains on another level, above and beyond purity. The deserving person or community will be granted holiness at God's will. The pure person has potential but has not yet won the key to the prize. Ambiguities and inconsistencies in the biblical texts leave the holy pursuer at a loss as how ultimately to gain that key. Different hermeneutics of holiness, even within the biblical texts, offer different answers.

In recent years, notions of purity and impurity have been discussed at length by scholars such as Jonathan Klawans (*Impurity and Sin in Ancient Judaism*) and Christine Hayes (*Gentile Impurities and Jewish Identities.*)[11] Like Klawans and Hayes, I trace an intellectual and exegetical history of a biblical concept. While they focus on purity and impurity, I focus on holiness. Nevertheless I am beholden to both authors for their insights and categorizations, for an understanding of biblical and post-biblical purity constructs is essential for comprehending paradigms of holiness. Purity exists for the sake of holiness. How one understands the dynamic between the two is a key to one's construct of holiness. Klawans argues that the biblical texts present two competing notions of purity (one "ritual" and one "moral").[12] I argue that the biblical texts also present several paradigms of holiness, which are in part dependent on these two different systems of purity.[13] What is of interest to me is not so much when and where the two categories of purity cross paths (this is Klawans's study) but when and where the paradigms of holiness intersect with the various systems of purity. For when there is confusion between the categories of purity and holiness, sexuality is often present and even the agent of that confusion.

Sexuality becomes the fulcrum for many of the prevailing post-biblical hermeneutics of holiness because of sexuality's presence in various forms in the biblical systems of purity defined by Klawans. Semen, for instance, is a physical pollutant that must be removed in order to achieve "ritual" purity so as to protect the holy presence of God (e.g., Lev. 15). Removing an impurity renders one pure, for God's protection, but does not change one's status vis-à-vis the holy. Forbidden sexual practices, such as bestiality, sleeping with a menstruant, and incest all fall into the category of "moral" impurity that opposes holiness (e.g., Lev. 18, 20). Avoiding the latter practices renders one "morally" pure, which then allows one to enter the holy community. Hence, pure behavior here does have something to do with the possibility of advancing to a holy status. But later texts (e.g., Jubilees) instruct the Israelites to behave purely in order to protect an ascribed holiness in the people, not just in God. Hence, purity here also protects an innate holiness. Thus, the differences between purity as a protective fence around God's holiness and purity as a protection around Israel's holiness begin to collapse. Furthermore, when a purity practice (e.g., avoiding incest or bathing after the voiding of a "ritual" impurity such as semen) becomes a means to achieving holiness in and of itself, a new hermeneutic of holiness and sexuality emerges. Hence, Aphrahat's choice of celibacy (chapters 5 and 6), and the Rabbis' suggestions of ethnic endogamy, on the one hand, and sexual restraint, on the other (chapter 7) fall within a several-centuries-long continuum of exegetical discourse on proper marriage partners, sexuality, purity, and holiness.

This book traces that discourse from the biblical texts through the Second Temple literature and early Christian writings into the Jewish (rabbinic) and Christian (Syriac) exegetical writings of the fourth century.

Within these texts and traditions I highlight two prominent paradigms. In the first, the holiness of Israel is assumed (that is, God ascribes holiness to them) and hence their sexual practices protect their innate holiness. In this case, in order to maintain one's God-given holiness, one must limit one's marriage partners to other members of one's holy community (endogamy). In the second, achieved holiness is the goal. That is, whether or not one might be of an ascribed holy community, the community also maintains that there are means or methods to improve on, elevate, or change one's holy status. One often achieves or gains this holiness through sexual restraint. The notion that the ability to stand in God's presence, to participate somehow in divine holiness, requires some sort of sexual restraint pervades the achieved-holiness construct. In contrast, for the person whose holiness is ascribed—gained at birth—endogamy proves to be the best protection.

As Martha Himmelfarb has argued, the biblical phrase "a kingdom of priests" expresses an important tension that is central to understanding ancient Judaism.[14] This phrase refers to the notion that Israel, the nation, is or becomes holy through God's choosing of it at Sinai, in imitation of God's "choosing" the priests from among Israel to be God's holy servants. The tensions Himmelfarb describes between priests by birth and those who win priesthood by merit map outwards to all of Israel (whether "Jewish" or "Christian"), when Israel considers itself to be holy as a "kingdom of priests." Are they holy by birth or did they do something to deserve to be called holy? While Himmelfarb focuses on the priesthood, the present study moves toward an exploration of the figure of Moses, for at Sinai he manifests himself as the leader of this newly chosen "kingdom of priests." But the question often raised about him by later authors is: why was he chosen from among Israel, if he himself was not a priest?

Moses—the prophet of God, the leader of the Hebrew Exodus from Egypt, and the one biblical character allowed to speak "mouth to mouth" with God—arises as the exemplary holy man because of his sexual choices (in his case giving up his married life). And it is here that we see an enduring fusion or cross breeding between notions of holiness—both ascribed (given to Moses by God) and achieved (attained by Moses through his sexual choices). We also see a fusion here between holiness and purity. At Sinai, God instructs Moses to direct the people to prepare themselves for Revelation. They must purify themselves by washing their clothing and abstaining from sexual contact for three days. An exegetical tradition as old as Philo, if not older, suggests that if the Israelites had to be celibate for three days, Moses, who was constantly in God's presence must have had to give up his conjugal life for his leadership role. Moses rises as both unique in his role and as a model to follow. For the Rabbis, he is Moses our teacher (*Moshe Rabbeinu*), the model rabbi who passes on rabbinic lore and law to his faithful disciples and spiritual descendants, the Rabbis, who represent and lead the descendants of holy Israel, the Jews. For Aphrahat, Moses is the quintessential mystic—the one human being who achieves the ultimate mystical goal: communion (or even union) with the divine. Moreover, Moses' achievements can be emulated by his followers, the *ihidaye* (single-minded ones), by copying his behavior at Sinai. The celibate Moses on Sinai, a tradition upheld by both the Rabbis and Aphrahat, suggests a culminating fusion of the various paradigms discussed in this book: singular devotion to God, sexual purity, and holiness. Finally, Aphrahat's laudatory praise of Moses places Aphrahat more solidly in his Aramaic milieu and differentiates him from his Greek and Latin counterparts.[15]

Holiness and Ethics

Scholars who discuss "moral" impurity (even as a separate category from "ritual" impurity) often describe it as an impurity created by sin. Thus, one can talk about the "defiling nature of sin." But what happens to this person so defiled? If he were already holy, does he lose his status? If one manages to avoid all the sins enumerated, can he become holy? If so, does this mean that anyone can become holy? This line of thinking often leads to a seemingly related conclusion: if sin (general or specific) is equated with "moral" impurity and "moral" impurity stands in opposition to holiness, is the holy one sinless? That is, if one can be sinless, is one necessarily holy? Moreover, while one can certainly argue that the levitical holiness code is in part an ethical code, it is more difficult to determine whether all biblical hermeneutics of holiness contain the same or any ethical component.[16] The post-biblical discussions of holiness are equally opaque and difficult to understand on exclusively ethical grounds. If one begins with the premise that an Israelite is inherently holy (as many of the post-biblical texts do), how can she lose her status through sin? Or, from another angle, do all sins tarnish holiness, or just grievous sins? Furthermore, to suggest an exclusively ethical or moral understanding of holiness is equally misleading.[17] At times it can be claimed that holiness is linked to "good behavior," but at others it is not. I have chosen to avoid such terms as "sin" and "moral" in order not to be tied to a notion of holiness as strictly (or even remotely related to) an ethical code of behavior. Moreover, the authors examined here do not necessarily link their ideas of holiness to ethical or moral behavior and I do not wish to do so for them. For the authors and exegetes of this study, holiness remains an indescribable, yet quintessentially valuable attribute of God, an embodiment of divine power. The focus of this book is not the ethical implications of holiness but, rather, its sexual implications. That is, how sexual practices, when mapped onto notions of holiness, become markers of community identity.

Holiness and Asceticism

Even within the biblical texts, I argue, it is possible to foresee the tendency to link holiness with sexuality that develops among certain groups in the post-biblical period. I contend that for these exegetes who pick up on this particular hermeneutic, they also integrate it into the foundations of their ascetic practices.[18] Elizabeth Clark, in her book *Reading Renunciation*, argues that certain Western Church fathers read their already established ascetic practices back into the biblical texts, rather than exegeting it out of the text. She argues that they were compelled to read asceticism back into the biblical texts in order both to further support their practices and to reclaim the rather procreative-oriented Hebrew Scriptures as truly Christian and hence ascetic.[19] Yet Clark concedes, in contrast to the flow of much modern scholarship on Christian asceticism, that asceticism was not imported from the outside culture, such as Hellenism, nor was it motivated by politics or social pressures.[20] Rather, she understands Christian asceticism as a phenomenon or tendency already present in the New Testament writings. The very first generations of Christians read and understood their developing Christian canon in various ways. Some chose to understand Paul, for instance, in a more ascetical way than others. These Christians then composed their own ascetically inclined tracts, such as the *Apocryphal Acts of the Apostles*, which present Christianity as a sexually renunciative religion. Others, such as the authors of the Pastoral Epistles, promote an anti-ascetic practice.[21]

Yet both groups claim dependence on Paul, and thus if we can argue that Paul pushes the envelope toward or around ascetic practice, can we ask what motivates Paul? I would like to suggest that some element of Paul's "ascetic" roots (that is, not whether he was or wasn't ascetic, but that others perceived him to be) can be linked to the constructs of holiness that evolve out of the Hebrew biblical and post-biblical literature. Like Clark I do not wish to impose an outside motivation toward asceticism on my subjects, yet in contrast to Clark, I wish to uncover, if possible, an internal motivation—one based on their reading and interpretation of Hebrew Scripture. Thus, while I also agree with Clark that the late ancient Christian theologians attempted to "asceticize" the more procreative elements of the Hebrew Scriptures, I argue that a native ascetic tendency also existed within these texts side by side with the more pronounced procreative elements. This element was particularly wrapped up within ancient biblical notions of holiness, a tendency that was picked up most avidly among the Aramaic-speaking (and reading) Christians. I wish to emphasize here that asceticism did not appear on the scene as something new in the fourth century but has deep roots in the biblical texts and particularly in the early interpretive history of some of those texts.

In Aphrahat's case, then, one could similarly suggest that Aphrahat "read renunciation" back into his biblical texts. Yet, I would argue that his theology of asceticism is more strongly linked to an exegesis of text, particularly of holiness, rather than a retroactive eisegesis as Clark posits for her Church fathers (Origen, Jerome, and Chrysostom). I further claim, in part, that this is due to Aphrahat's Aramaic (non-Greco-Roman) background. I attempt to show here that the ascetic practices of Syriac Christians are inherently tied to their hermeneutics of holiness—that is, to their exegetical and scriptural reading strategies. In other words, without arguing for or against "outside influences," I suggest that Syriac Christian asceticism can, in part, be traced back to very early exegetical expansions on notions of holiness and community derived from a reconfiguration of the various biblical hermeneutics of holiness that worked best in an Aramaic linguistic context. Moreover, Moses plays a primary role in these exegetes' ascetical imaginations.

Following a different line of argument, Kathy Gaca points to the primacy of the Septuagint in earlier Greek ascetical writings. Namely, she suggests that Greek Christian ascetic practices can be tied directly to their septuagintal readings. Gaca, arguing against what she calls the "continuity thesis," in which she counters Foucault among others, claims that Paul, Philo, Clement, and Tatian's ascetic tendencies are essentially more dependent on the Septuagint than on any other Greek or Hellenistic philosophical writings. Likewise, social historians miscalculate the possible rationales for Christian asceticism when they underestimate their philosophical and biblical theoretical underpinnings. Nonetheless, Gaca leaves plenty of room for cross-fertilization and philosophical enhancement from the various Hellenistic philosophies she examines in parallel to her Church fathers. While I strongly disagree with many of Gaca's specific readings of the Septuagint and the way it was interpreted in the Greco-Roman milieu, I support her argument that the Hebrew Scriptures, in whatever version or translation, played an important if not primary role in many Church authors' formative ascetical theologies. The Syriac Christian trajectory is but one very strong example.[22] In the end, Gaca argues that Paul and Philo are not moral philosophers under the influences of the Stoics and Pythagoreans but, rather, function as acculturated Greeks, for they read their Bible in Greek and this is what influences them most.

It is the particular nuances of the Greek biblical text that most directly affect their particular sexual politics. Gaca focuses on the commandment against adultery and its placement among the ten commandments as primary support for the ascetic tendencies of Paul and Philo. In contrast, for Paul at least, I argue that it is Paul's understanding of holiness, as inherited from his Second Temple Jewish background, that most influences his thinking on sexuality. Finally, it also seems fair to argue that it is Paul's hermeneutic of holiness, in Aramaic garb, that also proves foundational to Syriac Christian ascetic practice.

While most authors who study Christian asceticism focus on its manifestations in the Greco-Roman world, I focus on Syriac Christianity because of its Mesopotamian-Aramaic milieu.[23] Syriac Christianity develops an ascetic practice and theology essentially different from its Greco-Roman counterparts in that sexual renunciation appears as fundamental to Syriac Christian belief (at least in its earliest forms as embodied in the *Acts of Judah Thomas*, for example) and is founded on an enduring image of the oneness of the believer's dedication to God. These two concepts are interrelated in Syriac Christianity: it is because of the theology of oneness that sexual renunciation becomes fundamental. So, while the existence of asceticism, and particularly the practice of sexual asceticism in Syriac Christianity, does not differ greatly from other Christianities— sexual renunciation can be found in most forms of early Christianity—its centrality and theological underpinnings in Syriac Christianity set it apart.

The Syrian Orient was most likely evangelized by Aramaic-speaking Christians probably not before the late second century.[24] No matter from where these missionaries originated, they most likely propagated an already ascetic Christianity (again as the *Acts of Judah Thomas* seems to testify, for Judah came from some place else to India). Nevertheless, asceticism is soon incorporated into the very core of Syriac Christian belief and practice. While early scholars such as Arthur Vööbus and Robert Murray argued that celibacy was a requirement for membership in the early Syriac Church almost from the beginning, this argument has been modified by others such as Sidney Griffith. Nonetheless celibacy certainly was a highly valued Christian practice.

Peter Brown suggests that there must have been something specific to the Syrian East that differentiated it from the Greco-Roman world that allowed this sort of asceticism to flourish during the second and third centuries, for the East was not only home to the Syriac churches, but also other ascetic groups such as Manichaeans and Marcionites. Brown surmises that the lack of large Greco-Roman cities in the Syrian hinterland, the harsh life there, no anti-Christian persecutions (in the early centuries at least), and the larger and more prosperous Jewish communities all added up to create a culture receptive to asceticism.[25]

Yet the lack of Greco-Roman culture, particularly its sense of moderation in all parts of life, and other cultural landmarks, can only be part of the answer.[26] Early Christianity did not land in a vacuous countryside, but into a thriving civilization with a distinctive, Aramaic culture of its own. The cities may not have been distinctly Greco-Roman, but they were vibrant in their own multicultural landscape. The Jewish communities thrived and suffered as the other communities did along with the economic fortunes of the Persian Empire. Certainly the culture of the East (or perhaps Christian reaction to the cultures of the East) fostered the growth of an ascetic Christianity, but it is equally possible that the ascetic tendencies of Christianity were already in place when the first missionaries arrived in the Syrian Orient. I suggest that those tendencies grew out of native Aramaic exegesis on a shared biblical text, as well as a dependency on an already asceticized Paul, and continued to flourish in the Aramaic cultural submilieu of Persian Mesopotamia. In other words, I posit a native Hebrew biblical ascetic tendency, found within its various hermeneutics of holiness, that is expanded upon and developed first by Jewish readers of Scripture and then by Christian readers, especially Paul. Moreover, these hermeneutical trajectories manifest themselves strongly within the Hebrew and Aramaic Jewish and Aramaic Christian writings of the third and fourth centuries.

Finally, the early Christians, particularly the Aramaic/Syriac speaking ones, were not the only biblical exegetes to connect holiness, sexuality, and asceticism. The early Rabbis, or some segment of that grouping, equally imagined the importance of that three-way equation. Not just that holiness and some sort of sexual practice go hand in hand, but more specifically that some restriction on sexual practices is innate to holy living or holy acquisition. Steven Fraade was the first to suggest that the Rabbis (and their predecessors among Second Commonwealth Jews) possessed and developed their own native asceticism.[27] Following on the pioneering scholarship of Steven Fraade, Eliezer Diamond, in his work, *Holy Men and Hunger Artists*, further establishes rabbinic ascetic patterns, based in notions of *perishut* and *nazirut*, especially in the area of food and fasting. While his argumentation does not link these practices strictly or exclusively to a hermeneutic of holiness, he establishes that the early Rabbis were no strangers to asceticism. Building on Diamond's framework, I show that the Rabbis were not strangers to sexual asceticism, either. Moreover, their sexually restrained practices often descend from their hermeneutics of holiness and compare in striking ways to Aphrahat's hermeneutics of holiness and sexuality—both of which are firmly grounded in Scripture and revolve around the image of Moses.

In short, Syriac Christian asceticism, as manifested in Aphrahat, and early rabbinic asceticism share an Aramaic biblical tradition and cultural milieu that bring their scriptural exercises closer together while differentiating them both from the biblical interpretive practices and cultural influences of the Greco-Roman West.

Holiness, Sexuality, and Community Boundaries

While one could argue that sexuality and holiness are linked exclusively on exegetical grounds, that argument would ignore the social-historical context in which these exegetes lived. Every one of the constructs of holiness presented here develops out of a need to create community boundaries. Each exegete faced real or perceived opponents who laid claim to or somehow threatened Israel's holiness. The Deuteronomist uses the threat of uncontrolled sexuality as leading to idolatry to draw borders between Holy Israel and its unholy neighbors. Ezra constructs his notion of the holy seed—which cannot mix with unholy seed—in order to designate the returning Judaeans alone as representing true Israel. Paul suggests that Christian holiness necessitates certain types of (restrained) sexual behavior, both to protect the Christian's holy status and also to mark her differentiation from the non-Christian. Aphrahat, too, looks to sexual renunciation as a means to differentiate Christians from Jews. So while these exegetes depend on biblical prooftexts to support the nexus between holiness and sexuality, their focus on sexuality also proves to be an indispensable tool for constructing community identity. Sexual practices come to the fore in this endeavor of boundary building because they can easily be defined and monitored. The competition for God's exclusive attention (holiness) combines practically with social mores (sexual practices) to produce defendable community borders.

Daniel Boyarin argues in his book, *Borderlines*, that constructing tangible borders was a major endeavor of both Jews and Christians in the early centuries of the Common Era.[28] This endeavor manifested itself particularly strongly among Christians who created categories of "orthodoxy" and "heresy" with which to police the boundaries of Christianity. Thus, "Judaism" was created as an opposing heretical religion that was out of bounds. Boyarin argues that, at first, the early Rabbis accepted this differentiation and attempted to create their own external boundaries and internal heresiologies (*minim*) among traditionally ascribed Jews. *Minim*, therefore, were not necessarily Christians or Jewish-Christians, but ethnically ascribed Israelites who did not follow rabbinic law. As the borders between "Christianity" and "Judaism" firm up (especially for the Christians), the later Babylonian and Amoraic rabbis retreat from their own internal heresiologies, allowing all Israelites to remain within the category of Israel, despite their theological deficiencies. In short, the Tannaitic rabbis borrowed the Christian construct of heresiology, creating a Jewish or rabbinic "orthodoxy" in parallel to developing Christian orthodoxy, while the later Amoraic rabbis rejected this Christian notion of "true religion" for an older notion of ethnicity and culture.[29] Building on Boyarin, I argue that one can follow these developments, within both Judaism and Christianity, through their various and evolving hermeneutics of holiness. Moreover, when a particular construct of holiness includes all Jews, or Christians within a particular community, this construct can be further manipulated to create internal hierarchies. Holiness cuts both ways: on the one hand, it establishes firm boundaries between us and them, but, on the other, it allows for internal hierarchies of holiness and authority as well. To wit, our fourth-century exegetes, intellectual elites of their respective communities, begin to maneuver their understandings of holiness achieved through sexuality as a means to improve on their own status within their communities, often in line with the biblical priestly hierarchies in which the holier priests among Holy Israel remain closer to God. He who can claim the highest level of holiness wins. Thus, these exegetes also bolster their own authority within their communities. Aphrahat, as much as the fourth-century Rabbis, concerns himself with internal hierarchies as well as external borders.

Thus, this book concerns holiness and sexuality and the exegetical constructs built to support such a link, particularly within the Aramaic-Persian milieu. The book does not propose to discuss sexuality or holiness in all of their respective manifestations in the ancient texts, but, rather, to focus on and unpack those moments when holiness and sexuality merge into one theological concept and exegetical framework. I am also most interested in those manifestations of sexuality that assume sexual restraint or renunciation and become a religious practice of asceticism. Moreover, I attempt here to suggest social and political matrices in fourth-century Persian Mesopotamia for which these hermeneutics proved most useful.[30]

While the material treated in this book leads up to and culminates in the fourth century, I feel it necessary and compelling to understand the whole trajectory of biblically based holiness from its biblical roots. As this is a book focused on biblical exegesis, I include rather detailed chapters on the biblical and post-biblical and other exegetical material that precede the fourth-century context. While I find this material interesting in and of itself, I also believe it impossible to truly understand the fourth-century hermeneutics of holiness and sexuality without a thorough examination of the literature upon which these hermeneutics clearly depend. Each text or set of texts emerges from its own peculiar cultural milieu. Yet there remain connecting themes. By examining the earlier texts in detail I hope to show the multiplicity of interpretive possibilities that lay before my select few fourth-century authors. Moreover, I wish to demonstrate that because of or perhaps despite these many options, certain routes or trajectories of exegetical choice can be traced and mapped out from the biblical texts through the centuries to our late ancient authors.

Prologue to the Fourth-Century Context

Aphrahat: The Persian Sage

Aphrahat, the Persian Sage, has been overlooked by scholars of many fields. Within studies of the early Church, Aphrahat and his fellow Syriac writers have been ignored in part because of the vast literature of the Greco-Roman world and in part owing to basic language barriers. Yet even within the more narrow field of Syriac studies, Ephrem, Aphrahat's more prolific and younger contemporary, enjoys a wider readership than Aphrahat.[31] While this study does not intend to examine the whole of Aphrahat's writings, *The Demonstrations*, I hope in a small way not only to show Aphrahat's centrality to understanding fourth-century Syriac Christianity but also to illuminate how his compositions are essential for a more complete picture of both early Church history and rabbinic culture.

Although we know little about Aphrahat the man, his writings show him to be an educated and engaged student of the Bible. He neither reveals his sources nor quotes his teachers, but speaks from his own authority. He appears to have been a man of ecclesiastical position in the fourth-century Persian Church. Aphrahat's *Demonstrations* were read continuously, if sporadically, throughout the next ten centuries among the Eastern Churches, and at least one Western writer references his compositions.[32] An anonymous manuscript of the fourteenth century lists "the sage Aphrahat who is Jacob bishop of Mar Mattai."[33] This is the only source that gives a locale for Aphrahat—and a thousand years after his demise at that. Although it is impossible to prove, this anonymous manuscript may preserve an older tradition that was lost to other manuscripts. The monastery at Mar Mattai is or was on Mount Elphah, also known as Maklob, or Sheikh Matta;[34] it is east of the Tigris River in northern Mesopotamia, in what is today Kurdistan. Lack of an earlier recorded witness to Aphrahat and Mar Mattai, however, makes this association tenuous. The use of both the names Aphrahat and Jacob might suggest that the Persian Sage actually had two names: Aphrahat, his given name, and Jacob, the name he took either on conversion or when he was consecrated into the priesthood or bishopric, a known practice in the Syriac Church.[35]

It is possible that Aphrahat was a monk, priest, or even a bishop as some of the sources claim (although the last title may have been added subsequently in order to lend him additional authority).[36] Aphrahat's *Demonstrations* show that, at the very least, he was a thinking and educated man with a vast knowledge of the Scriptures. Demonstration 14, which is a condemnation of the corruption within the Church, especially of its higher ranked clergymen, indicates that Aphrahat had "pulled rank" himself. He addresses the other bishops and clergymen as equals: "We bishops, presbyters, deacons and all of the Church of God," corroborating his potential bishophood. In addition, John Gwynn claims that Mar Mattai's seat, Aphrahat's supposed bishopric, at or near Ninveh, was second only to that of Seleucia-Ctesiphon (when the hierarchy was established in later years), perhaps giving Aphrahat the additional clout needed to chastise other bishops if needed.[37] Although it is not clear whether Aphrahat was born a Christian or converted at an early age, he became a master of its traditions and texts, a teacher to his flock, and a protector of his Church's reputation.[38]

There are twenty-three "demonstrations," or homilies, in total; Aphrahat himself states at the end of demonstrations 10 and 22 that the total number of demonstrations (twenty-two) matches the twenty-two letters of the Syriac alphabet. In addition, a twenty-third "epilogue" demonstration concludes the whole work. Aphrahat composed at least the first set of demonstrations in response to a parishioner's question concerning the true Christian faith.[39] Aphrahat, answering this question directly in his first demonstration, "On Faith," continued to outline other Christian duties and practices in the next nine demonstrations, addressing topics such as charity, fasting, prayer, wars, members of the covenant, penitence, the resurrection, humility, and pastors. Three of the second twelve demonstrations cover similar themes, but nine center on issues of conflict with the Jews. Four of these argue against the Jewish ritual practices of circumcision, Passover, the Sabbath, and dietary laws, while the last five constitute a rebuttal of Jewish criticism against Christianity on issues such as the Messiah, virginity, the call of the Gentiles, the dispersion of the Jews, and the election of Israel. The twenty-third demonstration chronicles righteousness and salvation from Adam to Aphrahat (based on the concept of the "grape-cluster" in Isa. 65:8).

It is equally important to note what the demonstrations do not contain. They do not deal with Arianism, the "heresy" most threatening to the Church in the West, nor with the decisions of the Nicene Council, which had convened only a decade before the composition of the first demonstrations. The Persian Church might simply have been outside of the jurisdiction of the council, or the concerns of the Nicene fathers might not have been of interest or threatening to Aphrahat.

Luckily for the historian, Aphrahat dates his writings. At the end of demonstration 22 he writes:

> These twenty-two discourses have I written according to the
> twenty-two letters of the [Syriac] alphabet. The first ten I wrote in the

648th year of the Kingdom of Alexander the son of Philip the
Macedonian [337 CE] as is written in the end of them. And these
twelve last I wrote in the 655th year of the Kingdom of the Greeks
and of the Romans, which is the Kingdom of Alexander [344 CE] and
in the 35th year of the Persian King.[40]

In addition, demonstration 14 is dated to the year 655 of Alexander (344 CE), and
demonstration 23 is dated to the year 656 of Alexander (345 CE). One can see
from the dating that there is a hiatus of seven years between the writing of the
first ten and the second twelve, and that all the demonstrations concerning Jewish topics are among the latter half. Aphrahat, content to discuss the Christian
life in 337, turned to controversy with the Jews in 344 to combat the spiritual and
physical onslaught brought on by the Persian anti-Christian persecutions. Some
Christians who were not martyred at the hands of the Persians might have opted
for conversion to Judaism as a mechanism of survival. Since the Jews did not
appear to discourage this trend, Aphrahat may have felt compelled to do so.[41]
The narrative quoted at the opening of this chapter may exemplify the type of
"encouragement" Christians received from their Jewish neighbors. The Jews
could boast that they were "holy"—that is, protected by God and endowed with
divine blessing—while the Christians, because of their celibacy were "impure,"
or cursed by God, and to be persecuted by the Persians for their "unholy" beliefs
and practices.

This book's discussions focus mainly on Aphrahat's two demonstrations
that concern celibacy: demonstration 6 and demonstration 18. Demonstration
6, "On the Members of the Covenant," addresses Aphrahat's fellow celibates
who form a core elite for his Church. Aphrahat's main concern here is promoting uniformity of practice among already committed celibate Christians.
His latter demonstration (18), "On Virginity and Holiness," comes from among
his polemical writings composed at the height of the persecutions. In this demonstration Aphrahat must defend his earlier position against supposed Jewish
procreative arguments.

Yet, in both compositions Aphrahat not only projects traditional Syriac
Christian exegetical support and uniquely promotes his own interpretive
course. Indeed, when faced with a Jewish procreative argument—one that is
both dependent on Hebrew biblical support and apparently *attractive* to his
parishioners, he is forced to turn to Hebrew biblical support for sexual renunciation. Nevertheless, he does not limit his innovative reading only to his
polemical works. Aphrahat presents us with a new and creative reading of biblical
text in the name of traditional Syriac Christian practice. When Aphrahat, as
well as other Syriac Christian patristic authors, are more widely studied within

the larger field of early Church writings, a more nuanced notion of Christian biblical exegetical practices emerges. This study demonstrates how Aphrahat's hermeneutic of holiness broadens our understandings of Christian exegetical strategies for supporting sexual renunciation.[42]

Yet what appears as unique and new to fourth-century Syriac Christian biblical exegesis resonates widely in the rabbinic literature, revealing Aphrahat's importance to any comparative project. Aphrahat uses biblical traditions and interpretive strategies found within the rabbinic corpus (but not necessarily originating there) to defend his position against a supposedly Jewish one. The parallels and crossovers speak to a wider cultural literary milieu that Aphrahat shares with the Rabbis. While Ephrem sits on the border between Persia and Rome, imbibing Greek as well as Syriac traditions, Aphrahat situates himself firmly in a Persian Aramaic cultural context that is more readily comparable to the Babylonian rabbinic context. Yet both Aphrahat and Ephrem are firmly of the fourth-century Syriac Church. When scholars speak of the fourth-century Syriac Church they always turn to Aphrahat and Ephrem as the only extant writers of this century, yet Aphrahat's comparatively meager produce is usually overshadowed by Ephrem's broad corpus. Aphrahat's exegesis is often lumped together as an addendum to Ephrem's interpretive thought process rather than as a separate entity.[43] Their differences are overlooked and individual contributions obscured. Studying Aphrahat in isolation can only deepen our understanding of the breadth and variety of Syriac exegetical traditions.

Aphrahat among the Rabbis

Aphrahat and the fourth-century Babylonian rabbis were contemporaries in and around Ctesiphon/Mahoza, near modern-day Baghdad in the Mesopotamian river valley. Yet no consensus has formed among scholars concerning the nature of Aphrahat's relationship with rabbinic Jews and Judaism. In the early twentieth century, Saloman Funk, Louis Ginzberg, and Frank Gavin all concluded that Aphrahat was a "docile pupil of the Jews" since his style and exegesis closely followed the rabbinic literature.[44] Yet the assumption that Aphrahat created his writings by borrowing from the rabbinic literature may be altogether false, as pointed out by Jacob Neusner. As Neusner notes, any similarities between Aphrahat's texts and the Rabbis' do not necessarily mean that Aphrahat borrowed from the Rabbis.[45] Other factors may have played a role in the similarities between Aphrahat and the rabbinic literature—among them, older traditions and common milieus that could have affected both Aphrahat and the Rabbis' writings such that it appears as if one might have copied from the other.[46] In fact, Neusner's textual analysis concludes that Aphrahat had nothing to do with rabbinic Jews: Aphrahat neither copied nor learned an exegetical style from rabbinic Jews. Because Aphrahat never mentions rabbis, rabbinic schools, or the oral law, Neusner is convinced that Aphrahat knew no rabbinic Jews. According to Neusner, Aphrahat's critiques of Judaism are not by observation of fourth-century Jews necessarily, but of Jews of the Bible.[47] Neusner does not deny that Aphrahat knew any contemporary Jews, only that the Jews he would have met were nonrabbinic, or "Yahwistic," probably descendants of the converts of the royal house of Adiabene or even the ten tribes of Israel who had been exiled to northern Mesopotamia.[48] This region, Neusner claims, was far enough away not to have been influenced by the rabbinic stronghold of the south.[49] (Southern Mesopotamia, or Babylonia, was home to most of the region's Jews, rabbis, and academies. The dividing line between north and south ran somewhere northwest of Pumpeditta, where the land between the rivers widened.)[50]

While I do not completely disagree with Neusner's analysis, I am not convinced, however, that the northern Jews were completely isolated from their southern coreligionists. Other scholars have shown that northern Mesopotamia was home to a number of rabbinic Jews. There are several references within rabbinic writings to Jews who lived in or hailed from "the north." We read of Ya'akov of Adiabene who asked Rav Hisda a question about a mishnah, and Zuga of Adiabene who twice added a teaching to a talmudic discussion that the other rabbis did not know.[51] Furthermore, the Rabbis of the south, as well as their Palestinian contemporaries, traveled through the northern regions on their journeys between Palestine and Babylonia. Traveling preachers and rabbis most certainly would have stopped along the way in these Jewish communities since the journey back and forth to Palestine could not be accomplished in a day. They may very well have traded lessons in rabbinic teachings for lodging and food.

In addition, clear evidence exists for a second-century rabbinic academy in Nisibis, a major city about 100 miles to the northwest of Aphrahat's supposed diocese of Mar Mattai (near Ninveh).[52] The Jewish community there was weakened in numbers by the fourth century, possibly owing to a growing Christian presence.[53] If the Jewish community had been "rabbinic" in the second century, it would be unlikely that it would have reverted to "pre-rabbinic" or "Yahwistic" in the fourth century. Moreover, Nisibis' expanding Christian population might have turned to Aphrahat for guidance, and that, very likely, would have drawn that bishop into closer contact with the Jews of Nisibis. Granted it would be difficult to say who exactly was a rabbinic Jew even in the fourth century—let alone the second—as rabbinic Judaism itself was an evolving phenomenon in these centuries. As scholars such as Daniel Boyarin have been arguing for the last few years, it would be very hard to peg down any Jew before the fourth century as "rabbinic," given that the thing we call "rabbinic Judaism" was an emerging phenomenon.[54] Yet any Jew, post 70 CE (and probably many Diaspora Jews pre-70), in order to continue living a Torah-based life, must have engaged in some sort of interpretive enterprise. What we have in hand today descends from rabbinic circles, but surely they were not the only interpreters of biblical texts, just the lucky ones to have their legacy survive. Moreover, I wish to argue that that which we call "rabbinic" today might not have been exclusively "rabbinic" in the second to fourth centuries. I do not imagine any Jewish community that did not attempt to interpret the biblical texts in some way. Thus, Aphrahat and his community fit squarely into the larger shared Aramaic biblical interpretive milieu. What I call "rabbinic," for lack of another term, most likely encompasses a larger variety of Jewish (and other) interpretive adventures in these locales and centuries.

It is evident from Aphrahat's writings that while he may have spent most of his time in the north, he also communicated with the Christian communities in the south, specifically in Ctesiphon, the seat of the Catholicos in later centuries.[55] Mahoza, a suburb of Ctesiphon, was home to Rava, a leading rabbi of the mid-fourth-century generation. It is possible that Aphrahat addressed the problems plaguing the southern Christian community in its struggle with a large and vibrant rabbinic Jewish populace while at the same time dealing with a similar phenomenon in the north. Lastly, while it is true that Aphrahat does not mention the Talmud or the rabbinic academies in which it was studied, he does refer to a Jewish wise man with the same title as the Rabbis referred to themselves: ḥakham.[56] Yaakov Elman has also argued that Mahoza, being a suburb of the capital city, was a very cosmopolitan town. The Jewish community and its rabbinic leaders, such as Rava, were not immune to its influences. He also suggests that there is evidence that "interfaith dialogue" was not uncommon among its religious leaders. Hence, Mahoza/Ctesiphon presents itself as a possible place of meeting, sharing, or influencing—conscious or not—between religious communities.[57]

Thus, while Neusner rightly criticizes Funk, Ginzberg, and Gavin for over-emphasizing the parallels between Aphrahat and the Rabbis, he seems to go too far in the other direction in his attempt to show Aphrahat's complete isolation from rabbinic or other Jews. I believe that there is evidence to show that Aphrahat and the Rabbis or other Jews were in closer contact than he would have us believe, even if their contact was through third parties. While Aphrahat may not have had personal relationships with rabbis, certainly his parishioners knew other Jews, for this is how most of his narrations are reported, as our opening quote illustrates. Although Aphrahat did not meet a rabbi or a Jew himself, in this case, he clearly heard a story about "one of the members of our Church" and a "Jew."

One must also consider Marie-Joseph Pierre's claim that the "Jew" in Aphrahat's writing is a literary fiction, written for internal consumption only. Pierre contends that Aphrahat's community suffered from Judaizing—the Christian practice of keeping Jewish rites and rituals such as the dietary laws and Passover—and that, hence, the Jewish arguments that Aphrahat records did not come directly from fourth-century Jews but, rather, from descendants of Jewish converts, or "Jewish-Christians," eliminating the possibility that Aphrahat maintained contact with *any* Jews, rabbinic or other.[58] In short, Pierre has claimed that while Aphrahat's style and some of his doctrines appear similar to rabbinical formulations, in actuality they were inherited from "Jewish-Christians" and other early Jewish converts to Christianity.[59]

In trying to detect whether the Jews in Aphrahat's writings were real or imagined, it's helpful to consider that, as a rhetorician and author, Aphrahat most likely created the Jewish sage in his writings with whom he conversed. The conversations between Aphrahat and the sage must be considered fictitious or, at best, composites. But they are probably also dependent on live encounters experienced or retold that Aphrahat combined and recast in his essays. The opponent in question, however, most likely represents some version of fourth-century Judaism and the Jews who practice it in Aphrahat's day: no mention is made of "Jewish-Christians" or Jewish converts, while again and again Aphrahat addresses the Jews in his writings or instructs his readers to answer back to the Jews with these arguments that he puts forward. In fact, he specifically noted a number of times that his purpose was to arm his readers for verbal combat with the Jews, for their arguments confused the Christians.[60] Furthermore, Aphrahat's first ten homilies do not polemicize against Judaism. It is only after the onset of the Persian regime's anti-Christian persecutions that he takes up the subject, suggesting that the issue at hand was not mere Judaizing but a more serious issue of "backsliding" all the way into Judaism. Christians were more likely converting or returning to their native Judaism in the face of martyrdom than simply Judaizing.

Establishing that Aphrahat or his parishioners knew or associated with Jews remains a separate issue from whether those Jews were rabbinic. As I noted above, certainly not all people who called themselves Jews in the fourth century could be defined as "rabbinic" even by fourth-century standards. Rabbinic literature and culture was still in its formative stage and remained fluid. Although the Rabbis who composed the material may have had a sense of self, there is no telling how many non-rabbis looked to the Rabbis as final arbiters of things "Jewish." Nevertheless, the rabbinic material is all we have to go by for defining "Jewishness" in this period. That many of Aphrahat's "Jewish" statements and claims also appear in the rabbinic literature only suggests that they are also rabbinic, but not that they are exclusively rabbinic. We do not know how far rabbinic ideas permeated the general Jewish cultural outside of rabbinic circles, nor how large those circles were. In the end we can only say that it is more likely than not that, given the geographic and literary crossovers, Aphrahat's Jews were rabbinic in some manner.

The issue of audience and rhetoric is inherent in any of our ancient Christian documents concerning Jews and Judaism. Many scholars have convincingly argued that later fourth-century writers, such as Ephrem, Chrysostom, and Augustine, "think through" Jews and Judaism to get to another point (often against competing Christian doctrine). What they say about Jews and Judaism may not actually reflect historical reality.[61] No doubt this is in part true with Aphrahat as well. His purpose, after all, is to teach Christians how to be Christians. What interests me in the end is not so much whether or to what extent Aphrahat's Jews are real, but whether Aphrahat's biblical exegesis reflects a cultural reality in which both Jews and Christians participated.

Ultimately, I suspect that Aphrahat's community had dealings with Jews of some sort and in this way were exposed to the fourth century's variety of Judaisms. Aphrahat in writing his *Demonstrations* responds to the confusion his parishioners felt when confronted with other manifestations of a biblically derived religion that did not seem so different from their own. This Christian community at least still suffered some sort of separation anxiety. They were concerned about theological beliefs and doctrines, which were more integral to their self-identification than whether or not to follow biblically based ritual observances such as the Sabbath. Second, through the contacts established between the communities there must have been interchange of ideas and biblical traditions and interpretations—not necessarily between Aphrahat and a rabbi, but between common Christians and Jews. Yet I hesitate to say that the *only* means by which Aphrahat acquired traditions or texts that have parallels in the rabbinic literature would have been through direct interchange with rabbis or rabbinically influenced Jews, given that Aphrahat and the Rabbis share a cultural literary milieu from which these similarities most likely arise. So, while Pierre argues that Aphrahat's seemingly "rabbinic" texts come from former Jews and "Jewish-Christians" in his community, I posit an even broader field of possible exchange, discovery, and mutual development. While Neusner makes a similar claim, this claim for him is proof positive of absolutely no active interchange between Jews and Christians in fourth-century Mesopotamia. I prefer not to exclude all possibilities of actual dialogue or intellectual cross–fertilization.[62]

My reading of Aphrahat convinces me that Aphrahat is neither a "docile pupil of the Rabbis" nor completely ignorant of rabbinic Judaism. He neither descends from rabbinic circles nor copies wholesale from their texts, nor is he so geographically and intellectually isolated that he has no knowledge of the Jewish exegetical developments in his day (whether he recognizes them all as "Jewish" or not). Rather, he clearly shares biblical traditions, exegesis, and interpretive strategies with his rabbinic contemporaries through the broader literary milieu of Aramaic-speaking peoples of Persian Mesopotamia. Aphrahat writes in Syriac, a dialect of Aramaic not far removed from the Aramaic of the Rabbis. The biblical text he reads (or has memorized) is also probably in Aramaic or Syriac, again not so dissimilar from the Hebrew and targumic biblical versions of the Rabbis. Furthermore the parallels between Aphrahat and the Rabbis are not restricted to his polemical material but appear throughout his writings. It seems quite possible to me that Aphrahat and his contemporaneous rabbis had access to similar biblical interpretive collections and "libraries" that they depended upon equally to develop their exegesis and theology. Under these circumstances it would not be surprising to find similar interpretive patterns and traditions.

While it is not my purpose to equate Aphrahat's "Jewish" exclusively with "rabbinic," I see no reason to exclude "rabbinic" from whatever Aphrahat understands about "Jewish." Moreover, I believe he provides us with an opportunity to study what we have already determined "rabbinic" from another angle. How innovative is the rabbinic material? How unique? What other cultural influences come into play in its development? I will argue that some of Aphrahat's sources are "proto-rabbinic" or even early rabbinic—that is, they stem from interpretive collections that end up within the rabbinic corpus in one form or another but also have literary lives outside the rabbinic circles. The evolution of these traditions within Aphrahat's writings in comparison to their contextualization and development within the rabbinic corpus provides us with a new perspective on the development of rabbinic modes of thought and interpretation. Aphrahat's reading of text and tradition can illuminate other options of interpretation not followed through in our present rabbinic literature or even to highlight undercurrents present but not developed fully. In other places Aphrahat's *Demonstrations* simply illuminate the biblical traditions, interpretive methodologies, and literary idiosyncrasies that he shared with the Rabbis through their common Aramaic milieu in fourth-century Persian Mesopotamia. In sum, I posit that Aphrahat and the Rabbis share a matrix of text, tradition, language, and literary culture that shapes their exegetical output. For the purposes of this study I also submit that, even if they never met face to face in open discussion, this common matrix propels them into parallel and overlapping discourses on holiness and sexuality, which often depend on the same exegetical units and strategies. This shared cultural milieu allows for cross-fertilization without direct interaction. The "Jewish" arguments that pollinate Aphrahat's anti-Jewish discourse really represent only part of this cultural interchange. While some actual exchange—person to person—surely took place, Aphrahat's *Demonstrations* reveal a more deeply rooted shared literary tradition.

The Aramaic-Mesopotamian Context

Though widely spoken by many peoples in the area, Syriac (one of many dialects of Aramaic) evolved into an almost exclusively Christian language in the first centuries of the Common Era. In tension with Jewish Aramaic and Gentile and especially Christian Greek, Syriac proved useful as an independent Christian linguistic and cultural vehicle. Furthermore, by adopting a distinct and non-Greek language, Syriac Christian authors had other literary traditions of their own to emulate, draw on, or contradict. Syriac Christians were free to pursue their theological and other writings in a different literary milieu than many of their Greek Christian counterparts. Thus, Syriac Christian texts must be studied within the larger Aramaic literary context, as well as in comparison to developments in Greek and Latin Christianity. Aphrahat, as one of the earliest known Syriac Christian authors, proves essential to this program.

The fourth-century writers Aphrahat and Ephrem centered on sacramental and devotional rituals of an elite celibate community. These writers marked several transitions in Syriac Christian development. By the mid-fourth century, when these two writers flourished, celibacy was no longer a prerequisite for baptism (as it appears possibly to have been for some elements of the early Syriac Church); instead, celibacy was reserved for an inner core—the *bnay qyama*—the few, the elect, the elite at the center of the Church. Married householders were now a part of the Church, not outside it. The yearning for the next world was pushed to the background as the day-to-day existence, maintenance, and expansion of the Church predominated. Along with this functional transition the theological explanation for celibacy changed as well. Celibacy was no longer a mechanism to change the world, but a physical manifestation of the single-minded-one's (*iḥidaya*'s) dedication to God. Celibacy became the starting point for Aphrahat, not the end point. Furthermore, celibacy—which was taken for granted in the early manifestations of Syriac Christianity—found itself in need of support, explanation, and apology. Aphrahat appeared on the scene at a theologically defining moment.

Nevertheless, Syriac and its Christianization did not evolve in a vacuum, but in the Aramaic culture of the Near East. While Hellenistic influences may have been minimal, others were in abundance. Whatever the origins and later stimuli, whatever the subsequent innovations in the Syriac language, Syriac Christians could not remain unaffected by the surrounding cultures—even as they tried to differentiate themselves from them. This is nowhere more true than in the theological arena. As an Aramaic dialect, Syriac remains closer linguistically to Jewish Aramaic and Hebrew than to Hellenistic Greek. The Syriac Christian Bible translations develop analogously to the Jewish Aramaic Targums as interpretive texts, transmitting extra-biblical traditions as well as translations. While some scholars even claim that the Peshitta at core is originally a Jewish Targum translation later adopted by the Christians and abandoned by the Jews, as was the Septuagint before it, M. P. Weitzman disagrees. Weitzman contends that the Peshitta is a direct translation from the Hebrew by Syriac-speaking Christians. Yet he allows that even these translators must have depended on or consulted a wide rage of sources, including targumic and Greek translations, as well as other extra-biblical sources that would have been available to all biblical scholars in the Aramaic milieu.[63]

In the Syriac-speaking East, as opposed to the Greek-speaking West, Christians pursued their biblical studies and theological speculation in a linguistic, literary, and cultural milieu more similar to that of the Palestinian, and later the Babylonian, rabbis (both of whom wrote in similar dialects of Aramaic and Hebrew) than to their Greek-speaking coreligionists. Whether or not Aramaic-speaking Jews and Christians exchanged biblical readings, their shared literary heritage and linguistic culture further provoked similar interpretive methods and biblical traditions. These traditions and methods did not necessarily lead to similar practices (i.e., sexual renunciation), but the methods for interpreting text and using text as support for religious practice remain constant. Hence, while I argue that Syriac asceticism, in part, can be traced to ancient biblical interpretive traditions, I also suggest that once asceticism was established in the Syriac Church, the way in which it is presented, discussed, and supported by its fourth-century proponents relates more to their rabbinic exegetical practices than to Greco-Roman Christian hermeneutics.

Nevertheless, I believe it quite possible that there might have been an "exchange" or, better, a borrowing of early Jewish interpretive traditions that postdates the earliest inceptions of Christianity, takes place in Syrian territory, and further enhances the similarities found in Syriac and rabbinic biblical interpretive tradition. Robert Murray, while arguing for a link back to Qumran sectarian Judaism (which I do not agree with), nevertheless suggests the mechanism and place for such a transfer of influences: Nisibis.[64] Nisibis was a city on the crossroads from East to West—a thriving metropolis where goods and ideas were readily accessible. Up until the mid-second century there was an active Jewish community that supported an academy. This community and academy disappears by the mid-fourth century, when Christians and their schools dominate the city. While it is possible that many Jews simply moved south to other centers of Jewish learning and prosperity as Nisibis was increasingly Christianized, it is equally possible that many of those Jews converted to Christianity—taking their learning, texts and biblical traditions with them. By the time they "reappear" in Aphrahat, we can trace developmental trajectories. The tradition of Moses' celibacy may very well be one of those well-traveled and translated Aramaic traditions.

This book is divided into three parts. The first two parts are shorter and deal with the earliest texts. Part I (chapters 1 and 2) examines the Hebrew biblical and Second Temple literatures' various hermeneutics of holiness and attempts to trace trajectories of holiness from the Hebrew biblical texts into these post-biblical writings. I use the term "Hebrew biblical" to refer to texts that are part of the standard canonized Hebrew Bible. "Second Temple literature" refers to all those writings that fall between the close of the Hebrew biblical canon and the start of the rabbinic writings, within the Jewish context, and the New Testament writings, within the Christian context. "Post-biblical literature" refers generally to the writings of the Second Temple period, with the exception of those texts written in the Second Temple period that are included within the biblical canon (Ezra and Daniel, for example) and those texts that are also literature of the Second Temple period but are included in the Christian canon (Paul, for instance). I generally include the New Testament literature in the broader category of early Christian writings rather than in Second Temple literature. The category of early Christian writings, for the benefit of this study, stretches only into the fourth century.

The second part of the book (chapters 3 and 4) moves into the early Christian literature, starting with the New Testament writings. I focus my attention almost exclusively on Paul in chapter 3, as he is an essential link between the earlier writings of the Second Temple period and the developing Christian literature. Chapter 4 focuses on early Syriac Christian writings, as background to Aphrahat.

Part III (chapters 5 through 7) centers on the writings of Aphrahat, the rabbinic literature, and the interrelatedness of their various hermeneutics of holiness. Here, we find the shared literary and cultural influences of the Mesopotamian-Aramaic milieu in which these two exegeting communities flourished. It is also here that Moses appears as holy-protagonist.

PART I

I

In the Beginning

Holiness in the Bible

The Bible presents us with several different and conflicting paradigms of holiness. The pentateuchal (Torah) texts, which have been
subdivided by scholars into various strands, J (Yahwist), E (Elohist),
P (Priestly), and D (Deuteronomical), each carry different and often
opposing narrative traditions, theological notions and linguistic
variations. The various understandings of holiness that arise out of
the different historical, cultural, and literary strata of the text remain
in unresolved tension within the unified whole that makes up the
pentateuchal texts. Notions of the holy divide more or less straight-
forwardly between the priestly writings (P) and the nonpriestly
writings (J, E, and D). In this case "nonpriestly" includes non-
pentateuchal texts such as Samuel 1 and 2 as well. In the Pentateuch,
the priestly writings (P) stand out from the other Torah traditions for
their distinctive and more developed theology and terminology of
holiness.

Martha Himmelfarb, in her book *A Kingdom of Priests: Ancestry
and Merit in Ancient Judaism*, argues that the tensions biblical and
post-biblical writers negotiate, between an Israel holy by birth
(ancestry) and an Israel (or individual Israelites) whose holiness is
achieved through piety (merit), are key to understanding ancient
Judaism.[1] In this book, I make a similar claim for the tensions
surrounding holiness among ancient and late-ancient Jews and
Christians. How they define themselves vis-à-vis the holy is key
to understanding their self-identification. I will distinguish between

what I call *ascribed* holiness, a holiness granted by divine decree, and *achieved* holiness, a holiness acquired through obedience to divine laws. In both cases, I focus on personal (human) holiness rather than God's holiness. Furthermore, I pay attention only to those laws that have to do with sexuality. All subsequent biblical commentators build on these tensions already apparent in the biblical texts.

In addition, I emphasize the biblical distinctions between cultic purity and holiness. Integral to this discussion here is the biblical Hebrew root word קדש [QDS], which in its adjectival form describes things holy—whether ascribed or achieved. P deploys QDS exclusively as a descriptive of God and God's "things" (the sanctuary, the land, etc.) QDS usually translates as "holy" or "sacred." I will be using those English terms interchangeably here. In the nonpriestly texts, however, QDS can also signify "to purify (for cultic purposes.)" The priestly writers usually avoid this connotation. In this chapter, I examine when the various biblical authors deploy QDS to describe God and the divine possessions; when they use it to categorize the people of Israel (whether by ascription or achievement) and when they use QDS to signify cultic purity. Furthermore, I show how the biblical redactor allowed the various definitions of QDS to remain in ambiguous tension from text to text.

Yet, as will become evident even within the later biblical literature, these multiple constructs of holiness afford opportunities for the late- and post-biblical authors to combine or deliberately (con)fuse the various usages of QDS, as well as the (once) distinctive notions of purity and holiness. The historical or literary differences between the textual strata P, J, E, and D do not matter (nor really exist) for our ancient and late-ancient exegetes, yet as a modern reader I find it helpful to understand how the biblical texts come to have so many conflicting understandings of holiness and purity, and looking at the different categorizations of biblical text—P, J, E, and D—can aid this process.

You Are a Holy Nation to Me: Ascribed Holiness

All the biblical authors by and large reserve QDS to designate things, people, space, and time that belong exclusively to God. Thus, the adjective *qadosh* or the noun *qodesh* best translate as "holy" or "sacred." The holiness in question relates to the ultimate and exclusive "Holy One" [*haqadosh*]: God. God and all that belongs to God can only be described as *qadosh*. As Baruch J. Schwartz asserts, it is the element of specialness and separation from all others that essentializes God's holiness. *Qadosh* means, first and foremost: "'separated,' 'belonging to,' 'designated for,' [God]. . . . [and is] most often approximated by the terms 'holy' and 'sacred'. . . . [*qadosh*] expresses [God's] transcendent divinity, namely, the idea that [God] is all together separate from the created earth, 'totally Other.'"[2] When the biblical authors apply *qadosh* to others—people, places, objects, or time—they mark them as separated out and designated for God (ascribed). Hence, God chooses God's holy days, holy people (priests, Israel), sacrifices, and shrine. They are ascribed by (or to) God and all belong to God and stand out as different from any other nation's feasts, sacrifices, priests, and the like. While only God is intrinsically holy, other things can be consecrated to God through ritual means and can thus be *made* holy.[3] Interestingly, the term *qedushah* ("holiness") does not actually appear in the Hebrew biblical text, hence the abstract concept of holiness is not at issue as much as separating holy objects from profane objects.[4] Understanding QDS to connote "separated/dedicated" as an essential part of "holy/sacred" illuminates the "otherness" of things *qadosh*.

Nevertheless, the various Torah traditions carry conflicting understandings of the mechanisms of QDS as holiness. What does it mean for an individual or object to be holy? How does one become holy? In the nonpriestly traditions, Israel comes by its holiness through election (ascription). Once God chooses Israel to be God's possession at Sinai, the people of Israel become once and for all a *qodesh*, a holy object of God. They are chosen; they are designated "other"—that is, separated from the nations and dedicated exclusively to God. For example, D construes Israel's election as a *fait accompli*, a historic event that took place at the time of the patriarchs (e.g. Deut. 7:6–8). E places Israel's complete election in the future and links it to the covenant—namely, if the Israelites agree to follow God's laws, God will make them into a holy nation by choosing them to be God's exclusive worshipers and servants (e.g. Exod. 19:5–6). While Israel must follow the covenantal agreement, God reserves the exclusive privilege to ascribe the holy status to Israel. God confers holiness upon Israel through its relationship to God as the divine's elected worshipers. As God's servants, and in fulfillment of their covenant, the Israelites observe God's commandments; yet keeping the commandments does not make Israel holy—rather, Israel's election consecrates its people.[5] As Schwartz notes, "To be sure, the maintenance of Israel's holiness depends indeed upon obedience to YHWH's commandments. He can even rescind their holiness if they disappoint him. But the holiness is the status itself; it was conferred upon them by YHWH, when He chose them from among the nations of the world, and the obligation to obey his commands derives from it."[6] This ethnocentric conception may derive from popular Israelite religion and thus stands in opposition to other priestly understandings of holiness.[7]

The priestly texts present an alternate vision of holiness—a vision that itself subdivides into two substrata. According to biblical scholars, the priestly texts are derivative of two different priestly schools, chronologically separated by several generations but woven together at a later date. Hence, the book of Leviticus divides roughly into two parts: P (Priestly Torah—chapters 1–16) and H (Holiness School or Code—chapters 17–26).[8] While P primarily concerns itself with priestly relationships to the Holy One, H focuses on the behavior of the larger Israelite community. Israel Knohl suggests that H was devised as a revision of P, taking into consideration certain social developments.[9] In the end, for the purposes of this study, the differences between P and H's understandings of holiness matter most, not the historical underpinnings. Whether an author focuses holiness on God, the priests, or the whole people depends on which biblical paradigm he chooses. Since I am primarily interested in constructs of holy-peoplehood, how these authors manipulate the various understandings becomes of central interest to me.

In P, God ascribes holiness to his "things" alone—namely, God's name, God's Sabbaths and festivals, God's servants (the priests), God's house, and sacrifices dedicated to God (e.g., Exod. 31:13; Lev. 15:31; Lev. 20:3). As a result, only the priestly class (among Israel) can call themselves holy (e.g., Exod. 29:1), since God elevated them from the other Israelites. Although God alone is intrinsically holy (read: "other"), God can emanate (in the sense of "radiate") holiness to the priests, sacrifices, feasts, and so on that come into the divine presence.[10] The Israelites' "chosenness" does not confer holiness (neither dedication nor otherness), and they can participate in God's holiness only through their representatives, the priests. Here again, observing the commandments, a requirement of the covenant, does not confer holiness on the people. Things and people can be *qadosh* to God (dedicated to God), but God also emanates holiness to objects, thereby claiming them as God's and imbuing them with an otherness that is qualitatively more numinous than just separation or dedication.[11] The P texts describe the mechanism of these dedications through blood rituals and sacrifice that designate Aaron and his sons as the first priests. In P, only the priestly class is holy and they acquire that status by ascription.

Be Holy for I Am Holy: Holiness Achieved

In contrast, in H, *all Israel* is called to be holy, not just the priests (e.g., Lev. 19:2). In this sense, they are called upon to achieve holiness through their own actions. God not only emanates holiness to the whole nation by residing in its midst but also commands the people to consecrate themselves through the commandments so that they can receive God's emanations.[12] While God, the ultimate Holy Being, consecrates at will (the priests, for instance), H presents the biblical laws as *the* means by which the people sacralize themselves— namely, the mechanism through which the people convert themselves into *qodashim*, or holy things. In opposition to D, which presupposes the people's holiness through ascription, and P, which does not assume the people's holiness at all, H proposes that the people become holy by keeping God's laws and there by "tuning in" to God's holy emanations.[13] H in essence suggests that lay Israelites can make themselves as holy as the priests. The commandment "be holy" becomes a dynamic goal, not a given. Following the commandments gives the people the opportunity to participate in and benefit from God's holiness that is the exclusive domain of the priests in P. Thus, H proposes a different understanding of holiness through achievement. In some sense, H can be understood as semi-parallel to E in which holiness is conditional. Nonetheless, I wish to differentiate between God's threatening to take away the Israelites' ascribed holiness if they do not obey the law (E) and the not-yet-holy people gaining holiness through their own achievement (H). This issue of access to holiness will be key to understanding later constructs of Holy Israel.

The key to H's construct is obedience. The obedient Israel becomes holy; the disobedient Israel profanes itself and God's name. When Israel complies, God's holiness manifests itself all the more through Israel's "wholly otherness." But when Israel disobeys, it not only returns to commonness (undifferentiation from the other nations) but further profanes God's name as well. God's reputation depends on the "good behavior" of God's servants.[14] These texts, in differentiating between holy behavior (obedience) and unholy/profane behavior (disobedience), distinguish between a holy people and the unholy/profane peoples (everyone else). The Israelites are holy not merely by virtue of their chosenness (as is presumed in E and D) but also because they are commanded to behave differently from their neighbors. The unholy behavior highlighted in H (sacrificing children to Molekh, adultery, incest, etc.) supposedly characterizes both the Egyptians (among whom the Israelites resided for several hundred years) and the other Canaanite nations that the land spewed out before the Israelites. But these texts do not limit themselves to delineating only "unholy" behavior; they provide examples of "holy" behavior as well: keeping the Sabbath and honoring one's parents, for example (both from the decalogue). Holy behavior distinguishes and separates the Israelites from the people of neighboring nations and marks them as "other." Proper behavior—cultic, social, civic, and domestic—creates holiness/otherness and holiness provides community identity. Chosenness and holiness translate into prosperity and blessing because a holy people make room for God to live in their midst and

God's presence guarantees them prosperity and blessing. This priestly paradigm of holiness by achievement closes any option of underachievement. One cannot choose to remain common; one must always strive for holiness. There remains no neutral space between the holy behavior of Israelites and the unholy behavior of their neighbors. But if the Israelites succeed they will be like a whole nation of Yahwist priests. All Israel, not just the priests, will benefit from God's holy presence and participate in the divine emanations.

Yet, perhaps to help differentiate between the achieved holiness of the nation and the ascribed holiness of the priests, H formulates further restrictions on the priestly class because they are holy to God. Among other strictures, H legislates limitations in qualified marriage partners for priests. In part to ensure the genealogical purity of the priestly line, but also perhaps to help distinguish priests from the laity, H forbids the priests from marrying women who have been previously married or sexually active. The only exception to this rule seems to be an allowance for widows to remarry common priests. If a priest disobeys this particular legislation, he profanes his children—namely, his sons will not be able to serve as priests because their father has adulterated their lineage. This issue of endogamy and proper marriage partners for Holy Israel will invigorate several later discussions.

Sanctify/Purify Them . . . Do Not Go Near a Woman: Semen Pollution, Holiness, and Super-Purity

The biblical texts supply us with one more construct of holiness that does not easily fit my other categorizations of ascribed or achieved, for in the biblical context it has more to do with purity than holiness. But because of a linguistic twist of fate, among later exegetes it has everything to do with holiness and particularly holiness defined through sexuality. Hence, I discuss it in full here.

Up until this point I have tried to keep the notions of purity and holiness separate, as they remain distinct notions within biblical theology. I have minimally discussed purity within its priestly context—that is, through the eyes of the priestly writers—and in this case through the perspective of H. Namely, impurity is that thing that Israel creates when it disobeys God's laws and behaves like the Canaanites. Here, impurity stands in opposition to holiness. But this is not the case for P. In P, impurity is anathema to the holy, but it is not its opposite (e.g., Lev. 15:16–18). There, the opposite of holy is common or profane; the opposite of impurity is purity. Moreover, the means that create impurity and the mechanisms that neutralize its effects differ between P and H.

Two issues are of primary interest to my discussion:

1. In P, impurities can be and should be neutralized by prescribed rituals (ablutions, time, or sacrifices), hence these impurities are often referred to as "ritual" impurities. Israel as a community moves between impure and pure via these rituals, but it does not move between common and holy, for in P all (lay) Israel is always common.
2. In H (Lev. 17–26), the impurities caused by bad behavior (often called "moral" impurities), are irredeemable. Once generated, they cannot be neutralized through ritual means. Only exile (of the people) or destruction (of the land) can right the wrongs done. In this paradigm, impure behaviors stand in opposition to holy behavior.

The link between the two ("ritual" and "moral") impurities is that they both affect the holy. An accumulation of either (or both) will cause either God (the Holy One) to leave the sanctuary or camp and take the divine blessings with him, or cause Israel to be spewed out of its land, thereby also severing its connection to divine blessing. While I acknowledge a difference between the two systems of P and H, by and large I will refer to them as one as I think my various writers view purity, in all its manifestations, as a united antagonistic front against holiness. Yet, where they differentiate between the two, so will I.

The "ritual" purity system of P (as opposed to the "moral" purity system of H) plays nary a role in my story except for one glaring exception, to which we turn our attention now. As with the various understandings of holiness, the nonpriestly texts often present their own notions of purity. By and large, purity is a system that functions in parallel to holiness, but purity and holiness are not one and the same. The system prescribed in P makes this abundantly clear. There, purity functions as a means to protect the holy. Israel is instructed to maintain purity in order to keep God's holy presence in its midst. The Israelites do not change their status vis-à-vis the holy by being pure—only their ability to approach it. They remain common, whether pure or impure. The nonpriestly biblical narratives in general have a looser notion of this sort of purity. Purity is something one does in order to handle holy items such as a sacrifice. The nonpriestly biblical writers do not provide all the details of what constitutes impurity nor its purification processes, as the priestly texts do. In contrast, P lists the causes of impurity (naturally occurring bodily issues such as menstrual blood and semen, as well as corpses and certain skin diseases), as well as the mechanisms through which one neutralizes the effects of these impurities (time, ablutions, and sacrifices).

The nonpriestly texts tend to focus on only one impurity: semen pollution and the need to be purified of it if one wishes to bring sacrifice at an altar to

God or otherwise "enter" God's presence.[15] Moreover, making matters more confusing, and hence significant to our discussion, the nonpriestly texts often utilize a QDS-root word to signify that purification process. While P avoids QDS as "pure/purify," the other biblical writers often deploy QDS as "holy/ sanctifying" *and* QDS as "pure/purify" in the same sentence or passage.[16] Hence, these texts allow for one to purify oneself (QDS) in order to "meet one's maker," the Holy One (QDS).[17]

Those passages in which the authors use QDS to signify "purify" often appear narratively at a moment of preparation before a divine encounter. In I Samuel 16:5, for instance, Samuel purifies (QDS) Jesse and his sons before they offer sacrifice together: "And he [Samuel] said: 'Peace, I have come to sacrifice to YHWH, purify [hitqaddshu] yourselves and come with me to sacrifice.' And he [Samuel] purified [vayeqaddesh] Jesse and his sons and he called them to sacrifice."[18]

Samuel does not consecrate Jesse and his sons to God but, rather, cultically prepares them (through physical purification) to approach the altar. Presumably offering sacrifice at a sacred shrine assumes purity of some sort, however our text neglects to specify either the offending impurities or the mechanisms of purification. Similarly, in Joshua 3:5, Joshua directs the people hitqaddashu, for "tomorrow God will perform miracles in your midst." God's immanent "arrival" in the camp calls for purity, here signified by QDS. Again, in Numbers 11:18, the people are called upon to prepare/purify themselves, for God will descend into the camp the next day to pour his spirit onto the elders and to bring the promised quail upon a wind.

In another instance, in 1 Samuel 21:4–6, David and his men are on the run (or in hiding) and hungry. David approaches the priest at Nob (a local shrine) and demands food:

> 4. "Now then, what have you got on hand? Give me five loaves of bread—or whatever is available." 5. The priest answered David, "I have no common bread on hand; there is only consecrated [qodesh] bread—provided the young men have kept away from women." 6. In reply to the priest, David said, "Women have been kept from us since my going out the day before yesterday. The vessels of the young men were purified [qodesh] even though the journey is a common one; even today they are purified [yiqddash] in their vessels."[19]

In reply to David's request for food, the priest notes that he has only consecrated bread on hand. The priest in turn asks if the men have refrained from sexual contact with women. David answers yes, indeed, for three days the men's "vessels" have been qodesh. One could understand, from his statement that the men's vessels (whatever those are) have been dedicated (to God), but "purified" makes more sense syntactically. Furthermore, the "vessels," *kelim*, are often understood to be weapons (the men are at war, after all); but given the reference to sexual abstinence, I suggest that the vessels should be understood as sexual organs or the clothing that covers them. By refraining from sexual intercourse for three days the men have not defiled themselves (or their clothing) with semen.[20] In their present physically pure state they would be allowed to eat consecrated bread.[21]

The quintessential passage—the one that gives us the most information—is Exodus 19:10–15. Here, we have both a use of QDS (twice) and two specific ritual prescriptions: washing of clothing and refraining from sexual activity. Because we will also be discussing this passage several times later in this book, it will prove useful to examine it in detail here. Exodus 19:10–11 and 14–15 read as follows:

> 10. And YHWH said to Moses, Go to the people, and purify them [*veqiddashtam*] today and tomorrow, and have them wash their clothes. 11. And be ready for the third day; for on the third day YHWH will come down in the sight of all the people upon Mount Sinai. . . . 14. And Moses came down from the mountain to the people, and purified [*vayeqaddesh*] the people; and they washed their clothes. 15. And he said to the people, Be ready by the third day; do not approach a woman.[22]

In this passage we find Moses on the mountain receiving instructions from God several days before Revelation. The Israelites remain at the foot of the mountain in their camp. But before that momentous event God commands Moses to go to the people and purify them (*veqiddashtam*) and have them wash their clothing so that they will be ready for the third day, on which "YHWH will come down in the sight of all the people upon Mount Sinai" (vv.10–11). Moses goes to the people, and he purifies the people (*vayeqaddesh et ha-am*), and directs them to launder their clothing but also adds another instruction, "do not approach a woman"—that is, refrain from sexual intercourse. While many English translations render the Hebrew *veqiddashtam* (v. 10) and *vayeqaddesh* (v. 14) as "sanctify," they are better understood as "purify." Following Baruch Schwartz's argument as noted above, one key to understanding QDS as "purify" is through the syntax. Something that is to be sanctified must be sanctified to or for God. Here, God does not instruct Moses to "QDS the people to me (God)" but, rather, just to "QDS them." Hence, the connotation must be "purify"—for all holy things belong to God. Sanctity in the biblical context cannot stand on its own. One cannot claim to have sanctified something or someone—only to have sanctified (separated out for or dedicated) them *to God*. In this context, the Israelites have already been sanctified by God (or will be in the future) when God declares that they "will be for me a holy nation [*goy qadosh*] and a kingdom of priests" (Exod. 19:6). Hence, when God sends Moses down the mountain to prepare the people for their divine audience, that preparation entails purification, not sanctification. They prepare themselves in order to be able to withstand meeting God's holiness (the source of all things holy) face to face. In order to survive such an encounter with the Holy, the people must purify themselves—that is, rid themselves of those things that God's holiness finds anathema. In this case, the laundering of their clothing and the refraining from sexual relations is part and parcel of that purification process. So at this momentous occasion just before Revelation, the people prepare themselves "to meet their maker" through certain physical purificatory rites, particularly those that rid them of semen pollution.

These nonpriestly texts also reveal a notion of holiness as danger.[23] This narrative repeatedly insists that Israel be prepared—lest God's holiness destroy them. While Israel waits impatiently at the bottom of the mountain for either Moses to return or God to reveal Godself, God carefully, insistently, and repeatedly instructs Moses to keep first the people and then the priests away from the mountain, lest the Lord "break out upon them" (Exod. 19:22, 24). God takes care of his own, yet his holy presence is dangerous. Even in their purified state the people are at risk if they get too close. The priests, who will come even closer to God's presence, must be especially careful to purify (QDS) themselves, lest they be destroyed. In the nonpriestly narrative texts, one protects oneself from God's *qedushah* (holiness), yet prepares oneself for encountering that holy presence through "*qiddshut*" (purification). I label this sort of purity "superpurity" because in these narratives, it seems to carry an extra heavy imperative and potential for larger disaster if not followed precisely.

In sum, these narratives provide illustrations of moments when individuals or all of Israel must prepare themselves for an encounter of some sort with God. These very special occasions require an extreme level of physical or ritual purity. In 1 Samuel 21 and Exodus 19, temporary sexual abstinence—as a means to control semen pollution—arises as the most appropriate purification process. Yet these texts do not always or completely reveal the rationale behind these requirements. It is assumed that human bodily impurities, such as semen, are anathema in some way to God's presence and must be neutralized through purification rites before a divine encounter. At the same time, God's holiness presents clear dangers to the underprepared. God's presence, though courted, is also potently deadly. Purity affected through ritual means protects the people from the dangers of God's holiness, as well as readies them for cultic service.

As we shall see in the following chapters, the danger of semen pollution remains a live issue to many later writers in one form or another. The Qumranites protect their desert encampment and projected holy city from semen pollution by keeping their wives (with whom and for whom they "produce" semen) out of the camp and holy city.[24] The early Rabbis consider how and when to purify themselves from semen pollution before they give up on it all together. Yet, early Christian writers, inspired by the dual usage of QDS (which they most often read in translation) purposefully fuse the two meanings, creating a new notion of sanctification through semen pollution avoidance—namely, sexual renunciation, which we will discuss in greater detail in the next chapters. These primarily Christian readings, which transform this biblical purity paradigm into a new construct of holiness achieved through sexual renunciation, can be found, nonetheless, in Jewish exegetical sources as well. This is the subject of the last two chapters.

Holiness and Sexuality

The Torah as we have received it, then, presents us with several competing and seemingly incompatible paradigms of holiness. E and D posit that the people Israel are holy by virtue of their chosenness. P allows that only the priests are truly holy. And finally H offers the opportunity for all Israel to achieve holiness, but it must work at it for it is not a given. The "ritual" and "moral" purity paradigms discussed above come into play as they interact with these two notions of ascribed or achieved holiness. The pentateuchal redactor, in combining the various Torah traditions and harmonizing the narratives, leaves the theological differences side by side in uneasy coexistence. Later readers will capitalize on the varieties of holiness by homogenizing them or choosing one over the other. In some cases, the notion of ascribed holiness becomes primary; in others, achieved holiness proves more salient; and in certain cases, an uneasy harmony is constructed between the two.

Yet, wittingly or not, these biblical texts lay the groundwork for what I am calling a hermeneutic of holiness and sexuality. That is to say, I see here the seeds of a variety of understandings of holiness that is inextricably linked to sexual practices. A priest must limit whom he can marry, all Israel must avoid certain bad sexual practices (incest, adultery, etc.), and certain occasions of divine revelation require temporary sexual abstinence. Together in various combinations, these biblical prescriptions suggest to later authors that sexuality plays a large role in defining a community's relationship to God. Therefore, understanding how biblically derived communities define themselves and their community vis-à-vis the holy can be discovered through an examination of that community's sexual practices. Hence, my hermeneutic lens is sexuality.

In this case I do not construe sexuality as sexual orientation as in modern discourse but, rather, as either union of proper marriage partners or whether one is actively sexual or not. Nor do I assume that sexuality is the only means by which one can understand a community's notion of holiness; however, I do argue that it is central to that construct. We begin to see this transformation already in the biblical texts. In the rest of this chapter, we will study the examples laid out by Ezra and Ezekiel. Ezra gives us a model of ascribed holiness, but as I will suggest he does not ignore achieved holiness but, rather, transforms it into a subset of ascribed holiness. Ezekiel presents us with an example of achieved holiness gone awry. The "super-purity" paradigm discussed above does not interest these later biblical writers, but will become central to our post-biblical exegetes, particularly in the Christian community.

Ascribed Holiness Solidified

Ezra's Holy Seed

Ezra, a late biblical book that chronicles the exiled Judeans' return to their land and city in the fifth century BCE, ushers in a new era and paradigm of Israel's holiness that, in turn, influences many of the para-biblical writings of the Second Temple period. Ezra depends here on the prophet Jeremiah primarily and follows the deuteronomical notion that Israel gains holiness through ascription and that its behavior derives from that status. Yet both Jeremiah (2:3) and Ezra (9:2) take this concept of a holy nation one step further than the pentateuchal texts in decreeing that Israel, as a holy nation, or seed, can be desecrated in the same manner as any of God's other sancta—namely, through outside forces.

In Jeremiah's paradigm, it is the other nations, Israel's enemies and conquerors, who have "consumed" Israel like forbidden first fruits, who are guilty of that desecration.[25] As a result, Israel turns from God to idolatry and thus brings ruin upon itself. But Ezra reverses the equation. Israel, the holy seed, has desecrated itself by further importing the "enemy" into itself through intermarriage. In both images Israel the holy nation is a sanctum, a holy thing of God that must be or should have been protected from desecration. Ezra, here, combines the deuteronomical image of the holy nation that should remain separate and distinct from the nations of the land with the priestly notion of sancta contamination. Ironically, this same priestly paradigm does not include Israel among God's sancta—thus Ezra's innovation.[26] Furthermore, according to the levitical paradigm, a sanctum, once desecrated, cannot be reconsecrated, only replaced.[27] Yet, Ezra posits that Israel, if it rids itself of its foreign spouses (the cause of its desecration), will not lose its holy status. In essence, Ezra posits that Israel, a holy seed, must protect itself first and foremost from profanation. Endogamy ensures the purity (i.e., unadulterated state) of the holy seed.

Concerning profanation of the holy seed, Ezra (9:1–2) returns to the non-priestly paradigm of a Holy Israel with a twist. He claims:

> 1b. The people of Israel and the priests and Levites have not sepa-
> rated themselves [lo'nivddelu] from the peoples of the land whose
> abhorrent practices are like those of the Canaanites, the Hittites, the
> Perizzites, the Jebusites, the Ammonites, the Moabites, the Egyptians
> and the Amorites. 2. They have taken their daughters as wives for
> themselves and for their sons, so that the holy seed has become
> intermingled [vehit'arvu zera' ha-qodesh] with the peoples of the land;
> and it is the officers and the prefects who have taken the lead in this
> trespass [ba-ma'al ha-zeh].[28]

Ezra presents Israel not only as holy but as a *qodesh* in its own right—a free-standing holy thing, a holy seed, a sanctum. As such, it must be protected (or in this case, protect itself) from desecration. If profaned, Israel loses its special status and would find itself no different from the surrounding people. In other words, Israel would no longer distinguish itself, nor separate itself out for God (holy), but remain common—indistinguishable from any other nation. As Christine Hayes argues, Ezra's primary concern is protecting the "holy seed" of Israel from profanation.[29] Every Israelite who has returned from the Exile is a member of the holy community—each carries a holy seed. If other, common seed becomes mixed up with the holy seed, then the next generation of holy seed is rendered common, too. Ezra 9:2 states that: "the holy seed has become intermingled with the peoples of the land." As H. G. M. Williamson suggests, this phrasing recalls Leviticus 19:19 (within the holiness legislation), in which the priests ban the breeding of two different types of animals, the sowing of two types of seed together, and the weaving together of two different kinds of fiber. The Israelites, in intermingling their "seed" with other "seed," profane their offspring in mixing the unmixable.[30] Furthermore, Ezra calls this inter-mingling a *ma'al*, often translated as "transgression," but should be here understood as "sancta contamination" or "sacrilege," for which a specific sacrifice, an *asham*, is needed as reparation.[31]

The mixing of the profane with the sacred is an offense against God that can be repaired only through a guilt offering. As Jacob Milgrom explains, the import of Leviticus 5:14, which instructs that when any one is "inadvertently remiss with any of the Lord's sancta," he is guilty of a *ma'al*, an offense against God (for he has "messed with" God's holy things)—he must bring a reparation sacrifice, an *asham*. The sacrifice invokes God's forgiveness for offending God, and "repays" God for the item now profaned and useless to God.[32] Indeed, the Judeans who acknowledge their guilt (of offending God through illicit mixing of seed that occurred in their mixed marriages) "offered a ram from the flock to expiate it" (Ezra 10:19).[33]

Nevertheless, this explanation does not completely illuminate how Ezra understands exogamy to constitute a *ma'al*. It is clear, I think, that he refers to the mixing of the unmixable, or *kilayim*, which is banned in Leviticus 19:19. But is *kilayim* a *ma'al*? Perhaps it is not technically included in the thought processes behind Leviticus 5 (P) but, rather, is implied through its inclusion in the holiness code of Leviticus 19 (H). As Milgrom notes, the category of *miqad-shei YHWH* in Leviticus 5:14 is ambiguous and undefined by that text. Only by comparing it contextually with other biblical and nonbiblical texts can Milgrom determine that this phrase refers to a very broad category of anything that belongs to God from the time it is dedicated until it is consumed.[34] Clearly, Ezra builds from both of these paradigms, positing that Israel, the holy seed, is a sanctum of God that can be desecrated like other sancta (sacrifices, temple furniture, etc.); that it has been desecrated through another illicit action (*kilayim*, the mixing of the unmixable—in this case, human rather than agricultural holy seed with profane seed); and that the people themselves are the guilty ones for they have been "inadvertently remiss" with one of the Lord's sancta—his holy seed, Israel. In essence, the Judeans do not profane themselves irrevocably, nor individually, but, rather, their intermarriages affect the community at large, particularly their offspring. Their children by foreign wives are profane (because they were procreated from a mix of seeds), and hence they cannot be counted among the holy.[35] Therefore, Ezra expels the children with their mothers from the holy community. The Judeans' offense has more to do with the future community than with the existing one—for if the present community produces only common (mixed) seed, there will be no one to carry on the holy seed and the community will die out.

Christine Hayes describes Ezra's notion of profanation in terms of genealogical purity.[36] Ezra is the first biblical author to describe Judean/Israelite (rather than just priestly) identity along genealogical lines. Ezra claims that "Israeliteness" comes through birth only. In order to ascertain who is "in" and who is "out," Ezra checks the priestly genealogical books. Yet, rather than a simple racist or blood-purist ideology, Ezra couches his construct in cultic terms. Israel is holy; as such, it can be desecrated by admixture, as described above. Nevertheless, Ezra also incorporates the genealogical purity restrictions of the priests to further his point. In Leviticus 21, the common priests are required to avoid certain spouses (harlots and divorcees). The high priest is additionally warned to marry only virgins from "among his people." (Whether this means among Israelites or among the priestly class or just his particular family/clan, the text does not elaborate.) Ezekiel 44:22, however, further restricts the (Zaddokite) priests to marry only virginal Israelite women.[37] H links these spousal restrictions directly to holiness. The wrong spouse would profane the priest's lineage, rendering his offspring common and unfit for the priesthood. Endogamy, therefore, preserves the priestly prerogative of holiness throughout the generations. Ezra, having democratized holiness among all Israel, likewise advises endogamy to preserve all Israel's holiness past the present generation. In Ezra, a non-Israelite spouse renders an Israelite's children non-Israelite. Ezra thereby solidifies Israel's ascribed holiness (E and D) and prescribes behavior (endogamy) accordingly following the priestly patterns (P and H). In so doing he also highlights the developing link between proper sexuality (in this case, marriage partners) and holiness.

Holiness Protection

Ezra, like the Deuteronomist, perceives a further and chronic danger for Israel if it does not continue to separate itself from its neighbors. For this reason, he develops a parallel system of protection of the sanctum from defilement. These present peoples of the land, like the ancient Canaanites before them, follow abominable ways. The Canaanites' abhorrent practices polluted the land to such an extent that it spewed them out. Referring back to the Canaanites while also implicating the present peoples of the land, Ezra notes that Moses said, "[t]he land that you are about to possess is a land unclean through the uncleanness of the peoples of the land, through their abhorrent practices with which they, in their impurity, have filled it from one end to the other" (Ezra 9:11).[38] As Jonathan Klawans has noted, peoples of the land (both present and past) generate irredeemable "moral" impurity, not manageable or contagious "ritual" impurity.[39] These abominable practices include the "big three" sins of sexual impurity, murder, and idolatry, as outlined in H.[40] Idolatry rises as Ezra's primary concern, for by alluding to Deuteronomy 7:2 (the biblical verse most closely approximating Ezra's list of forbidden marriage partners among the Canaanites), Ezra also includes the deuteronomical rationale for avoiding these peoples—the fear of being lead astray into idolatry—within his own paradigm.[41]

While Ezra accuses the present Gentiles of generating impurity, he does not argue that their impurity affects Israel's status directly, for he emphasizes the effects on the land, not the people.[42] Rather, he argues that the presence of the Gentiles among the Judeans presents the Judeans with the opportunity to learn and copy the Gentiles' abhorrent ways, thereby threatening *their own* security on their land with *their own* impure behavior, which defiles the land. To wit, Ezra claims that the present peoples' practices are *like* those abhorrent practices of the ancient Canaanites. He does not make the claim that they are Canaanites—only that they practice the same bad habits. While one must assume that he implies that the present peoples of the land are defiling the land as well, he provokes the Israelites not to copy the Gentiles lest they be responsible themselves for defiling the land. Hence, in addition to outlawing marriage with the present peoples of the land for fear of profanation, he adds another rational—or hedge of purity—that they should completely separate from these peoples so as not to learn their ways and imitate them so as to be the cause of their own exile (through the impure act of idolatry). For, if Ezra's concern was that the impure behaviors of the peoples were going to cause the Judeans' exile (either by defiling the Judeans contagiously or the land), Ezra would have had to require the complete expulsion of those people from the land.[43] This obviously was not politically expedient, or even possible, since the retuning Judeans were probably well outnumbered. In essence, Ezra rationalizes that only complete separation will prevent the Israelites from copying, let alone marrying, Gentiles.[44]

Yet this notion of separation can also be read in another way. Ezra claims that the Judeans have not separated from the peoples of the land, using the term *nivddal*, "distinguish." As we learned above, the notion of holiness subsumes a category of separation. In Deuteronomy, the Israelites manifest their ascribed holy status by distinguishing between themselves and all others. In contrast, in Leviticus, the Israelites actively achieve their holy status by following God's commandments, which include not imitating the abominable ways of the Canaanites. Ezra, starting with the assumption that Israel is already holy, presumes that separation is a necessary outcome of that designation. Ezra does not practice separation/distinction in order to become holy (H) but, rather, presumes separation because one is already holy (D). But more than just a manifestation of Israel's holiness, separation actively protects Israel from damaging its holy status, both from profanation (through exogamy) and through defilement (by imitating the impure behaviors of the Gentiles).

In short, then, I posit that Ezra understands the separation of Israel from the present peoples of the land to operate on several levels. First, he is concerned with the profanation of the holy seed—an innovation on his part—through the illicit mixing of two unmixable seeds. This mixing of seeds creates genealogical impurity/profanation—common or profane seed. Second, he is concerned with the continuing process of preserving the purity of the land as an abode for the holy people (through rigorous maintenance of behavioral purities), which can be accomplished only through the necessary separation from the other peoples and their impure ways. Finally, he simply assumes separation is a necessary outcome of holy chosenness. The holiness code suggests that one achieves holiness by separating oneself from the other nations both by following God's distinctive commandments *and* by avoiding the impure behavior characteristic of those nations. Ezra, in contrast, presumes the Judeans' holiness is inherent already. Thus, this separation merely preserves their already God-given holy status while at the same time preventing exile by avoiding the defiling behaviors that pollute the land. Protecting Israel's purity and its holy status through avoiding the impure behaviors that defile the land does not create holiness for Israel, but it is cast as a hedge of purity around Israel's inherent holiness. Profanation of the seed, defilement of the land, and certainly both combined would bring disaster to Israel. Separation occurs both when one is holy and as a means to protect one's inherent holy status in a holy land. Ezra carefully keeps his categories of holiness and purity distinct, all the while arguing that the lack of either will prove detrimental to Israel's survival in the land—distinctive behaviors, particularly in the realm of marriage and sexuality, prove key to both.

Israel the Prostitute

In the late-biblical and Second Temple literature we find further developments in the ideologies of purity and holiness, particularly those that link holiness with proper sexuality and improper sexuality with impurity. Whether following a hermeneutic of ascribed holiness (such as Ezra) or achieved holiness (H), sexual practices play a large role in these constructs. Ezra and the late prophets Jeremiah and Ezekiel sit on the chronological and theological divide between the biblical and post-biblical/Second Temple worlds and are instrumental in formulating or influencing new constructs of holiness. Yet even within these biblical texts and the constructs already discussed, sexuality, whether referring to sexual practices or sexual partners, emerges as a focus, if not the central focus. We saw above that genealogical purity, which protects the lineage of the holy priestly line (H), involves limited marriage partners for priests (no widows, divorcees, etc.). Yet Ezra, by democratizing this priestly construct further, applies marriage-partner limitations to all Israel because of its holiness. Second, two out of the eleven chapters of the holiness code (H) focus almost exclusively on sexual conduct—namely, further limitations on marriage partners even among lay Israelites. Finally, the prophetic focus on Israel's idolatry

and its metaphorical transformation into a form of religious *zenut*, or prostitution, have had great influence on certain segments of Second Temple literature and post-biblical hermeneutics of holiness and its inherent relationship
to sexuality.[45] I will focus the rest of this section on these sexual prohibitions
and the prophetic language of religious *zenut* because they are so successfully
combined by the later Second Temple writers.

As we saw above, Leviticus 18 and 20 delineate forbidden sexual relationships, among them adultery, bestiality, homosexuality, incest, and sexual congress
with a menstruant (also known as the forbidden consanguineous relations, or
the *gilui 'arayot*, in later rabbinic writings). Already in these priestly texts we
perceive a heightened sense of proper sexual behavior and general ethical behavior. Idolatry, which plays a larger part in the prophetic writings, appears here
only as a subcategory of general unjust behavior. Chapters 18 through 20, though
focusing on exploitative sexual and other socially unjust behavior, includes legislation against Molekh worship that defiles the sanctuary and profanes God's
name (Lev. 18:21; 20:3). Among other things, to be holy one must avoid all sorts
of improper sexual partnering: incest, adultery, bestiality, homosexuality, and the
niddah (the menstruant).[46] Noncompliance among Israelites creates an impurity
that defiles God's sanctuary and the land upon which the Israelites live. An over-
accumulation of this sort of impurity will eventually spew the people out—as it
spewed out the Canaanites before them. Leviticus 18:30 explicitly states that this
sort of bad behavior was endemic among the Canaanites, and the Israelites
should be sure to avoid it in order to (a) differentiate themselves from them and
(b) ensure their continued safety in the land. It is important to note that while
these bad sexual behaviors defile the land and sanctuary, they more importantly
prevent Israel from achieving holiness. I am less interested in categorizing this
sort of impurity than I am in highlighting its opposition to holiness. Proper
sexual partnering (among other things) is a mechanism by which Israel can
make itself holy. Illicit sexual partnering, by its defiling nature, makes one into
a Canaanite (or the equivalent thereof). An Israelite is one who strives for holiness, a Canaanite can or does not. Thus, Israel both achieves its holiness and
differentiates itself from its neighbors. Nevertheless, forbidden consanguineous
relations and Molekh worship stand out as the most offensive to God because
they damage the cult.[47] Sexual offenses defile the individuals involved and pollute the land, idolatry affects the sanctuary and God's reputation. Yet the two are
subtly linked not only by virtue of adjacency in the legislation but also through
the metaphor of religious prostitution.

While in Leviticus, harlotry per se is not defined as polluting, in certain cases
it is profaning. Women who prostitute themselves suffer grave punishment.
Leviticus 19:29 directs: "Do not degrade [profane] your daughter by making her

a harlot, lest the land fall into harlotry and the land become full of depravity." Also, Leviticus 21:9 notes that the daughter of a priest who commits harlotry profanes both herself and her father and she receives capitol punishment for her crime. In other words, the promiscuous woman creates community chaos (illegitimate children), but the priestly daughter disqualifies her progeny from continuing in the priestly line. In essence, the offspring of harlotry, because of their questionable lineage, cannot be included in the community. This is particularly important for the priestly daughter because only the priests are inherently holy, by levitical standards. As we noted above, genealogical purity is an issue for priests only in the levitical texts. Yet, Ezra extends the qualifications to all Israel. In Leviticus at least, harlotry is not a sexually offensive behavior (such as incest) that pollutes the land, but it does profane the woman's children and her father's priestly line.

H links Molekh worship (which includes "giving one's children" to this god of the underworld) and sexual harlotry, in that these acts both profane Israelite children. Molekh worship further damages God's reputation and hence affects the worshipers as well (they disqualify themselves from God's care). Other biblical writers further associate Molekh worship (and other idolatry or foreign worship) and sexual harlotry through the metaphor of religious *zenut* (prostitution). Israelite worshipers of Molekh and other foreign gods, by virtue of their unfaithfulness to God, "play the harlot" with these gods. In so doing they profane God's name and their children, as well as defile the sanctuary. The Israelites sin through idolatry (polluting God's sanctuary), but the metaphor of sexual prostitution emphasizes the damage they cause to the community as a whole.

The language of sexualized sin and unfaithfulness is not limited to the priestly texts. Both Exodus 34:16 and Deuteronomy 31:16 talk of Israel "lusting" after, or "playing the harlot," with the foreign gods that they will find in the land of Israel. The Hebrew word used is *zanah* "to commit fornication" or "to be a harlot."[48] The Torah text deploys the term figuratively to describe Israel's unfaithfulness to YHWH. The Israelites will forget their covenantal agreement to worship only God in order to "take up" with the Canaanite gods. Israel in particular will continue to worship YHWH along with their other idols, tarnishing God's exclusive reputation. Hayes labels this unfaithfulness religious *zenut*. Israel, in worshipping other gods, is likened to a prostitute who has many sexual partners. All idolatry, through the linked images of Molekh worship (giving children to a foreign god) and sexual prostitution (the profaning of one's seed through admixture), thus becomes profaning to Israelite worshipers—they disqualify themselves and their children from God's protection.

The prophets take this metaphor for unfaithfulness a step further by connecting Israel's unfaithfulness/prostitution to pollution, as well as profanation, further imbricating the two notions. Jeremiah, for instance, compares Israel's behavior to the wife who is twice divorced but wants to go back to (or be taken back by) the first husband (Jer. 3:1). The Deuteronomist calls the remarriage of a twice-divorced wife to her first husband impure and an abomination before God (Deut. 24:1–4). The wife has "disqualified" herself from returning to her first husband after she has been married to a second husband. Following Milgrom's argument that the incest laws protect women from sexual exploitation, here too the twice-divorced wife is protected from being handed back and forth between two men.[49] Remarriage to a former spouse is codified here as a form of sexual impurity similar to adultery or incest. Similarly, Israel, by "sleeping around" with the foreign gods, has technically disqualified itself from being taken back by YHWH. Jeremiah specifically classifies Israel's idolatry as a type of harlotry (Jer. 3:1, 2) that pollutes the land. Building on H's paradigm in which Molekh worship defiles the sanctuary, Jeremiah posits that all idolatry defiles the land as well. Through religious *zenut* (idolatry), Israel has polluted the land, making itself abhorrent to God and the land uninhabitable.

In the previous section we saw that Jeremiah also accuses Israel's enemies of profaning Israel. The acts of outsiders profane Israel, but its own "prostitution" disqualifies it as well as defiles the land. By assuming that remarriage to a former spouse defiles and Israel's idolatry equates with prostitution, Jeremiah posits that Israel's idolatry not only profanes God's name and defiles the sanctuary but also defiles the land, which will eventually spew the Israelites out. Hosea likewise accuses Ephraim/Israel of harlotry and impurity (Hos. 6:10), adultery (7:4), and "mixing" with the other peoples (7:8). Here, Israel profanes itself through harlotry/idolatry. Idolatry and harlotry merge to create a hyper-detrimental behavioral impurity that affects the people and their land.

Ezekiel, utilizing the biblical texts before him, pushes this metaphor of Israel's sexual unfaithfulness to its fullest potential. The language of impurity further penetrates his discussion of Israel's infidelity. Unlike Jeremiah, Ezekiel does not hold that all Israelites are holy, thus he cannot claim that they profane themselves by their actions; rather, he must concentrate on their polluting behaviors. Hence, he shifts his metaphor from prostitution to adultery (Ezek. 16:30–34). Ezekiel saves his most virulent language for Israel's idolatrous acts. He compares the faithless people of Jerusalem to a whore who fornicates with anyone who comes her way. Israel, in turning to other gods and other forms of worship, particularly those of its neighbors, behaves as promiscuously as a harlot. Jerusalem, the poor bedraggled, rejected orphan that God takes under his wing and raises to young adulthood, turns on her husband/caretaker to court other lovers among the nations. Yet, Ezekiel also accuses her of adultery, for she offers the gifts that God gave her to other gods. Most abhorrent, she sacrifices her children as offerings to her fetishes.[50] At other times, Ezekiel compares Israel's unfaithfulness more directly to an overabundant sexual appetite—for she did not even bother to accept payment for her lovers but went to them freely; she is more willing adulterer than desperate prostitute. Israel's covenantal agreement to worship YHWH exclusively maps favorably onto a marriage contract in Ezekiel's imagery.[51] As adultery, rather than or in addition to prostitution, Israel's idolatry falls squarely into the bad behaviors of H.

Leviticus, of course, reminds us that the particular behaviors that undid the Canaanites were the forbidden consanguineous relations. By calling Israel's idolatry and unfaithfulness adultery, Ezekiel places its crime within this same category, which he calls more generally (zenut), or "fornication," but manifests itself much like the levitical (H) "moral" impurities.[52] Ezekiel 16:36 easily merges the two concepts of zenut and forbidden consanguineous relations into one: "Thus said the Lord God: Because of your brazen effrontery, offering your nakedness [ervatekh] to your lovers for your harlotry [betaznutayikh]." Rather than suffering victimization at the hands of a male householder's whim, Israel (a "married" woman) willingly and wantonly gives herself to her lovers, and thus brings destruction upon herself through the impure behavior of adultery. She is worse than the philandering patriarch because she willingly goes to her lovers. Most important for our discussion, however, is the merger of zenut and the forbidden consanguineous relations. As defined in Leviticus, these relations do not include prostitution (probably because the legislation is directed at a male audience). Rather, it is a list of inappropriate marriage partners for the male Israelite householder. Presumably the male Israelite can have sexual contact[53] with many other nonrelated females as long as they are not already married to someone else. Yet, in Ezekiel, the image of harlotry/adultery prevails—a particularly female-gendered image. Ezekiel uses both notions (harlotry and adultery) to describe Israel's idolatrous behavior. Israel is an adulterer because of its infidelity to God; Israel is likened to a prostitute because Israel has taken many lovers/foreign gods. Yet in combining the two notions of zenut and the forbidden consanguineous relations, Ezekiel does not forgo the impact of the latter; rather, he implicates the polluting nature of the latter onto the former. Israel pollutes itself, the land, and the sanctuary all the more now that its idolatry is defined as adultery (prostitution profanes the individual, but adultery pollutes the land and sanctuary as well). Ezekiel embellishes and strengthens H's language of impurity and sexuality in his prophecies of Israel's unfaithfulness and resultant destruction. Israel defiles itself, God's name, and God's sanctuary with its sexualized idolatrous abominations. While Israel's crime is idolatry/worshiping foreign Gods, Ezekiel's metaphor of sexual promiscuity, prostitution, and adultery highlights and demonizes Israel's failings.

According to the biblical texts, Israel defiles the land and the sanctuary, bringing disaster upon itself through idolatry, but Ezekiel's more nuanced metaphor of sexualized disobedience only adds to the growing sense of necessary proper sexual behavior as somehow linked to chosenness or holiness. For one can only imagine if the disobedient and idolatrous Israel compares well to a prostitute or adulterous lover, how much more a faithful Israel could be cast as a chaste, sexually pure, or even celibate lover/spouse. These images and notions of sexual purity play themselves out in many of the later texts, including the patristic and rabbinic writings. While constructing codes of proper sexual behavior that either descend from one's chosenness and protect it or elevate one to holiness, many exegetes also focus on perceived improper sexual behavior (particularly of others) as the cause of irredeemable impurity or even profanation that would necessarily negate any possibility of holiness. Nevertheless, even for those authors for whom Israel's holiness is a given, Ezekiel's redefinition of *zenut* inspires many later writers from the author of Jubilees to Paul.

Conclusions

In sum, then, I understand the biblical texts to provoke three different hermeneutics of holiness. Holiness ascribed, holiness achieved, and a third phenomenon, to be manipulated by later readers: holiness as a derivative of protection from semen pollution ("super-purity"). This third paradigm becomes central to the fourth-century writers. I focus the rest of this book on the biblically exegeted link between holiness and sexuality and its developments. Ezra gives us one fine example of an expanded notion of ascribed holiness. The book of Jubilees, examined in the next chapter, gives us another.

The notion of achieved holiness transforms itself further in two ways in these and other subsequent biblical texts. In the one we see "holiness achieved" becoming a notion of "holiness protection" for the already holy. Ezra again provides the example. In the other, the metaphor of sexual infidelity becomes the marker of Israel's downfall. Israel loses its special status vis-à-vis God—namely, its holiness—through sexualized sin. That is to say, the real sin is idolatry or polytheism, but our authors construe it as sexual sin. In behaving like the Canaanites, Israel defiled the land and indeed was spewed out into Exile. Nevertheless, these authors, and many later ones, who strongly suggest that Israel failed to achieve holiness still wonder whether Israel nonetheless managed to retain its ascribed holiness. We will see how this tension is resolved in the following chapters. The book of Jubilees proves essential to this transformation.

2

Holy Seed or Holy Deed

Sexuality, Holiness, and Purity in Second Temple Literature

Notions of holiness and sexuality move in several different directions in the literature of the Second Temple period. This chapter by no means can capture all the nuances; however, I focus on what I see as the main trends, particularly those that carry over, at least thematically if not directly, from the biblical literature and that in turn influence the late-ancient hermeneutics of Aphrahat and the Rabbis. As we examine the Second Temple literature, we will discover that three main themes rise to prominence. In one trend, Israel continues to be depicted as a holy seed, a sanctum of God. Here, the avoidance of *zenut*, described variously but usually meaning the act of marrying a forbidden (and often foreign) partner, becomes the focal point of preserving one's God-given (ascribed) holy status. In another trend, holiness achieved through obedience to the law prevails. Sexuality does not figure remarkably in this Second Temple period configuration, yet obedience to the law becomes a dominant trope in late-ancient hermeneutics and hence remains pertinent to my discussion. Finally, in a third trend, semen pollution arises as the main obstacle to preserving a pure place for God to reside among his holy people. While these three trends develop along separate lines in this period, it is in their multiple combinations that they influence or invigorate the holiness debates in the late-ancient period.

The literature of the Second Temple period is notoriously hard to date. Most of the texts I discuss here fall into the range of second-century BCE to first century CE. It is not my primary goal to place these texts in any chronological relationship to each other but, rather, to look for overlapping and divergent themes of holiness and sexuality.

Holy Seed: Holiness Ascribed

Ezra's notion of a holy seed that cannot be adulterated with unholy seed merges with Ezekiel's construct of idolatry (disobedience to God) as religious prostitution, or *zenut*. This fusion results in *zenut*'s transforming into a sinful category (disobedience) of its own. In its simplistic form, all idolaters (those whom one is not supposed to marry), particularly women, become prostitutes (*zonot*). In other forms *zonot* refers to all forbidden marriage partners among Israelites of any sort (be they of a different class, priestly, nonpriestly, or of a forbidden consanguineous relationship). *Zenut* then becomes a catchall term for the act of marrying a forbidden partner. The precedence set by the H authors, who limited marriage partners for priests because they are holy to God, develops into a broader trend applied to all Israel. Israel, a holy sanctum in and of itself, must also place restrictions on whom Israel can marry.

In the book of Tobit, for instance, Tobit counsels his son Tobias to be aware of all *porneias*,[1] and to take a wife only from the seed of his fathers (4:12). Thus, Tobias can expect to be as blessed as Abraham, Isaac, and Jacob. Though this author does not use the language of holiness, he clearly divides between "us" (we are the sons of prophets) and "them" (those who are not). Moreover, the act of taking a foreign wife is considered an improper sexual relation, while endogamy comes with the blessings of Abraham.[2] In the Aramaic Testament of Levi, Levi similarly warns his sons away from *zenut*—namely, marrying a woman outside the family—because of his holy status. As Christine Hayes argues, in this case Levi warns his sons not only about non-Israelite women but also about marrying women outside the priestly line. For the priest, then, any nonpriestly woman is a *zonah*—a forbidden marriage partner.[3] Hence, the sons of Levi should marry only within their clan in order to preserve their holy and priestly status.

In contrast, the Damascus Document uses *zenut* to describe a whole host of illicit sexual partners, not specifically foreign or nonpriestly women. Rather, it accuses the Jerusalem priesthood of not following through on some basic rules of consanguineous relationships.[4] The authors of the Damascus Document expand their understanding and application of those rules and accuse anyone who does not follow through of *zenut* (disobedience). Hence, in the Second Temple period, *zonah* becomes a technical term for "a forbidden marriage" or a "forbidden marriage partner" of any sort (not just a foreigner), and *zenut* is the term for the act of marrying or have sexual relations with a *zonah*, though neither lose their original meanings entirely.[5] In Ezekiel, *zenut* metaphorically represents Israel's disobedience and points to idolatry. In the Second Temple literature, *zenut* becomes disobedience through sexual deviance.

In the following section we study two texts in depth that help transform *zenut* into a more insidious crime by classifying it as the worst of all "moral" impurities and, in this case, as intermarriage.

Jubilees

The book of Jubilees, composed in Hebrew during the second half of the second century BCE, was probably written by an Israelite priest of the Maccabean period who took issue with the priestly establishment over the sanctity of Israel.[6] The Jubilean author, like Ezra, assumes first and foremost that Israel is and always will be a holy sanctum of God.[7] The Israelites' holy status derives not only from Sinai but also from God's transformation of Jacob into Israel. Throughout the text the author refers to Israel (the people) and Jacob/Israel (the person) as the "holy people," "holy descendants," and "holy offspring."[8] God hallowed them and chose them (or Jacob) to be his own special possession (Jub. 2:18–33). In the same manner that God sanctifies the Sabbath and the angels—namely, separates them out for himself—so too God hallows Israel (Jub. 2:1, 24). All Israel, as descendants of Jacob, inherit their holiness from Jacob (as his "seed"). Hence, their holiness is native and ascribed from above. This closely follows both the nonpriestly pentateuchal traditions and Ezra. Echoing Exodus 19 and Genesis 17, the Jubilean angel informs Abraham and Sarah that Isaac will generate the holy seed. He will become "the Most High's portion, and all his descendants will settle in that land which belongs to God, so as to be the Lord's special possession, chosen out of all the nations, and to be a kingdom of priests and a holy nation" (Jub. 16:18). Isaac's descendants (through Jacob) are chosen, priestly and holy. Likewise, due to this special relationship with God, God requires Israel to follow the covenantal laws. Circumcision, Sabbath observance, and dietary restrictions loom large for this author's understanding of the covenant because these commandments ensure the separation of Israel from its neighbors. Yet they also protect the people from losing their holy/separated/elevated status. "[E]veryone who keeps the Sabbath day will be holy like the angels" (Jub. 2:17) really means for the Jubilean author that everyone who observes the laws of the Sabbath will remain holy—namely, preserve their God-given (ascribed) holy status. Keeping the positive commandments and avoiding profaning or defiling behavior is key to keeping and protecting their holy status, but it does not create the status in and of itself. Only God can hallow. Israel works exclusively to protect itself from contamination. For the Jubilean author, as in Ezra, holy protection comes first and foremost through endogamous marriages.

Recall that in Ezra's paradigm, because all Israel is holy seed, mixing any holy seed with unholy seed (via intermarriage) profanes (i.e., degrades) the resulting generation of holy seed. The children of mixed holy-unholy sexual unions are impure, alloyed, not fully native Israelite and cannot be included in the holy community of Israel. Hence, Ezra directs the returning Judeans to expel their foreign wives, as well as the children of those marriages, for neither qualify as holy seed. However, the Judean men, despite their lapses in marriage partners, remain holy. As Hayes argues, the Jubilean author moves well beyond Ezra with a much more complex argument for endogamy.[9] In effect he argues that miscegenation (the act of sex with a foreigner) in and of itself pollutes the Israelite partner and the land. The sexual relations conducted in an exogamous marriage cause impurities in the same manner as idolatry and consanguineous relations do. In this way, the sexual act both profanes (makes common) the children and pollutes the parents and the land. The community must excise such families in order to preserve themselves.

The Jubilean author comes to this conclusion through a complex reading of the biblical texts. First, he moves all Israel into the same holy category as the priests, since according to Exodus 19:6 they are "a nation of priests." Second, he applies the priestly marriage restrictions to all Israel analogously. Martha Himmelfarb argues that the author of Jubilees is particularly concerned with the practices of all Israel, not just the priesthood, and hence he insists that if all Israel is a nation of priests, they should all act accordingly.[10] If the biblical texts forbid the priests from marrying certain types of women (widows, divorcees. etc.), so too, the Jubilean author claims, does the Bible forbid all Israelites, in their "priestly" mode, from marrying foreigners. Following Ezekiel, who prohibits all non-Israelite women to the Zaddokite priests, the Jubilean author similarly prohibits Israel, as a priestly nation, from marrying all non-Israelites. Third, the Jubilean author relates this law to the biblical law against Molekh worship found in Leviticus 18:21 and 20:3. There, the texts forbid the Israelites from "passing their seed/offspring over" to Molekh. While in the biblical context this probably refers to child sacrifice to this god of the underworld, the Jubilean author assumes it means giving one's children in marriage to an idolater (read: all Gentiles) and thereby creating more Gentile (read: unholy) seed. Hence, Torah law, according to Jubilees, forbids all intermarriages between a holy Israelite and an unholy Gentile.

Fourth, and most importantly for this study, the Jubilean author labels intermarriage *zenut*, something Ezra never does. While the biblical texts, particularly the late prophets, metaphorize Israel's "love affair" with foreign gods as religious *zenut*/prostitution, Jubilees moves in the opposite direction, declaring *zenut* to be sexual relations with foreigners and the more serious crime. Israel suffers because of its intermarriage rate, not its idolatrous acts. Whereas the practice of idolatry creates impurity in the land and among the people in the biblical texts, *zenut*—intermarriage and the miscegenation that comes with it—becomes the greatest creator of pollution among the people and hence the biggest threat to Israel's holiness and its security in the land. The Gentiles' idolatrous practices, while certainly detrimental to themselves, are not the main reason they cannot marry Israelites. They cannot marry Israelites simply because they are not Israelites. Israelite seed is holy, while Gentile seed is profane. Here, the Jubilean author moves beyond the religio-social reasoning put forward by some biblical authors that marrying an idolater will necessarily lead an Israelite to idolatry. Rather, like Ezra, he builds a fence of purity around Israel's holiness.

This Jubilean "prooftext of endogamous marriage"[11] descends from a legalistic reading of the biblical narrative of Dinah's abduction that further interweaves the priestly code into the biblical narrative. While recasting the biblical tale in unambiguous moral terms—Dinah was violated and defiled, Levi and Simeon were in their rights to destroy Shechem, there is no discussion of "conversion" through circumcision of the males—the Jubilean author builds his case against intermarriage. First, he claims:

> And if there is a man in Israel who wishes to give his daughter or his sister to any foreigner [lit.: man who is of the seed of the Gentiles] he is to die. He is to be stoned because he has done something sinful and shameful within Israel. The woman is to be burned because she has defiled the reputation of her father's house; she is to be uprooted from Israel. No adulterer [lit.: fornicator?][12] or impure person is to be found within Israel throughout all the time of the earth's history; for Israel is holy to the Lord. Any man who has defiled [the seed of Israel] is to die; he is to be stoned. (Jub. 30:7–8)

A daughter of Israel who marries a Gentile should be treated like the priestly daughter who prostitutes herself (Lev. 21.9), for all daughters of the priestly nation Israel are priestly daughters. In the biblical legal context, the promiscuous priestly daughter profanes herself and her father and deserves death by fire. Thus Dinah, representing all daughters of Israel, profaned herself and all Israel (for Israel/Jacob also stands in for the whole nation).[13] Yet, more than describing her actions as just desecrating her children (who will not be able to be counted among the priestly nation), the Jubilean author defines Dinah's relationship with a Gentile as defiling, for she has committed *zenut*, a forbidden sexual act. Dinah causes impurity to exist in the midst of Israel. Hence, the Jubilean author calls for the death of all who intermarry. The very existence of such impure behavior within the community detrimentally affects the whole community. Biblical prostitution, which profanes the priestly line, becomes forbidden intermarriage and defiling to the land, to individuals, and to the sanctuary, in this Jubilean interpretation.[14] In a strange reversal, Dinah has become the *zonah*: not just a girl who has prostituted herself but also the counterpart to the "foreign" wife. In this case at least, the Jubilean author is egalitarian: foreign spouses of both genders are forbidden marriage partners. The Jubilean author further supports his contention through the examples of the Watchers (angels who mixed with humans) and the generation of Noah. The angels and the humans indulged in *zenut* through sexual relations with forbidden partners, which wrought divine destruction on the earth.[15]

Like Ezra, the Jubilean author constructs a hedge of purity around the holiness of Israel. Yet, as Hayes notes, he improves on Ezra's paradigm by subsuming the very act of miscegenation into the category of *zenut*.[16] Following Ezekiel's sexualized language of disobedience (idolatry equals adultery or prostitution and is called *zenut*), he transforms Ezra's notion of intermarriage as leading to impurity (in this case, idolatry) into the notion that the very act of miscegenation produces impurity in and of itself. Sexual congress with a Gentile generates impurity on the land analogously to idolatry. This impurity all the more threatens the security of the whole Israelite community. Exogamy becomes a double-edged sword, for it can both profane/defile the holy seed and pollute the holy land. More precise perhaps than Ezra, who only presumes the defiling of the land by idolatry, the Jubilean author assumes that all cases of *zenut* (intermarriage) also defile the offending individuals, as well as the land and the sanctuary.

The Dinah story provides another key to our author's manipulation of impurity as well. The biblical narrative describes Dinah as "defiled" by her sexual relations with Hamor. While *timeh* in the biblical passage probably connotes "shame or humiliation," Jubilees reads it as pollution.[17] Dinah's sexual relationship with Hamor produces impurity in the same way as any other sexual offense, as well as parallels the Watchers' "illicit intercourse," for the Jubilean author compares Dinah's act to that of a fornicator: "let no adulteress [fornicator?] or any uncleanness be found in Israel." While the language of this passage is unclear—is she an adulterer (not likely) or a fornicator?—the author probably refers to the more general category of *zenut*, under which adultery, and now miscegenation, are subsumed. Likewise, Esau may have profaned his children by taking a foreign wife, but he also defiles himself and the land through his sexual relations with her. Moreover, the residents of Sodom and Gomorrah not only defile themselves through "fornication and impurity" they also court their own destruction by these impure acts.[18] By categorizing miscegenation as *zenut* and a generator of impurity, the Jubilean author builds a high hedge—a protection—around Israel's holy status. Israel profanes and defiles itself through exogamy. Moreover, the whole community is affected by an accumulation of impurity in the land and/or in the sanctuary through miscegenation.

Jubilees appears to have been a popular text at Qumran, and the earliest of the Qumran literature, to which we turn next, profited from its interpretive precedents. Yet not all the sectarians agree with the Jubilean paradigm; indeed, they create different and competing hermeneutics of holiness.

4QMMT

A Halakhic document discovered among the Dead Sea Scrolls, 4QMMT constructs a hierarchy of holiness in which all the people of Israel are "holy" but that the sons of Aaron are "most holy." Following Jubilee's exegesis, this document also concludes that there should be no mingling between holy seed and profane seed. It may also suggest that there be limited mingling between holy seed and most holy seed. Although the text is fragmentary, the following section can be reconstructed:

75. And concerning the practice of illegal marriage [*zonot*] that exists among the people: (this practice exists) despite their being so[ns] of the holy [seed],
76. as it is written, Israel is holy [Jer. 2:3]. And concerning his (i.e., Israel's) [clean ani]mal
77. it is written that one must not let it mate with another species; and concerning his clothes [it is written that they should not]
78. be of mixed stuff; and he must not sow his field and vine[yard with mixed specie]s.
79. Because they (Israel) are holy, and the sons of Aaron are [most holy.]
80. But you know that some of the priests and [the laity mingle with each other] [as well as]
81. [And they] unite with each other and pollute the [holy] seed [as well as]
82. their own [seed] with women whom they are forbidden to marry [*zonot*]. Since [the sons of Aaron should . . .][19]

Citing Jeremiah 2:3, the text claims "Holy is Israel" while Aaron and sons are "most holy."[20] Similarly to Ezra and Jubilees, intermarriage here interferes with the preservation of Israel's holiness. Following Jubilees, the 4QMMT author labels the Israelites' mixed marriages as *zenut/zonot*, or fornications or illegal marriages, and its effects as defiling the holy seed of Israel. Yet, the true import of this accusation is more beholden to Ezra's exegetical evaluation of intermarriage than to Jubilees'. The author borrows Ezra's language of "mingling" and directly relates it to the biblical prohibitions of *kilayim*, or forbidden interminglings. Leviticus 19:19 proscribes the interbreeding of different clean animals, the interweaving of linen and wool in fabrics, and the sowing of two different types of seed in one field. The 4QMMT author positions intermarriage here as a similarly forbidden intermingling. As Ezra notes, Holy Israel, when it mixes its holy seed with profane seed of the non-Israelites, profanes its seed—that is, its offspring. Yet 4QMMT, like Jubilees, accuses the Israelites and the Aaronites (the priests) of defiling (rather than profaning) their seeds (holy and most holy, respectively). 4QMMT uses the language of Jubilees (*zenut*, or defiling), but exegetes from Ezra's notion of profanation by intermingling. Whether the author confuses the two concepts or attempts to harmonize them, the upshot is the same: profanation and defilement both damage the holy seed, the community of Israel.

The next passage of 4QMMT (Qimron C4–9) follows Ezra's *ma'al* (sacrilege) construct, which argues that intermarrying Judeans desecrate their holy seed (i.e., children), which belong to God. Yet unlike Ezra, 4QMMT continues to label intermarriage as *zenut*. 4QMMT may also retain a more metaphorical reading of *ma'al*—one of transgression of God's law. It is not that the Israelites have simply defiled themselves (through *zenut*) or just profaned their holy seed, but that they have disobeyed the express word of God not to intermarry. While it can be shown that the biblical texts do not support a general ban on intermarriage, the Second Temple literature, of which Ezra, Jubilees, and 4QMMT are a part, claim it to do just that.[21] Ezra turns to his notion of sacrilege of intermingling (Lev. 19:19); Jubilees finds support in aligning intermarriage with *zenut* (Gen. 30 and Lev. 18:21); and 4QMMT, in the next passage, turns to yet another proof-text: Deuteronomy 7:26. There, God forbids the Israelites from taking a *to'evah*, an "abominable thing," into their homes. The *to'evah* presumably represents an idol; yet our author understands the prohibition to focus on idolaters, not just their idols, and assumes the import of the passage prohibits Israelites from bringing idolatresses (foreign women) into their homes as wives.[22] The language of abomination nevertheless links this argument to the original accusation of *zenut*—for it, too, is abominable before God. Illegal marriage not only profanes the holy seed but also courts destruction and exile, as the abominable behavior of the Canaanites caused their exile. It is best, the text advises, to separate completely from the peoples of the land.

While the rest of the 4QMMT text deals with issues of "ritual" purity that affect the sanctuary, these discussions add no more to our discussion on the holiness of the people or of individuals. These authors clearly differ with their opponents[23] on the exact interpretation and implementation of certain ritual purity laws having to do with access to the Temple itself. Therefore, I suggest that this short portion explored above falls within the category of Ezran and Jubilean hermeneutic, in which the people Israel are considered genetically holy (ascribed). They did not do anything to achieve this holiness—it was granted to them; yet, they must protect themselves from losing it or damaging it. In this case, intermarriage profanes the holy seed, rendering the products of these intermarriages common and not holy—the children of intermarriage cannot be counted among the holy people. Finally, 4QMMT upholds the Jubilean argument that exogamy/miscegenation is *zenut*, the most pernicious and deadly of impurities. The author brings it in here, in a discussion of purity and the Temple, surely, because he, like the author of Jubilees, holds that impurity caused by intermarriage is more damaging to the sanctuary than any other "ritual" impurities, which can be neutralized, because *zenut* cannot be neutralized.

While *zenut* as intermarriage remains a minority or extreme position in the sectarian literature of the Second Temple period, it also becomes a catchall term for illicit sexual behavior, however that behavior is defined. But no matter how it is defined, *zenut* defiles individuals, the land, and the sanctuary, creating grave concern for those who care to protect either the sanctity of the people or the Temple. The Damascus Document, for instance, accuses the Jerusalem priests of several specific kinds of *zenut*. But this *zenut* translates better as variations of the forbidden consanguineous relations than as illegitimate foreign-born marriage partners, as it is understood by Jubilees and 4QMMT. The Jerusalem priests err in three ways: (1) they take more than one wife (in sequence, not at the same time); (2) they sleep with their wives while the wives are still menstruants; and (3) they marry their paternal and maternal nieces.[24] Each accusation derives from a broad extrapolation of biblical law. For instance, the biblical texts do not forbid a man from taking more than one wife, either at one time or in succession. Rather, he is only forbidden from marrying two sisters or a woman and her daughter at the same time or in sequence.[25] The Damascus Document text supports the one-wife rule by turning to two other biblical texts: Genesis 7:9, which describes the animals going into the ark "two by two," and Deuteronomy 17:17, which admonishes the prince not to "multiply wives to himself." (As we shall see, the one-wife issue will resurface in early Christian texts, while a menstruant's status vis-à-vis her husband will occupy the Rabbis' interpretive imagination. The Rabbis will also follow through on extending the forbidden consanguineous relations in a gendered equal manner.) The Damascus Document labels these actions *zenut* and claims that they are the cause of the pollution permeating Jerusalem and the Temple. Thus, like the Temple and War Scrolls, the Damascus Document appears more concerned with the purity of the Temple than of the people. The priest's *zenut* may or may not disqualify him from the priesthood (or the Israelite community), but it surely pollutes the Temple, making it uninhabitable for God. A major theme of this sectarian community's dispute with the Jerusalem priesthood centers on the supposed pollution of the Jerusalem Temple by all sorts of impurities.

Finally, by the end of the Second Temple period, *zenut* as a category is stretched, particularly in Paul's hands, to refer to all illicit sexual relations. As we shall see, Paul—influenced perhaps by earlier Second Temple manipulations of *zenut*—places *zenut* (translated as *porneia* in the Greek) in opposition to holiness in several of his letters. Yet, as we shall see, Paul's *porneia* can take on various definitions. At times it means "marriage to a non-Christian," at times it means "polygamy" or "more than one wife (even sequentially)," and at others it refers to the forbidden levitical consanguineous relations. Nevertheless, Paul is equally beholden to another biblical paradigm further developed at Qumran: holiness by achievement. Paul's *porneia* always opposes a holiness gained through obedience to the law—in this case, the divine law as understood through the Jesus event. I will discuss Paul in more detail in the next chapter.

Holy Deeds: Holiness Achieved

The "full-blown," sectarian literature from Qumran presents us with a very different hermeneutic of holiness than most other Second Temple Jewish literatures.[26] These sectarians view only themselves, among Israel, as holy. In their texts they never call Israel a holy seed or a sanctum of God. For these Qumranites, Israelite birth lineage no longer qualifies one for holiness. Rather, these sectarians deem most of Israel (if they were indeed once holy) as now defiled and disqualified. Only those who belong to the Yahad, or Community, can call themselves holy. But again it is not by birth alone that one enters this community but, rather, by achievement and intention. Anyone who "enters the covenant" of the Yahad agrees to abide by the rules of the Community. The "rules of the Community" translates as the Yahad's own idiosyncratic interpretation of the biblical covenant. A "member of the covenant" agrees to be fully obedient to God's covenant, as understood by the Yahad. Hence, any Israelite is eligible to join through obedience to their interpretation of the covenant and any member can be excluded by his disobedience.[27] Righteous Israelites achieve their holiness through full compliance to the Yahad's particular form of covenantal understanding.

Nevertheless, the Yahad rarely describes itself as "holy", for it uses *qodesh* (noun—with or without the demonstrative) more often than *qadosh* (adjective) as a modifier. The Yahad prefers to call its members *anshe ha-qodesh* (people of the holy); the community *yahad ha-qodesh* (community of the holy) or *edat ha-qodesh* (congregation of the holy); and its governing body *etzat ha-qodesh* (council of the holy). While many translators render *qodesh* as "holiness," I wonder if that is the most accurate translation. While *qodesh* is a noun as opposed to an adjective (*qadosh*), it is not necessarily an abstract noun. In biblical Hebrew, *qodesh* usually refers to God's things. The priests are *qodashim* (holy possessions of God), the Sabbath is a *qodesh* (a holy day to God). I suggest that here, too, the *qodesh* is more concrete—namely, it refers to the divine covenant itself. The Yahad members enter into this covenant and thereby become people of the holy covenant. The council rules by the covenant and the congregation abides by its laws. The Yahad defines itself, and the members differentiate themselves from all other Israelites, by their complete and perfect obedience to the divine covenant. Yet, by entering into the holy covenant I am not sure they make themselves individually into *qodashim*—holy things of God, as described in Leviticus. At best the community is a *qodesh*, but not the individuals outside of their membership in the community. The Community Rule states that:

> And when someone enters the covenant to behave in compliance
> with all these decrees, enrolling in the assembly of the holy, they shall
> examine their spirits in the Yahad, one another, in respect of his
> insight and of his deeds in law, under the authority of the sons of
> Aaron, those who freely volunteer in the Yahad to set up His covenant
> and to follow all the decrees which He commanded to fulfill, and
> under the authority of the majority of Israel those who freely
> volunteer to return within the Yahad to His covenant.[28]

In this passage, "entering the covenant" and "enrolling in the assembly [or congregation] of the holy" parallel each other. Furthermore, they equate with "follow[ing] all the decrees which He [God] commanded." The passage emphasizes that these members freely join up—they are not compelled, nor are they born into membership; they must intentionally "sign up" by agreeing to abide by the covenant as interpreted by the Yahad. The Yahad's interpretation of the covenant is not just one of many possible interpretations, but The Truth, the *only* possible way to participate in God's covenant with Israel. While not explicitly stating that the members of the Yahad are holy, the community marks itself by correctly fulfilling the stipulations of the holy covenant. They alone, among Israelites, therefore identify with, possess, and benefit from that covenant. Certainly one cannot be holy, no matter one's behavior, outside the confines of the Yahad. Martha Himmelfarb has argued that the Yahad, in intensifying the biblical purity laws, manifests a hope that all Israel will become more priestlike without accepting the Jubilean construct that all Israel is necessarily a priestly nation. Thus, they evince their own struggle with the tension between merit and ancestry.[29] Certainly, if one considers the Qumranites to descend from priestly circles, and to concern themselves with bad priestly behavior in Jerusalem that was defiling the sanctuary, they would necessarily struggle with the problems of ascribed holiness. The priests in Jerusalem are holy by definition, but according to the Yahad, they do not deserve to be so called.[30]

Following H's paradigm of obedience leading to holiness, the Yahad believes that they now have an exclusive hold on "holy" Israeliteness. Similarly, membership in the Yahad comes through proper behavior rather than or in addition to birthrights. The Damascus Document notes that Abraham "was counted as a friend for keeping God's precepts and not following the desire of his spirit. And he passed (them) on to Isaac and Jacob, and they kept (them) and were written up as friends of God and as members of the covenant forever."[31] Rather than passing on holy *seed*, Abraham passes on holy *deeds*—God's precepts. Abraham was not chosen randomly by God, but because he was worthy. The Yahad counts Abraham's obedience to all of God's laws as the measure of his worthiness. Likewise, the Yahad members must deserve their membership—they must achieve it. Once gained, it must be maintained. Holiness acquired through achievement is a dynamic ongoing process. Hence, the Yahad members achieve holiness only as a community that together maintains and practices the covenantal laws.[32]

Nevertheless, the Yahad does not decamp to Qumran just because they follow a different interpretation of the law; rather, purity—particularly incursions of impurity (caused by disobedience to their interpretation)—arises as a major concern and focus. All those Israelites who do not belong to the Yahad are impure. They are not intrinsically impure, but have defiled themselves through disobedience. Basically, because they do not follow the Yahad's interpretation of the law, they create impurity by everything they do. Presumably their defilement is reversible, but only if they submit to the authority of the Yahad. If this is the case, then the Yahad evinces here a fusing of the biblical "ritual" and "moral" purity paradigms, as Jonathan Klawans has argued.[33] What is of import to them, obviously, is their ability to "control" impurities. The Yahad focuses particular attention on the behaviors of the Jerusalem priests in Jerusalem who have defiled the Temple through their negligence and stubbornness in misinterpreting the law. The Community Rule constructs a dichotomy between the *anshe ha-qodesh* (people of the holy) and everyone else who is deemed unclean:

> No holy person [*ish ha-qodesh*] should support himself on any deed of futility, for futile are all those who do not know the covenant. And all those who scorn His word He shall cause to vanish from the world.
> All their deeds are impurity [*niddah*] before Him and they are impure [*tameh*] in all their possessions.[34]

The non-Yahad Israelites defile themselves because they do not "know the covenant"; their ignorance necessarily leads them into all sorts of errors that cut them off from God. They head irresolutely into disaster, for God will destroy all those who have futilely abused his covenant. The Yahad members, on the other hand, "know the covenant" and pursue purity through that knowledge. That is, they know how to preserve purity in their midst so as not to offend God. Obedience to the covenant encompasses both the need to follow all the ethical laws (social justice, fair treatment of one's neighbors, etc.) and the ritual laws that pertain to cult practice and purity. However, since the Yahad has removed itself from Jerusalem and refuses to partake in the sacrificial worship in what they perceive to be a defiled Temple, purity takes on a different role in their way of life. If the Jerusalemites pollute their city and shrine through willful negligence, then the Yahad must recreate an alternate pure space outside of Jerusalem for God and his representatives, the angels, to reside. The Yahad as a group becomes that pure space. It is not clear whether they also claim to be a holy space—a replacement for the Temple. Assuming they model themselves on the biblical war camp and/or on the encampment around Sinai—both of which were temporary and pure spaces, yet not holy ones[35]—then presumably here, too, they wish only to create a temporary pure space, not a replacement for the Temple. While they call themselves the Community of the Holy, I have also suggested that the Holy in that equation is not the community per se, but the covenant; hence, they may also create a pure place for the holy covenant to reside.

In sum, these "full-blown" sectarian texts from Qumran construct the Yahad as an exclusive holy community by achievement, in that they retain or gain their holiness (as a community), not by ascription but by vigorous and meticulous observance of the holy covenant. In addition, they hold that only their interpretation of the law leads to holiness. Hence, all who interpret and observe the law differently (e.g., the Jerusalem priesthood) are no longer holy. Correct interpretation of biblical text and its ensuing practices (the prize for which is holiness) further motivates the late-ancient Jewish and Christian exegetical communities, as we shall see in the following chapters. These later communities, however, differ from the Qumranites in their focus on individual rather than communal holy achievement.

One last Qumranic hermeneutic is important for us to study here—not so much due to its direct influence on any particular late-ancient writer but for its thematic relationship. For this construct is an important link between the "super-purity" discussed in the last chapter and the holiness as sexual abstinence that we will discuss in the next. This paradigm, which I label "QDS as super-purity," proves important to the Rabbis and Christians alike. Yet it is important to note that those Qumranic texts that focus on super-purity do not always label it QDS.

Super-Purity: God's Holiness Protected

In the Temple Scroll and the War Scroll, two other sectarian texts, the people of Israel remain a holy people by ascription, in contrast to the scrolls discussed above. Moreover, these texts neither concern themselves with ways to achieve holiness, nor to maintain that holiness by meticulous observance of the law, nor with protecting it from defilement through *zenut*. Rather, the Israelites' roles in these texts focus on how to manage their "ritual" impurities in order to preserve a pure space on earth in which God can reside. The Temple Scroll obviously focuses on the Temple, while the War Scroll concentrates on the war camp in which the Israelites prepare for their end-time battles and the holy angels visit as moral support. While the authors of these texts consider Israel to be holy to God, they do not describe Israel as a freestanding sanctum that needs protection of its own (or at least they show no interest in protecting it as such). Israel's impurities, particularly the "ritual" impurities, affect the Temple or war camp (holy space) more than themselves (holy people). These texts read as if they represent or complete the divine revelation to Moses at Sinai (not in addition to that revelation, as Jubilees purports to be). God often speaks to Moses in the first person in order to emphasize these texts' revelatory and authoritative nature. The Temple Scroll, for instance, follows more or less the outlines of Deuteronomy, "improving" on it as it feels warranted, often by harmonizing the D texts with P texts and paradigms.

As noted above, "ritual" impurities and their potential effects on holy space invigorate these scrolls' authors. Following P, they perceive Israel's main job as managing its impurities so that God or the divine angels can reside in a pure space.[36] In order to do so, the Temple Scroll expands the boundaries of holiness from the Temple into the city (following Ezekiel's example), forcing all "unessential personnel" (nonpriests) outside the city limits. Furthermore, it places strict limitations on who can come in and out of the city, as well as what activities can be conducted within its walls. Similarly, the War Scroll limits the war camp to essential personnel—the warriors and the angels.[37]

Nonetheless, both the war camp and the Temple city remain vulnerable to human-created impurities. Here, semen pollution and human waste stand out as the most problematic. Although excrement and urine are not levitically defiling, they are so defined by the Deuteronomist in conjunction with the war camp. The War and Temple Scrolls clearly build from both biblical precedents. Furthermore, because the city and camp were most likely populated exclusively by men, semen pollution rises as another fulcrum of purity concerns. Both texts legislate mechanisms to prevent semen pollution. What interests me here is how semen pollution is treated differently from other "ritual" impurities. This, for me, continues and expands on the biblical paradigm of "super-purity" that I described above, which intensifies the dangers of this one impurity and, hence, the legislation created to neutralize it and keep it far from the Holy. Thus, in the Temple Scroll, all sexual relations happen outside the city limits. Any priest who pays a conjugal visit to his wife must remain outside the city for three days. Likewise, a man found "unclean in his flesh" cannot go into battle that day, according to the War Scroll. While Leviticus and Deuteronomy legislate that semen pollution remains contagious only until the evening (and after appropriate ablutions), the Temple Scroll, following the precedent of Israel at Sinai (Ex. 19), advocates a three-day purification process.[38]

In sum, then, the Temple City, and the Qumran war camp, which are places where holy beings reside, must be "super-pure" in a way analogous to the encampment around Sinai and the biblical war camp. Sexual restraint, as a precaution against semen pollution, looms large in this construct. Israel remains holy in these texts' hermeneutics of holiness, but its sexual practices do not affect that holy status. Rather, sexual congress—because of the semen pollution it incurs—is distanced physically from the camp, Temple, and its surrounding city. As a result, the priestly class that lives in the city necessarily practiced sexual restraint while in the city and certainly for the duration of their service. But nothing prevented them from keeping a wife and family outside the city limits, whom they could visit when "off duty" for more than three days. Of course, it must be remembered that the Temple Scroll projects a utopian vision of Jerusalem that never was put into effect. Similarly, the War Scroll keeps unessential personnel (women, children, and feeble old men) outside the camp—not because they are inherently impure, but rather because they would be creators of unnecessary impurity and because they are not warriors. The camp must be "super-pure" in this case, because the angels, God's representatives, are present. The text calls the angels "holy-ones of God" or the "congregation of your holy-ones."[39] And it is because *they* are present in the war camp that the camp must be kept free of impurities.

The War Scroll clearly follows the deuteronomic precedent that the people are holy because God chose them to be so. Yet, the War Scroll, like the Temple Scroll, does not use either holy-seed or holy-deed terminology. Similarly, sexuality relates to issues of "ritual" purity and the purity of the war camp, rather than purity caused by illicit sexual behavior. Women and young men are excluded from the camp, I submit, for the same reasons as in the Temple Scroll—for fear of semen pollution. Men preparing for imminent war in the war camp necessarily must refrain from sexual contact, yet when not at war they can resume their normal sexual, family, and domestic lives. Most important for us, this "super-purity" is presented as (1) a requirement for contact with the holy, or (2) being in a holy being's presence; yet in and of itself, it is not a marker of holiness—neither ascribed nor achieved. Remarkably, in the Temple and War Scrolls, the absence of impurity, particularly that caused by semen, is never connoted with QDS, only THR. Thus, these scrolls avoid the semantic issues the original texts present when using a QDS root to signify purity from semen pollution.[40] Yet, they treat it with more deference: those impure through semen pollution must wait three days for purification (as at Sinai), rather than one day, as stipulated by Leviticus. Thus, it continues to be viewed as a more intense or virulent form of impurity that requires extreme precautions, and thus the absence of semen pollution is not just purity but becomes "super-purity."

Epilogue: Qedushah and Purity, Both Spiritual and Physical

In contrast, while QDS in most of its manifestations in the "full-blown" sectarian documents usually translates as some form of "holy," there are several instances where it is better rendered as "pure" or "purify." In these cases, QDS signifies one element of the total purification process (both physical and spiritual) that a person must undergo before entering the Yahad. It always parallels THR in these formulations, and hence does not always connote "super-purity" as I have defined it in every case. For instance, the Messianic Rule states:

> And if there is a convocation of all the assembly for a judgment, or
> for the Yahad council, or for a convocation of war, they shall purify
> themselves during three days [*vaqiddshom sheloshet yamim*] so that

everyone who comes is prepared for the council. . . . No man defiled
by any impurities of a man shall enter the assembly of these [the men
of renown]; and no-one defiled by these should be established in his
office amongst the congregation . . . for the angels of the holy
[*malakhei qodesh*] are among their congregation.[41]

When the Yahad gathers for special convocations—a call to war, a judgment, or
a council meeting—the members must properly prepare themselves. In this
case, they are called upon to purify themselves for three days. This no doubt
imitates the call to "super-purity" before Revelation at Sinai. Similarly, the purificatory rites focus on semen pollution. Nobody with a defilement "of a man"
can enter the assembly of the Yahad—because the angels are also present
among them. Here however, unlike the Temple and War Scrolls, the Messianic
Rule echoes the biblical text: *vaqiddshom shloshet yamim*. As at Sinai, the people
do not *sanctify* themselves, but only "super-purify" themselves in order not to
offend God (or worse be destroyed by God's holiness). Here, too, the presence
of the angels (representing God) requires "super-purity," connoted in this text
with QDS. Finally, given the reference to three days' purification with QDS, the
act of purifying probably includes some water ritual in imitation of Sinai. Nevertheless, it is important to note that while this passage focuses on Sinai, it does
not mention Moses, who becomes central—because of this very same biblical
passage—to our later exegetes.

The next passage, from the Community Rule, similarly deploys QDS to
connote "purify" but intends a more spiritual usage:

He will not be rewarded [*yizkeh*] by the acts of atonement, nor shall
he be purified [*yitaher*] by the cleansing waters [*mei niddah*], nor shall
he be made pure [*yitqaddesh*] by seas or rivers, nor shall he be purified
[*yitaher*] by all the water of ablution. Defiled, defiled [*tameh*] shall he
be all the days he spurns the decrees of God, without allowing
himself to be taught by the Yahad of his counsel.[42]

The use of QDS in this passage again refers to purifying, for it parallels the
other three THR words. Moreover, one does not sanctify oneself "by seas or
rivers" but, rather, purifies oneself (i.e., by ablution in the live waters.) This
passage, as Jonathan Klawans notes, exemplifies the Yahad's complete homogenization of the various kinds of biblical impurity. A person who does not
follow the dictates of the Yahad (i.e., correct behavior) is impure, defiled. No
matter how many baths, ablutions, or other physical purificatory rites he
undergoes, he cannot rid himself of these impurities. Rather, he must repent
of his ways and follow the ways of the Yahad; then, his ablutions will be

efficacious (likewise, his true repentance will not "hold" unless he also undergoes physical baptism).[43] Hence, the passage continues:

> For it is in the spirit of the true counsel of God that are atoned the paths of man, all his iniquities, so that he can look at the light of life. And it is by the holy spirit of the Yahad [ruaḥ qedushah la-yaḥad], in its truth, that he is cleansed [yitaher] of all his iniquities. And by the spirit of uprightness and of humility his sin is atoned. And by the compliance of his soul with all the laws of God his flesh is cleansed [yitaher] by being sprinkled with cleansing waters [ba-mei niddah] and being made pure [lehitqaddesh] with the waters of purity [ba-mei dukhi].[44]

A person never fully regains purity until he has repented of his sins. Yet, in effect this atonement can be affected only through the "true" council of the Yahad—that is, by following the Yahad's covenantal understanding. When he has fully complied with the laws of God and removed himself from all sin (disobedience), then his flesh can be purified by water. Here, again, QDS is used in parallel to THR to represent physical purificatory rites by ablution; nonetheless, this text links both QDS and THR to "sinlessness," or the state of being in total compliance with the Yahad's interpretation of divine law. Although it seems that the sectarians here deploy QDS and THR similarly to connote "purify," later readers (whether of these texts, the biblical texts, or other exegetical texts) subsume these notions of "ritual" purity into their notions of holiness. While I cannot argue for any direct influence between the Dead Sea Scrolls and later exegetes, I only wish to show here the apparent interpretive possibilities practiced in the Second Temple period. "Super-purity" is connoted biblically by QDS, but by both QDS and THR at Qumran. This sort of purity almost always assumes an absence of semen pollution as basic to that status. Moreover, one enters this super-pure state (by removing or preventing semen pollution) in order to enter God's presence (Exodus, Joshua, Samuel, Temple Scroll, War Scroll, Messianic Rule). The Community Rule, however, presents us with an already evolved sense of "super-purity," for there it does not refer only to physical purity but also to a broader sense of "sinlessness." That is to say, a person is physically purified (with QDS) only after he has repented of all his sins, takes counsel with the Yahad itself, and agrees to abide by its interpretation of the divine law. Only then is the purified person allowed to partake in God's true covenant and become a member of the holy community, the Yahad. The Yahad's (con)fusion of the various purity paradigms represents a new hermeneutic of holiness in which all kinds of impurities (not just those enumerated in H) stand in opposition to holiness.

Finally, the evidence gathered here does not, I think, suggest that the Qumranites were necessarily a mindfully celibate community but, rather, that they developed a heightened sense of the dangers of semen pollution. Therefore, in this chapter I chose not to discuss the writings of the several other Second Temple Jewish writers, such as Philo and Josephus, who may or may not provide some evidence to the contrary. This book is not a history of ascetic practice; hence, references to Jews who may or may not have been ascetic do not interest me here, even if I show interest in ascetic Christians. Rather, this is a history of holiness. Thus, where discussions of holiness and asceticism (or other sexual practices) converge, I pay attention. This convergence does not happen in the Hellenistic Jewish literature. By and large, their understanding of ascetic practice (particularly celibacy) stems from Greco-Roman notions of the same, not from biblical precedents. Josephus does not call the Essenes' celibacy "holy." The one possible exception is Philo's depiction of Moses as a celibate priest; this text will be discussed in full in chapter 6. And while Josephus uses purity terminology to describe the Essenes, his reference point again is Greco-Roman rather than biblical.[45]

Conclusions

In the post-biblical literature of the Second Temple period we have traced three developments in hermeneutics of holiness and sexuality. In the first, based on Ezra, all Israel is inherently holy and must be protected—as a community of individuals—from profanation and defilement. Intermarriage with non-Israelites rises as the fulcrum of danger for all Israelites. The mixing of (holy) Israelite seed with (profane) non-Israelite seed creates more profane (Gentile) seed, thereby diminishing the Israelite seed and, with it, its population. Jubilees likens the very act of miscegenation to other sexual sins (incest, etc.) that both defile the land and the individual. In this way, even the ascribed holy parents who produce profane seed thereby render themselves disqualified from holiness. In many ways this is simply an anti-assimilationist tactic. Yet, by placing their group-survival discourse within a theological discussion, these ancient writers imbue their group identity with cosmic overtones and further distance the non-Israelites and "bad" Israelites from holiness. The language of *zenut* helps these authors define and patrol these borders. As we shall see, Paul will similarly capitalize on *zenut* as a boundary marker to create his own community identity.

Some Qumran literature (4QMMT) follows and strengthens Jubilees' hermeneutic by further homogenizing the dangers of profanation and defilement to the people of Israel, while other Qumran literature moves in another direction entirely. Convinced that they have a (re)newed and exclusive covenant with God, the Yahad excludes all who do not follow their interpretation of biblical text from the holy community. Only those who willingly "enter the covenant" under the Yahad's guidance can be considered part of the holy community. Sexuality, however, does not appear more important here than any other divine commandment. Only compliance to the whole of the law makes a person worthy of entering the Yahad. Nevertheless, proper sexuality plays a different role in protecting holy or "hyper-pure" space. In the early Yahad's strident construct of holy space, active sexual relations and women are distanced from the center of activity—the Temple—as a precaution against semen pollution. Normal procreative activities continue, but take place outside the limits of Jerusalem and the war camps. Nevertheless, this utopian image strengthens the biblical notion that semen pollution (and the sexual relations that produce it) prevents a person from entering holy space or holy presence.

Ezra, Jubilees, and the literature of Qumran clearly reflect their Second Temple provenances, in which purity issues rise to the fore in the polemics between competing Judean communities. Yet, the destruction of Jerusalem and Qumran around 70 CE brings a quick end to the Qumran settlement and its potential influence, as well as to most of the purity debates. That literature remains hidden for 2,000 years. Although scholars have posited links between the Dead Sea Scrolls and early Christianity, particularly the Eastern and Syriac varieties, little evidence for such a connection survives. Ezra's holy-seed paradigm, innovated as the Second Temple was being rebuilt, falls out of favor with that Temple's demise. Nonetheless, the notion that protection from *zenut* is key to religious (holy) community cohesion and identity resurfaces in the early Christian literature. Paul, clearly a product of the Second Temple period himself, for instance, worries about the effects of *porneia* on the Christian community. In the New Testament texts we will discover how some early Christians shifted the hermeneutic of holiness away from intermarriage but remained concerned with how certain sexual practices continued to protect one's holiness gained through achievement (in this case, faith and baptism). We will turn to these texts in the next chapter. Likewise, the Rabbis expand on the biblically prohibited consanguineous relations, as well as the limited marriage partners for priests, to create their own construct of holiness protected by limited marriage partners. In contrast to Ezra and Jubilees, the Rabbis never advocate a strict endogamy as the only means to protecting nascent Israelite holiness.

In the following chapters we shall see how all of these paradigms transform, reconfigure, and overlap in the early Christian and rabbinic writings. For the Rabbis, Israel is always holy, yet at the same time they allow for more porous borders than Ezra could have imagined. Nevertheless, the Qumran-like notion that achievement/obedience is also a key to holy access comes to the fore, both in the early Christian literature and the rabbinic writings. Both of these literatures differentiate themselves from Qumran in that the door to holy access is opened to all (or most) who inquire. Conversion to Holy Israel is no longer limited to native Israelites by any post-70 CE group that considered themselves descendants of the ancient Israelites. Moreover, these new hermeneutics of holiness are deployed yet again by our late-ancient writers to fortify and define the ever-changing and emerging borders between what they would like to differentiate more clearly as either "Jewish" or "Christian."

Finally, the notion that active sexuality and holiness do not mix persists and evolves among Jews and Christians alike. As we shall see, some Christians take notions of asexuality and holiness to an extreme by renouncing all sexual activity. The Rabbis, for their part, both uphold the notion of sexual restraint in the face of holiness and also reconstruct holiness to fit their notions of married sexuality, individual spirituality, and religious authority. Thus, holiness and sexuality play a large role in how fourth-century Jewish and Christian communities defined themselves internally and externally.

PART II

3

Holiness Perfected

Pauline Constructs of Holy Community

In the Pauline literature, we learn of a different kind of holiness, one granted to a new community—the community of Messiah believers. In describing those who believe in the Messiah as "saints" and "holy ones," these texts add a new element to ancient hermeneutics of holiness by positing Christians as a new holy community. Thus, the definition of holiness expands to include not only the Israelites, defined by their heritage from ancient Israel (holy nation of priests, chosenness, etc.), but also the community of Christian believers through their new-found faith in Jesus.[1] Paul argues that native-born Israelites can claim their nascent, ascribed holiness as long as they also believe in the salvation offered through Jesus. Non-Israelites gain access to (achieve) holiness through their faith alone, for despite their birth, they best obey (achieve) the will of God. Israelites who do not believe lose their status. Thus, Paul opens the possibility of holiness to all, and he puts severe qualifiers on any notion of ascribed Israelite holiness. True holiness is achieved, not ascribed, and it is achieved only through faith. Interestingly, it is in the Pauline literature that this reconfigured notion of sanctification achieved through faith nonetheless intersects with sexuality most thoroughly. Very much in line with Ezra and Jubilees, Paul and his imitators present images of Christian holiness that must be protected from pollution. In 1 Corinthians, for instance, Paul uses similar purity language to the other Second Temple Jewish writers studied in the last chapter, in order to focus on sexual sins that he claims defile the now holy body of the individual

Christian. A Christian body, for Paul, is both a piece of the corporate body that forms the community of believers and an individual sanctuary within which the holy spirit resides. *Porneia*, Paul's Greek translation of *zenut*, arises (as among the Hebrew writers we have studied so far) as the most dangerous of pollutions. But as we shall see, in Paul's hands *porneia* can mean more than one thing.[2] I concentrate on these texts that introduce this new understanding of holiness and sexuality because they are also the texts that invigorate the later Christian interpreters I discuss in the next chapters. And while Paul addresses these letters to primarily Gentile communities, he supports his arguments with biblical notions of holiness achieved.

You Were Sanctified and Justified: Achieved Holiness in a New Context

In his letters, Paul transforms notions of holy community. In these writings a new paradigm of holy achievement emerges in which only people who accept a certain theological tenet can count themselves "in." Faith, more than law or birth, marks the nascent Messianic/holy community's boundaries. Among Israelites, birth no longer counts for anything unless it also comes with faith in the Messiah.[3] Behavior, likewise, does not guarantee access if it is not undergirded by faith. One achieves holiness, or access to holy community, first and foremost through belief; and Paul reckons this belief as obedience to God—that is, through faith the community of believers best fulfills the will of God. Similar to the Qumran sectarians, Paul suggests that any Israelite can "see the light" and join the community by accepting its theological system, for one who obeys God is holy. Hence, here Paul falls in line with the H hermeneutic that promotes holiness as achievable through obedience to the law. Paul, however, understands that obedience to be faith in Jesus rather than obedience to specific laws. Yet, in vast distinction to the Qumranites, Paul opens the doors to all, no matter what their birth origins. Gentiles and Jews alike achieve holiness (membership in the holy community) through faith; and their faith is reckoned to them as righteousness (obedience to God). Using the example of Abraham, Paul argues in Romans 3 that God considered Abraham an obedient servant (righteous) already when he believed God, not just when he later acted on that belief. Hence, Paul too claims that anyone's belief in the Christian message equals obedience to God and thereby sanctifies the believer—that is, it brings him or her into the holy community.[4] Nonetheless, while faith binds the members to their new and holy community, they also define themselves against what they have left behind: sin and impurity.

Paul represents this dichotomy between sin/impurity and righteousness/ sanctification in Romans 6:19, when he remarks: "For just as you once presented your members as slaves to impurity and to greater and greater iniquity so now present your members as slaves to righteousness for sanctification."[5] Here, impurity and sin stand in opposition to sanctification and righteousness. Obedience (faith) leads to sanctification, disobedience (faithlessness) to impurity. And as he notes in v.22, sanctification (belonging to God) leads to eternal life. Through their faith, the new believers "sell" themselves to God, exchanging their slavery to sin for slavery to God. In so doing they become holy, belonging to God. Impurity and sin must be left behind. By aligning sin with ("moral") impurity, Paul follows the logic of the levitical holiness code. God and holiness stand across a gaping divide from sin and impurity. Yet Paul adds another element: Christian obedience does not mean obedience to the letter of the levitical laws. In the levitical context, the act of avoiding all "moral" impurities made an Israelite holy. For Paul, the act of faith makes a person holy: faith in Jesus is the true access key to God and God's holiness. Only those who believe in Jesus have truly fulfilled God's law. Nonetheless, Paul contrasts this new-found path in holiness with the levitical path to unholiness: sexual sin and impurity. With this new direct route to holiness, sin and impurity necessarily remain behind. Similarly the author of Ephesians (1:4) aligns holiness and blamelessness. Removal from sin puts one closer to holiness, belonging to God. Sin and impurity stand in unequivocal opposition to Christian faith and community, holiness, and God. Likewise, the author of 1 Peter takes Paul's understanding of Leviticus and concretizes it: "As obedient children, do not be conformed to the passions of your former ignorance, but as he who called you is holy, be holy yourselves in all your conduct; since it is written, 'you shall be holy, for I am holy'" (1 Pet. 1:14–16). Being holy, obedient children and being faithful means also physically distancing oneself from sin and impurity. 1 Peter points to an element more apparent in other Pauline letters—that holiness is based on proper conduct as well as on faith. I return to this point below.

In Romans, Paul seems to indicate that, in crossing the boundary from unholy to holy, one also crosses from impure to pure. Since the holy and impure do not mix, once one transfers to the side of holiness, the holy need not worry themselves about the impure. Impurity goes hand in hand with faithlessness, as the one is the result of the other. But when faith is present, impurity dissipates. This proves not to be exactly true in several of Paul's other letters as it is in 1 Peter. There, Paul concerns himself with the continuing vulnerability of the human being to pollution, despite the newfound faith that sanctifies him or her. Furthermore, pollution comes through impure behavior, whether by insiders or by outsiders. In 1 Thessalonians, for instance, Paul divides the world between "us" and "them." And while "they" can cross over and become one of us through conversion, "we" can fall back into being one of "them" (by imitating their impure behavior) and lose out on the benefits of that conversion, eternal life. Thus Paul writes:

> For you know what instructions we gave you through the Lord Jesus.
> For this is the will of God, your sanctification [hagiasmos]: that you
> abstain from prohibited sexual relations [porneias]; that each one
> of you know how to take a wife for himself in holiness [hagiasmôi]
> and honor not in lustful passion like the Gentiles who do not know
> God . . . for God has not called us to impurity [akatharsia], but in
> holiness [hagiasmôi]. (1 Thes. 4:2–7)

In 1 Thessalonians, Paul constructs a barrier between "us" and "them." "We," or those called by God to holiness, differ from "them," or those who do not know God. We are sanctified, they are not. We take wives in holiness and avoid *porneia*, they indulge in *porneia* and thereby render themselves unclean—unfit for God. Paul builds a dichotomy between holiness/taking wives in holiness and *porneia*/impurity. However he understands *porneia* here (I would argue that it translates *zenut*—but does not necessarily mean intermarriage; see discussion below), it stands in contrast to taking wives in holiness. Those who indulge in *porneia* cannot be holy because *porneia* defiles; hence, to be holy (and to take a wife in holiness) means to avoid *porneia*. Similar to the other Second Temple biblical exegetes discussed in the last chapter, Paul advocates an avoidance of some sort of sexual behavior, which he labels *porneia*, as a means of protecting the holy—in this case, the Christian believer and, by extension, the whole (holy) Christian community. A member of the faith community is holy, yet if he "screws around,"[6] he becomes like "them" and necessarily no longer one of "us." A person who indulges in *porneia* disobeys the law and fails to protect his holy status gained through faith.

In this passage, *porneia* and *akatharsia* (prohibited sexual relations and impurity) are placed in direct opposition to *hagiasmos* (holiness or sanctification).[7] The latter cannot exist where the former flourish. In order to fulfill one's destiny one must be holy, for it is God's will that one be sanctified. But how is one to achieve that goal? By avoiding *porneia*, which is presumably best accomplished by taking wives in holiness. Although Paul does not further elaborate on the particulars of *porneia* or *hagiasmos*, he makes it clear that the former is endemic and native to the non-Christian Gentiles and the latter is the marker of distinction for the Christians. While Paul speaks more generally of holiness before this passage ("how holy and righteous and blameless was our behavior to you believers"; and "so that he may establish your hearts unblamable in holiness before your God" [1 Thes. 2:10, 3:13]), he connects holiness here deliberately with sexuality within legitimate Christian marriage. It most likely refers to limiting marriage partners to nonconsanguineous relations, as per Leviticus 18–20.[8] The heathens, who do not know God, do not know to restrain and focus their sexuality within legitimate marriages. Presumably they allow themselves to follow their passions, which would necessarily lead them to sexual deviance such as adultery, incest, bestiality, and homosexuality—in other words, to commit *porneia*. *Porneia* here, I believe, best translates as all those "customs of the peoples of the land" that are condemned in Leviticus 18, particularly the prohibited sexual relations.[9] Finally, according to several of the Gospel narratives, Jesus specifically condemns divorce and remarriage. Following the role model of Adam and Eve, who were made for each other by God, all couples should marry but once and for life. Jesus concludes preachings on the subject (in Matt. 19:9) by noting that "whoever divorces his wife, except for *porneia*, and marries another, commits adultery (*moichatai*)."[10] The one-wife rule may be part of Paul's construct in 1 Thessalonians as well, for Paul strives to draw distinct lines between Christian and pagan practices. The Gentiles indulge in *porneia*, the Christians do not. Moreover, taking a proper wife—and perhaps only one and for life—distinguishes the Christian from the non-Christian. In so doing Paul expands on his notion of *porneia*. On the one hand, the person who takes a wife in holiness cannot also indulge in *porneia*; on the other hand, if monogamy best opposes *porneia*, *porneia* comes to signify adultery, polygamy, and even remarriage as the most sexually deviant. Recall that the Damascus Document[11] constructed a similarly restrictive paradigm, making remarriage an equally forbidden sexual partnering (like incest) that pollutes the sanctuary.

Larry Yarbrough argues that Paul's program—taking a wife in holiness as a distinguishing marker from the non-Christians—stems from Hellenistic Jewish moral philosophy. Paul, however, firmly grounds his ruling as a manifestation of God's will.[12] That is to say, taking a wife in holiness is a commandment from God. Fulfilling this commandment, therefore, becomes part and parcel of their sanctification—that which distinguishes them from others. It is possible, therefore, to understand Paul as advocating a one-spouse policy as the best means to distinguish between (holy) Christians and (non-holy) others. That he aligns these distinctions with purity/impurity all the more drives the issue home and aligns any other sexual or marriage patterns as *porneia* and inherently impure. Here, Paul shows himself clearly aware of other trends in holiness thinking as manifested at Qumran and in Jubilees, in which *zenut/porneia* refers to a whole host of sexual no-no's that affect one's holiness detrimentally.

Do Not Join with the *Pornê*: Holiness Protected

Paul, certainly a solid reader of sacred text himself, let alone most likely versed in its Second Temple interpretations, nonetheless is not alone among New Testament writers in his concerns about impurity, and especially *porneia,* with or without reference to holiness. While the Gospels do not focus on the holiness of the new community (for in part they still see themselves as of the "old" community), they do struggle with the issue of purity. Yet, as Jonathan Klawans argues, Jesus, as presented in the synoptic Gospels, prioritizes "moral" purity over "ritual" purity.[13] The Gospel of Mark, for instance, contrasts these impurities in this manner:

> "Do you not see that whatever goes into a person from outside
> cannot defile since it enters, not the heart but the stomach, and goes
> out into the sewer?" (Thus he declared all foods clean.) And he said,
> "It is what comes out of the person that defiles. For it is from
> within, from the human heart that evil intentions come: improper
> sexual partnering [*porneiai*], theft, murder, adultery [*moicheiai*],
> avarice, wickedness, deceit, licentiousness, envy, slander, pride,
> folly. All these things come from within and they defile a man."
> (Mark 7:18–23)

Sin, unethical behavior, and disobedience to God's law defile a person more than physical impurities such as semen, menstrual blood, and the eating or touching of unclean animals. Unlike those Qumran texts that equate "ritual" impurity with "moral" impurity (the one is a manifestation of the other), the Gospel texts demote and/or void bodily-produced impurities in an effort to emphasize the ultimate importance of good, just, and righteous behavior between people. The levitical golden rule (love your neighbor as yourself), combined with several of the decalogue's more universal decrees (no theft, murder, adultery, coveting), become this Gospel's code to proper behavior, which also protects a believer from defilement and keeps access to God, the Holy One, alive. Furthermore, *porneia* as a catchall term for improper sexual behavior here resembles the late biblical and post-biblical writers' transformation of *zenut* into a similarly general-use term. What for Ezekiel was a metaphor for idolatry became for Jubilees a representation of real idolaters and foreigners. Yet, the Gospel writers and Paul, more inline with the "full-blown" Qumran documents, refocus *zenut/porneia* as a general term for all sexual deviance. And whether these behaviors typify non-Christians or not, they are to be avoided by Christians for their own sakes.[14]

Paul more stridently advocates for pure behavior as an absolute necessity than other New Testament writers. The Christian believer aims not just to access the holy community but also to access God's kingdom, which Paul claims is just around the corner. Impure behavior, then, not only denies one access to the holy community on earth but also bars one from the kingdom of heaven. For these early Christian writers, the holiness of the community on earth reflects the potential holiness of its members once they enter heaven. Hence, Paul lays down the law: the ticket to heaven is pure behavior—namely, proper interpersonal (particularly sexual) behavior motivated by faith. Pure behavior alone cannot get one into heaven; rather, it functions as a protective barrier around one's faith. Paul writes:

> Now the works of the flesh are obvious: improper sexual partnering
> [*porneia*], impurity [*akatharsia*], licentiousness, idolatry, sorcery,
> enmities, strife, jealousy, anger, quarrels, dissensions, factions, envy,
> drunkenness, carousing and things like these. I am warning you, as I
> warned you before, those who do such things will not inherit the
> kingdom of God. By contrast, the fruit of the Spirit is love, joy, peace,
> patience, kindness, generosity, faithfulness, gentleness, self-control
> [*enkrateia*]. There is no law against such things. (Gal. 5:19–23)[15]

According to Paul, those things that defile a person resemble the levitical impure behaviors. Actions that lead to injustices defile. Paul admonishes his readers to behave purely in this world so that they have access to the next world. Larry Yarbrough further argues that Paul, in 1 Corinthians, shows particular concern for intra-community behavior. Creating impurities within the community through improper behavior toward each other outweighs any other concern for outside influence.[16]

While the texts cited above lump together a full litany of impure behaviors that defile and bar a person (especially a believer) from eternal life, Paul elsewhere emphasizes the extremely defiling nature of sexual sin in particular. In these passages, Paul deploys the term *porneia* in several different ways, as well as builds his case for holiness protection using variously reconstructed biblical paradigms. First, he more firmly dichotomizes between improper sexual behavior and holiness; but then, like Ezra and the Jubilean author, he creates a model of holy-community endogamy. Moreover, as we have already seen in 1 Thessalonians, *porneia* (that which the Gentiles do) stands in stark opposition to Christian monogamous (and therefore holy) marriages. Sexual sin (albeit understood slightly differently in each passage) stands in particular opposition to holiness and holy community. Hence, I think it unfair to Paul to insist that he consistently understands *porneia* to be only one kind of sexual sin.[17] Rather,

I believe he perceives a whole variety of sexual sins—all called *porneia*—to be avoided at all costs as the most polluting sin a Christian believer can commit. And while I attempt here to divide his definitions by text, it would be equally unwise not to acknowledge that Paul can be free and easy with his definitions and sometimes mean more than one thing at any one time with any given term, for each letter addresses a different community with its own particular issues. Paul did not set out to write a systematic theology, but to put out theological and community fires as they flared up. Finally, Paul plays with two paradigms simultaneously. On the one hand, when one becomes a Christian one leaves behind one's sinful behavior, thus a Christian defines himself as distinct from his neighbors and holy because he does not indulge in *porneia*. On the other hand, once holy, a Christian must protect himself and his community from pollution usually caused by *porneia*. Danger lurks inside and out of the community and is pinned to proper behavior.

So, for instance, in 1 Corinthians 5–6, Paul proves himself more concerned with defilement within the community than from without. Here, Paul concerns himself less with "us" and "them" (as he does in 1 Thes.) and more with the believers' own bad behaviors, which create pollution within the community. Using the example of the man who lives with his father's former wife, Paul attempts to show that this action, incest, defiles not only the incestuous man but also the whole community. Moreover, pollution is an internal and insidious matter. This incestuous man is not an outsider but, rather, a misbehaving insider. Paul writes:

> Do you not know that the wrongdoers will not inherit the kingdom of God? Do not be deceived; *pornoi*, nor the idolaters, nor adulterers [*moichoi*], nor sexual perverts [*malakoi*][18], nor sodomites, nor thieves, nor the greedy, nor drunkards, nor revilers, nor robbers—none of these will inherit the kingdom of God. And this is what some of you used to be. But you were washed [*apelousasthe*] and you were sanctified [*hegiasthête*] and you were justified [*edikaiôthete*] in the name of the Lord Jesus Christ and in the Spirit of our God. (1 Cor. 6:9–11)

In this passage, the *pornoi*—the adulterers and the other sexual "deviants" listed here—all line themselves upfront with the idolaters. All other disobedience comes in second. Moreover, all of these bad behaviors were manifest among Paul's Gentile readers, according to Paul—until they converted. Paul equates the Gentiles, as does the Jubilean author, with impure behavior. They are naturally inclined to idolatry and, hence, also to adultery, incest, murder, and theft. The Christians, therefore, differentiate themselves from their former Gentile selves and their former Gentile cohorts by their pure behavior.

Now, after they have been justified by their new faith and cleansed through baptism of the effects of these impure behaviors they used to do, and are thereby sanctified—that is, rendered members of the new holy community— they must not fall back into defiling behavior. Such actions will disqualify them from their recently achieved pure and holy status.[19] The Corinthians gained access to the community by choosing to believe in Jesus; they are cleansed of all their former sins by the baptismal waters and become sanctified, in that they are now members of the holy community. Yet, they can backslide if they do not continue on a sinless path of activity. Alternatively, the issue may not be backsliding but, rather, overstepping or going beyond what Paul originally told them—that is, by joining this new community they free themselves from the social mores of the old. Yet, as Yarbrough cogently argues, Paul is particularly obsessed with community order and seemliness in 1 Corinthians. How the believers behave among themselves and to each other is as important as how they deal with outsiders.[20] Like the Jubilean author, Paul concerns himself here primarily with protecting the holy community from itself. The Gentiles' impure behaviors remain a separate issue. At worst, the Gentiles set a bad example for the Christians, but their impurity is not contagious. According to Paul (and Ezra and Jubilees), the only impurity that can affect the holy community is self-inflicted.[21]

Again, in the above passages Paul does not specify what exactly constitutes *porneia*. Nevertheless, given that this passage comes as support for his arguments against allowing an incestuous man to continue living within the community (among other arguments), he makes abundantly clear that his notion of *porneia* here more or less dovetails with the forbidden levitical consanguineous relations. For, one purpose of 1 Corinthians 5–6 purports to be to condemn a man, a member of the holy community in Corinth, who has taken up residence with his stepmother (a levitically forbidden relationship[22]). As Dale Martin has argued, Paul proves himself here to be particularly concerned with bodily pollution. In Martin's astute estimation, Paul understands the human body to be particularly vulnerable to pollution, disease, and invasion from outside forces, especially the satanic.[23] Martin, however, contends that Paul's fear of pollution is based primarily on a popular Greco-Roman ideology of the body as especially vulnerable to pollution and disease. Paul in this passage opposes what Martin calls the "Strong" in the Corinthian community—upper-class Christian converts—and their bodily construct, which understands the body to be more of a mini-cosmos with its own checks and balances to keep it healthy and in harmony with its environment than as a body vulnerable to invasion.[24] According to the Strong, that the man in question committed incest is none of their concern—his bad behavior clearly demonstrates only his own weaknesses.

Martin convincingly argues that Paul works with a completely different ideology of the body than the Strong of Corinth. He also suggests that the difference between the ideologies falls along class lines. The ideology of balance (the Strong) belongs to upper-class Greco-Roman sensibilities, and the ideology of invasions to popular and necessarily lower-class culture (the Weak). Paul, however, with his Greco-Roman popular pollution paranoia, sees the incestuous man as opening himself up to a specifically levitically derived pollution of forbidden relationships (something he claims that even the pagans avoid). Furthermore, Paul understands that that pollution, though created by the act of a lone individual, harms the whole community. For Paul further argues that the individual person connects through his shared holy *pneuma* to the body and spirit of Jesus, because Jesus replaces the sanctuary and land in Paul's construct; hence, what detrimentally affects the individual necessarily affects the corporate whole. So while Paul's notion of the body as vulnerable may merge with popular Greek notions of bodily pollutions, I suggest that his main point of reference is levitical and his main goal is preservation of the holiness of the community—a holiness as vulnerable as, if not more than, the individual's to the effects of impurity. Jesus' "body" is as vulnerable to the effects of impurity as the sanctuary and the land are in the Torah texts.

It is also possible to understand Paul as having further transformed the Ezran/Jubilean holy-seed rationale into a holy-body rationale in which he applies the Ezran/Jubilean notion of holy protection through defilement avoidance. For Paul claims that one avoids these unholy behaviors because a Christian's physical body, not just his *pneuma*, has become part of God and thereby is sanctified, too. He writes: "The body is not meant for *porneia*, but for the Lord and the Lord for the body . . . do you not know that your bodies are members of Christ?" (1 Cor. 6:13b, 15a). *Porneia*—defined here as illicit sexual relations—stands in opposition to holiness in a very stark and physical manner. A Christian body is first and foremost a member of Jesus' body (a metaphor for the Christian community), which cannot be defiled because of its holiness. Illicit sexual activity, because it is affected through, with, or on the body, more than any other illicit activity (theft, murder, bribery, etc.) affects the individual body but also the corporate body—that of both Jesus and the community—of which it is a part.

Yet Paul continues. If the Christian aims for unity with the holy body of Jesus, Paul demonstrates how inherently incompatible that unity is with sexual union with a *pornê*. He continues:

> Do you not know that your bodies are members of Christ? Should I therefore take the members of Christ and make them members of a

pornês? Never! Do you not know that whoever is united to a *pornê* becomes one body with her? For as it is written, "The two shall be one flesh." But anyone united to the Lord becomes one spirit with him. Shun *porneian*. Every sin that a person commits is outside the body; but the *porneuôn* sins against the body itself. (1 Cor. 6:15–19)

While most English translations (including the NRSV) render the Greek *pornê* as prostitute or harlot and *porneia* as sexual immorality or a sexually immoral person, they are all one and the same for Paul. While a *pornê* under certain circumstances, may indeed be just a prostitute, what defines the *porneuôn* for Paul is his behavior—a person who conducts illicit sexual relations. Since this passage in chapter 5 starts with reference to an incestuous man, I believe here in chapter 6 that Paul refers primarily to forbidden sexual partners (consanguineous and possibly others). The *porneuôn* is a person who conducts illicit sexual relations with a *pornê*, a forbidden partner. In this way, Paul only continues the evolution of the term *zenut*, now translated as *porneia*, which started in the late biblical period. Paul focuses not on prostitution (Christian men visiting professional female sex workers) but on Christians (though speaking in gendered language I think he refers to everyone) conducting illicit sexual relations such as incest or adultery (possibly with other Christians and, of course, this category could include general prostitution as well), for he highlights the dangers such relationships bring to the whole community. Citing Genesis 2:24, Paul argues that when one joins in sexual union with another the two become as one flesh. But when the "other" is an illicit partner, the union—the one flesh—is irrevocably defiled. The Christian, similarly, has become one spirit (metaphorically described as one body) with the Lord. How can the polluted body (through its physical union with the *pornê*—the forbidden sexual partner) also unite itself with Jesus, who is holy? If the Christian body claims membership in the larger corporate body of the Lord (read: the community), it cannot also unite itself with a *pornê* lest it (the Christian body) spread its pollution to the whole body.

As noted above, Paul compares both the real physical union of a person with a forbidden sexual partner [a *pornê*] and the spiritual union of believer and Jesus to the marital union of Adam and Eve. Paul understands this metaphor rather concretely, for the two bodies that join in such a union (whether physical or spiritual) exist as one unit—whatever failings exist with the one become part of the other. For Paul, this notion is bi-directional. On the one hand, the believers share in Jesus' holiness because he is holy; on the other hand, their bodily impurities will detrimentally affect that union—that is, dissolve it. Hence, Paul warns his readers that if they "contract" the impurity caused by sexual union with a forbidden sexual partner, they cannot also unite with Jesus because his holiness, like the holiness of the Temple, cannot come into contact with impurities. And to further this point, Paul makes yet another analogy: "Do you not know that your body is a temple of the Holy Spirit within you which you have from God?" (1 Cor. 6:19). The body is a vessel for the holy spirit. Like the Temple in Jerusalem, which functions as God's divine abode on earth, the vessel must be pure in order to receive the holy within it. *Porneia* creates pollution that defiles the body such that it no longer can house the holy spirit. In such a case, the defiled body must be removed from the community and the holy spirit from within it. Here, Paul echoes Qumranic concern for all pollution, but especially for "moral" pollution, which affects the Temple (and other holy space) all the while transferring the holiness of the Temple to the individual Christian bodies and the corporate community as a whole.

Christine Hayes argues (following Dale Martin) that Paul here not only contrasts the pure "sexual" unification of believer and Jesus with the impure sexual unification of believer with a *pornê* but also implies that (if one understands the *pornê* to be metaphorically a harlot, but in reality a non-Christian) the harlot/nonbeliever, who by her nature and "profession" is impure, can transfer her impurity to her many lovers. Hence, they are impure not only by their improper sexual behavior (sleeping with a "prostitute") but also by physically contracting her impurity. Hayes refers to this as carnal impurity. In Paul's hands, Ezra's holy-seed paradigm is transformed into a holy-body paradigm in which the individual body can contract "moral" impurities from others who are "morally" impure.[25] In so doing, Paul conflates the contagiousness of "ritual" impurity with the bad behaviors of "moral" impurity. The believer cannot have sexual relations with a prostitute/nonbeliever lest he defile himself by contact with a "contagious" person, rendering his union with Jesus null and void. Yet, as I argue above, one need not think of Paul's *pornê* here as a flesh-and-blood harlot, nor as a nonbeliever, because any forbidden sexual partner (even a previously chaste one) causes *porneia*. Remember, the case Paul sets before the Corinthians as prime example is incest: a man sleeps with his father's former wife. Furthermore, prostitution in and of itself is not a levitically prohibited sexual relation, nor does Paul imply that exogamy constitutes *porneia*. Paul simply innovates that the impurity caused by the action of *porneia* is contagious to others via their shared union with Jesus. The Christian partners in an illicit relationship create an impurity that can spread to the whole community in the same manner as any impurity "spreads" to the Temple or the land. Here, Paul argues that the pollution created by the union becomes part of the partners in the union, and it can pass from person to person as they are also in union with Jesus. For, in uniting with Jesus, they are all—as a community—one and the same "sacred space" in replacement or imitation of the Jerusalem Temple. In this case, the man who has an illicit relationship creates a pollution that can permeate the whole community, as he is also a part of that community in that he is a member of the corporate (and vulnerable) body of Jesus. (Although Paul condemns all forbidden partners—male and female—the term *pornê* remains specifically gendered and female, whether deployed as reality or metaphor.) Paul here proves himself unconcerned with contracting "moral" impurities through contact with non-Christians but, rather, with the ways Christians can create those same impurities even among themselves.

Finally, as Dale Martin argues, Paul, in the beginning of 1 Corinthians 7, constructs marriage as a further prophylactic against pollution.[26] Paul writes, "It is well for a man not to touch a woman. But because of cases of *porneia*, each man should have his own wife and each woman her own husband" (1 Cor. 7:1–2). While some in Corinth (the Strong, according to Martin) were probably arguing that it is better not to marry at all, to which Paul most likely agreed, he argues nonetheless that not everyone can be so restrained.[27] Better they should have a sexual outlet than be tempted into *porneia*—illicit sexual unions—and thereby damage the whole community. Moreover, as I noted above, Yarbrough argues that Paul shows himself obsessed with community seemliness, as his whole discussion of sexual pollution fits within his larger program of community cohesion.[28] Most of the issues Paul concerns himself with in 1 Corinthians have to do with the divisions within the community. Paul argues against the Strong's elitist tendencies—namely, that their claim to superiority is detrimental to the overall health of the community. Likewise, pollution of the corporate body results in community damage. Marriage, then, provides a legitimate outlet for a person's sexual urges and hinders his temptations to seek sexual contact with a *pornê*.

But the Children Are Holy: Holiness Ascribed through Parental Achievement

Nonetheless, as I noted in the preceding chapters, the biblical authors' propensity to metaphorize Israel's apostasy (worship of foreign gods) as prostitution or adultery led some Second Temple readers (though not Paul, as I argue below) to merge the notion of "spiritual" prostitution (alien worship) with the foreigners themselves who worship these alien gods. The author of Jubilees is but one example. And, while the Jubilean author would surely agree that the idolaters defile themselves through their idolatry, he excludes their potential redemption by declaring them inherently unholy as well. Their idolatry remains beside the point, for their impurity is not transformable (it cannot be rendered pure). Recently, Kathy Gaca has argued that the Greek translations of the Hebrew Bible's dual metaphors of "spiritual fornication" and "spiritual adultery" equally inform Paul's notion of *porneia*, in that the "biblical harlots" of the LXX (foreign worship) become real, in-the-flesh non-Christian potential spouses that Paul calls "harlots."[29] Hence, she argues, one should read Paul's *pornê* above not so much as a prostitute or even an illicit sexual partner on levitical terms but as a foreigner—that is, a non-Christian. Gaca further argues that Paul understands *porneia* to mean specifically heterosexual relations with Gentiles that either promote syncretistic worship of other gods or are in and of themselves ritualized worship practices dedicated to other gods and are always conducted with non-Christians (or non-Israelites in the LXX), by definition.[30] In other words, Paul's biggest fear is not the defilement of "moral" impurities (incest, adultery, etc.) but sexual relations that are in and of themselves or that will lead people to foreign worship because they are relationships with foreign (i.e., non-Christian people). Gaca understands Paul to translate *pornê* first and foremost as a "foreign women" rather than as a "prostitute" or as any other forbidden sexual partner.[31] While I think this notion of *pornê* as a foreign (and hence forbidden) woman may inform one of Paul's usages of *porneia*, it is not necessarily the primary meaning, as my reading of 1 Corinthian 5–6 and 1 Thessalonians 4 demonstrates. Elsewhere Paul may understand the *pornê* to be a threat because of her foreignness (1 Cor. 10:8, for instance), yet when he advocates a Christian form of endogamy as a protection around the community's holiness, though similar in many ways to Ezra and the Jubilean in exegesis, he does not there invoke a notion of *porneia*. Rather, holiness guides him to endogamy. Gaca's argument fits neatly with other Second Temple paradigms of endogamy (Ezra, Jubilees, Tobit), but Paul's hermeneutic differs in several significant ways from these earlier constructs, as I have already demonstrated.[32]

Gaca argues that Paul anchors this notion of *pornê* as foreign woman exegetically through his reading of the LXX pentateuchal narratives of illicit relations between Israelites and non-Israelites, particularly the episode at Shittim in Numbers 25 (1 Cor. 10). There, the Israelite nation is punished as a whole for allowing their men to "go a whoring" with the daughters of Moab. While the Hebrew biblical text remains ambiguous as to whether the real Israelite crime in this narrative is foreign worship, sexual relations with foreign women, or both, Gaca understands Paul to argue that the significant crime is sexual—because he labels the act there *porneia* (1 Cor. 10:8).[33] Yet, it is unclear from the very cryptic passage ("We must not indulge in *porneia* [*porneuômen*] as some of them did, and twenty-three thousand fell in a single day") what exactly Paul references with this verb. Does he mean the act of sexual congress with foreign women? Or the act of idolatry that followed? Or both? Gaca assumes both. That is, she assumes *porneia* refers here to both the illicit sexual acts (assuming they were illicit because the women were foreign) and the idolatrous worship. She further argues that Paul highlights the dangers of foreign spouses because they will necessarily lead the Christians to worship foreign gods or are in and of themselves already tainted because of their foreign worship. And while I would agree that this particular pentateuchal episode provides exegetical material for Paul here, in 1 Corinthians 10, it is not necessarily applicable to what he says in chapters 5–7; as I demonstrated above, Paul's hermeneutic is equally, if not more, embedded in a paradigm of purity. This is not to argue that Paul is sanguine about Christian–non-Christian mixed marriages—surely he is not—yet he does not label exogamy *porneia*; in fact, he calls some of these unions holy.

Paul (or perhaps a secondary author)[34] argues his case for Christian endogamy in 2 Corinthians 6:

> Do not be mismatched with unbelievers. For what partnership is
> there between righteousness and lawlessness? Or what fellowship is
> there between light and darkness? What agreement does Christ have
> with Beliar? Or what does a believer share with an unbeliever? What
> agreement has the temple of God with idols? For we are the temple
> of the living God. (2 Cor. 6:14–16)

Here, *porneia* figures not at all; rather, this author argues for a separation along genetic or species lines—following the logic of Leviticus 19:19. As Hayes notes, verse 14 implies that the "yoking" (in marriage) of a believer and an unbeliever can be equated with the levitical prohibition of mixing seed, yoking two different animals together, and the interweaving of flax and wool (Lev. 19:19).[35] The issue here is not impurity in the sense of pollution, but impurity in the sense of hybridity. Cross-breeding seed or cattle results in hybrids or mutts— non-purebreds. The levitical call to holiness includes all these prohibitions against illicit mixing. Similarly, the Christian community is different, hence it should not mix (in marriage) with those who are not like them. While Ezra understands the Judeans to be in a separate category of holy people, this author, too, positions the Christians in a category of their own as a distinct community. Moreover, the mixing with non-Christians (in marriage) would cause the Christians to lose their holy status, as Ezra argues for the Judeans. Note that 4QMMT uses this exact biblical passage to further support Ezra's holy-seed construct. Nevertheless, the author of this Pauline passage, while condemning these mixed marriages, does not label them *porneia* or impure—rather, they are simply untenable.

Yet, the conclusion to this passage implies something else about the impurity the Christians should avoid:

"Therefore come out from them and be separate from them, says the
Lord, and touch nothing unclean; then I will welcome you and I will
be your father and you shall be my sons and daughters, says the Lord
Almighty." Since we have these promises, beloved, let us cleanse
[*katharisômen*] ourselves from every defilement [*pantos molusmou*] of
body and spirit, making holiness [*hagiôsunên*] perfect in the fear of
God. (2 Cor. 6:17–18)

Nonetheless, this author argues that by implication, the non-Christians are impure—something that a Christian should not touch (here we see a borrowing from the paradigm of contagious impurities). The formerly Gentile, now Christian converts were also once impure/unholy as these are now, but they have made themselves holy by accepting Paul's teachings and thereby cleansing themselves of these impurities (idolatry). So while Paul in 1 Corinthians argues that Christians in and of themselves and their own bad behavior (incest) can pollute themselves, and by extension the community, here the author suggests that the Gentiles by classification are both profane and impure through their idol worship. Furthermore, he implies that the nonbeliever can contract this impurity through touch (i.e., marriage). In this case, Paul (or his imitator) *does* argue that sexual contact with a nonbeliever infects the believer with the same impurity. Yet he blames their idolatry (Belial) rather than their sexual behavior as the primary source of their pollution. The Jubilean author concludes similarly. In 2 Corinthians, the Gentiles defile themselves through their idolatry, but Paul does not condemn them for indulging in *porneia*, nor advocate that marrying one constitutes *porneia* for a Christian, even as he suggests they contract some sort of "moral" impurity from them.

In fact, despite this seemingly hard-and-fast ruling in 2 Corinthians (whether or not of Paul's hand), Paul elsewhere seems more lenient on the issue of intermarriage. In 1 Corinthians 7:10–14, he allows already consummated intermarriages to stand:

To the married I give this command—not I but the Lord—that
the wife should not separate from her husband (but if she does
separate, let her remain unmarried or else be reconciled to her
husband), and that the husband should not divorce his wife. To
the rest I say—I and not the Lord—that if any believer has a wife
who is an unbeliever and she consents to live with him, he should

not divorce her. And if any woman has a husband who is an
unbeliever and he consents to live with her, she should not divorce
him. For the unbelieving husband is made holy through his
believing wife, and the unbelieving wife is made holy through her
husband. Otherwise your children would be unclean, but as it is,
they are holy.

Paul, here, addresses the question of already consummated mixed marriages.
If it is so detrimental to a Christian's holiness to marry or have sexual relations with non-Christians for fear of profanation (or defilement), what should
one do in the situation where one member of a previously consummated
non-Christian marriage converts to Christianity? Need that person necessarily divorce his or her spouse? Ezra's answer would have been yes—even as
he did not believe in the possibility of conversion. (Apparently the Strong of
Corinth felt similarly.) Paul, however, says "not necessarily"—as long as the
non-Christian spouse does not object to continuing the marriage. Influenced,
perhaps, by Jesus' supposed ban on divorce—because once one has become
"one flesh" with another, there is no going back or exchanging of flesh—Paul
bends over backwards to preserve even partially Christian marriages.[36] Perhaps he retains some hope that the other spouse will eventually convert, too
(though he realistically does not expect that in every case).[37] Nevertheless,
Paul couches this concession in the language of holiness. One need not
divorce one's spouse because the children are "holy." And if the children are
holy, then somehow the non-Christian spouse must have been sanctified by
the Christian one. Yonder M. Gillihan explains this exemption as a legal
ruling.[38] While a Christian technically should not marry a non-Christian, the
fact that these marriages have already been consummated, and the fact that
the community insists on including the children produced by these marriages (and does not exile them as Ezra would have), shows that these
particular Christian–non-Christian marriages have been sanctioned retroactively.
Gillihan understands Paul's reading of legal marriages and particularly the
status of the children in the community in the context of the biblical *mamzerim*. Children of illicit sexual unions (*mamzerim*) are prohibited from
entering the Israelite community.[39] If such were true in the Christian community, then the children and the spouses would be banished, but since the
children are "in," then so too are willing spouses. The very fact that the community considers the children to be members of the holy community renders these mixed marriages legitimate—that is, their offspring are not
unholy. Though this appears to be circular reasoning, Paul elsewhere
appears unwilling to exclude anyone on legal/racial/social grounds (Jew/

non-Jew, free/slave, etc.), so it would follow that he would not necessarily wish to exclude people simply because of their parentage.[40]

Contra Gillihan, Hayes prefers to read Paul's "sanctified," not in the legal sense of "legitimately betrothed/married," but in what she calls a religio-moral sense of "cleansed from all impurities." Paul's legal fiction does more than simply allow the children to be members of the holy community, but it actually marks the non-Christian spouse as holy.[41] However, I do not think this is what Paul intends here. Perhaps reflecting an understanding of holiness similar to the one used in 2 Corinthians 6, his questioners ask, "if the mixing of holy and non-holy is forbidden—how can we continue in mixed marriages?" Paul retorts, however, "but the children are holy!" The whole point of the nonmixing rule is to keep the children from being rendered profane (mutts), yet the community has decided (though we do not know on what grounds) that they are purebreds.[42] Here, in his more universalistic mode, Paul refuses to exclude any child because of what formerly might have been considered illegitimate parentage. Yet, in so doing, Paul leaves the unconverted, yet supposedly sympathetic spouse in a precarious position. She or he is neither holy—a member of the community like his or her spouse and children—nor unholy, like other nonmembers. Moreover, one is left with a final question about the children: are they holy by achievement or by ascription? Has Paul created yet another category? Are children born to Christian parents automatically Christian? Paul does not address this issue here, but later communities surely solve this problem by requiring baptism for all Christians, no matter their birth. In 1 Corinthians, Paul proves himself flexible and inclusive in order to preserve order within the community. Perhaps with an eye to both Greco-Roman and Jewish legalized divorce, Paul wishes to distinguish the Christian community further by upholding the sanctity of all marriages made by Christians. Furthermore, in this passage, as in the rest of 1 Corinthians 5–7 and 1 Thessalonians 4, Paul does not equate intermarriage with *porneia*. Certainly he prefers Christians to "marry in the Lord" (1 Cor. 7:39), but he does not necessarily link exogamy with *porneia* (except perhaps in the case of 1 Cor. 10).

Conclusions

In the end, Paul stands by a notion of holiness achieved. He posits that holiness is achieved through the *act* of faithfulness. That is, by taking up faithfulness—believing in the Messiah—a community of holy people, the Christians, is created. Nevertheless, the holy body is vulnerable to pollution and, hence, the

Christians must keep up a vigilant stand against invading pollutants such as *porneia*. A holy person can lose his holy status through bad behavior. In Paul's estimation, sexual deviance remains the most damaging of the bad—and by their nature—polluting behaviors. At the same time, Paul makes a distinction between holy people and unholy people. While holy people are defined by their faith, unholy people are further defined by their impure behavior, as well as their unbelief. Hence, holy people must be further defined by their holy and pure behavior. In some cases, rather than just advocate that the holy avoid *porneia* and other unholy behavior, Paul suggests that there are specific holy behaviors that a Christian must pursue. In 1 Thessalonians, Paul promotes monogamous, lifetime marriages as one way to act as a holy person should. In this way, Paul continues and expands on earlier traditions that separate the holy from the profane and impure on sexual grounds. Yet, while simultaneously promoting endogamy along "genetic" lines (not mixing of seed), he rarely condemns exogamy as *porneia*. Most likely this is due to the porousness of Paul's community borders. Although it's important to keep pollutants out of the holy community, any Gentile can enter the community (avoid pollution) if she or he properly converts.

Finally, and by way of comparison, the author of Ephesians, no doubt a later reader of Paul, similarly emphasizes the notion that holiness requires protection from impurities, particularly *porneia*. For no *pornos* or impure person [*akathartos*] will be allowed into the kingdom of God (Eph. 5:5). He further upholds the notion that believers differentiate themselves from nonbelievers by their behavior. While not explicitly claiming that Gentiles are impure by nature, their ignorance and stubborn blindness lead them to defiling behavior. What the Christian believers have discovered is that their former defiling behaviors were keeping them out of God's kingdom. Yet the author of Ephesians has no difficulty instructing the believers to remove from themselves their "old nature"—that is, defiling behaviors—and put on a "new nature . . . created according to the likeness of God in true righteousness and holiness" (Eph. 4:24).[43] That is, this author implies that something does actually change in the very nature of the Christian when he or she becomes a Christian—that something has everything to do with proper and pure/holy behavior.

Furthermore, the author of Ephesians continues to expand on the holy nature of monogamous marriages. But in so doing, he creates a hierarchy within marriage, which is necessary to protect the holiness of the marriage (which comes from being both properly formed and monogamous). He points to the marriage itself and specifically to the hierarchical relationship between husband and wife as the fulcrum of holiness:

> Husbands, love your wives, just as Christ loved the church and gave
> himself up for her, in order to make her holy, by cleansing her with
> the washing water by the word, so as to present the church to himself
> in splendor, without spot or wrinkle or anything of the kind—yes,
> that she may be holy and without blemish. (Eph. 5:25–27)

In comparing the husband to Jesus, the "head" of the Church, the author renders the husband "head" of the wife and the family. And just as Jesus, head of the Church, sanctifies the Church, so too does the husband sanctify the wife. In preserving both the hierarchy and the fidelity of the marriage, the husband elevates the wife, just as Jesus separates out and glorifies the Church for God. For the wife, particularly, it is clear that her holiness rests on her husband's ability to keep her faithful to him. Presumably, too, the husband's holiness depends on his dual job of faithfulness to wife and Jesus.

It is this image of strict monogamy and lifetime partnering as a reflection of Christian holiness (and *porneia* as a manifestation of polygamy or remarriage) that both builds on Paul's hermeneutic and informs at least one stratum of the third-century Christian text, the *Acts of Judah Thomas,* to which we turn in the next chapter. Nevertheless, Paul's refined hermeneutic of achieved holiness (through faith) also combines with notions of semen pollution, paradigms of *porneia* as illicit sexual relations, and unrelated ideals of human incorruptibility to create a new and particularly (though not completely unique) Christian hermeneutic of sexual abstinence. In the next chapter we will see how the hermeneutic of *porneia* as illicit sexual partners merges with ideals of human incorruptibility as necessary preparation for salvation. In the fifth chapter we see how this hermeneutic of holiness (sexual renunciation) merges further with biblical notions of semen pollution and refined images of spiritual "marriage" between believer and God in the writings of Aphrahat. Finally, we will see how hermeneutics of achieved holiness and sexuality evolve among the Rabbis in both similar and dissimilar ways.

4

"Mother-City of All Evils"

Sexuality and Holiness in the
Acts of Judah Thomas

Celibacy—that dedicated act of renouncing sex and marriage for the duration of one's life—emerges as a religious vocation in the Syriac Christian tradition. This chapter examines early Syriac Christian writings to provide another window into nascent Christian thinking on sexuality and holiness, of which celibacy becomes such an important part. While the New Testament writings do not uniformly present an ascetic agenda, later Christian writers and practitioners often understand these earlier texts to do just that. In the Syriac Christian context, the full flowering of a hermeneutic of holiness as sexual renunciation can be found in the fourth-century writers Aphrahat and Ephrem. But because their hermeneutics (though innovative and unique) are dependent on the Syriac Christian authors that preceded them, this chapter takes as its focus the relevant work of these earlier authors. The chapters following this one then focus on the particulars of Aphrahat's hermeneutic of holiness and sexuality.

Let me explain the logic of this organizational choice further. In his *Demonstrations*, Aphrahat equates holiness (*qaddishuta*) with celibacy—that is, he argues that the only true way to achieve holiness is through sexual renunciation. Yet, there is a vast difference between Paul's constructs of holy community and Aphrahat's. This chapter, in an attempt to fill that gap, centers on the earliest Syriac Christian writings that uphold several different hermeneutics of holiness and sexuality as bases for their notions of religious community. While there are other second-and third-century texts that attest to Syriac

Christian ascetic practices, none earlier (as far as I can tell) than the *Acts of Judah Thomas* discusses sexuality in relationship to holiness or holy community.[1] The *Acts of Judah Thomas* testifies to a growing and distinctly Christian notion of holiness achieved that began with Paul. While Paul posited a holiness achieved through faith, but protected by proper sexual behavior, these authors tend to see sexual behavior as embodying that holiness rather than just protecting it. What interests us here is the different ways in which this holy achievement is exegeted from the biblical texts.

The earliest association between a QDS word (in this case *qaddishuta*, the abstract noun for "holiness") and sexuality in a Syriac text is in the third-century *Acts of Judah Thomas*. There, however, it presents itself within two different hermeneutics of holiness. The first, similar to Paul's, associates *porneia* (*zanyuta* in the Syriac) with improper sexual partnering but focuses on adultery (or more than one spouse) as the main culprit. Neither incest nor miscegenation invigorates this author's concerns. Rather, he focuses on promoting monogamy and condemning remarriage after divorce from or death of a spouse. Being a member of the holy community means having only one lifetime spouse. The second hermeneutic associates total sexual renunciation as an integral part of Christian faith. In order to follow the "doctrine of *qaddishuta*," one must renounce all sexual activities. Hence, in these *Acts*, holiness can mean living a married life with one lifetime partner *or* total sexual renunciation. As we shall see, the two hermeneutics remain in uneasy tension in the later redactions of the *Acts*, even as the second one rises to the forefront. Hence, I believe the *Acts* are the earliest direct linkage of total sexual renunciation and holiness (*qaddishuta*) in the Syriac tradition. As discussed in the next chapter the fourth-century writer Aphrahat seemingly picks up from where the *Acts* left off and presumes from the start that *qaddishuta* and celibacy are two sides of one coin: the one cannot exist without the other. Nevertheless, Aphrahat's hermeneutic diverges from the *Acts* at key points.[2]

Acts of Judah Thomas

The *Acts of Judah Thomas* is a difficult text to crack. While scholars agree that it was most likely written in Syriac in the third century, our earliest manuscripts preserve the Greek translation that must have been made shortly thereafter. The existing Syriac manuscripts clearly evince later emendations and catholicizing language.[3] I will cite the Drijvers English translation of the Greek unless otherwise noted, because it probably reflects a closer rendition of the original

Syriac text. Nevertheless, it must also be noted that "Syriac" ideology can be found in Greek language texts, as well as in Syriac language texts, as the category "Syriac Christian" also includes Greek-speaking Christians, in the same way that not all "Jewish" texts are composed in Hebrew.

The *Acts* is composed of thirteen praxeis, or chapters, that narrate Judah Thomas' life from the moment Jesus sends him on his mission to India until his martyrdom. The narration includes the apostle's stories, deeds, miracles performed, and conversion successes as he preaches the Christian gospel to members of the Indian upper classes. The *Acts*, as we have it today, represents a combination of older traditions concerning Judah Thomas' mission to India, some of which circulated separately. The *Acts* can be subdivided into two parts. The first seven acts constitute a loose collection of miracle stories connected to Judah Thomas' apostleship, while the latter six acts make up a more coherent narrative of Judah Thomas' evangelical mission to India, the upper-class converts he wins there, and his eventual martyrdom provoked by those conversions.[4] This latter part resembles popular Hellenistic romance novels, Christian novels, and other apocryphal acts of the apostles, such as the *Acts of Paul and Thecla*.[5] In these narratives the apostle converts upper-class women only to die at the hands of their jilted and disgruntled husbands. In the case of the *Acts of Judah Thomas*, a later editor redacted the various traditions into one longer narrative.[6] Thus, the collected miracle stories and the conversion/martyrdom cycle most likely circulated separately and were joined together at some later point. In addition, the hymns that are imbedded within the narrative—the hymn of the bride and the hymn of the pearl—both probably also enjoyed earlier and separate literary lives. Han J. W. Drijvers has argued that the *Acts* forms a highly redacted and polished literary unit, despite the fact that several of the subunits probably came into existence earlier and even circulated separately. The *Acts'* unifying theme is the mystery of and access to salvation.[7] While I agree with Drijvers that the major theme of the *Acts* focuses on presenting the correct path to salvation, I am not convinced that for a third- or even fourth-century audience the pieces all fit together neatly into one symbolic system and theology. As I have explained above, and will demonstrate more fully below, a closer reading of the different traditions embedded in the texts proves that the terminological connotations vary from act to act.

The *Acts of Judah Thomas* has been classified in a genre or collection of texts known as the Thomas tradition. Judah Thomas, as the main character in the text and his identification in these compositions as the twin brother of Jesus, bring the *Acts of Judah Thomas* together into this corpus with the *Gospel of Thomas* and the *Book of Thomas*. While most scholarly literature on these texts refers to them as the Thomas corpus, the character's name is Judah

Thomas. This is most likely a means of differentiating this Judah from Judah Iscariot. "Thomas" is a Greek derivation of *te'om/tama*, which in the Aramaic/Syriac means "twin." Hence, in the Greek text "Thomas," is also called "Didymus," as *didumos* means "twin" in Greek.[8] I refer to the character as Judah Thomas.

The *Acts'* relationship to these other two texts within this corpus, however, is hard to determine. Besides the common use of the Judah Thomas persona and his identification as a twin, there is little to go on. P. H. Poirier, however posits that there remains a loose cultural-literary relationship among the three books rather than a solid homogeneous literary trajectory that links the literature to the Edessa area. The *Acts* is clearly familiar with the *Gospel*, as it seems to cite *Gospel* passages, but there remains much in the *Acts* that is not found in the *Gospel*. And while the *Book of Thomas* appears familiar with both the *Gospel* and the *Acts*, a clear developmental trajectory cannot be traced from any one to the other. Rather, while one might place the *Gospel* chronologically earlier and the *Book* as later, Poirer suggests that all three texts evolve out of a similar milieu in which Judah Thomas as a twin of Jesus is a major theme, but they really share very little else in common.[9] Thus, the books are minimally related in that they share the major character, Judah Thomas, identified (in his very name!) as the twin of Jesus.

In the *Acts*, this twin notion is perhaps more developed than in the other texts. For instance, in the narratives Judah Thomas and Jesus often switch places (Jesus appears as Judah Thomas or vice versa). Moreover, the narrative plot line loosely follows Jesus' life pattern. However, in certain strata of the *Acts*, as opposed to the *Gospel* and *Book*, it is further expanded into a theology of twinship in which every convert to Christianity is a spiritual twin to Jesus as well.[10] Yet, it must be noted that this theme presents itself most articulately in the liturgical piece, the "Hymn of the Pearl." That the union between convert and Jesus is a union of "twins" can really only be inferred by the example of Judah Thomas, who is called a twin, and reading the narratives about such unions through the imagery of sibling reunion in the hymn. As Poirier notes, the twinship is defined by its metaphor in that, at the end of the *Acts*, even Judah Thomas denies his physical twinship with Jesus in order to emphasize his spiritual twinship.[11] But it is unclear, to me at least, how much of this spiritual twinship is projected on to the converts. In the other two works, Judah Thomas' twin status remains on the one hand, an identity marker, and on the other, an indication of his intimacy with Jesus and hence his authority. This twinship does not include the converts. Nonetheless, I am not so sure that the theme of spiritual twinship is so pronounced even in the *Acts* outside of the two incorporated hymns. Marriage to Jesus arises as an equally if not more dominant theme.

Thus, the notion of spiritual twinship of the Christian believer and Jesus, while innovative in the hymns imbedded within the *Acts*, builds on other notions of mystical union with and love/knowledge of God that lead to salvation as it appears in other Syriac and Christian literature. For another major theme of the *Acts* is conversion to the truth, through which the individual gains salvation. The *Acts* espouses a soteriology in which the individual can save him- or herself through knowledge. The individual who recognizes that humans were meant to be immortal can return to that immortal state. Jesus (sometimes doubling as Judah Thomas) serves as a role model and guide to this truth. Humans can be born again, as the first-born Son was born, and through this they become identical with one another.[12] Thus, the soteriology of the text is narrativized through many different, yet subtle types of twinning. Not only is Judah Thomas the twin brother of Jesus (and thus privy to his deepest wisdom) but also as his apostle he imitates and repeats Jesus' mission (evangelism and martyrdom), and finally he is the guide to each individual convert's spiritual twinship. In the *Acts*, the converts become spiritually identified, or one with Jesus, through their newly received knowledge and accompanying faith. Through his faith and knowledge, the Christian believer is reborn into a new level of human existence—life with Jesus. Yet, as I argue, this spiritual oneness is more often described as a marriage than as a duality. Judah Thomas doubles as Jesus (as teacher and guide), but his converts, "marry" him. They remain followers; they do not ascend to and become equals with Jesus or Judah Thomas.

Drijvers further suggests that another of the *Acts'* underlying themes, which unites the various acts and their motivations, is *enkrateia*, or the practice of sexual renunciation, and that the narratives all point in that direction—namely, that salvation can be attained only through or in conjunction with *enkrateia*. That is, the knowledge gained through faith is accompanied by specific life-changing practices—in this case, sexual renunciation. Nevertheless, a close reading of the narratives suggests that the redactor of the *Acts* was not as successful in smoothing over the inconsistencies between the traditions that he brings together in the *Acts* as Drijvers would have us believe. While the theme of *enkrateia* as the only means to salvation dominates the martyrdom cycle, several other narratives and the sermons that support them appear to promote other modes of achieving eternal life. Hence, the soteriology of the *Acts* is not as seamless as it might seem. Rather than presenting a singular encratic theology, the *Acts* presents divergent views that have been brought together by the redactor into one rather disjointed narrative. Yves Tissot, for instance, points to the fact that none of the miracle-story converts take on any form of *enkrateia* as part of their conversion. The miracle stories can be distinguished from the martyrdom narrative by their *lack* of an encratic theology.[13] Moreover, a careful study of the language of holiness and sexuality reveals two different paradigms of holiness at work in the *Acts*. Holiness—as the opposite of *porneia*, understood to be bad sexual behavior, such as adultery—better fits the *Acts'* miracle-story worldview, which focuses on reforming people's overall behavior (kindness to strangers, charitableness, etc.) in light of the miracles that this "New God" (so he is described in the text) performs through Judah Thomas. The miracle stories, therefore, manifest a hermeneutic of holiness more similar to that described in the earlier chapters of this book— an avoidance of certain polluting behaviors (though it highlights proper sexual behavior without censoring sexuality as a whole) that can block communion with God. The martyrdom narrative, however, produces a new hermeneutic in which holiness is linked to full sexual renunciation as part and parcel of the "New God's" soteriological plan. This connection is supported through a further connection between the corruptible body, death, and sexuality (in opposition to God, immortality, and incorruptibility), as well as a developing notion of spiritual marriage. Both of these notions can be traced back to the New Testament texts. And as H. W. Attridge aptly demonstrates, the *Acts* is particularly dependent on Christian Scripture in an intertextual relationship.[14] The *Acts*, as a composite text, presents two different behavioral policies to accompany its soteriology of knowledge.

This same soteriology—of knowledge and rebirth—manifests itself quite differently in the different strata of the text. In both, knowledge that Jesus is the Lord, the only one who can provide salvation into the next life, is primary. This newfound knowledge then provokes in the convert a need to live a different sort of life in the present. The differences between one's old life and one's new life are symbolically represented through various dichotomies: old and new, darkness and light, sickness and health, demon possession and release from demons, death and life/rebirth, idolatry and worship of the One God, nonsalvation and salvation. These themes are repeatedly dramatized particularly in the miracle stories, in that in every one someone dies and is reborn. Once reborn, the convert must also change his or her behavior. In the miracle stories, more often than not this change has to do with participating in more good works and living monogamous married lives. In the martyrdom cycle, the change is more radical: renouncing all sexual activity and especially married life.

Moreover, as with the place of sexuality, the concept of immortality is radically different in each part. In the martyrdom cycle, the convert lives her life on earth as if she were already immortal. Thus, she anticipates the immortality of the next and eternal life. *Enkrateia* plays a large role here, in that leaving earthly marriage for spiritual marriage is part of the overall package that faith in Jesus and an anticipation of the immortal life requires.[15] Nonetheless, in the miracle stories the next life is played down. Surely one converts to the New God (as he is called in the *Acts*) because he can provide immortality in the next life, yet what one does in *this* life remains crucial. Proper living, both sexual and social, commands attention. Good works and monogamous (controlled) marriage come hand in hand with faith here. Hence, the *Acts* as a whole displays a tension between salvation gained through good works (including proper marriage partnering) in this life and salvation demonstrated through living as if in the next life already (*enkrateia*).[16] This tension further highlights the ongoing slippage between sexual behavior as protection around one's holiness gained through faith and sexual behavior as manifestation of holiness achieved.

Drijvers further maintains that the *Acts* takes on certain soteriological themes that are already articulated in earlier Syriac writings, or writings that probably circulated in the East, such as Tatian's *Oration to the Greeks,* and narrativizing them.[17] In particular, Drijvers claims that the *Acts'* soteriology is directly related to Tatian's—but has been narrativized into the twin motif. Judah Thomas, the "twin" of Jesus, is sold as a slave to an Indian businessman, but carries his price with him—he has the means to buy his own freedom, which he eventually does. Through his freedom ("knowledge of the truth"), Judah Thomas is reborn. Judah Thomas then acts as a guide and spiritual light to his followers in India. Because Judah Thomas acts through the will of Jesus his Lord, he is also described as his twin. But like Tatian, who claims in his *Oration* to imitate Jesus in his rebirth, so too Judah Thomas and all his followers in their rebirth become "twins" of Jesus. Yet, this twin motif is clearest in the "Hymn of the Pearl," where an actual brother is mentioned, rather than in the narratives. For instance in the narratives, Judah Thomas several times advises his listeners to "put off the old man and put on the new," or to change their lifestyles completely, because they have been reborn anew, in that they have discovered their true nature after their conversion. The bridegroom, after his night vigil with Jesus who lectures him and his bride on the new faith, declares in the morning that he has recognized "who I was and who and how I now am, that I may become again what I was."[18] Through the guidance of Jesus (who doubles here as Judah Thomas), the bride and bridegroom realize that their true nature is immortal, but that they can only gain that status through their union with God, which is embodied in their love for God; but that union is a union metaphorized as a marriage, rather than as a reunion of siblings or as a spiritual twinning. In the hymn, this union is described both as a cloaking of the princely son in his native cloak and a reunion of same son with his brother in heaven. Yet, I think Drijvers stretches his analogy in both directions, in that Tatian is not alone in his soteriology of knowledge, nor does he ever call himself a twin of Jesus.[19] So, too, even in the *Acts*, one needs to read the narratives through the language and imagery of the "Hymn of the Pearl" to fully understand the spiritual twin concept. While Judah Thomas often switches places with Jesus, and claims to teach Jesus' wisdom, the convert's union with God is more often referred to as a marriage.[20]

The symbolic union of the soul with the holy spirit/*pneuma* is narrativized in several different ways in the *Acts*. It is symbolized as a marriage between the convert and the guide, Jesus. The female converts in these acts often construe their newfound relationship with God as a marriage. The young bride, in fact, assumes that her newfound love for God, manifesting itself as a marriage to Jesus, obviates all possibilities of any other marriages. Yet, the union is also described as the cloaking of the soul in a mantel of the spirit. This notion is well ingrained in the second of the two hymns that have been incorporated into the *Acts*—the "Hymn of the Pearl." In this hymn, the Word becomes a letter, which guides the protagonist (the wayward royal son) back to the royal cloak he left behind when he abandoned his parental home (heaven).

While Drijvers is surely correct to note the similarities between some parts of the *Oration*'s soteriology and the *Acts*', I do not believe Tatian is the sole or even primary influence behind these texts. The soteriology that is narrativized in these texts appears most forcefully in the two hymns that even Drijvers admits are later additions.[21] The rest of the narratives manifest as many differences as similarities to the *Oration*'s soteriology. And many of these themes find parallels in other literature, such as the *Odes of Solomon*, or can be traced to innovative intertextual readings of Scripture. Moreover, the *Acts* further narrativizes an element that is wholly missing from Tatian's *Oration*—those actions one must accomplish in order to embody that salvation. Drijvers misreads Tatian's *Oration* when he claims that it is an encratic text. While it is true that the martyrdom pericopes of the *Acts* spend much time and effort on enforcing sexual renunciation, the miracle stories, which are also beholden to this soteriology through knowledge theme, patently do not. Furthermore, a close reading of the *Oration* on its own merits shows that sexuality is a subject that Tatian never broaches there. Hence, a soteriology of or through knowledge need not necessarily be connected to encraticism, though it clearly provokes a change in behavior of some sort.[22]

Therefore, if one accepts a limited version of Drijvers' argument, that some part of the *Acts*' soteriology is similar to Tatian's, I claim that it is the *Acts* itself that adds and develops the sexual element as part and parcel of its salvation package. Acquiring knowledge or "the truth," after all, is a very ephemeral experience. The more compelling theme of the *Acts*, and I argue the dominant one, is holiness (*qaddishuta/hagiôsunê*) or proper behavior—that act which makes the individual's salvation real and manifest on earth. This is not to say that Judah Thomas does not preach the gospel of God's kingdom, but the more abstract notion of "truth" is often obscured behind the more tangible facts of sexuality and good works. Indeed, I argue that the *Acts*, as we have it today, presents two notions of that proper behavior: (1) good works and an absence of adultery and (2) total abstention from sexual relations. There is nothing specific in the *Oration* that advocates sexual purity, nor even sexual restraint.[23] Rather, only when a soteriology of knowledge and anthropology combines with other Christian notions of holiness as (primarily) sexual restraint (i.e., monogamous partnering) do we get a fusion of ideas that results in holiness as monogamous marriage or as celibacy. I argue, contra Drijvers, that Tatian is not responsible for the ascetic nature of the *Acts* but, rather, Tatian's soteriology (if the *Acts* is at all beholden to him) must be seen as merging with a larger mix of already existing hermeneutics of holiness and sexuality, which are more beholden to Paul, the canonical Gospels, and Leviticus. The miracle stories certainly carry these biblical traditions forward into another geography and literary landscape. The martyrdom narrative, however, presents something new: a direct conflict between earthly existence (marriage, children, sexuality, corruptibility, death) and a heavenly existence. While the opposition of the corrupt/mortal/earthly life to incorrupt/immortal/heavenly life can be traced directly to 1 Corinthians 15, the addition of sexuality versus asexuality seems to be the innovation of the *Acts*. I shall return to the discussion of sexuality and spirituality below.

Finally, while it is true that Tatian discusses the unity of the knowledgeable human spirit with the divine spirit, he does not call this unity a marriage. This theme of Christian faith as marriage most likely evolved out of early readings of the New Testament Gospels, where Jesus is described as the ultimate bridegroom, which the faithful attend as bridesmaids (to the marriage between the Church and Jesus). We can follow that development of marriage themes in the *Odes of Solomon*. But here the union is an esoteric love union between believer and God more than a celestial wedding ceremony attending by the believers as bridesmaids, as presented in the *Acts* and later in Aphrahat. Nonetheless, the language of in/corruptibility, which pervades the *Acts'* martyrology cycle, also relates back to this theme in the *Odes*. Hence, it behooves us to take a brief look at this earlier text.

Odes of Solomon

The *Odes of Solomon*, to be differentiated from the Herodian-era *Psalms of Solomon*, is probably the oldest known Christian writings in Syriac. James H. Charlesworth characterizes the *Odes* as an early Christian hymn book composed circa 100 CE, somewhere between Edessa and Antioch, in the Syrian East. In his estimation, the hymns attempt to articulate the formative experiences of a new theological paradigm—the advent of the Messiah. Although Christian, the *Odes* reveal deep Jewish sensibilities. The *Odes* often parallel biblical and apocryphal psalms and the Qumran *hodayot* literature in style and content, demonstrating the *Odes'* Jewish liturgical milieu through which the author attempted to articulate his joy in the advent of his Messiah. In essence, the *Odes* is truly a "Jewish-Christian" document, in that it appears to represent the liturgy of an ethnically Jewish community that has accepted Jesus as its Messiah.[24]

These hymns' central theme focuses on mystical union with God through the Messiah's love. The poet, perhaps echoing the biblical Song of Songs, refers to the Messiah as his beloved (*Odes* 7:1). By accepting the Messiah's love, the poet comes closer to God; through the Messiah's love, the poet finds truth and knowledge. The third hymn in this collection opens with a love poem to God and his son, the Messiah. Union with God, the Most High, is affected through the love of the Messiah. The lover/poet has found his beloved (the Messiah) and, hence, has found his way back to God—he is "no foreigner" to the Lord Most High and Merciful, God. The Messiah provides the means to return to God, to God's blessing, and ultimately, to salvation. Union with him who is immortal provides immortality for the lover/poet. This ode closes with an acknowledgment of the wisdom gained through this love: "This is the Spirit of the Lord, which is not false/ Which teaches the sons of men to know His ways. Be wise and understanding and vigilant. Hallelujah" (3:10–12). If I have understood this passage correctly, the Lord/Messiah teaches the men to know the ways of his Father— the Lord Most High. Love of the Messiah brings divine wisdom and God's truth to the lover.

Sexual renunciation does not appear to be a requirement for this mystical union. Neither celibacy nor *qaddishuta* is the subject or even subtheme of the *Odes*.[25] There is no language of protecting the union or distinguishing it from earthly unions through sexual renunciation. It would be difficult to classify this text as sexually ascetic at all. Rather, the odist expresses his joy for the mystical union with God, with his body, and his words. He stretches out his hands in prayer (*Odes* 21:1, 27:1, 35:7) and is embraced by the immortal life (28:7). The odist expresses neither remorse nor distaste for his body. His body joins his soul in celebrating the Messiah's love and salvation (26:2–4). The union of human body and soul with God does not inspire the odist to reflect on his own sexuality at all. His closeness to God sparks no anxiety about marriage duties or sexual activity. The union, in fact, is effected outside community bounds. It is an individualistic experience.

Yet, the notion of "putting on" the spirit pervades the *Odes*, as it does Aphrahat's sixth demonstration and the "Hymn of the Pearl" in the *Acts of Judah Thomas*. Not only do the believers put on God's holiness but, as seen in *Odes* 3, they also put on the love of the Lord, God's grace (4:6), and the name of the Most High (39:8). In other odes, the believers also put on the Messiah. In 7:4, the poet writes: "He became like me, that I might receive Him/In form He was considered like me, that I might put Him on." Finally, immortality becomes part of the new wardrobe. In *Odes* 15:8, he notes that: "I have put on incorruption through His name/And took off corruption by His grace." Incorruption, perfection, and immortality parallel each other throughout the *Odes*, albeit without any mention of sexuality.

This putting on is also complemented by the notion of the indwelling of the holy spirit. This notion is best described in *Odes* 33:5–13. The perfect Virgin here is the holy spirit personified, who simultaneously enters into and is put on by the believer. She is opposed to the Corruptor, who is death. The holy spirit/perfect Virgin, therefore, represents life—eternal life. The believer who puts on the holy spirit, or allows it to dwell within, gains eternal life and salvation. Thus attired, the believer becomes immortal in the next life because she chooses to walk with God in this world, where "walking with God" translates into belief in Jesus as God's Messiah. Gaining eternal life is the believer's ultimate aim—union with God, the ultimate source of life, the believer's goal. The odist earlier notes that "immortal life embraced me/And kissed me./ And from that (life) is the Spirit which is within me/And it cannot die because it is life" (28:7–8). The spirit is life and life with God (who is the source of the spirit) is eternal.

While the language of incorruptibility appears only sporadically in Aphrahat's writing, it pervades the *Odes* and, as we will see, the *Acts of Judah Thomas*, as well. While in the *Acts*, it is clear that corruptibility and sexuality go hand in hand, that connection is not as apparent in the *Odes*. Rather, in the *Odes* the believer becomes immortal, incorrupt, and perfect through his faith. Salvation gained through faith in/love of the Messiah translates into eternal life. Eternal life is life with the Immortal one (God/Messiah) and Life is incorruptible. He writes: "For in the will of the Lord is your life/And His purpose is eternal life/ And your perfection is incorruptible" (*Odes* 9:4). The Messiah, who is Life, is contrasted with Satan, who is the Corruptor (death). Those who walk with the Corruptor will perish; those who choose the Messiah will be immortal (*Odes* 33). As we will see below, the language of corruptibility comes to be closely associated with sexuality and death—but they do not appear to be so tied down here. This is not to argue that sexuality is not already assumed to be a part of corruptibility, but it is not so expressed here.

Additionally, in *Odes* 42:7–9, the Messiah's love and benevolence are also compared to the love a bridegroom bestows on his bride. Jesus throws his yoke of love over his believers like a bridegroom protects the bride with his arm. The bridal feast is compared to Jesus' abode where the faithful reside. Hence, the exacting image of a celestial marriage, which replaces earthly marriage, does not appear here. Marriage is a freer metaphor, which is manipulated in both positive and negative directions, by the poet. Neither image promotes a necessary abandonment of earthly marriage as a result of the believer's faith. Furthermore, the language of corruptibility and death versus incorruptibility and eternal life are not here linked with sexuality explicitly, even as life is represented by a virgin and death by a carousing bridegroom. These images may lead later readers to make such connections, but I think they are latent to nonexistent in the worldview of the poet.

So while the *Acts* shares themes in common with Tatian (a soteriology of knowledge) and the *Odes* (union with God imagined as a marriage, language of in/corruptibility, and a notion of "putting on" a new life), its literary repertoire appears much broader and as beholden to Scripture than to any other developing Christian literature. The *Acts* is a compilation of texts, traditions, and soteriologies and symbolic systems. Moreover, the *Acts'* rising advocation of first sexual restraint and then sexual renunciation is an innovation—or at least an early witness to these developing practices—in the history of Syriac Christian literature. I focus the rest of the chapter on the *Acts'* various hermeneutics of holiness and sexuality in order to illuminate this development in the history of Syriac Christian asceticism.

Hermeneutics of Holiness and Sexuality in the *Acts of Judah Thomas*

Judah Thomas goes to India in order to convert the natives to the new Christian faith and he is particularly successful among the urban upper-classes. Although Judah Thomas preaches to the masses all over the countryside, and many are converted, only the conversions of a few upper-class Indians are recorded in full detail. Each of these elongated narratives of conversion (except one) includes some element of sexual restraint within the conversion process. In several cases (Mygdonia, Tertia, Vizan, the young bridal couple), the converts clearly give up all sexual relations in order to partake in the new life that Judah Thomas offers them. The hapless husband of Mygdonia complains about this "doctrine of *qaddishuta*" that Judah Thomas preaches, in which husbands must sever themselves from their wives and vice versa. His wife refuses to sleep with him anymore, claiming that sexual intercourse is anathema to her new status as a believer in the Christian Messiah. She will not "give herself to corruption" again. But in others (the youth who kills his prostitute-lover, the demon who possesses the betrothed woman), certain sexual practices only are at issue, such as adultery and polygamy. The prostitute who is killed by her lover (and brought back to life by Judah Thomas) reports of her visit to hell that she saw the places of torments for those who pervert the proper union of intercourse as appointed by God and for those who did not preserve their virginity but gave themselves to lust—before they were married—and for those who indulge in prostitution (both the women and their male clients). Here, in the miracle narratives, sexual relations per se are not condemned but, rather, only having more than one sexual partner is. In the first case of Mygdonia (in the martyrdom cycle), all sexual intercourse is forbidden to her after her conversion. In the second case (miracle narrative), only illicit sex is condemned—sexual relations that are not appointed by God namely, adultery, incest, prostitution, and premarital sex. Yet these latter texts introduce a new understanding of sexual purity: lifetime monogamy. *Porneia* (*zanyuta*—in the Syriac), or sexual impurity, here constitutes sexual relations with anyone other than one's legitimate (and only) spouse. In all of these narratives (miracle and martyrdom), "filthy intercourse" or "impure union"—whether defined as adultery or sexuality—opposes holiness (*qaddishuta* or *hagiôsunê*) eternally.[26]

This conceptual inconstancy probably highlights both the composite nature of the *Acts* and its transitional position within the developing theology of *enkrateia*. I examine first the narratives in which *qaddishuta/hagiôsunê* connotes "legal sex" and, second, those texts in which *qaddishuta/hagiôsunê* is clearly aligned with total sexual renunciation. I argue that the first category of narratives relates back to legal definitions of holiness and purity in the post-biblical Old Testament apocryphal literature such as Jubilees, the Testaments of the Twelve Brothers, and some of the Qumran literature, but especially as they are filtered through the New Testament texts. The second set of narratives develops from and depends on the earlier construct but also transforms it yet again into a new paradigm in which *qaddishuta* takes on celibacy as its sole manifestation by fusing the levitically based paradigm with yet another construct of human sexuality most likely created out of a fusion of various Pauline notions of the perishable, earthly body and images of mystical union/marriage, as well as more developed notions of incorruptibility and immortality as displayed in the *Odes of Solomon*.

Monogamy: The Mother-City of All Good

In the *Acts of Judah Thomas*, chapters 17–29, King Gundaphorus hires Judah Thomas to build him a palace. But instead of a mortar-and-brick building, which stands on solid earth, Judah Thomas builds him a palace in heaven. This edifice is created from Judah Thomas' efforts to feed, console, and heal the poor of India with the money the king supplied him to construct the palace. Judah Thomas' good works, supported by the finances of the king, builds the king a heavenly palace that he can inhabit only in the next life. At first the king is aghast, angry and distraught over these circumstances. He understands only that Judah Thomas has swindled him out of his construction fees. While the king contemplates how best to punish Judah Thomas, the king's brother sickens and dies. The angels take the brother's soul up to heaven to see the king's palace. He is then allowed back to earth to report on the splendor of the eternal palace to the king, his brother. Only then does Gundaphorus accept and understand why Judah Thomas spent his money on the poor. He begs to be converted to the new faith so that he can enjoy that palace in the next life.[27] In the process of converting the king and his brother, Judah Thomas preaches what will become a standard sermon that will repeat itself in various forms throughout the *Acts*:

> Men and women, boys and girls, youths and maids, vigorous and aged, whether you are slaves or free, *abstain from improper sexual behavior [porneias] and avarice and the service of the belly; for in these three heads all lawlessness is comprised.* For improper sexual behavior [*porneia*] blinds the mind and darkens the eyes of the soul, and is a hindrance to the right ordering of the body, turning the whole man to weakness and throwing the whole body into sickness. Insatiate desire brings the soul into fear and shame, since it is within the body and plunders the goods of others, and harbors this suspicion, <that if it restore> the goods of others to the owners <it will be put to shame>. And the service of the belly plunges the soul into cares and anxieties and sorrows, <since it becomes anxious lest it come to be in want, and reaches out for what is far from it>.[28]

"Abstain from sexual immorality [Gk: *porneias*; Syr: *zanyuta*] and avarice and the service of the belly; for in these three heads all lawlessness is comprised," preaches Judah Thomas. As I noted above, the conversion stories usually contain a narrative of sexual activity that needs to be refined. This is the only case in which we have no indication of the main protagonist's sexual life. Nevertheless, Judah Thomas forewarns him not to indulge in sexual immorality, avarice, or service of the belly, for these three sins lead to greater lawlessness and evil. The notion that there are several "cardinal" sins and that sexual immorality or some illicit sexual activity is one of the most cardinal is not unique to the *Acts*. Similar lists appear in Jubilees, the Qumran literature, the New Testament literature, and other noncanonical literature. Recall that Mark lists sexual immorality (*porneia*), theft, murder, adultery, avarice, etc., as actions that defile a person. Jubilees claims that *zenut*, (illicit sexual relations), uncleanness, and iniquity lead to the downfall of Noah's generation and the flood.[29] Yet, this particular pericope of the *Acts*, while condemning these three practices, does not couch its discourse in the language of impurity and holiness (as Mark and Jubilees do). God is not the reference point for proper behavior here. This, however, is only an aberration in the retelling of this passage. When the litany of sins is repeated later in the *Acts*, it is aligned directly with a notion of holiness. Yet, in these passages the sexual relations, which best embody holiness, differ. Also, noteworthy is the fact that when the king and his brother convert, their behavior toward their subjects changes radically—in that they take up the lives of itinerant philanthropists—but their sexuality is never broached.

The pericope of the youth who kills his lover is more explicit in terms of which kind of sexual acts are defiling and offensive to God. In this narrative (chap. 51ff), a young man kills his lover because she refuses to give up her other lovers. In this pericope, the young man hears Judah Thomas preaching the new faith and doctrine, accepts it, converts, and then returns to his lover (who also happens to be a prostitute) in order to convert her, as well. But what he asks of her is not to renounce sexual relations entirely but only having sexual relations with other men (she is a prostitute, after all). What he wants to establish is a monogamous relationship with her. When she refuses, he kills her because he "could not see her commit adultery with another."[30] And while it is the murder that exposes the youth (his hands shrivel as he reaches for the Eucharist), Judah Thomas forgives him this sin when he explains his reasoning and even resurrects his girlfriend, whose journey through hell reinforces Judah Thomas' message, as we shall see below. Thus, this passage dismisses the murder in order to focus on what it deems more important: multiple sexual partners.

This narrative, similarly to 1 Thessalonians, aligns Christian faith with the practice of monogamous sexual relations. Judah Thomas' preaching at this point in the narrative further reinforces this notion. This is how the Greek text relays Judah Thomas' preaching, how the youth hears it, and what he attempts to do in order to follow it. According to the youth, Judah Thomas preaches: "Whoever shall unite in the impure union, and especially in adultery, he shall not have life with the God whom I preach." The youth then surmises and recounts to Judah Thomas: "Since then, I loved her greatly, I besought her and tried to persuade her to become my consort in chastity (*hagnea*) and pure (*kathara*) conduct, which thou thyself dost teach; but she would not. Since she was unwilling, then I took a sword and slew her, for I could not see her commit adultery with another."[31] Judah Thomas preaches against "impure union,"[32] while the youth asks his lover to live a life in "chastity and pure conduct." What is impure union to Judah Thomas? What does chastity and pure conduct mean to the youth? The latter clearly points to monogamous sexual relations for the youth; the former has something to do with adultery—the opposite of monogamy. Judah Thomas' subsequent preaching gives us a further clue and relates back to the earlier preaching to King Gundaphorus:

> Each of you, therefore, put off the old man and put on the new, and
> abandon your first way of life and conduct. And let them that steal
> steal no more, but live by labouring and working. Let the adulterers
> no longer practice sexual immorality [*porneuetôsan*], that they may
> not utterly deliver themselves to eternal punishment; for with God
> adultery is exceeding wicked, above the other evils. Put away also
> avarice and falsehood and drunkenness and slander, and do not
> return evil for evil. For all these things are strange and alien to the
> God who is preached by me. But walk ye rather in *faith* [*pistei*] and
> *meekness* [*praoteti*] and *holiness* [*hagiôsunê*][33] and *hope* [*elpidi*] in which
> God delights, that ye may become his kinsman, expecting from him
> the gifts which only some few receive."[34]

Judah Thomas preaches a total lifestyle change—one is to become a new person, turn over a new leaf, conduct one's actions, behavior, and particularly one's relations with others in a completely different fashion. Judah Thomas calls for an end to robbery, adultery, lechery, avarice, falsehood, drunkenness, and slander. Adultery, however, is in a category all its own, for it is "above the other evils." It is the worst of all possible sins against another human because it is also the most odious to God. Later, Judah Thomas will label it the "mother city of all evils."[35] This passage highlights the problematics of having more than one sexual partner (namely, that it is the greatest evil before God). This heightened concern for monogamous sexual relations echoes both Paul's claim that improper sexual partnering (whether adultery or incest or both) is the worst offense one can commit against God (because the body is a temple that "houses" God) and the Gospels' statements against divorce and remarriage. General sexual immorality and adultery seem to merge into one category of sexual offense: multiple sexual partners. This homogenization is reinforced by the fact that the *Acts* uses "sexual immorality" and "adultery" interchangeably at times. If *porneia* is the worst of all behavioral impurities, then adultery is the worst of *porneia*.

Furthermore, in line with the earlier literature (both Jewish and Christian), sexual sins are here placed in highlighted opposition to holiness. In the Greek *Acts*, Judah Thomas calls upon the youth to live a life in faith, meekness, holiness (hagiôsunê), and hope; the youth in turn calls upon his lover to live a life with him in chastity (hagnea) and pure (kathara) conduct. Faith, humility, holiness, and hope in the Lord translates into chaste, monogamous, and, therefore, pure sexual relations for the youth and his lover. Judah Thomas' impure unions stand in opposition to the youth's chaste and pure unions through monogamous marriage, which stand together with holiness. Someone who wishes to participate in the community of believers—the new holy community—must conduct himself in a manner so as not to offend the Holy One, God. In this pericope, holy behavior translates to monogamous sexual relations.

The Acts' emphasis on proper sex (as opposed to no sex) is furthered through the visit to hell, which the murdered lover must endure before being resurrected by Judah Thomas. As she relates her underground journey, it becomes clear that most of those being punished, tortured, and imprisoned in hell have committed grievous sexual sins—basically, following the established lists we have seen elsewhere. They have perverted the intercourse of men and women; they have committed adultery and prostitution; finally, they have indulged in sex with virgins (presumably with more than one lover). Those who have chased after virgins have indulged in premarital sex (and most likely premarital promiscuity). Along with these sexual sinners are a host of nonsexual sinners—thieves, slanders, the immodest, greedy, unjust, and those who generally run after evil. But they are added almost as an afterthought. The lion's share of hell is occupied by those who did not restrict themselves to one sexual partner in their lifetime.

This pericope's "impure union," then, is in part based on the levitical notion of proper sexual partnering, though most likely filtered through later texts such as Jubilees and the New Testament writings. These early Christian writers, including the author of the Acts, focus on eternal life—a very different end result than the one envisioned by the biblical and early post-biblical Jewish writers, who concerned themselves more with preserving their presence in the existing world. In Leviticus, proper sexual behavior (among other things) allows the Israelites to "be holy" like God and to survive in this world; in this part of the Acts, qaddishuta/hagiôsunê—that is, "pure unions"—allows the practitioner into eternal life and the kingdom of heaven with God in the next world. Holiness, or the fulfillment of God's command to "be holy," translates in this part of the Acts to "pure unions" of monogamous relationships. Prostitutes and adulterers will not get into Judah Thomas' heaven; rather, holiness gained through proper sexual partnering is the promise of eternal salvation. Walk in holiness, preaches Judah Thomas, not in adultery. Judah Thomas flips Paul's equation (shun porneia) to its positive side and restricts its parameters further: be holy, follow hagiôsunê—that is, marry or cohabit with one (legitimate) partner so as to avoid eternal damnation. Paul's concern for protecting the body, which is a pure vessel for the holy spirit, does not surface here. Rather, the protective act (avoiding *porneia*) merges with the declaration of faith. Holiness comes through *porneia* avoidance.

Nevertheless, it must not be forgotten that *hagiôsunê* can only be attained *after* one converts to the new faith. The youth, after all, comes to the conclusion that he must live a chaste and pure life only after he acquires the knowledge that comes through faith and, hence, wishes to protect that faith so that he can gain eternal life. Monogamous relations without faith mean nothing. However, the *Acts'* extensive discourse on sexual morality overshadows the priority of faith. The issue that trips up the youth in the first place is his sexuality, not his faith. The passage that sits foremost in his memory is not "believe in Jesus and gain eternal life" but "whoever shall unite in the impure union, and especially in adultery, he shall not have life with the God whom I preach."

It is my contention, then, that the notion of *hagiôsunê*, as described in this pericope of the *Acts of Judah Thomas*, descends from distilled readings of the levitical holiness code in which holy behavior is placed in irreconcilable opposition to impure behavior, which is described as sexual sin above all other sins. In Paul, *porneia* can refer to the whole host of levitical improper sexual partners; yet, in Thessalonians we see it referring to polygamy. In this pericope of the *Acts*, "impure union" points to adultery, or multiple sexual partners, above all. Paul, however, maintains a clear divide between faith, which brings one into the community, and pure sexual behavior, which keeps one there once admitted. Sexual purity is a protective fence around one's faith. The *Acts* seems to merge the two notions into one. Proper sexual behavior not only protects the faithful but also somehow maintains or solidifies, or even embodies, their holy status as well. Sexual uprightness looms larger than faith in Judah Thomas' sermons. This becomes particularly apparent in the passages in which *hagiôsunê* equates with total sexual renunciation.

Sexual Renunciation: The "Doctrine of Holiness"

In several narratives of the *Acts of Judah Thomas*, sexual abstinence, rather than monogamous marriage, arises as the only means to holiness. In the first conversion narrative of the *Acts*, Judah Thomas calls upon his Lord, Jesus, to lead a just-married young couple to what is "useful and profitable" to them. Jesus appears in the bridal chamber just in time to prevent the couple from consummating their marriage. Jesus (appearing in the form of Judah Thomas and calling himself the twin of Judah Thomas) counsels the young couple as follows: "And know this, that if you abandon this filthy intercourse you become holy temples, pure and free from afflictions and pains both manifest and hidden, and you will not be girt about with cares for life and for children, the end of which is destruction."[36] Mimicking the language of Paul, Jesus/Judah tells the young couple that they can become "holy temples" for God. He requires them only not to indulge in "filthy intercourse." Filthy intercourse does not translate here, as it does in Paul, to a levitical notion of sexual immorality. Rather, it becomes clear from the narrative that Jesus/Judah refers to all sexual intercourse. Sexual renunciation is presented as the only means to creating that holy temple in which the spirit can dwell. Nevertheless, our text does not explain how it is that all sexual intercourse is "filthy" and therefore defiling of their holy temples/bodies. Rather, Judah Thomas switches rationales in mid-sentence and descends into a diatribe against earthly marriage and child-bearing. For the downside of indulging in "filthy intercourse" is the heavy burden of child-bearing and rearing, the opposite of a "pure" life free from domestic cares. Even proper acceptable sexual partnering cannot prevent one from suffering under the load of family and domestic woes. Mortality overshadows purity here. He continues:

> But if you get many children, then for their sakes you become
> robbers and avaricious, (people who) flay orphans and defraud
> widows, and by so doing you subject yourselves to the most grievous
> punishments. For the majority of children become unprofitable,
> possessed by demons. . . . Even if they are healthy, again will they be
> unserviceable, performing useless and abominable deeds, for they
> are caught either in adultery [moicheia] or in murder or in theft or in
> unchastity [porneia], and by all these you will be afflicted.[37]

Sexual activity produces children; children produce nothing but pain and agony. Caring for children turns parents into thieves and oppressors of the poor (presumably as they scramble to provide for their offspring). Worse yet, these ungrateful progeny usually turn out poorly. If they are not possessed outright by demons, they will try their best to vex and worry their already anxious parents. Most likely they will turn to those cardinal sins we have come by before: murder, adultery, theft, or unchastity (porneia). In short, children bring more sin into the world.[38] Rather than suffer all this, Jesus/Judah counsels the young couple:

> But if you obey and keep your souls pure [hagnas] unto God, you shall
> have living children whom these hurts do not touch, and shall be
> without care, leading an undisturbed life without grief or anxiety,
> waiting to receive that incorruptible and true marriage (as befitting

for you), and in it you shall be groomsmen entering into that bridal chamber <which is full of> immortality and light."[39]

Here, "purity" is understood as the "undisturbed life"—namely, a life dedicated to God and "purified" of all other cares, burdens, and anxieties. If one can free oneself from the strings and commitments of domestic life, one is then free to dedicate oneself as a perpetual bridesmaid or groomsman who waits on the bride and bridegroom as they enter the eternal marriage chamber, heaven. The only way to guarantee such freedom is to deny oneself any sexual relations, which naturally bind one to family and household. Moreover, as the bride explains to her father on the morning after, she has discovered her true husband. She, in accepting Jesus as her savior, is bound in another marriage, one that lasts forever, which prevents her from consummating a physical marriage on earth. Virginity and faith go hand in hand, but not explicitly because of holiness; rather, sexuality is a casualty of her newfound faith. While the pure asexual body (purified of all domestic cares) is compared to a holy temple, the connection between that holiness and sexual renunciation is muddled. Rather, heavenly marriage (whether of Jesus and the Church or the virgin to Jesus) replaces earthly marriage, and earthly marriage is described in the most derogatory manner. One cannot participate in an earthly marriage and expect to gain salvation as well. In other sermons, Judah Thomas will attempt to combine the two paradigms into one, such that holiness equates to sexual renunciation. There, a new theological theorem develops in which total sexual renunciation bridges the widening divide between the mortal, earthly and corruptible, and the immortal, incorruptible and heavenly. This distinct hermeneutic eventually merges with the sexual-morality-for-the-sake-of-holiness paradigm.

Moreover, in this pericope, faith comes after sexual renunciation. The young couple, only after listening to Jesus' sermon on pure asexual bodies that allow one into the celestial bridal chamber and, hence, to immortality, "believed the Lord and gave themselves entirely to him and refrained from the filthy passion and so remained throughout the night in that place."[40] The young couple accepts faith in Jesus only after he has lectured them on sexual renunciation. Celibacy is their access key to faith in Jesus. Yet, the complete imbrication of sexual renunciation and faith is most strongly manifested in the conversion narrative of Mygdonia.

Mygdonia, the wife of Charisius, a close relative of King Misdaeus, a native Indian king, goes out one day to hear the new apostle preach in the streets. Because of the great crowds of people, her servants cannot carry her palanquin within earshot of Judah Thomas. Yet Judah Thomas, who sees the servants attempting to push the others aside, comes closer to scold Mygdonia because she should not think that she deserves the right of way. Among other things, Judah Thomas preaches to the crowd a variation on his now standard sermon:

> Abstain then first from adultery, for of all evils this is the beginning,
> <and from murder, because of which the curse came upon Cain>
> then also from theft which ensnared Judah Iscariot and brought him
> to hanging, <and from intemperance, which cost Esau his birthright
> and from avarice> for those who <yield themselves to avarice> do not
> see what is done by them; and from ostentation <and from slander>
> and from all disgraceful deeds, especially those of the body, <and
> from the horrid intercourse and couch of uncleanness>, whose
> outcome is eternal condemnation. For this (disgraceful deeds of the
> body) is the mother-city of all evils. And likewise it leads those who
> walk proudly into slavery, dragging them down to the depth and
> subduing them under its hands that they may not see what they do;
> wherefore their deeds are unknown to them. But do you <walk in
> holiness, for this is choice before God, more than any other good>
> and become therefore pleasing to God.[41]

The Greek text, which seems defective at this point, is reasonably amended by additions from the Syriac, though one should keep in mind that the Syriac may manifest later additions as well. Nonetheless, this sermon contains the same elements of Judah Thomas' theology that we have seen before. A litany of sins, which must be avoided, begins once again with adultery. Other disgraceful deeds, but especially deeds of the body, bring eternal condemnation to the practitioner. The Syriac makes it clear that deeds of the body are "horrid intercourse and the couch of uncleanness." Barring the possibility that this is a later addition to the Syriac, the rest of the narrative bears out the notion that sexual intercourse of any sort is proscribed. At minimum within the sermon, "disgraceful deeds of the body" such as adultery are "the mother-city of all evils." Furthermore, all of these evils are opposed to holiness. "Walk in holiness" means do not partake in all those evil actions. Although the Greek text may be unclear here about what holiness means, it more forcefully opposes some form of sexuality further along in the passage when Judah Thomas continues:

> For this [holiness] is choice before God, and leads to eternal life. For
> this [holiness] before God is the mother-city of all good. For those who
> do not contend in Christ's stadium shall not attain holiness [hagiôsunê].
> And holiness appeared from God, abolishing improper sexual behavior
> [porneia], over throwing the enemy, well pleasing to God.[42]

The mother-city of all evils (disgraceful practices of the body) opposes the mother-city of all good: holiness that leads to eternal life. *Hagiôsunê*, which comes from God, not only opposes *porneia* but also abolishes it. It will become clear from the narrative that *porneia* here translates to *any* sexual activity and *hagiôsunê* assumes sexual renunciation. Nevertheless, the sermon itself, out of its narrative context, does not necessarily advocate total sexual renunciation but simply the avoidance of sexual impurity (*porneia*). Judah Thomas concludes his sermon, as he did earlier, admonishing his listeners to "abide therefore in holiness, and receive freedom from care, and be near meekness, for in these three heads [holiness, meekness and temperance] is portrayed the Christ whom I proclaim to you. Holiness is a temple of Christ, and he who dwells in it receives it as a habitation."[43] Following Paul, he calls the pure human body a temple for Christ to dwell in. But rather than concluding with "shun *porneia*," Judah Thomas emphasizes the "walk in *hagiôsunê*."

Judah Thomas' sermon to Mygdonia—in the Greek at least, when taken out of context of the narrative—is really no different from his earlier sermon to the youth who killed his lover. Here, as there, sexual immorality opposes holiness. Holiness cannot exist where there are "disgraceful deeds of the body." Even the fact that holiness abolishes *porneia* can be read in line with traditional levitical theology: holy behavior (proper sexual partnering) does away with unholy behavior/*porneia*/*zenut*/incest, adultery, and so on. Or, *porneia* could be read simply as an interchangeable term for adultery, which is, after all, just another form of illicit sexual relations. Moreover, this particular episode is prefaced with the following statement: "But we have received this commandment from the Lord, that what does not please us when it is done by another, this we should not do to any other man."[44] While this statement reflects the sentiment of the "golden rule" (Leviticus 19:18: Love your neighbor as yourself), it more closely parallels the New Testament version as evoked by Matthew 7:12: "So whatever you wish that men would do to you, do so to them; this is the law and the prophets." However, unlike Leviticus and Matthew, Judah Thomas' dictum is cast in the negative: do not do (we should not do). This version evokes more closely the wording of Hillel in the Babylonian Talmud: "What is hateful to you, do not do to another, this is the whole Torah."[45] Despite these interesting parallels, what is of importance to us here is that Judah Thomas subsumes his sermon to Mygdonia under the category of the "golden rule." In essence, all he is preaching is kindness to others. This framework fits perfectly within the notion that holiness is good behavior (toward others). Nevertheless, as I have demonstrated, the *Acts* manifests an intense interest in proper sexual behavior as part and parcel of that good behavior.

Yet this very interchange of adultery and *porneia* (which we witnessed already in the episode of the murdering youth) in this last sermon allows for the profound practical change that the Mygdonia narrative espouses: *hagiôsunê* here, as we shall soon see, stands for total sexual renunciation, not just monogamy. *Porneia*, a less specific term than adultery, which up until now has represented sexual immorality (i.e., forbidden sexual relations), here takes on an expanded notion encompassing all sexuality. That is, *all* sexual relations are viewed here as forbidden sexual relations. Judah Thomas' sermon placed in the context of the narrative makes it clear that the practical lesson of the sermon is that all who accept Jesus as their Messiah must also give up all sexual relations. The rationale, here, is that holiness opposes all sexuality, for all sexual relations are forms of *porneia*, and *porneia* defiles and keeps one away from the holy.

When one reads the Mygdonia cycle along with the first conversion narrative of the young couple, one can trace this transformation of *porneia* from sexual immorality to all sexual activity and of *hagiôsunê* from absence of sexual immorality to absence of sexual activity. How did this happen? Clues to this transformation can be found in the continuation of this narrative. The opposition of earthly to celestial marriage, found in our first pericope of the bridal couple, is further developed in the Mygdonia narrative. Hence, in the Mygdonia cycle we see two different constructs of proper sexual behavior merging more successfully than they did in the earlier pericope of the bridal couple. In the first construct (miracle stories), *porneia* opposes holiness. In the second (martyrdom cycle), all sexuality opposes salvation. The *Acts'* redactor maps the one onto the other in this pericope such that *all* sexual activity comes to oppose holiness.

We witness this fusion in the next episode of the pericope. When Judah Thomas finishes preaching, Mygdonia throws herself at his feet, begging to be converted to the new faith and to become "a dwelling place" and a "holy temple" for Jesus. Yet, in reply, Judah Thomas instructs her:

> Rise up from the ground and compose thyself. For this added adornment
> shall profit thee nothing, nor the beauty of thy body, nor thy garments.
> But neither the fame of the honour that surrounds thee, nor the power
> of this world, nor this sordid communion with thy husband shall avail
> thee if thou be deprived of the true communion. For the pomp of
> adornment comes to nothing, and the body grows old and changes, and
> garments become worn out, and authority and lordship pass away,
> accompanied by punishment for the manner in which each has
> conducted himself in it (lordship). And the fellowship of procreation also
> passes away, as being indeed matter of condemnation. Jesus alone
> abides for ever, and they who hope in him."[46]

Here, we find ourselves again in a completely different paradigm of sexuality. Although Mygdonia asks to be a holy temple for Jesus, Judah Thomas reminds her that sex, husbands, upper-class authority and privilege, clothing, and the human body all grow old and wither with time and eventually pass away, for they are earth-bound, corruptible, and perishable. Only Jesus and those who believe in him are incorruptible, immortal. Sexuality comes to represent all that is human, bodily, earthly, corruptible, and dispensable. Life with Jesus is an asexual and out-of-body experience. Yet, the believers remain in their bodies on earth. Sexual renunciation is their way of marking themselves as soteriologically differentiated from other humans on earth. They do not reject sexuality simply in order to protect their holy temples/bodies from cultic defilement (through *porneia*) but, rather, because sexuality keeps one mortal. Nevertheless, this soteriological action is equated with holiness when it is mapped onto the *porneia/hagiôsunê* dichotomy. Although the text is not specific here, one can presume that Paul's language of imperishable heavenly bodies lies behind this developing understanding of sexuality. It is not a huge stretch to think of a mortal, earthly body as also sexual and that a heavenly one would necessarily be asexual. But the exact development of this thought process is not apparent here.

The Mygdonia narrative continues to weave between the two paradigms. Convinced and converted, Mygdonia returns home but she refuses all intercourse with her husband, who remains dumbfounded and petulant until the end of the narrative. Mygdonia's husband, when confronted with his wife's refusal to continue conjugal relations with him, pleads with her to be reasonable. In answer to her husband's pleas for "reason," Mygdonia responds:

> He whom I love is better than thee and thy possessions. For thy
> possession is of the earth and returns to earth; but he whom I love is
> heavenly, and will take me with him into heaven. Thy wealth shall
> pass away, and thy beauty shall vanish, and thy robes and thy many
> works; but thou (shalt remain) alone with thy transgressions < . . . >
> Remind me not of thy deeds towards me; for I pray the Lord that thou
> mayest forget, so as to remember no more the former pleasures and
> the bodily intimacy, which will pass away like a shadow; but Jesus
> alone abides for ever, and the souls which hope in him. Jesus himself
> will set me free from the shameful deeds which I did with you.[47]

Mygdonia dichotomizes between her former life with her husband and her present life with her new lover/husband, Jesus. The former life of married sexuality is shameful, earth bound, temporary, and ephemeral. It has a beginning and an end in this world. By contrast, life with Jesus is eternal life, heavenly bound and forever. Only those who place their hope in the Messiah can gain that life. Mygdonia's sexual relations with her earthly husband, likewise, bind her to the earth and do not allow her to rise to heaven. In explaining her new faith to her husband, Mygdonia relies heavily on the heavenly/earthly paradigm. After receiving baptism at the hands of Judah Thomas, Mygdonia further lectures her hapless and distraught husband:

> Thou hast seen that [earthly] marriage, which passed away <and
> remains here (on earth)>, but this [heavenly] marriage abides for
> ever. That [earthly] fellowship was one of corruption, but this
> [heavenly one is one] of life eternal. Those [earthly] attendants are
> short lived men and women, but these [heavenly ones] now remain to
> the end. . . . That [earthly] bridal chamber is taken down but this
> [heavenly one] remains for ever. That [earthly] bed was spread <with
> coverlets>, but this [heavenly one] with love and faith. Thou
> [Charisius] art a bridegroom who passes away and is destroyed, but
> Jesus is a true bridegroom, abiding immortal for ever. That [earthly]
> bridal gift was money and robes that grow old, but this [heavenly one]
> is living words which never pass away.[48]

Mygdonia, here, further solidifies her original dichotomy by comparing her new life with Jesus to a marriage. Marriage to Jesus is better than marriage to Charisius because the latter passes away with death and the human bridegroom is destroyed (by death). Heavenly marriage, by contrast, is eternal because the heavenly bridegroom is eternal. This marriage extends beyond the grave and grants the bride immortality, in that she will reside with her husband in his home, heaven, after her death on earth. Yet, by construing her newfound faith as a marriage, Mygdonia obviates all possibility of marriage to an earthly husband. On one level that would be adultery, and the shameful deeds that Mygdonia performs with her earthly husband (sex) constitute *porneia*—illicit sexual relations. Nevertheless, this rationale is not put forward specifically, but Mygdonia surmises that her sexual relations even before she found Jesus are shameful because she understands all sexual relations to be corruption. That is to say, they belong to an earthly existence. She refers to neither *porneia* nor holiness; rather, she plays between heavenly marriage and corruptible earthly marriage, death on earth and immortality in heaven.

Charisius, however, only understands that his wife wants to leave him for another man, a man who advocates celibacy against all logic of nature and society. When he retells his narrative of woe to the king, he describes the new Christian doctrine in stark and simple terms. He describes Judah

Thomas as one who "teaches a new doctrine, saying that none can live except he give over all his possessions and become a renouncer like himself; and he is zealous to make many partners with himself."[49] While the Greek does not portray any notion of holiness here, the Syriac labels the new doctrine a "doctrine of *qaddishuta*"—a doctrine that calls for giving up all of one's possessions, including one's spouse. This becomes clear in what follows. Charisius states further that Judah Thomas teaches: "It is impossible for you to enter into the eternal life which I proclaim to you, except you rid yourselves of your wives and likewise the women of their husbands."[50] The new Christian faith requires total sexual renunciation of its practitioners. Yet, the Syriac text labels this renunciation—which is based on the earthly/ heavenly divide—*qaddishuta*, or holiness. Another convert, Siphor, the king's captain, explains the new doctrine thus: Judah Thomas, after healing the captain's wife and daughters (from demon possession), did not demand any reward but, rather, counseled that he should live in "faith and holiness, that (men) may become partakers with him in what he does." Furthermore, Siphor explains to the king that "[t]his he teaches, to worship and fear one God, the Lord of all, and Jesus Christ his son, that they may have eternal life. . . . And he teaches that this God is holy and powerful, and that Christ is life and giver of life. Therefore, he charges those who are with him to approach him (God) in holiness and purity and love and faith."[51] Faith and holiness come together here as foundational tenets of the Christian doctrine. If one has faith in the holy God, then one should interact with God "in holiness" because God is holy. That holiness is understood here to be celibacy is assumed by the author and explained later by Judah Thomas when he is questioned by the king.

The king accuses Judah Thomas of teaching an evil doctrine because it teaches its adherents, according to the Syriac, to "keep themselves pure."[52] Judah Thomas defends his position by comparing Jesus to a king and his believers to a king's retinue. Would the king want his soldiers and attendants to escort the king in dirty garments? He continues:

> If thou then, who art an earthly king, and dost return to earth, dost
> require that thy subjects be seemly, how canst thou be wrathful and
> say I teach ill when I say: Those who serve my king must be holy
> and pure and free from all grief and care for children and useless
> riches and from vain trouble? For indeed thou dost wish thy sub-
> jects to follow thy behaviour and thy ways, and thou dost punish
> them if they scorn thy commands. How much more must those
> who believe in my God serve him with great holiness and purity and

<chastity>, free from all bodily pleasures, adultery and prodigality, theft and drunkenness and service of the belly and (other) shameful deeds?[53]

In one fell swoop, Judah Thomas combines the various rationales for sexual renunciation. First, sexual renunciation is purity and holiness; it is a seemly act that honors the king. Sexuality is described as "dirty" and the purity of sexual renunciation as "clean." If read against the levitical notion of purity and holiness, this purity is a state of offenselessness before God, honoring God by not being impure. Holiness is that position gained through avoiding impurities. Judah Thomas subsumes the two into one homogenous category of "seemliness," a status fit for honoring and serving a king. Nevertheless, Judah Thomas' first explanation does not explain why or how one gains holiness or purity through sexual renunciation. It is only assumed to be so, as his second rationale states. Second, Judah Thomas invokes the notion that the sexually renunciant and otherwise ascetic life—a life free from children, family, and personal possessions of any sort—is a life free from trouble. It is simply a better life than the domestic one that is burdened with worries and anxieties. Third, he reminds the king that a life of holiness is a life free from sin: adultery, prodigality, theft, drunkenness, and service of the belly. Like the king's servants who follow the king's every commandment, the followers of Jesus follow his every commandment, which includes sinlessness (no adultery, theft, etc.). Holiness, then, is obedience to the divine commandments as well. Yet, sinlessness/holiness here also assumes celibacy, for lack of "bodily pleasures," and "shameful deeds" most likely refer to sexual intercourse. (Mygdonia often refers to the sexual relations she had had with her husband as shameful deeds and pleasure of the body.) The only rationale that Judah Thomas does not invoke here is sexuality as corruptibility. Nevertheless, he brings it into his discourse with his last words to the king: "This [earthly] life is given in usufruct, and this time changes; but that [eternal] life which I teach is incorruptible."[54] In short, Judah Thomas merges two different paradigms—the one, which places *porneia* against holiness, but understands *porneia* to describe illicit sexual relations only; and the other, which places all sexual activity in the earthly realm, which stands in irrevocable opposition to the heavenly eternal realm. The resulting equation lines up holiness with sexual renunciation. The *Acts* constructs a syllogism in which holiness is to *porneia* as incorruptibility is to sexuality. If holiness and incorruptibility are one, since they both belong to God and the eternal life God promises, then so, too, are *porneia* and sexuality. Sexuality, which is the embodiment of the earthly existence, in that the earthly world exists and continues through sexual relations between humans, must be overcome in order to gain access to the heavenly world where holiness resides. Behaving in a holy manner, befitting a member of the holy community, translates to sexual renunciation because sexuality represents everything that is nonheavenly and, hence, unholy.

Conclusions

Is holiness achieved through celibacy? The reader of the *Acts* is left with a very strong impression that Christian faith and sexual renunciation are fundamentally related, if not one and the same thing. The author reinforces this notion by aligning celibacy with holiness through a fusion of two different paradigms of sexuality. Recall that in his first sermon to Mygdonia, Judah Thomas notes "[f]or this [holiness] is choice before God, and leads to eternal life. For this [holiness] before God is the mother-city of all good."[55] Holiness, understood in this pericope to be the practice of celibacy, leads to immortality. Mygdonia, when trying to fight off her husband's attentions, cries out: "Lord God, Master, merciful Father, Savior Christ, do thou give me strength that I may overcome Charisius' shamelessness, and grant me to keep the holiness [*hagiôsunê*] in which thou dost delight, that I too through it may find eternal life."[56] Holiness (understood to be sexual renunciation) again holds the key to immortality. Siphor, however, is probably closer to the earlier theological mark when he remarks "that this God is holy . . . therefore he charges those who are with him to approach [God] in holiness and purity and love and faith."[57] Neither statement, however, explains in and of itself why holiness should equate so readily with celibacy. To find the answer, we must do a closer reading of the text.

Holiness is equated with celibacy through the narratives, rather than through the sermons. The underlying exegetical construct of holiness and sexuality, displayed in Judah Thomas' sermons, does not necessarily lead to the conclusion that holiness equates with *total* sexual renunciation. Rather, holiness (*hagiôsunê/qaddishuta*) continues to be a form of protective purity, in which only certain types of sexual relations are proscribed. (Holiness stands in opposition to *porneia*—however it is defined.) Nevertheless, the author, or perhaps redactor of this text, forces the notion that holiness requires sexual renunciation by pushing this purity paradigm into the dichotomy between heaven and earth through the narratives of women who forgo their husbands and marriage for Judah Thomas' new religion.

Aphrahat, writing a century or so later, starts his discourse on celibacy from the position that *qaddishuta* translates best as celibacy. Furthermore, he exegetes this equation directly from Exodus (something the *Acts* does not do). In so doing, he builds on the biblical notion that sexuality because of semen pollution is impure and that the absence of sexual activity produces a state of purity—which he calls *qaddishuta*. Hence, Aphrahat's explicit exegetical support for celibacy is patently different from that of the *Acts'*. Yet, at the same time, many of the non-biblical rationales for celibacy found in the *Acts* (the heavenly/earthly divide, celestial marriage motifs) also resonate within Aphrahat. Aphrahat situates himself within the Syriac tradition, and many of his explanations for sexual renunciation echo and build on the *Acts* as well as other early Syriac Christian writings. We will turn to Aphrahat's notions of sexual renunciation and holiness in the next chapters.

PART III

5

Wedding Garments and
Holy Yokes

Celibacy and Holiness in Aphrahat, the Persian Sage

In mid-fourth-century Persian Mesopotamia, a curious Christian man writes a letter of inquiry to his local Christian authority.[1] In his letter he asks: What are the basic tenets of our faith? What is a Christian to believe and how is he to behave? Aphrahat, known as the Persian Sage, in the Syriac tradition and the authority in question, composes a total of twenty-three essays, called *The Demonstrations,* over several years in answer to this request. He organizes *The Demonstrations* following the twenty-two letters of the Syriac alphabet. The first ten hold together thematically and chronologically as a first installment. Aphrahat himself dates the composition of these first ten to the year 337, and he notes that they should be considered as one piece. Aphrahat devotes the first four to Christian faith, love, fasting, and prayer. The fifth deviates from the rest in that it focuses on the mid-fourth-century military and political confrontations between the Roman and Persian Empires. With the sixth, entitled, "Concerning the Members of the Covenant," Aphrahat returns to his theme of Christian virtues and issues, and he focuses there on the practice of celibacy—that practice that distinguishes the "members of the covenant" from others. It is here, within his discourse on sexual renunciation, that Aphrahat first brings up the notion of holiness. This chapter attempts to unravel Aphrahat's rather complex, and at times confusing, hermeneutic of holiness and sexual renunciation. In this demonstration, celibacy operates on several levels. First, similar to Paul and the *Acts of Judah Thomas,* celibacy functions as a fence around the Christian body within which the holy spirit dwells and protects it from pollution. Whereas Paul insisted on avoiding *porneia*, and Judah Thomas advocated monogamous marriages, Aphrahat makes the claim that celibacy is the best protection against all impurities. I argue that Aphrahat makes this claim, first, by combining his understanding of "moral" purity (obedience) as a protection around the body/temple with the biblical paradigm of "super-purity," which focuses on an absence of semen pollution in order to stand in God's presence; and second, Aphrahat presents celibacy as a marker of holy achievement above and beyond the holiness gained through faith, baptism, and membership in the holy community. The Christian ascetic, through his or her sexual renunciation, upgrades his or her holy status to a higher level. If the Christian laity is holy, he or she is more holy. Thus, Aphrahat creates an internal hierarchy of holiness that is not unlike the biblical priestly one and that is also parallel to similar hierarchies forming in emergent rabbinic Judaism in the same decades, which I will discuss in the last chapter.

Aphrahat continues his exposition of Christian virtues in the remaining four demonstrations (of the original ten), and covers topics such as repentance, the resurrection, humility, and pastors. Seven years later, in the heat of military confrontation between the Persian and Roman Empires and under the pressures of an ensuing government-sponsored persecution of the Christians, Aphrahat sits down to dash off another twelve demonstrations.[2] While several of these essays return to Aphrahat's earlier theme and focus on the topics of alms, surviving the persecution, and death and the afterlife, nine of these twelve form a strident polemic against Judaism. While the details of this polemic are not the subject of this study, it is important to note that it is within this debate that the subject of celibacy arises again.[3] Aphrahat's eighteenth demonstration, "Against the Jews Concerning Virginity and *Qaddishuta* (Holiness)," complements his sixth, "Members of the Covenant," in that in "Virginity and *Qaddishuta*" he expands on his hermeneutic of holiness, which he expresses and promotes in "Members of the Covenant" but never fully explains exegetically. "Virginity and *Qaddishuta*," furthermore, places celibacy and sexuality squarely at the forefront of the wide-ranging conversations on holiness that inform both Jewish and Christian notions of holy community and sexual behavioral practices in mid-fourth-century Persian Mesopotamia. The pan-community element will be discussed in greater detail in the following chapters that focus on the rabbinic writings and fourth-century Jewish hermeneutics of holiness and sexuality. As we shall see, Aphrahat and the Rabbis share much literary material and exegetical discourse in common. This chapter however, focuses on Aphrahat's hermeneutic of holiness as it is articulated in his sixth and eighteenth demonstrations, and how it draws and expands upon and reconfigures early Syriac Christian traditions.

Bnay Qyama: Members of the Covenant

Aphrahat's sixth demonstration, "Concerning the *Bnay Qyama* (members of the covenant)" and eighteenth ("On Virginity and *Qaddishuta*/Holiness") are the only two demonstrations that express Aphrahat's hermeneutic of holiness. Not surprising, these two demonstrations also focus on sexuality. Faith, charity, love, and prayer are all valued Christian virtues, but in Aphrahat's construct celibacy draws closest to holiness—in fact, it is holiness. Aphrahat addresses these demonstrations not to the Christian community at large but more specifically to its ministerial and spiritual core, the *bnay qyama*. Scholars have noted that the Syriac-speaking Church integrated sexual abstinence into its theological core very early on, and that in some of its earliest incarnations it appears that celibacy was a prerequisite for baptism.[4] Certainly the upshot of the *Acts of Judah Thomas*—that sexuality stands in the way of salvation—points in that direction. Yet, by the time Aphrahat writes in the mid-fourth century, sexual renunciation is limited to an internal elite: the *bnay qyama*. From Aphrahat's writings, it is evident that noncelibate Christians also belong to his church. However, in the sixth demonstration he makes it abundantly clear that the celibate *bnay qyama*, "the members of the covenant," because of their sexual renunciation, are far superior to the married parishioners. These men and women make up an elite spiritual and ministerial core to Aphrahat's community. Demonstration 6 focuses exclusively on the superior spiritual status gained through this religious vocation. Married folk remain on the periphery. In demonstration 18, however, Aphrahat allows that God also created and blessed marriage, but that God appointed it as spiritually inferior to celibacy. Thus, Aphrahat creates a hierarchy of holiness in which all Christians are holy by faith and baptism, but the *bnay qyama* are more holy by virtue of their celibacy. Aphrahat's equation of holiness and celibacy, as well as his hierarchy of holiness, are not unique in fourth-century Christianity (see discussion below), yet I think his exegetical pathways distinguish him from others.

Nevertheless, in demonstration 6, Aphrahat at times slips into rhetoric that implies an all-or-nothing attitude toward sexuality, indicating, perhaps, that in explicating his hermeneutic of holiness, Aphrahat draws on earlier hermeneutics that excluded all possibilities of sexually active Christians (such as the Mygdonia cycle of the *Acts of Judah Thomas*). Whether exclusive to the elite few, or as a requirement for all (and there is some slippage between notions in Aphrahat's theological musings), holiness—or perhaps super-holiness—is best achieved through sexual renunciation, and this is the primary religious vocation of the *bnay qyama*. This chapter focuses on Aphrahat's hermeneutic of holiness and sexuality as expounded for his fellow celibates. As we shall see, his understanding of holiness is bound up in several other interpretive mechanisms and scriptural images and traditions that together inform his theological stance.

In Aphrahat's exposition, the *bnay qyama*, or "the members of the covenant," constitute the spiritual nobility of the Syrian Christian community. Men and women both belong by renouncing their sexuality. In choosing to devote themselves to God they, therefore, necessarily give up their conjugal lives. Celibacy and/or virginity is an essential characteristic of this inner group. Their celibacy embodies their vocation—divine service—and thereby becomes a marker of their elevated status within the Church. Their vocation, often called *ihidayuta*, or single-mindedness, is thus intertwined with their sexual renunciation that Aphrahat labels *qaddishuta*, or "holiness." Their celibacy also represents the *qyama*, or covenant, to which they belong and which identifies them as "elect" within the community. In Aphrahat's construct, *qyama* (covenant), *qaddishuta* (celibacy), and *ihidayuta* (vocational service to God) go hand in hand. The spiritually superior (the *bnay qyama* also called the *ihidaye*) achieve their hierarchical status (their *qyama*) through their practice of *qaddishuta* (celibacy). While all Christians are members of the holy community by virtue of their faith and baptism, in which they receive the holy spirit, some Christians achieve a higher level of holiness through sexual renunciation. These are the *bnay qyama* and *ihidaye*. Like the biblical priests, the *bnay qyama* and *ihidaye* stand before God in perpetual service. In so doing, their whole community enjoys continual communion with God via the spiritual elite's devotion and service. In addition, Aphrahat suggests that this elite not only serves God and God's community on earth but can also ascend to heaven in mystical transportation. Celibacy proves key to that ascent's possibility.

In this homily, Aphrahat refers to his readers interchangeably as *bnay qyama* (members of the covenant), *ihidaye* (single-minded ones), *qaddishe* (holy ones or celibates), and *btule* (virgins). The *ihidaye* are single-minded in that they completely devote themselves to God to the exclusion of all else—especially family and social and economic commitments. Yet, as their name indicates, they also imitate or represent on earth the *Ihidaya*— God's Only Begotten One, Jesus—in that their asexuality (not participating in sexual activity) evokes a foretaste of heaven. As we will see below, the immortals who reside in heaven are also asexual.[5] Scholars have noted that the term *ihidaye*, "single ones," carries several interconnected meanings, for it can connote all at once:

(1) singlehood (celibacy or bachelorhood), (2) singleness of mind or purpose, and (3) a special relationship of emulation and representation of the *Ihidaya*, God's Only Begotten One, Jesus.[6] The very title these men take on with their vow of celibacy reminds them, and the larger Christian community, of their unique association with God. That is, through their celibacy these men not only imitate Jesus' singlehood and dedicate their life to God but also represent a type of the restored humanity that Jesus exemplified.[7] The devoted ones, or *ihidaye*, become an upper class within the community because they represent to the rest of the community "true humanity," or what they will become as restored humanity in the eschaton. These people imitate life in heaven, and in that imitation seem to have a foot already across the celestial doorway. It is to this inner group of heavenly-tuned people that Aphrahat addresses himself. Their single-minded devotion to the Only Begotten One of God is called *ihidayuta*. The *btule* are (male) virgins; the *qaddishe* are celibates—that is, men who have had sexual pasts but have since renounced their sexuality. While the *btule* never marry and the *qaddishe* renounce already consummated marriages, they both count themselves among the *ihidaye* and *bnay qyama*.

The term *qaddisha* and its relative *qaddishuta* pose the most interesting and challenging questions. Grammatically conjugated from the Syriac root, QDS, they most often connote "holy one" and "holiness," respectively. In Aphrahat's text, a "holy one" (*qaddisha*) is primarily a "celibate one," but it can also refer to the Holy One, God suggesting an intimate connection between the holy ones and the Holy One. The other term, *qaddishuta*, while literally translated as "holiness," also functions as a technical term for celibacy. Moses serves as primary example, for he "loves" *qaddishuta*, which Aphrahat explains as meaning he left his wife for God. Thus, celibacy is that action that best defines the holy ones. How are the two related? How does "holiness" translate to celibacy? Why are men who forgo their consummated married lives to become *ihidaye*, devotees of God, called *qaddishe*, when men who never marry in order to become *ihidaye* are simply *btule*, virgins? While I argue that Aphrahat uses *btule*, *qaddishe*, and *ihidaye* interchangeably, in origin *qaddishe* and *btule* seem to have been separate categories. The origin may even lie in the exegesis that Aphrahat utilizes in demonstration 18, concerning Moses' celibacy, even as he continues not to distinguish between *btule* and *qaddishe* (they are both holy) in his own writings. In demonstration 18, however, Aphrahat never questions the assumption that *qaddishuta*/holiness equals celibacy (whether virginal or not) nor constructs an exegetical or even philological basis for *qaddishuta* as celibacy. This equation stands as an unalienable truth for Aphrahat, and his readers that needs no further explanation. Aphrahat composes this demonstration for the benefit of his already committed celibate cohorts, who understand and appreciate the value of sexual renunciation. He brings in the equation as further support for how the *ihidaye* should practice their vocation of *ihidayuta* (single-mindedness). In this case, Aphrahat strongly suggests not only that they must practice *qaddishuta* (celibacy, which is intimately connected to their Christian faith and promise of salvation) but also that they should further protect their *qaddishuta*—while all the more enhancing their *ihidayuta* (their religious vocation of single-hood)—by physically separating themselves from all associations with women, family, and commerce. In the same way that *qaddishuta*—celibacy—is construed as a means to protect one's soteriological state, *ihidayuta* safeguards one's state of *qaddishuta,* or holiness. The best way not to be tempted into sexual relations—the opposite of *qaddishuta*—is to separate oneself from the temptations—namely, women and family. In separating physically from home and hearth one also highlights one's other-worldly status of *ihidayuta*. Finally, *qaddishuta*, in its holy mode, can also connote "separation" or "dedication," in and of itself. The *ihidaye* dedicate themselves to God while also separating themselves from the mundane—family, business, and other social/human ties. The question remains, however, as to why or how celibacy also embodies this holy separation.

Seven years later, when the subject of celibacy as *qaddishuta* arises again in Aphrahat's writings, it emerges from a heated polemic against Jews and Judaism. There, Aphrahat must bolster his argument against the apparently successful Jewish propaganda for marriage and procreation. There, Aphrahat produces exegetical proof that *qaddishuta* does indeed translate to celibacy and is on superior theological grounds than procreation. Here, however, he does not feel the need to be so explicit. Nevertheless, he constructs an argument that supports the notion that celibacy is already understood to equate with holiness, states that *qaddishuta* is a necessary and important element of *ihidayuta*, and sets out to further uphold that integral relationship for the benefit of his readers. Thus, demonstration 6, while focusing on both the theological underpinnings of Christian sexual renunciation and the practical means to preserve and advance one's celibate vocation once chosen, emphasizes the latter. Demonstration 18, in contrast, must unequivocally establish that holiness is better accomplished through celibacy than through procreation. In demonstration 6, Aphrahat argues that celibacy, as a religious vocation, rests on the three pillars of Christian salvation: baptism, *qaddishuta*, and *ihidayuta*. As we shall see, Aphrahat models the latter two both theologically and practically on Moses and Jesus.

It is important to note that when Aphrahat discusses sexuality, he does not primarily mean sexual lust but, rather, marriage and procreation. To renounce sex means to forgo family and children. There is no space in Aphrahat's paradigm for sexuality outside of marriage. The purpose of sexual abstinence is not so much to overcome human passions as to separate the *iḥidaya* from human society and to perfect one's *qaddishuta*. Sexuality and marriage produce children, family, kinship, and economic interdependence. Sexual renunciation cuts the strings that tie a person to a socioeconomic unit and to the mundane world. This is not to say that Aphrahat does not recognize the problematics of human sexuality and lust. He addresses this very issue when he suggests that it is best for all *iḥidaye* to live alone so as to avoid the pitfalls of sexual tempta-tion that draw one into society. Nonetheless, this emphasis on separation, rather than on passion, further distinguishes Aphrahat from his Greco-Roman counterparts, who were more influenced by Greek philosophical notions of bodily control.

Although this demonstration's general theme elevates sexual renunciation as the key to the *iḥidaya*'s vocation, a subtext promoting strict separation of the sexes permeates Aphrahat's discourse as well. Clearly, those who have already committed themselves to the celibate life understand its value and do not need to be reminded of it. Yet, some of these same men and women choose to live in "spiritual marriages" with celibate partners. Apparently these people believe that their celibacy makes them immune to human passions such as lust and sexual desire. Aphrahat severely criticizes this practice of celibate men and women sharing domestic quarters. Yet, throughout the ancient Christian world these mutually beneficial partnerships and households proved popular.[8] The women supervised the domestic duties while the men provided the women with some sort of social legitimacy and protection. On other occasions, these men and women might have traveled together in the business of spreading the gospel. Peter Brown suggests that these renunciants believed that their bap-tism had changed them—transformed their human sexuality. He writes, con-cerning these men and women that "Christian baptism had brought an ability to live at ease with each other. The presence of the Holy Spirit ensured that the fearsome current of sexuality that had once flowed through their bodies was safely disconnected. No treacherous spark now jumped between the once-charged poles of male and female."[9] Somehow the vow of celibacy allowed these people to live in mixed company without any fear of sexual temptation. Several generations removed from these earlier attempts at living out a Chris-tian life on earth, Aphrahat, however, finds these arrangements unacceptable. It is unseemly for unmarried men and women to live together where the temp-tations for sexual contact are too great. Better the couple should marry legally than burn with unrequited lust or, worse, indulge in that passion. Vowing sexual renunciation does not change the sexual nature of the human being, and salvation itself is no protection. In fact, Aphrahat argues the opposite: their changed status as "saved" must be protected by sexual renunciation, but since their human nature and sexual needs have not been transformed, they must be all the more vigilant to keep themselves away from sexual temptation. As Aphrahat demonstrates, sexual temptation, more than arrogance, pride, gluttony, or greed, opens the door to the Evil One. As soon as a person leaves an opening for the Evil One to attack, he will. Nevertheless, Aphrahat's subtext of sexual temptation reinforces his supertext that family life (i.e., the sexual life)—and its reflection in domestic partnerships of any sort—is incompatible with the spiritual endeavors of the celibate *ihidaye.* To be an *ihidaya*—single-minded—also means to be single, or unattached, available to God alone. Aphrahat finds these "spiritual marriage" arrangements untenable not only because of the temptations they provide but also because the domestic arrangements, no matter how mutually effective and convenient, undermine the singleness of purpose inherent in *ihidayuta.* Furthermore, the simple domestic arrangement of one man and one woman living together looks too similar to the basic family unit of society from which the *ihidaye* supposedly escape.

The one-sided nature of his diatribe against "spiritual marriage," in which all women, even celibate women, pose a terrible threat to celibate men, exposes Aphrahat's true audience: the men.[10] Aphrahat remains most concerned with protecting the integrity of the male *ihidaya*'s religious vocation.[11] The women's spiritual needs are peripheral to Aphrahat's discussion. While he speaks directly to the women only once as *bnat qyama,* "daughters of the covenant," he most often refers to them as female virgins: *btulata.* In Aphrahat's construct, it seems that only virginal women can belong to the "covenant." The other categories of *qaddishe* (those who love *qaddishuta*) and *ihidaye* remain male-gendered. Women are probably not included in the latter because of its gendered parallel with the male Messiah/Jesus. Yet, Aphrahat does not seem to allow for nonvirginal celibate women among the *qaddishe,* either. First, when he addresses women, he addresses them only as *btulata* (virgins), never as *qaddishata* (holy ones). Adam Lehto has argued that Aphrahat's use of terminology is inexact, and one should not jump to conclusions about the lack of nonvirginal women celibates in his community based on his free-floating and unregulated language. Hence, he argues, that one cannot prove, from Aphrahat's terminology alone, whether there were also nonvirginal female celibates who claimed some religious vocation through their celibacy.[12] Nonetheless, I do not refute this point. My claim is, rather, that Aphrahat's otherwise male-focused lens makes it absolutely clear that *he* has no interest in such women (the nonvirginal celibate types) nor in their spiritual needs, if they did indeed exist. And while he acknowledges female virgins, his primary interest is protecting the male *ihidaye* from their worst temptations: women of all sorts, virginal, celibate, or sexually active. Second, Aphrahat's diatribe against all women (discussed in more detail below) does not seem to allow for a redeeming position for women who have married or produced children. If they remain virginal they retain some status, but once they have descended to becoming "daughters of Eve," there seems to be no return for them. Third, Aphrahat's lack of interest in non-virginal celibate women's spiritual abilities or needs contrasts greatly with the third-century *Acts of Judah Thomas*, in which Thomas targets all women for conversion, whether virgins, wives, or mothers.[13] Fourth, his exemplary biblical examples of those who love *qaddishuta* are all male. He might have, for example, made use of the prophetess Anna from Luke 2:36–38, who outliving her husband by many years dedicates those years of widowhood to divine service in the Jerusalem Temple. This is not to say that there were no nonvirginal celibate women in his congregation, only that he does not address them or their needs, nor consider their religious vocational potentials. The only place where he seems to acknowledge the existence of female nonvirginal celibates is when a husband and wife together vow to live a celibate life but continue to dwell together. But even here he is more concerned with the backsliding of the husband than of the wife. As we will see below, Aphrahat models *qaddishuta* on Moses, and perhaps that gendered model also works to exclude the women. With this homily, Aphrahat reminds his primarily male readers why they have renounced sexuality, demonstrates how to protect their celibacy from sexual temptation, and encourages them in their endeavor.

"Concerning the *Bnay Qyama*," is long-winded and rambling, yet replete with theological expositions, biblical exemplars, and practical advice. The images flow from this sermon in a stream-of-consciousness manner, overwhelming the reader with a flood of narrative, biblical interpretations, theological images, and vocational pep talk. Yet, Aphrahat's sixth demonstration reveals a theology of salvation that is also intimately connected with sexual renunciation. Like the *Acts of Judah Thomas*, Aphrahat at times seems to espouse the position that celibacy is *the only* means to protect or maintain one's soteriological status gained at baptism. He argues that the *bnay qyama* must become celibate after baptism because sexual renunciation is the only means to protect their potential Christian salvation. This extreme theological stand most likely reflects, on the one hand, an earlier position in which celibacy was a requirement for baptism in some elements of the Syriac Church;[14] and on the other, an attempt on his part to differentiate between the spirituality of the laity and that of the elite. In Aphrahat's construct, celibacy becomes for the elite few, the *bnay qyama*, a religious goal in and of itself—something to work toward after baptism that brings the practitioner even closer to God and to the realization of that salvation promised at baptism. While the noncelibate Christian is promised salvation in potential at baptism, the Christian who takes on celibacy with baptism some-how acquires a foretaste of the salvation via his celibate life on earth. Aphrahat's argument weaves back and forth between the earlier position of essential sexual renunciation and sexual renunciation as a higher spiritual goal, creating a reli-gious vocational agenda for his readers. In so doing, he often blurs the notions of celibacy as a necessary protection around salvation gained in potential at baptism and celibacy as an optional means toward actualizing that salvation on earth for the elite few. At times, it seems as if he argues that without celibacy a Christian does not even gain that salvation in potential. Hence, Aphrahat's dis-course leaves the married Christians (particularly the women) in an ambiguous position: are they really Christian?[15] While Aphrahat concedes that marriage is blessed in demonstration 18, his discourse in both demonstrations brings that blessedness into highlighted tension. Yet, by reading demonstration 6 intertex-tually through demonstration 18, I argue that he essentially creates a hierarchy in which he places married men and women (and perhaps even celibate women) on lower levels of holiness within the community.

I have subdivided the rest of this chapter into three sections that concern the main theological paradigms Aphrahat brings to the practice of religious vocational celibacy: Christian salvation, qaddishuta, and ihidayuta. The way he interweaves these various theological positions further underlines the tensions between them and the ambiguous position in which he leaves the noncelibate Christians. These ambiguities seem of little concern to Aphrahat, for his sermons are directed at the already celibate. Aphrahat's notion of holy community hinges on how qaddishuta is interpreted. As will become clear, Aphrahat's hermeneutic of holiness (as celibacy) draws on several different par-adigms of holiness and sexuality.

Christian Salvation

In demonstration 6, the attainment of salvation pervades Aphrahat's whole discourse on sexual renunciation. Christian salvation is available to all takers through baptism. Sexual renunciation functions here as a protection—a fence, if you will—around Christian salvation already gained or achieved in potential for those who are able. Some earlier Syriac Christian paradigms would have required all baptized Christians to renounce their sexuality. This appears to be the case in the Mygdonia cycle of the *Acts of Judah Thomas*, which we examined in the last chapter. There, sexuality is earthly and opposed to a heavenly immortal life—the life a Christian gains at baptism. Yet, even if in Aphrahat it is clear that only the *bnay qyama* must be celibate after baptism, in demonstration

6, Aphrahat's argumentation does not always move beyond the "fence" category. Once the *bnay qyama* have gained salvation through confession of faith and baptism, that newfound status (of "saved") must be safeguarded from corruption and damage. Celibacy rises as the best means to that end—it is the best fence an *iḥidaya* can build around his soteriological status. Reminiscent of the Jubilean author who earlier advocated endogamy as the primary means for protecting the holiness of the people Israel, on the one hand, and 1 Thessalonians and the miracle pericopes of the *Acts of Judah Thomas*, which promoted monogamy, on the other, Aphrahat likewise argues that celibacy protects the holy spirit, which the *bnay qyama* receive into their physical bodies at baptism, from defilement.

Nevertheless, throughout Aphrahat's discourse, the once-distinct notions of holy achievement (baptism) and holy protection (celibacy) fuse such that at times it appears as if the *bnay qyama*'s salvation, at least, is gained or enhanced through sexual renunciation above and beyond baptism. More strongly than the martyrdom cycle in the *Acts*, Aphrahat presents celibacy as an essential Christian act that more than protects—it also sanctifies the practitioner. The *bnay qyama*'s holiness is gained through celibacy, as well as baptism. For the *bnay qyama*, at least, celibacy becomes a religious goal in and of itself, not just a practical way to maintain a new soteriological status already gained through other means. With this discourse of enhanced holy achievement and sexuality, Aphrahat opens a new avenue for greater spiritual advancement. All Christians are holy by virtue of membership in the community of faith and through baptism, but the *bnay qyama* are holier. Sexual renunciation becomes their main means of distinction. Like the biblical priests, sexual differentiation goes hand in hand with superior holiness in relation to the whole of the holy community.

Aphrahat utilizes three different, but interconnected images to express his constructs of salvation gained. The first is the image of the celestial marriage, in which the *bnay qyama* function either as brides to the Messiah or as bridesmaids to the Church, who marry the Messiah. In either case, the brides and bridesmaids forgo earthly marriages because they are intended for heavenly ones. The second is the notion of clothing—one puts on the "holy garment" or the holy spirit at baptism. This garment, however, must be protected from impurities. The third connects the first two through the image of the wedding garment one wears to the celestial wedding feast. The heavenly wedding banquet is the consummation or actualization of the salvation gained in potential at baptism. The wedding garment doubles as the holy garment or holy spirit one must put on before being allowed to attend the wedding feast. The opportunity of being clothed in something other worldly is open to all, yet

Aphrahat insists that once clothed, the garment must be protected from stains.

Wedding Imagery

Wedding imagery pervades Aphrahat's text and is the first that the reader encounters when reading this demonstration. Jesus is the Bridegroom who is about to come to his wedding banquet in order to consummate his marriage to the Church (the community of believers). The Christians then are the wedding guests. They are those who have been invited by—and have accepted the invitations of—the apostles. Aphrahat distinguishes the iḥidaye from among all the invited guests by comparing them to the virgins who attend the bride (here the Church) in her wedding procession to the wedding feast. Marshaling the extant New Testament imagery (particularly from Matthew), Aphrahat encourages his listeners to be like the wise virgins who keep their lamps full and at the ready so that they could rise and join the nuptial couple at their feast when the Bridegroom arrives. Aphrahat opens this demonstration with the following exhortation:

> Watch the time of the Glorious Bridegroom that we should go in with
> him to his bridal chamber [gnona] (Matt. 25:10; Luke 12:36).
> Prepare the oil for the lamps so that we can go out and greet him in
> happiness (Matt. 25:4–7).[16] Let us prepare provisions for our dwelling
> for the road which is narrow and straight (Matt. 7:14). Let us throw
> out and keep away from us all uncleanliness/filth [ṣa'uta] so that
> we can wear the wedding feast [meshtuta] clothing.[17]

The key here is readiness, for it is not clear when the Bridegroom will appear and hence the virgins must be continually watchful and prepared. In the image of the New Testament Gospel virgins, the male iḥidaye also construe themselves as continually watchful and ready. Presumably, if they are busy elsewhere (at home with a spouse, for instance) they will miss the call to the wedding feast. Virginity, or celibacy, is then the best means to placing oneself at the ready for the Bridegroom's arrival, for it both embodies and symbolizes detachment from worldly cares and burdens. The iḥidaya as virgin has no other obligations to family, no domestic responsibilities, but can sit tight and await the Bridegroom. Aphrahat concludes this section with a similar notion:

> He who is invited by the Bridegroom should prepare himself (Matt.
> 22:1–6; Luke 14:16–20). He who has lit his lamp should not let it go

out (Matt. 25:7–8). He who expects the shouting should take for
himself oil in his vessel. He who guards the door should wait/expect
his Lord.[18]

While the earthly virgin/bridesmaid would presumably become a bride at her
own earthly wedding someday, the *iḥidaye* are instructed to live in the moment
of virginal bridesmaid-hood—on the edge of expectation. Perpetually ready,
single, and prepared with lamp and oil to greet the ever expected Bridegroom,
the *iḥidaye* live their lives as if the Bridegroom could appear at any moment.
Proper preparation translates into the ability to transcend earthly life at a
moment's notice.

While the celibate men play the virginal bridesmaids and/or wedding
guests at the celestial wedding, Aphrahat construes his female virgins as the
actual brides of the Messiah.[19] In this paradigm, each individual *btulta* presents herself as if she were a bride of the Messiah. As such she, though only
betrothed—the marriage will be consummated only at the end of days, which
in Aphrahat's estimation is actually just around the corner—is already "promised" for "marriage" and hence cannot consummate an earthly marriage to an
earthly spouse. Two notions work side by side here. The first notion suggests
merely that a person (particularly a woman) can be married only to one spouse
or serve one master at a time. If one is betrothed to the Messiah, then one
cannot contract any other marriage—earthly or otherwise—for this would be
equivalent to serving two masters/husbands at once. This notion echoes
Matthew 6:24, in which Jesus reminds his listeners that they cannot serve
God and mammon at the same time. Aphrahat similarly exhorts his (virgin)
female readers to proclaim themselves fully occupied by their commitments
to the celestial Bridegroom. Although they have already forsaken earthy marriages, these virgins must also avoid spiritual marriages (other than to the
Bridegroom). If an *iḥidaya* should approach one of them and ask for her
domestic services (in return for his protection), she should reply to him: "to a
royal husband am I betrothed, and Him do I serve. And if I leave His service
and serve you, my Betrothed will be wroth with me and will write me a bill of
divorce."[20] Even a nonsexual spiritual marriage fragments a virgin's dedication to the Messiah, for she would be expected to take care of her domestic
partner as well. The second notion concerns the great difference between an
earthly marriage and the celestial marriage for the female spouse. The virgin
betrothed to the Messiah enjoys an eternal marriage, for she is betrothed to
an immortal husband (who by implication shares his immortality with his
bride). In contrast, a mortal husband provides his mortal wife with pain,
agony, and grief. Aphrahat writes:

And all those pure [female] virgins those that are betrothed to the
Messiah shall light their lamps and with the Bridegroom they go
into his marriage chamber [*gnona*] [Matt. 25:7–10]. All those who
are betrothed to the Messiah distance themselves from the curses
of the law and separate themselves from the punishment on the
head of the daughters of Eve. They do not belong to men such
that they would receive the curses and experience the pains [of
childbirth]. They are not reckoned for death because they did not
provide children for him [death]. Instead of a mortal man they
betroth themselves to the Messiah. Instead of birthing children
they take for themselves a name which is better than sons and
daughters [Isa. 56:4–5]. Instead of the laments of the daughters of
Eve they sing hymns of the Bridegroom. The wedding banquets[21]
of the daughters of Eve are for seven days; but those of the Bridegroom never pass away. The adornments of the daughters of Eve
are of wool that wears out and disintegrates; but their [the virgins']
garments never wear out. The beauty of the daughters of Eve
withers with age, but their beauty in the time of the resurrection
will be renewed.[22]

Aphrahat divides all womanhood into two categories—the virgin brides of the
Messiah and the daughters of Eve. It is not a favorable comparison, for the
daughters of Eve carry heavy curses and punishments; they suffer immeasur-
able burdens and pain. Childbirth, death, the dominance of a mortal husband,
and the laments of wifedom all besiege a married, sexually active daughter of
Eve. Moreover, a daughter of Eve eventually loses her beauty and withers with
age. Such is not the case with a virgin bride of the Messiah, who is freed from
childbearing and rearing and serving a mortal husband. By betrothing herself
to the Messiah a virgin gains a sense of immortality—her clothing and youthful
blush never fade away. How this is all accomplished is not explained but, rather,
it is implied through the union with the immortal husband. Moreover, it seems,
for Aphrahat at least, that there is no redeeming category of formerly-sexually-
active-but-now-celibate women. Once involved in sexual activity a woman
cannot redeem herself by forgoing marriage, as the men do. This differs markedly from the *Acts,* in which Mygdonia, a married woman, becomes a model of
conversion. Although the comparison remains—the bride of Christ lives an
immortal and glorious life while the bride of a human husband suffers innu-
merable burdens—the *Acts of Judah Thomas* allows and even encourages the
married women (Mygdonia and Tertia) to abandon their mortal husbands,
Aphrahat assumes that once married, the mortal woman cannot change her

spiritual status. While elsewhere Aphrahat seems to acknowledge that a married couple could chose to live a celibate life together, Aphrahat does not seem to recognize the former wife's celibacy as a religious vocation. Only female virgins have religious vocational status. Clearly, the act of childbearing detrimentally marks a woman, in Aphrahat's estimation. That is not to say that they cannot be saved, or confess to being Christians, but they cannot be members of the covenant—the *bnay qyama*. The restricted choices for women are further emphasized when Aphrahat labels the virgins "pure." By contrast, the married woman appears thoroughly and irredeemable tainted. The virgins' purity is clearly tied to their virginity.

While some might argue that these servants of God sacrifice their marriages or the possibility of children and posterity on earth in pursuit of their spiritual goals, Aphrahat argues the opposite. There is no sacrifice, particularly for women. One cannot compare apples and oranges. The life of a married woman is curses and suffering—childbirth and family care bring nothing but physical stress and emotional letdown. The daughters of Eve constantly gripe about their unhappy condition, but the *bnat qyama* fill their days with hymns to the Messiah. While Aphrahat writes ostensibly to promote segregation among the already celibate, he also not so subtly reinforces the superiority of virginity over marriage and procreation. In this case, the virgin female enjoys an easier, carefree life while the wife and mother necessarily suffers in her predicament.[23] Note again that sexual passion is not of primary concern but, rather, childbirthing and childcare. Nonetheless, at least in this context, once tainted by sex and procreation a woman cannot redeem herself. In Aphrahat's paradigm, she is either a virginal bride of the Messiah or a sexually tainted daughter of Eve. Nonetheless, the notion that there is a great unbridgeable gap between earthly and heavenly marriage relates back to the *Acts of Judah Thomas*.

Yet Aphrahat's discourse remains distinctly different from the *Acts* in one remarkable way: while invoking the imagery of earthly versus heavenly marriage, he refrains from using the language of corruptibility and mortality. Surely the notions are there behind this passage (the daughters of Eve bring death into the world), but his language remains oblique. Aphrahat's mystical wedding imagery far overshadows any underlying notion of death and mortality as part and parcel of earthly marriage. Moreover, he does not follow through on the *Acts'* mapping of *hagiôsunê/qaddishuta* as absence of impurities (in Judah Thomas' case, monogamous marriages) onto the great divide between earthly (death, corruption, mortality) and heavenly (life, incorruptibility, immortality) that results in an equation of *qaddishuta* with celibacy. As we shall see, Aphrahat exegetes his equation from elsewhere even as he proves himself steeped in the same marriage imagery as Judah Thomas.

Finally, it is interesting to note that, while separating the men into the category of bridesmaids and the (virgin) women into the category of brides, Aphrahat
makes use of the same New Testament passage as textual support (Matt. 25:10)
for each. Both the men and the women live in the image of the Matthean virginal
bridesmaids, yet they function differently. The brides marry the Bridegroom, the
bridesmaids accompany the Bridegroom (Jesus) and the Bride (the Church) to
the wedding feast. Nevertheless, Aphrahat's text emphasizes the wedding
chamber (*gnona*) over and above the wedding feast (*meshtuta* or *ḥlula*).[24] These
brides and bridesmaids actually enter the marriage bedroom where the marriage
will be consummated. It seems to me that Aphrahat makes a qualitative leap by
focusing on the wedding chamber rather than on the feast. Everyone is invited to
the feast, but only the brides and the bridesmaids enter the wedding chamber.
Those who are so privileged are, of course, the *bnay qyama*. The spiritual elite
move closer to God at the eschaton. Aphrahat remarks elsewhere that the bridesmaids who go out to greet the Messiah and who put on the holy garment will sit
"at the head of the table."[25] The *bnay qyama* occupy a place of honor at the wedding feast. The wedding chamber as special privilege places the male *iḥidaye* who
imitate female virginal bridesmaids in a strange position. Do they enter the
chamber as participants or as witnesses? Are they equal to the brides here? Do
virginal women (as brides) outrank virginal or celibate men (as bridesmaids)?
Aphrahat does not go there—and maybe he never intended his image to be decon-
structed in this manner. *Gnona* could just be an equivalent for *meshtuta,* in his
mind. And yet, I think he attempts to establish a hierarchy of privilege between
the *bnay qyama* who ascend closer to God in the wedding *chamber* than the rest of
the community at the wedding *feast*.

The combined imagery of virgin bridesmaids attending the celestial wedding and virgin brides participating in the celestial wedding itself reinforces
Aphrahat's notions of salvation and celibacy. Yet here, sexual renunciation
remains a side effect of conversion. Baptism necessitates renouncing one's
sexual relations, but celibacy itself is not construed vocationally. Brides and
bridesmaids are by nature virginal and do not actively choose to become celibate.
Yet, when the wedding imagery is combined with the clothing imagery, we see
yet another paradigm of salvation and celibacy emerge. This one, however,
builds on the notion that celibacy creates a means of protection around one's
soteriological status. Celibacy here becomes an active pursuit.

Clothing Imagery

Sebastian Brock has argued that in Syriac literature the theology of incarnation
and salvation are expressed in the language of putting on clothing. Adam and

Eve were created with "garments of glory"[26]—clothing of immortality that they lost when they disobeyed God's command. Had they stayed in the Garden of Eden they would have remained immortal. Yet, what they lost in essence was not just immortality but the image of God within them—the holy spirit. The Messiah then put on a human body (a descendent of Adam) in order to return the original garments (the holy spirit and immortality) to humans. This return-ing occurs at baptism, for the Messiah sacralized all baptismal waters (when he was baptized) by leaving the garment within the waters of the Jordan. The Christian convert then takes up and puts on the garment from the baptismal font. From the moment of baptism the convert (re)gains the holy spirit and salvation. This salvation, nonetheless, is only in potential, to be realized in full at the eschaton. And yet, when the eschaton arrives, the convert becomes some-thing more than the first Adam. Christian salvation is more than just a return to paradise; it is also a continuation to an eschatological paradise.[27] The notion of the holy spirit investing the new convert is described in the early Syriac language as "putting on" the holy spirit or a holy garment of some sort.

Aphrahat demonstrates both the notion of putting on the holy spirit and the parallel metaphor of putting on a holy garment in his writings. For instance he writes:

> For we receive the spirit of the Messiah from baptism. For in that
> hour in which the priests call to the spirit, the heavens open and it
> descends and hovers on the waters (Gen. 1:2). Those that are baptized
> are clothed in it; for the spirit keeps away from all that are born of the
> flesh until they come to the birth by water and then they receive the
> holy spirit.[28]

At baptism, when the convert is "born anew," she or he regains that which Adam and Eve lost at their expulsion from Eden—the holy spirit. Aphrahat describes this investment as being clothed in the holy spirit. Similar images appear in the *Odes* and the *Acts*.

Aphrahat further transforms the notion of the received holy spirit into a metaphor of clothing when he notes that the holy spirit (now personified) when it returns to heaven (after the body's death) will state before God: "the body into which I went and which put me on from the waters of baptism has kept me in *qaddishuta.*"[29] Again, Aphrahat constructs a parallel between the spirit that invests itself into the baptized convert and the convert's body that "puts on" the spirit at baptism.

Yet, Aphrahat further narrativizes the notion of salvation through invest-ment of the holy spirit into the baptized via the image of the garments of glory, which he refers to as "celestial wedding garments," "clothes that are not made by human hands," and "holy garments." The convert receives salvation in potential at baptism that will only be realized at the eschaton, which is here described as a celestial wedding between the Messiah, the Bridegroom, and his bride, the Church. Only those who are properly attired will be let into the celestial banquet hall to celebrate the wedding. Aphrahat, therefore, exhorts his readers to "throw out and keep away from us all uncleanliness/filth [ṣa'uta] so that we can wear the wedding feast clothing."[30] Wearing the proper attire—the wedding garment—that is acquiring the holy spirit is a prerequisite for attending the celestial wedding. Further on he notes, "Let us put on the holy garment so that we may rest at the head of the table. He who does not wear the wedding garment [lbusha d-meshtuta] is sent out to the furthest darkness (Matt. 22:13)."[31] Again, Aphrahat emphasizes the essentiality of the wedding garment/holy spirit invested. He who has not been baptized and has not received the holy spirit/put on the holy wedding garment will not be able to attend the wedding feast/be saved at the eschaton. As he later (all but) declares the kingdom come—among other signs of the times he claims—"the garments that were not made by hand are ready."[32] Referring to the garments of glory that were made by God for Adam and Eve, Aphrahat emphasizes the imminent possibility of the Bridegroom's return and the necessity to be "prepared"—that is, putting on the wedding garments or being invested with the holy spirit. The wedding garment, which is also called the "holy garment" and the "garment that was not made by [human] hand," clearly represents more than festive dress appropriate for a wedding. It is other-worldly, holy and not made by normal human processes of weaving of wool or the tanning of leather. It comes from elsewhere and is given to humans by some other outside source. It is a metaphor for the holy spirit they receive at baptism.

The Christian believer must acquire his or her wedding garment/garment of glory/holy spirit/ticket to salvation before she or he enters the wedding feast/the realization of the eschaton. Proper preparation, therefore, includes baptism (conferral of the "ticket" or garment). Putting on the wedding garment, therefore, embodies the notion of promised salvation that is realized at the celestial wedding of the Bridegroom to the Church at the end of days. Yet the acquisition of the garment is not the end of the story, since it is only a ticket to the show but not the actual event. In the meantime, the baptized must take care of the garment bestowed. Several times Aphrahat reminds his readers to protect their garments from impurities. As cited above he writes: "throw out and keep away from us all uncleanliness/filth [ṣa'uta] so that we can wear the wedding feast clothing."[33] Thus, one must actively protect and care for one's holy garment/holy spirit. This notion of purity protection will be better understood after we review Aphrahat's parallel construct of the body as a temple for the holy spirit.

Purity of Body: Body as Temple

Aphrahat describes the Christian body as a temple of God twice in this demonstration, but repeatedly manipulates the terminology of purity around the body within which the spirit resides. The body as a temple must be pure in a manner similar to God's physical temple, the temple in Jerusalem. Whereas the Israelite priests kept the Jerusalem Temple free of impurities so as to protect God's holy presence in the Temple, so too must Christians protect their bodies in which the holy spirit has been invested at baptism. So argues Paul in 1 Corinthians. Working with Paul's paradigm of purity, toward the end of his opening exhortation, Aphrahat states: "He who calls himself a temple of God (1 Cor. 3:16), let him purify [ndakke] his body from all impurities [tanputa]."[34] Building on the biblical construct of temple as the divine abode on earth, which requires strict rules of purity, the human body, the Christian temple of the holy spirit, now acquires these specific requirements. Hence, the body/temple must be "clean" of "impurities." But what are these impurities? Paul at least gives us an indication of what in his mind constitutes defiling impurities: porneia, best rendered as illicit sexual relations and translated as zanyuta in the Peshitta Syriac, is that action that is most defiling to the temple/body. Such defilement causes the holy spirit to depart and the body to be destroyed. In Aphrahat's discussion of the Christian body, temple, wedding garments, and garments of glory—all which need to be protected from impurities—we are reminded of these passages in Paul, as well as those in the Acts of Judah Thomas, in which purity retains its levitically derived sense of proper sexual behavior. I suggest that, similar to the Acts, Aphrahat retains here traditions of purity as protection around Christian salvation.

For instance, toward the end of the demonstration Aphrahat writes:

> He who guards the spirit of the Messiah in purity [dakyuta] when
> it [the spirit] goes before the Messiah thus it will say to him—the
> body that I went into and which put me on from the waters of
> baptism guarded me in qaddishuta. The holy spirit will pressure the
> Messiah to resurrect the body that guarded it in purity [dakyuta].
> The holy spirit will wait to be reunited with it because that body will
> rise with praise.[35]

If one reads this passage through Paul, Aphrahat suggests here that when the time comes for a Christian to die, his or her portion of the holy spirit travels back to the Messiah and witnesses before him. If the spirit can testify that the body into which it was sent was pure (i.e., it never had sexual contact with the wrong partners—and remained so throughout its association with it)—then the Messiah will be pleased and resurrect that body at the eschaton. "Guarded me in *qaddishuta*" would then translate into "guarded the holy spirit from any defiling 'moral' impurities"—that is, the body/person obeyed God's directive to have sexual relations with approved sexual partners only. In other words, the body obeyed God's law, made him or herself into a "holy thing of God." Similarly, the body that puts on the holy garments protects itself from all impurities (*sa'uta*). The emphasis here is on the Christian body that was protected from impurities so that it could be a vessel for the holy spirit (and hence call itself holy, too).

Yet, Aphrahat's parallel usage of *dakyuta* and *qaddishuta* suggests another reading. These two terms, which I have translated as "purity" and "holiness," clearly mean one and the same thing to Aphrahat. They stand in opposition not to *zanyuta/porneia* but to *tanputa* and *sa'uta*. In the Peshitta Syriac (and I acknowledge this is an imperfect comparison, since we do not know which Syriac version of the Bible Aphrahat used), *dakya* is the equivalent of the Hebrew *tahor* (pure), while *tanputa* is used both for *tameh* (impure) and *to'evah* (abomination). *Sa'uta* does not appear there at all. While still building a notion of holiness (holy body) protection from Paul, perhaps even through the *Acts*, Aphrahat's terminology borrows also from "ritual" purity as much as from "moral" purity. In any case, all impurity, however defined, remains a constant danger to the holy body.

In what we have read so far, Aphrahat seems to understand *qaddishuta* (if not *dakyuta*) to be celibacy, rather than proper sexual partnering. The simple juxtaposition of the pure wedding garment next to the virginal brides and bridesmaids points in that direction. Aphrahat's discussion of purity as a necessary protection around the holy spirit, which is either invested in the body as in a temple or is worn by the body like a cloak on a virginal Christian body, leads one to the conclusion that sexual renunciation, as opposed to pure sexual partnering, functions as *the* safeguard against impurities. Yet, it remains unclear as to where along the line *qaddishuta* assumes celibacy rather than sexual ("moral") purity as its equivalent. The answer to that question may be found in Aphrahat's construction of Moses' sexuality, which exegetically plays on the dual meanings of QDS that are as apparent in the Syriac as they are in the biblical Hebrew and on an understanding from that narrative that sexual renunciation is a requirement for anyone who wishes to stand permanently in God's court. Hence, Aphrahat can easily merge his notions of a holy body that needs holiness protection (through avoidance of impurity) and a *qaddisha*, who must avoid semen pollution in order to stand in God's presence. Luckily for Aphrahat, both notions are represented by QDS in the biblical texts.

Qaddishuta

It is in demonstration 6 that we are introduced to the notion of *qaddishuta* as a terminological equivalent for sexual renunciation. Although the term *qaddishuta* appears earlier in the *Demonstrations*[36] it is here that Aphrahat first makes a direct link between *qaddishuta* and celibacy. He reminds his readers that "hence a man who wants to live in *qaddishuta*, his wife should not dwell with him such that he should not revert back to his former nature and be reckoned an adulterer."[37] A man, having chosen the celibate life, should necessarily separate himself physically (live in a completely different dwelling) from his wife lest he be tempted back into his former sexual habits. Living in *qaddishuta*—that is, celibacy—necessitates living apart from one's (former) sexual partner, thereby assuring that he remain "in *qaddishuta*." Breaking with his former family-based lifestyle also symbolically reinforces the great difference in status that the *ihidaya* has achieved. *Qaddishuta* on the technical level is the act of separating from one's wife and thereby forgoing one's conjugal responsibilities. As noted above, it is Moses who provides for Aphrahat his model of *qaddishuta*/celibacy, for in Aphrahat's exegesis Moses abandons his family life upon being "called" by God. Nevertheless, QDS, which forms the root word of *qaddishuta*, reminds the reader of other QDS words such as the *Qaddisha*, the Holy One, God. Relation to the holy—or holiness—remains an important part of the equation. Finally, in exploring Aphrahat's hermeneutic of *qaddishuta*, we uncover how he has subtly combined the different biblical constructs of QDS that we have been pursuing throughout this study.

Celibacy by Example: Demonstration 6

In demonstration 6, Aphrahat does not spell out for us this exegetical or philological link to the extent that we might wish (he will do so in demonstration 18). Here, Aphrahat notes that they—the *ihidaye*—can all learn from the example of Moses who, "from the time the Holy One [the *Qaddisha*] revealed Himself to him [Moses], he also loved *qaddishuta*. And from the moment that he was *etqaddish*—"sanctified"—his wife did not serve him."[38] That is, from the time that God called Moses to his service to be God's prophet to Israel, Moses renounced his marriage. Aphrahat reasons, thus, from the time that Moses began to serve God, the biblical text notes that Joshua served Moses. He writes: "For thus it is written that Joshua bar Nun was Moses' servant from his [Joshua's] youth.[39] Aphrahat understands from this text that if Joshua was serving Moses, then necessarily Zipporah was not! Obviously, Moses had abandoned his conjugal duties and domestic arrangements to take up a solitary existence (with the small help of Joshua, his second hand man) in order to better serve God. Abandoning his conjugal relations/marriage with Zipporah is here equated with "loving *qaddishuta*." What remains puzzling and unexplained in this exposition is Moses' "sanctification." When was Moses *etqaddish*? And how did this change of status transpire? What exactly does it mean to Aphrahat that Moses was *qaddish*? Is it just a translation of the noun *qaddishuta* into a verb? But how does he then understand celibacy not just as "loving holiness" but also as sanctifying the person who practices it? While not exactly addressing this question here, Aphrahat suggests more than just that Moses lived alone in order to protect his already assumed celibate state; rather, he pushes the notion that Moses chooses to become celibate and abandon his marriage in order to serve God better. Celibacy enhances Moses' divine service—in fact, his prophetic service necessitates it. In some, as yet unexplained manner, the *Qaddisha*, God, "sanctifies" Moses, prompting Moses to "love *qaddishuta*" and abandon his family life.

The uninitiated reader is left with an impression that *qaddishuta* is that status that Moses achieves by abandoning his marriage. In so doing he is also somehow able to better serve God, as well as enhance his own spiritual status. But in case the reader remains unconvinced, Aphrahat provides a further litany of biblical exemplars who follow suit or, better yet, never take wives in the first place. Each in his own way "loves *qaddishuta*," serves God, and therefore receives God's favor. Aphrahat marshals these biblical characters—all prophets, priests, and other authority figures—before his readers, the *ihidaye*, so that they may model themselves after their examples. They, too, should distance themselves from women, as these exemplary biblical men did when they chose divine service and hence *qaddishuta*. In so doing, Aphrahat suggests that prophetic calling/divine service in and of itself is incompatible with family life of any sort. In other words, to be a prophet, or to serve God on the highest level, requires sexual renunciation and separation from family life and dependency.[40] The nature of the divine calling necessitates this "sacrifice." While focusing on Moses, Elijah, and Elisha, Aphrahat includes several more authority figures on his list of *qaddishuta*-lovers. Following the example of Moses, Aphrahat continues with Joshua:

> Of Joshua it is further written, "he never left the tent" (Exod. 33:11). That is the earthly tent—in which no woman served—because the law did not permit women to enter the earthly tent. In order to pray, they come only as close as the entrance of the tent. They prayed and retreated.[41]

Concerning Joshua's marital status, Aphrahat claims that since Joshua served Moses from his youth, and that he never left the tent of meeting while serving Moses, and because women were not allowed into the tent of meeting, he must necessarily never have had the opportunity to get married. Hence, Joshua, albeit indirectly through his work for Moses, proves to be another example of *qaddishuta*—sexual renunciation. Aphrahat's reference to the women is odd. Nowhere does the Bible specifically state that women were not allowed into the tent, yet twice the biblical text mentions women who served at the entrance to the tent.[42] Perhaps Aphrahat understands that because they serve at the entrance they necessarily were barred from entering the tent.

Following Joshua, Aphrahat turns to the biblical priests and states: "Concerning the priests, [Moses] commanded them to remain in their sanctity [*qaddishuta*] during their times of service—and not to know their wives."[43] Aphrahat contends that the priests were required to be celibate—that is, "remain in their *qaddishuta*," during their days of service. Again, the Bible makes no connection between the priests and celibacy while on duty. Although the priests are restricted in whom they can marry, they are not otherwise restricted in sexual practices.[44] There, in order to be holy, the priests are instructed to marry virginal women only. Perhaps Aphrahat refers to the week-long ordination process in which Aaron and his sons are required to stay in the tent of meeting segregated from all nonpriestly outsiders, their families included.[45] Aphrahat's argument may simply develop in his own mind from the idea that the priests are holy, *qaddishin*. And if they are holy, they must carefully guard their holiness while on duty lest they be disqualified from divine service. Moreover, if for Aphrahat holiness/*qaddishuta* translates to celibacy, it is quite understandable for him to assume that holy men, like the priests, must necessarily remain celibate during their holy services. This simple translation seems to apply to Elisha below as well, for he too is called a holy man of God. But first Elijah:

> Look and see what is written concerning Elijah—that during the time he was upon Mt. Carmel and by the river Carith he was served by his disciple. And because his heart was in the sky, the birds of the sky brought him his nourishment. And because he carried upon himself the resemblance of the watchers of the sky [angels] it was these watchers themselves who brought him bread and water when he had to flee from before Jezebel. And because he directed all of his thoughts towards heaven he was taken up to heaven in the chariot of fire (2 Kings 2:11). And there he has his eternal dwelling place.[46]

Aphrahat furthers his argument through the example of the prophet Elijah. Not only is Elijah served by Elisha, and not by a woman, but also his heart is in heaven—that is, he is fully occupied with his service to God. The birds on Mount Carmel feed him, allowing him to survive without a wife. The watchers, or angels, mistake him for one of their own and protect him from Jezebel. Therefore, for his proper, celibate service, Elijah is taken alive to heaven in the fiery chariot. As we shall see below, being angelic, resembling the angels, or in close proximity to the angels also translates into *qaddishuta*, because the angels are holy (being members of the Holy One's entourage) and asexual, having no need for reproduction in their eternal existence. Elsewhere, Aphrahat even refers to Elijah as a virgin for he like Joshua never marries.[47] Elisha, however, is actually called a "holy man" by the biblical text:

> Elisha marched according to the steps of his master and when he lived in the upper chamber of the Shulamite[48]—he was never served but by his servant. Thus said the Shulamite woman: "That a holy prophet of God is he who passes by us regularly. Thus it is proper for his celibacy [*qaddishuta*] that we build him a second story room for his use" (2 Kings 4:9–10). And what served Elisha in this room? Only a bed, a table, a chair and a lamp.[49]

Elisha, too, is ministered to by his servant, even though he lived in the Shulamite's home. He writes: "Thus said the Shulamite woman: 'That a holy prophet of God is he who passes by us regularly. Thus it is proper for his celibacy [*qaddishuta*] that we build him a second story room for his use'" (2 Kings 4:9–10). Aphrahat implies from this verse that Elisha lives alone in this room, for he has all he needs there.[50] Any transactions he makes with the woman are through his servant, Gehazi, as the subsequent verses indicate. Yet Aphrahat (or his source)[51] amends the citation of 2 Kings 4:9–10. Like the Massoretic text, the Peshitta reads: "A holy prophet [Heb: man] of God is he and he passes by us regularly. We will fashion a small upper room, and we will put there a bed, a table, a chair and a lamp." Although Elisha is called a *holy* (MT: *ish qadosh*/P: *gabra qaddisha*) man of God, there is no mention of Elisha's *qaddishuta*/celibacy in either the Massoretic text nor the Peshitta. Clearly, for Aphrahat the whole purpose of building the addition is to provide Elisha with a segregated living space where he can live in *qaddishuta* even while enjoying the Shulamite's hospitality. Hence, Aphrahat (or his source) puts this sentiment into the words of the Shulamite.[52] Again, the *qaddishuta* may simply develop from Elisha's description as a holy man or prophet. And since Aphrahat already assumes that *qaddishuta* is celibacy, it is again easy for him to surmise that he was.

Finally Aphrahat concludes with two examples from the New Testament, John the Baptist and Paul:

And what can we say concerning John [the Baptist]? Even though he
lived among the people he guarded his virginity perfectly and received
the spirit of Elijah. The blessed Apostle [Paul] said again concerning
himself and Barnabas: "Could we not eat, drink and travel with women?
Rather that is neither convenient nor adequate" (1 Cor. 9:4–5).[53]

After Aphrahat explains all of these prophetic examples, he turns to New Testament images. John the Baptist guards his virginity in virtue, though he dwells
among the people and thus receives the spirit of Elijah.[54] Paul and Barnabas,
while traveling among the peoples, also choose to remain bachelors. Aphrahat
infers that all of these men who served God were necessarily celibate or virgins
and therefore lived separate from women and family.

The men on this list exemplify for Aphrahat appropriate models of celibacy. All these biblical characters illustrate how one should live a life in *qaddishuta*, in single-sex accommodations or, better yet, in solitude. These men come
together as exemplars of service to God in one capacity or another. Moses, Elijah, and Elisha are prophets: the priests serve the cult of God; Joshua serves
Moses and then takes over his position; John the Baptist works in the image of
Elijah; and Paul is an apostle of the Messiah of God. In order to fulfill their
various callings as men of God, these men all avoided or retreated from marital
entanglements. Together they provide proof that full dedication to God necessitates sexual renunciation. Again, there is nothing here that specifically targets
sexuality or sex per se but, rather, points to marriage and family as competitive
duties to one's spiritual inclinations. Whether these men avoided marriage or
abandoned family and wives either temporarily or permanently, they all exemplify "loving *qaddishuta*," for they are all celibate. Yet, they also model the
proper behavior for the *ihidaye* because they all devote themselves to God as
well—these biblical men practice *ihidayuta*, or single-minded service to God.
In so doing, they "religiously" avoid entanglements with, or simple dependence
upon, women. Hence, Aphrahat's list of biblical characters who practice *qaddishuta* also exemplifies models of *ihidayuta* as well.[55]

Celibacy by Exegesis: Demonstration 18

Yet, Aphrahat does not reveal his true exegetical understanding of *qaddishuta*
as celibacy until demonstration 18. In the heat of debate against his Jewish
competition, Aphrahat carefully explicates, with the support of pentateuchal
prooftexts, how his position is superior to that of the Jews.[56] In "Virginity and
Qaddishuta," Aphrahat attempts to counter what seems to be a convincing
Jewish argument: that God commanded all humans to procreate. Aphrahat

responds with the following argument. First, he concedes that, yes, God blessed marriage and procreation, but that God also offers something better: *qaddishuta*. Aphrahat's reading of Exodus 19 inspires him to suggest that God creates a means for people to come even closer to God than the mere fulfillment of divine commandments (of which "be fruitful and multiply" is just one) allows. Adam Lehto has argued that the underlying theme of the whole *Demonstrations* is the law—a law that by and large follows the decalogue, but is filtered through the teachings of Jesus. Rather than emphasizing the abrogation of the law, Aphrahat appreciates the Christian need to affirm the law, albeit with a Christian (and ascetic) gloss. Celibacy arises as just one manifestation of this law.[57]

Moses' example of celibacy, mentioned briefly in demonstration 6, becomes in demonstration 18 a full-fledged manifestation of God's command at Sinai to Moses to "purify the people." In effect God "calls" Moses to celibacy. The issue for Aphrahat here is not purity, in the sense of protecting the body from impurities so as to keep the holy spirit within (Paul), but in the sense of preparing the body to enter God's presence (Moses). Commenting on Exodus 19:14–15, "And Moses went down from the mount to the people, and sanctified the people [*qaddesh l-'amma*]; and they washed their clothes. And Moses said to the people, 'Be ready [*hwaytun mtayybin*][58] by the third day; do not go near a woman'"; Aphrahat writes:

> And concerning virginity and [*qaddishuta*], I will persuade you that
> even in that nation [Israel] they [virginity and *qaddishuta*] were more
> loved and preferred before God . . . [for] Israel was not able to receive
> the holy text [*petgama qaddisha*] and the living words that the Holy
> One [*Qaddisha*] spoke to Moses on the mountain until he had
> sanctified [*qaddsheh*] the people for three days. And only then the Holy
> One spoke to them. For He said to Moses: "Go down to the people
> and sanctify [*qaddesh*] them for three days" (Exod. 19:10). And this is
> how Moses explained it to them: "Do not go near a woman" (Exod.
> 19:15). And when they were sanctified [*etqaddashu*] these three days,
> then on the third day God revealed himself. . . ."[59]

In the biblical narrative, God commands Moses to physically *purify* (not sanctify) the Israelites for several days before the law is revealed. Yet, I have translated the Syriac—which like the Hebrew can mean either "purify" or "sanctify"—as "sanctify" because I believe that is how Aphrahat reads the text, as I will explain. Back in the biblical narrative, God then directs Moses to tell the people to wash their clothes and, thus, prepare themselves for three days. Moses, in transmitting these instructions, adds "be ready . . . do not go near a woman." In other words, the people should abstain from sexual activity as part of the overall purificatory and preparatory process. In the biblical text, the action that *seems* to fulfill the requirements of *qaddesh l-'amma* is the washing of their clothing (presumably to rid them of residual semen pollution). Moses' additional "do not go near a woman" appears to be a precautionary prescription added to "be ready" in the next verse. Nevertheless, Aphrahat reads *qaddesh l-'amma*, "purify the people," and *hwaytun mtayybin*, "be ready," as one. The directive "do not go near a woman" qualifies "purify the people" rather than, or perhaps in addition to, "be ready." Aphrahat assumes these two verses to mean: "purify the people through sexual renunciation and be ready for the third day."

But does Aphrahat understand *qaddesh l-'amma* to mean "purify the people" or "sanctify the people"? In the passage from demonstration 18 cited above (as well as the passages from demonstration 6 discussed in the preceding section) it could easily mean "purify." And in essence, all Aphrahat might be arguing is that the celibate are more "ritually" pure—or even permanently "ritually" pure—and therefore able to stand before God at all times, as Moses did, and that this is a good thing.[60] And yet, the overall tenor of this polemical demonstration points in the opposite direction. If we return to the introductory passage of this book, the Jews (according to Aphrahat) claim that they, the Jews, are *qaddishin* (holy and obedient) because they procreate, and the Christians are *tam'in* (impure, unholy, disobedient) because they do not. This quote appears here as the culmination of this argument in demonstration 18:

> I write you my beloved concerning virginity and holiness
> [*qaddishuta*] because I have heard from a Jewish man that
> insulted one of the brothers, members of our congregation, by
> saying to him: You are impure [*tam'in*] you who do not marry
> women; but we are holy [*qaddishin*] and better, [we] who procreate
> and increase progeny in the world.[61]

If this Jewish complaint is understood as a critique against those who do not fulfill God's law, then it is best to understand *qaddishin* as "holy" and *tam'in* as its opposite, "unholy." The Jews claim that they are holy because they follow God's laws, while the Christians are not because they disobey. The Jews, therefore, have access to God in a way that the Christians do not. Hence, I believe Aphrahat reads "sanctify" rather than "purify," for he needs to counter the argument that Christians do not have access to God.

If one were to read QDS as pure, then Aphrahat's counterargument would be that they (the Christian celibates) are pure (*qaddishin*) because they do not procreate, but the Jews are *tam'in* because they do. But Aphrahat never actually calls the Jews impure. Rather, he argues that the Jews misunderstand the biblical text. They think that they are holy (*qaddishin*) because they obey God's word by procreating. In effect, Aphrahat cannot counter that argument. What he does instead is show that God actually gave another "commandment" at Sinai—one that says "be celibate," which bears greater weight. The Christian celibates are themselves *qaddishin* (i.e., obedient or better) because they follow *that* commandment. Hence, Aphrahat's answer to the Jews is that the Christians are not *ṭam'in*—that is, scofflaws—but that they achieve holiness through other means, and in Aphrahat's estimation, in a better manner. Aphrahat demonstrates that his method is better not only because God calls it holy but also because it is a prerequisite for standing in God's presence. God may have commanded procreation, but celibates are closer to God, for they answer God's "call" to holiness in the same manner as Moses—through sexual renunciation. God's love for *qaddishuta* (celibacy) at Sinai translates celibacy from purity to holiness.

In his interpretation of this passage, Aphrahat establishes his hermeneutic of holiness: one sanctifies oneself (i.e., obeys God's word) through the act of sexual restraint, for is that not what God directs Moses and Israel to do at Sinai? The intermediate details of "wash your clothing" are lost in this alternative reading. The sense of readiness or being prepared is also subsumed into the notion of sanctification through compliance. With this reading, Aphrahat contends, against the Jews, that God "loves" *qaddishuta* (that is, celibacy) because God demands it of the Israelites at this point in the biblical narrative. Hence, he can argue that celibacy is equal, if not superior, to procreation for it embodies holy action, answering a divine call—an action needed for drawing near to God. This is the exegetical link that is missing from Aphrahat's earlier text in demonstration 6. Moreover, with this exegesis Aphrahat further transforms the hermeneutic present in the *Acts of Judah Thomas*, for his notion of purity focuses more directly on sexual renunciation than on proper sexual partnering or corruptibility and mortality. Rather, he argues for better obedience (answering God's call) with a positive command (be celibate) derived from Exodus 19:15, rather than from Paul's "avoid *porneia*." Nevertheless, Aphrahat further supports his argument by suggesting that Moses sets a fine example for all to follow:

> For Moses was speaking and God answered him with a voice.
> Israel stood on that day in terror, fear and trembling. They fell on
> their faces, for they were unable to bear it. And they said to Moses
> "Let not God speak with us so, that we may not die" (Exod. 20:19).
> O hard-hearted one who is vexed by these things and stumbles!

> If the people of Israel, with whom God spoke only one hour, were
> unable to hear the voice of God until they had sanctified [*etqaddish*]
> themselves three days, even though they did not go up the mountain
> and did not go into the heavy cloud; how then could Moses, the man,
> the prophet, the enlightened eye of all the people, who stood all the
> time before God, and spoke with him mouth to mouth, how was it
> possible that he be living in the married state?!^{62}

Aphrahat here constructs a logical deduction from the narrative of the text as
he understands it. If the Israelites were required to be prepared and sanctified
(*etqaddish*) through sexual restraint for three days, just so they could hear God's
voice and receive God's word only once, how could Moses, who stands continuously in God's presence, be sexually active? He must necessarily refrain from
sexual contact at all times. Although Moses renounces his sexuality permanently because of his constant proximity to God, Aphrahat opens up this possibility to all Christians, for this is how he concludes his exegetical reading:

> And if with Israel, that had sanctified [*etqaddish*] itself for only three
> days, God spoke, how much better and desirable are those who all
> their days are sanctified [*mqaddshin*], alert, prepared and standing
> before God. Should not God all the more love them and his spirit
> dwell among them?^{63}

Would it not be wonderful, he claims, if we all could be like Israel on those
three days, if not like Moses: prepared, sanctified, and continuously standing
before God? Would not God love us more (than the nonsanctified, noncelibate)
and dwell among us? Here, Aphrahat lays out his fundamental claim: not only
does God demand celibacy prior to a singular divine encounter (for purity reasons) but through Moses' example God further calls (those who are able) to
celibacy, which is the preferred status of God's beloved, elect, chosen people,
for God dwells among them. God loves *qaddishuta* (celibacy). The act of
remaining pure—following the example of Moses—translates those celibates
from pure to holy. Those Jews, then, Aphrahat contends, who claim they fulfill
God's commandments and claim to be God's holy people because they procreate (i.e., obey God's law), are greatly mistaken. While Aphrahat will never
condemn married procreation entirely (it, too, was created by God), God clearly
prefers celibacy for he calls it holy.^{64} And in the greater hierarchy of holiness,
the celibate proceed to the top.

Probably to Aphrahat's great frustration, the biblical text never explicitly
commands, "Be celibate" in the same manner as procreation is so commanded:
"Be fruitful and multiply." Yet with this exegesis Aphrahat comes as close as he

can to a divine directive. God's love for the *qaddishin* (celibate) suggests divine commandment. Aphrahat not only construes celibacy as a divine directive but also strongly suggests that it is *the only*, or the most significant, commandment that sanctifies a person. In this way Aphrahat establishes firm boundaries between "Jewish" holiness (marriage) and "Christian" holiness (celibacy). In the end, celibacy remains the only means to true sanctity and divine blessing. The Jews, by missing the significance of Moses' move, misunderstand the whole import of the biblical text. Holiness comes not through procreation, Sabbath observance, or dietary laws but by following the simple example of Moses' celibacy. In the end, Aphrahat argues not only against the value of Jewish practice but also for the religious (and scripturally based true) significance of the *bnay qyama*'s practice for Christians. Jews may marry and call it holy, but don't you Christians believe them! Scripture supports the notion that celibacy, demanded by God at Sinai and called holy, is more valuable before God—in fact, it is the only means to accessing God's presence. Aphrahat remains aware that not all Christians can or will want to become *bnay qyama;* hence, he notes that Christian marriage is also blessed, as it was also created by God. But in so doing, he not so subtly notes that celibacy is on a higher spiritual plane because God calls it holy. Marriage is a blessed action, but not a sacred one.

Although this interpretation of Exodus 19 appears only in Aphrahat's later work, one can assume that it lies behind his earlier statement that Moses "loved *qaddishuta*" and therefore was not served by his wife. In that context, Aphrahat presumes that he does not need to prove that Moses loved *qaddishuta*, nor that *qaddishuta* equals celibacy; rather, he wishes to show that once Moses became a practitioner of *qaddishuta*, he did not live with his wife (for Joshua served him in her stead). Aphrahat's overarching purpose at that moment in demonstration 6 is to undermine the practice of "spiritual marriage," in which celibate men and women share domestic arrangements. Furthermore, in assuming that *qaddishuta* equals celibacy, Aphrahat can easily transform the earlier Syriac paradigm of *qaddishuta* as proper sexual partnering into sexual renunciation. Better than the *Acts*, however, Aphrahat produces a biblical prooftext to support his contention. Finally, we see that in transforming celibacy into a divine commandment, Aphrahat can counter the Jewish marriage and procreation lobby. Implicit in his argument is the biblical notion that holiness comes from fulfilling the divine commandments. Aphrahat claims that his commandment is celibacy—because God calls it holiness in the biblical text—and one-ups the Jewish argument.

Jeremy Cohen argues that, despite the fact that the biblical text considers procreation, as stipulated in Genesis 1:28 to be a blessing, the Rabbis construct it as a religious obligation, a *mitzvah*, or commandment. In rabbinic hands, procreation becomes equally incumbent on all male Jews as circumcision.[65] Aphrahat's discussion of celibacy as commandment reflects this same transition in many ways. On the one hand, the words he puts into his Jewish opponent's mouth indicate that some Jews felt strongly that procreation was a commandment of God, even if not in the same legal sense that the Rabbis construe. On the other, Aphrahat presents his celibacy as a religious obligation for him and his fellow iḥidaye. Moreover, he positions it in opposition and as superior to, as well as superceding, procreation. For, the first "Jewish" critique he counters in demonstration 18 accuses the Christians of being accursed because they do not follow God's commandment to procreate:

> But you do something that God did not command such that you receive
> a curse and increase barrenness. You hinder birthing, the blessing of
> the righteous. You do not take wives and you do not become wives for
> men. You hate birthing the blessing given from God.[66]

While Aphrahat continues to call procreation a blessing, he clearly understands some Jews to construct procreation as a divine commandment, not just as a result of divine blessing. According to this text, birthing, or procreation, is both a blessing and a commandment, and the Christians both disobey God's word and are cursed because in so doing they work actively against the blessing of fertility. Cohen claims that the Rabbis go so far as to connect procreation and salvation, in that the Messiah would not come until all the predetermined souls had been embodied through birth.[67] Here, Aphrahat's Jew accuses the Christians of undermining God's blessing and plan and perhaps suggests that they also endanger their salvation in so doing.[68]

Other Christian Examples

While I argue that Aphrahat's hermeneutic of holiness is unique among Christian exegetes, he is not alone in equating holiness with celibacy. Other Christian authors come to the same or similar conclusions by using different prooftexts. Aphrahat distinguishes himself, however, by (1) subsuming all notions of holiness into a larger construct of obedience to God's law; (2) by his focus on Moses rather than on Paul; and (3) through his transformation of the event at Sinai into a call to celibacy, which is called holiness.

Elizabeth Clark argues that some Greco-Roman Christian writers, in an effort to "asceticize" the Hebrew Scriptures, homogenize the once distinct priestly purity paradigms to such an extent that "to be holy" (H) comes to mean "to be (ritually) pure" (P), especially sexually pure (i.e., celibate). And hence, they understood that celibacy or virginity was the only way one could be pure, holy, and inoffensive to God. Indeed, they translate the whole of levitical purity law, which applies in its biblical context to the people as well as the land and the sanctuary, to the Christian body, thereby focusing attention on those bodies' sexuality. Reading these texts intertextually with New Testament notions of perfection (Matt. 5:48) or living without blemish (Phil. 2:14–15), these exegetes understood that all of the ritual purity laws of P were promulgated in order to allow the Israelites physical access to God. Furthermore, they read "to be holy" as "to be close to God," rather than in imitation of God or simply as compliance.[69] Whereas I argue that Aphrahat emphasizes the obedience inherent in holiness (by choosing to be celibate one is obeying God's command), these authors understand celibacy first and foremost as a "commandment" of Paul. That is to say, they learn the importance of celibacy from Paul, and only latter explain that importance through Old Testament texts.

Tertullian, for instance, supports Paul's contention that it would be better to refrain from sex before prayer with an intertextual reference to Leviticus 11:44 ("Be holy for I am holy").[70] Though Paul says nothing about holiness in 1 Corinthians 7:4, Tertullian assumes it is there, and perhaps he has Exodus 19 in mind because that is the obvious place where sexual restraint and holiness come together—though he may only be thinking of other passages in Paul. Clement, on the other hand, bends over backwards to negate this association. Reading allegorically, he claims that both Paul and Moses only wanted to discipline the people, not to advocate sexual renunciation. He is very careful in his analysis of Exodus 19 not to mention holiness; but more important, he notes that semen pollution cannot possibly be an issue for Christians, as all purities were abrogated with the new dispensation. Clement writes to counter Tertullian-like arguments and claim Paul back for the married Christians and away from the growing ascetic community.[71] Clement, a man of his time and culture, carefully advocates for a moderate and serene Christian model.[72]

Clement, however, remains an isolated moderate among more radicalizing Christian exegetes in the East. Origen, Clement's successor in Alexandria, finds purity inherent to his understanding of holiness and celibacy. Suppressing sexuality proves a more focused means to release from social binds, for Origen.[73] Although it is hard to categorize just one hermeneutic of holiness out of Origen's vast writings, he provides some interesting comparisons. For instance, Origen provides the exact exegesis that Clement tried to counter when he links Exodus 19:15 and 1 Corinthians 7 intertextually, to argue that Moses and Paul agree concerning sexual purity—namely, that when Paul advocates refraining from sex before prayer he is thinking of Moses' directives to the Israelites at Sinai. But even as he posits more strongly that active sexuality and communion with God are anathema to each other, he too never condemns

marriage completely. Furthermore, he, like Aphrahat, homogenizes the meanings of "purity" and "sanctity." In his homily on Exodus 19, Origen writes:

> "Descend, testify to the people and purify [*purifica*] them today and
> tomorrow, and let them wash their garments and let them be prepared
> for the third day" (Exod. 19:15). If there is anyone who assembled to
> hear the word of God, let him hear what God has ordered. After he has
> been sanctified [*sanctificatus*], he ought to come to hear the word: he
> ought to wash his garments . . . no one, therefore, can hear the word
> of the God unless he has first been sanctified, that is unless he is "holy
> in body and spirit," unless he has washed his garments.[74]

In this passage, Origen reads "purify" and "sanctify" as the same thing: they
both mean one should wash one's garments. This (con)fusion of the two concepts happens already in the LXX translation when QDS in Exodus 19:10 is
rendered as *hagnison* (from *hagnizô*, "to purify"), while the QDS in Exodus
19:15 becomes *hegiasen* (from *hagiazô*, "to sanctify"). Thus, sanctification here
requires the washing of clothing. Yet, in addition to the purity-now-sanctification
inherent in the garment washing, he also seems to imply a spiritual reading of
washing—that is, the washing of the garments also represents the spiritual
washing (cleansing of sins) that one must do before one can put on the celestial
wedding garments—for Origen also connects the washing of the garments
with the wedding garments one wears to the celestial wedding feast. All this
activity points to holiness. But the laundry is only the beginning:

> Hear, therefore, now also the kind of sanctification [*sanctificationis*]:
> You shall not approach," the text says, "your wife today or tomorrow,
> that on the third day you may hear the word of God." This is what the
> Apostle also says: "It is good for a man not to touch a woman."
> Marriage, nevertheless, is a sound remedy for those who need its
> remedy for their weakness.[75]

Moses' sanctification through sexual restraint melds perfectly with Paul's dictum to refrain from women for the sake of prayer. To be holy, to be close to God,
to be in a proper state to pray to God, one must refrain from sexual activity
because it is defiling. All Pauline notions of proper sexual partnering are lost. I
presume here that he also advocates full sexual renunciation, for those who are
able, though he, too, makes a small concession for the weak. For Origen, sexual
activity is defiling and such pollution prevents one from approaching God,
especially in prayer. Holiness, closeness to God, opposes all forms of impurity,
but especially those caused by sexual impurity. Origen's exegesis is awfully
close to Aphrahat's, but Aphrahat's focus is wholly on Moses, both what he says

and what he does, with no recourse to Paul. Obviously in a polemical treatise aimed at Jews or Jewishly sympathetic Christians, recourse to the New Testament would be of little help. But even as he builds a case for celibacy for his elite Christian readers (the *bnay qyama*), a case replete with other New Testament images (celestial marriage, wedding garments, garments of glory), his specific hermeneutic of holiness and sexuality descends first and foremost from his reading of Exodus 19. He further distinguishes himself from these other exegetes in that he emphasizes the obedience inherent in holiness over and above the purity that nonetheless informs his practice—celibacy—even if he is unaware of it. While Origen understands Moses at Sinai to teach that impurity is incompatible with the holy, Aphrahat claims that Moses at Sinai teaches obedience to God's call. In the following discussion we shall see how he imbeds this hermeneutic in his discourse of *ihidayuta*, the practice of solitude or single-mindedness. The singly devoted *ihidaya* may be physically pure through his celibacy, but it is his obedience to God, through his celibacy, that marks him as a holy one and hence gains him access to God's presence.

Ihidayuta

The root of *ihidaya* is YHD or HD, meaning "one" or "single." Not only is the *ihidaya* single-minded in his approach to God, he is also alone or solitary. He lives by himself—namely, without a family or business connections. He lives alone in order to create undisturbed space and time for his vocation. As noted above, the YHD of *ihidaya* connotes both singleness of purpose (devotion to God) and singleness of being (a "family" of one). He is both alienated and isolated from society. The single-minded nature of the *ihidaya*'s calling requires the celibate to separate himself from family because domestic obligations distract him from his divine duties. There simply is not time enough in a man's day to serve God and family. Nevertheless, the early Syriac ascetics do not decamp to the deserts or mountains, as the early Egyptian monastics do.[76] They remain in the cities and villages in which they grew up—"in society" but not "of society."

Celibacy is construed here in both a practical and a theological manner. It is the means by which one separates oneself from family and domestic distractions and the embodiment and symbol of that separation. It is what enables the *ihidaya* to practice *ihidayuta*, as well as the sign of his *ihidayuta*. The *ihidaya* aims for complete existential alienation and physical isolation from family life and lifestyles. Celibacy represents the antithesis of accepted social behavior and sexuality. While sexual relations involve family, clan, village, and society, celibacy frees one from all such associations. Nevertheless, by birth one is a member of a family, clan, or village and one must constantly work to perfect one's ideological isolation and alienation. Celibacy provides, then, both the mechanism of alienation and the embodiment of the symbols of separation. Yet, the *ihidaya*, through his alienation and separation from society, which is manifested in his sexual renunciation, also anticipates his future life in heaven. How he lives his life on earth represents how he will live his life after the eschaton. Heavenly life is so "other" than earthly life that those already living in or anticipating that "other" life must live their life on earth markedly differently from everyone else in order to maintain their distinction.

Yet, as the practice of *qaddishuta* is modeled on the example of Moses, the vocation of *ihidayuta* centers itself on the illustration of Jesus. The *ihidaya*, as noted above, takes his name and calling from the *Ihidaya*, the Only Begotten Son of God, who was not of this world though lived in it for a short while. "Let us be strangers to the world" (Matt. 25:21), writes Aphrahat, "even as the Messiah was not of it."[77] Similarly, the *ihidaya* lives in the towns and villages of his native country but he does not participate in the social networks that support those communities. Moreover, the *ihidaye* must imitate the Messiah's perfected humanity. They must be humble, modest polite, civil, just, merciful, charitable, loving, faithful, and self-restrained in all of their interactions with other people. "Let us take upon ourselves the image of He who gives us life," writes Aphrahat. "When he was rich he made himself poor; when he was great he humbled his majesty; and though he lived in the heavens he had no place to rest his head."[78] Sections 9–10 of this demonstration focus on Jesus' perfected humanity—particularly his humility—which all *ihidaye* should imitate.

Aphrahat grounds his notion of *ihidayuta* in several different images: the holy yoke of the Messiah, likeness to the angels, emulation of Elijah, and the covenant to which the *bnay qyama* submit. All together these images embody or encourage for him this two-sided construct of alienation from (this world) and orientation to and anticipated participation in the next that is reserved for the more spiritually capable. Having become holy through sexual renunciation, the *ihidaye* must now actualize the other side of holiness—namely, his dedication to God and separation from the rest of society.

Yokes of the Covenant

The yoke imagined by Aphrahat in demonstration 6 is the harness of a beast of burden. It is a representation of the wooden bar and leather straps, which keep an ox or donkey under control of its master.[79] The animal cannot move without its master's directive. So, too, Aphrahat understands the biblical yoke. The harness is heavy, it is a burden. But most important, it connects the bearer directly to his master, God. God directs the actions of the yoke-bearers through divine commandments, and in return, those who fulfill God's commandments are "yoked" to God. Their actions reflect divine intention. Aphrahat focuses on the yoke's embodiment of sexual renunciation and its mechanisms of societal alienation.

In the middle of the first section of "Concerning the *Bnay Qyama*," Aphrahat writes: "He who puts on the yoke of the holy ones [*nira d-qaddishe*] distances commerce from himself."[80] One who is holy-yoked cannot participate in the daily business of his community. His vocation removes him from these worldly cares, and by association he cannot support a family, either. A yoked one is without family or trade, and hence by ancient sensibilities necessarily a virgin or celibate because he lives by himself. The holy-yoked one is therefore identified by his celibacy, while at the same time his celibacy becomes his vocation.

Furthermore, the yoked one is devoted only to one other—his Lord: "He who carries the yoke of the holy ones sits and is silent. He who loves silence waits for his Lord, for the hope of life."[81] The *ihidaya* sits and waits patiently and in silence for direction from his master, the Messiah. He cannot be preoccupied by other business lest he miss the divine call. The yoke he bears is the obedience he pledges to that Master to wait for his appearance. Celibacy, then, is the manifestation—the yoke—of their obedience. Similar to the virgin bridesmaid, the yoke-bearer is at the ready to greet his Lord on his return and to do his bidding. Aphrahat further likens the yoke-bearer to a tree planted firmly by a river: "He whose trust is in his Lord is likened to a tree that is firmly rooted by the stream" (Jer. 17:7–8); "He who trusts in humans receives the curse of Jeremiah" (Jer. 17:5–3).[82] An *ihidaya* who puts his trust in God, rather than in human endeavors, is strong like a well-watered tree, and someone who does not will wither like a bush in the desert (the curse of Jeremiah).

The *qaddishe* of *nira-d-qaddishe* (yoke of the holy ones) has often been translated as "saints," but it is better understood in its biblical Hebrew and classical Syriac sense of "holy ones," "sanctified ones," or "separated ones."[83] It connects the bearer to both his vocational practice of *qaddishuta*, celibacy, and to his Master, the *Qaddisha*. The yoke of the separated ones represents their special status in the Church. It is the outward sign of their superior spirituality. Sebastian Brock points out that alienation is key to this separation. An *ihidaya* is alienated from society—no possessions, no family, no home. Hence, a holy one is not only one who is separated, but is a foreigner to his own birth community because he has moved on to some other reality.[84] In this case, this is a reality that places the holy-yoked one in closer association with heaven and the eschaton. As God is "other," so is a yoke-bearer who serves God. Aphrahat also refers to the yoke as a "heavenly yoke," something that the disciple "receives."

This image of the yoke's celestial origins reinforces the yoke's essentiality as conduit of *qaddishuta* between the *Qaddisha* and the bearer of the *nira-d-qaddisha*. Loving or practicing *qaddishuta* takes on more theological depth with the holy yoke than the technical translation of celibacy implies. While it parallels the image of putting on the holy spirit, I argue that the yoke is not the holy spirit per se, but *qaddishuta* itself—celibacy—that element that distinguishes the *ihidaye* from the rest of the congregation. Obviously, the holy spirit is available to all who are baptized, but those who also accept *qaddishuta* at baptism accept upon themselves the holy yoke and thereby imbue themselves with superior status within the Church. The bearers of the holy yoke will sit at the head of the table at the celestial wedding feast. They will rejoice with the Messiah in God's heavenly sanctuary.[85]

Aphrahat further expands this image of the yoked one who sits separate from the community and devotes himself to God. He connects the image directly to virginity/celibacy and supports it with a biblical prooftext. While Aphrahat several times describes the yoke as the yoke of the Messiah, the yoke he evokes is not the light and easy yoke of Matthew 11:30 ("for my yoke is easy and my burden is light"). Rather, his yoke is heavy and burdensome and dependent on the yoke image of Lamentations 3:27:

> Thus, this counsel is proper and just and beautiful that I counsel
> myself and also to you my beloved *ihidaye*: that women we do not
> marry, and virgins (female) are not given to men. And those who love
> *qaddishuta* it is right, just and proper that even under pressure a
> man remains by himself; and thus it is proper for him to dwell as it
> is written in the prophet Jeremiah: "that it is good for a man to carry
> your yoke in his youth and sit by himself and be silent, because he
> received upon himself your yoke" (Lam. 3:27). Thus it is proper, my
> beloved, for he who carries the yoke of the Messiah, that he guard
> His yoke in purity [*dakyuta*].[86]

This biblical image invokes a heavy and restrictive yoke that anchors the bearer in his solitude. It is a burden he can carry only by himself. So while he calls it the yoke of the Messiah, the image he carries is the image of Lamentations.[87] The Peshitta language makes this connection easier by designating the yoke "your [i.e., God's] yoke," where the MT has only "a yoke." In this passage, Aphrahat sets up a parallel construct between those who do not marry (virgins) and those who love *qaddishuta* (celibates), and those who dwell by themselves and carry the yoke of the Messiah. The two underlying descriptives—sexual renunciation and sitting by oneself—are essential elements of *ihidayuta*. Perhaps, in contradistinction to Matthew, Aphrahat perceives that *ihidayuta* and *qaddishuta* are not necessarily "light and easy." Nevertheless, the image of the individual and isolated yoke bearer reinforces Aphrahat's push to separate the sexes, particularly the men from their former households.

The alienation implied by this image also fits Aphrahat's understanding of what it means to imitate the Master. "Thus [sitting in silence under the yoke is] proper for the *iḥidaye* those that receive the heavenly yoke and become disciples of the Messiah. Thus it is proper for them his disciples to become like their leader the Messiah."[88] The *iḥidaya*, who sits/lives alone under the burden of his celibacy, imitates the *Iḥidaya*, who was an "alien" on earth, but who came from a heavenly source. And yet, Aphrahat emphasizes that imitating the *Iḥidaya* does not just mean imitating his otherworldliness, but his perfected humanity as well. The Messiah was perfectly humble, modest, merciful, and just. Aphrahat dwells particularly on Jesus' humility and modesty—human characteristics that he recommends the *iḥidaye* study most carefully. Their superior spiritual status does not allow them arrogance or boastfulness, but just the opposite. Singleness of mind and purpose distances them from worrying about their reputations among other people.

Moreover, this holy yoke of the Messiah—like the holy spirit/holy garment—is also something that must be protected, or guarded in purity. The holiness of the yoke can be defiled and must therefore by kept from damaging impurities. As purity, *dakyuta*, is paralleled with *qaddishuta* in the discussion of the holy spirit above, so too are they linked here—only more so. *Qaddishuta* is no longer just a protection around the holy garment, but it is in need of further protection itself, for it too needs to be kept in purity. It has become a goal unto itself with all the requisite barriers and protections. *Qaddishuta* has moved beyond being a fence around salvation to be an end in and of itself—a spiritual goal for the Church elite. *Iḥidayuta* cannot be perfected without the holy yoke of sexual renunciation; sexual renunciation has become a religious vocation called *qaddishuta*, or holiness. The holy yoke is the bearer's means of direct association with the *Qaddisha*.

Finally the notion of covenant draws these images together. An alternative approach to understanding Aphrahat's commitment to celibacy is through the word *covenant*. Aphrahat's virgin ascetics have "yoked" themselves to God through their sexual restraint and call themselves the *bnay qyama*, or "sons of the covenant." The yoke is the embodiment of the covenant and the covenant is the "pact of sexual abstinence" that the covenanters submit to on becoming *bnay qyama*.[89] The covenant and the yoke are defined through ritualized physical behavior. The yoke and the covenant are the closest Aphrahat gets to a physical manifestation of his conceptualization of the divine law: celibacy.[90]

Much has been written about the various connotations of *qyama* in Aphrahat and other early Syriac literature. Most scholars conclude that, despite its many varied uses, its main meaning is "covenant." It is a covenant that the "covenanters" both submit to and are members of. Hence, the sons of the covenant are the people who simultaneously submit to the covenant (virginity) and are members of the holy community of believers or celibates, the *qyama*. Yet, Sidney Griffith points out that the base meaning of *qum* remains "to stand" or "to rise" and is also the root for *qyamta*, "resurrection."[91] He suggests that Aphrahat, aware of the multiple meanings possible in *qum*, plays between *qyama* and *qyamta*, thereby implicitly connecting the two. Hence, "sons of the resurrection" can be seen as a secondary, background meaning to "sons of the covenant."[92] Those who participate in the covenant thereby also represent the resurrection to come.

Without drawing any direct conclusions, Arthur Vööbus, among others, has compared this covenantal concept to that of the Qumran community.[93] While clearly there are parallels, I submit that the rabbinic material provides a more nuanced analogy, particularly when the images of yoke and covenant are invoked together. We will explore these images more carefully in the next chapters. We can make no real conjectures about the relationship between the Qumran community and early Syriac Christianity, even if it is agreed that Syriac Christianity evolved out of Palestinian Aramaic Judaism. Yet, Babylonian rabbinic Judaism thrived, along with Syriac Christianity, in the same centuries and geographic locations.

For Aphrahat, then, sexual abstinence is both the yoke and the covenant that the holy ones adopt and the means by which the covenanters attain *qaddishuta*/holiness, or true separation. Although perceived of as a burden, Aphrahat's yoke-bearers have their reward—in their celestial marriage to the Bridegroom. The yoke, embodied in their sexual renunciation, offers a means toward a higher level of salvation. The essentiality of sexual renunciation, its heavenly and therefore its holy characteristics for the *bnay qyama*, are further highlighted through Aphrahat's invocation of the angels and the prophet Elijah.

Angels

Another image that is closely entwined with the yoke image is that of the angel. Aphrahat writes, "He who takes on the image of the angels (Matt. 22:30; Mark 12:25; Luke 20:36) to humans he should be a stranger."[94] The image that the *ihidaya* assumes is the New Testament equation established in the synoptic Gospels that "in the resurrection they neither marry nor are given in marriage but are like angels in heaven" (Matt. 22:30). These New Testament authors make the assumption that angels necessarily are celibate because they do not marry. The need that earthly humans face to procreate and reproduce is not mirrored in heaven, where the angels reside. Angels are eternal and hence have no need to reproduce themselves in order to gain immortality, as humans do on earth.[95] Therefore, "taking on the image of angels" while still living on earth also translates into celibacy for Aphrahat. Making oneself a stranger to other humans goes hand in hand with this notion. Angels have no need for human company, for they dwell in the shadow of God. The *iḥidaya*, then, lives his life on earth as if he were an angel—an already divine being on earth—or at least in anticipation of his joining the angels in heaven at the resurrection.

In Aphrahat's mind, the two images of holy yoke and angels are closely linked, for he follows the above statement with this one: "He who puts on the yoke of the holy ones should distance himself from giving and taking (commerce)."[96] The angel-like *iḥidaye* and the holy-yoked ones similarly alienate themselves from human society, both socially and economically, because they have changed status. While not yet of the resurrection, they anticipate it on earth. Their celibacy both enables them to separate and symbolizes their vocational distance from human society, while at the same time representing their spiritual elevation within the community. They have already started out on the journey toward perfected humanity, which will only end at the eschaton.

Aphrahat further suggests that the *iḥidaye* and *qaddishe* will receive special treatment for their efforts when they do arrive in heaven. Because they were not served by women on earth, Aphrahat notes, "All those who do not take wives will be served [*meshtammshin*] by the watchers of heaven."[97] While it might seem daunting to some to give up the comforts of home, Aphrahat entices them with images of heavenly servants. He writes further:

> The protectors of *qaddishuta* will rest in the High One's sanctuary.
> The *Iḥidaya*—the Only Begotten One—that is from the bosom of his
> father—will rejoice with all those *iḥidaye*. There is no male nor
> female there, nor slave nor free, but everyone is a child of the High
> One (Gal. 3:28).[98]

The asexual nature of the angels—those beings who dwell in heaven already—is reflected back onto those Christian believers who will join them at the eschaton. Their sexual renunciation manifests their angelic-like status, and yet their *qaddishuta* must be protected—only the successful ones will rejoice with the Only Begotten One in the bosom of his Father. Again, we see the goal of the *iḥidaya* is not so much the protection of his holy garment but the safeguarding of his *qaddishuta*. An *iḥidaya* must be ever vigilant against temptation and backsliding.

Elijah

Another image—the image of the prophet Elijah—fits Aphrahat's growing paradigm of celibacy, alienation, and holiness. First, Elijah is not only celibate but also a virgin, according to Aphrahat's reading of the biblical text.[99] For that reason alone, he is exemplary and a perfect model for the *iḥidaye*. "He who loves virginity," writes Aphrahat, "should make himself in the image of Elijah."[100] Elijah never marries and takes himself to the hills in order to separate himself from society and better fulfill his prophetic role. Elijah, it seems, is also a perfect exemplar of the yoke-bearer, for he "sits in silence"—in this case, never complaining about bearing the hard burden of prophecy that God has bestowed on him. The above comment is followed immediately by "He who takes up/carries the yoke of the holy ones should sit and be silent. He who loves silence/solitude waits/expects his Lord the hope of life."[101] The *iḥidaya* should be a silent yoke-bearer, like Elijah. Moreover, Elijah clearly has a special relationship with God, for he never dies but is swept up to heaven in a fiery chariot. In Aphrahat's mind, Elijah's immortality embodies the *iḥidaya*'s aim, blurring the distinctions between this world and the next in hope of bringing the latter closer to fruition. If they imitate Elijah, maybe they too will be swept up to heaven alive—in the near and imminent future. Aphrahat contrasts this image of heavenly ascent with what he considers its opposite, domestic and this-worldly entanglement: "He who expects to be caught up in the clouds should not make for himself adorned chariots [on earth]."[102] If one has chosen to follow the example of Elijah and, to carry the yoke and hence, to live in celibacy and alienation, he most certainly must forgo even the ornaments of earthly life, such as horses and chariots.

The holy-yoked ones—the *iḥidaye*—resemble the angels and Elijah, in that they already have attained in some manner, or at least anticipate, life in heaven. They maintain this position by a studied alienation from the norms of human society—family life and commerce. Sexual renunciation stands out both as *the means* by which one achieves such a position and the *manifestation* of that achievement. An *iḥidaya* is known to others by his sexual renunciation. By labeling that behavior "holy," Aphrahat further highlights the function of sexual renunciation, separation from society, dedication to God, and of course a closer proximity to God's heavenly abode. As "holy ones," the yoked and celibate *iḥidaye* "belong" only to the Holy One. Stephanie Skoyes Jarkins argues that Aphrahat promotes a mystical ascetic program akin to the Merkavah literature. While Elijah stands as one example of ascent to heaven, Aphrahat wants no less than to imitate Moses' experience on Sinai, in which he stood in the heavenly cloud and communed with God "face to face."[103] Hence, Aphrahat's understanding of God's "command" to "be celibate" at Sinai remains key to this mystical experience and central to what it means to be an *iḥidaya*.

Conclusions: Transforming Fences into Ladders

Qaddishuta, in its Syriac origins, was understood to be a fence of proper sexual behavior around the purity of the Christian body because the body was a temple to the holy spirit. Yet, Aphrahat contends that *qaddishuta* is a direct commandment from God "to be celibate" that enables a practitioner to stand in God's presence. *Iḥidayuta*, then, can be construed both as the goal of celibate *qaddishuta* (single-minded devotion to God) and as a fence around that spiritual achievement of *qaddishuta*, or communion with God. Strict segregation of the sexes, then, functions for Aphrahat as a final fortification. Valorizing sexual renunciation as a positive sign of obedience and sanctification (more than just a fence) necessitates, for Aphrahat, a detailed exploration of the negative aspects of married life—the alluring opposite of *qaddishuta* and *iḥidayuta*. While faith, fasting, prayer, and charity all form important elements of an *iḥidaya*'s practice, celibacy poses the greatest risks and obstacles. Aphrahat, therefore, pays particular attention to the temptations to evil that regular association with women provides for men. Aphrahat's stated purpose is not to denigrate marriage, or even sex per se, but to persuade celibates to live in sex-segregated households. To this end—namely, keeping celibate men and women segregated—Aphrahat presents yet another argument. He pinpoints women, lust for women, and the resultant influence women have over their men as the source of all of men's problems. The Evil One, humanity's ultimate adversary, gains easy access to men through their womenfolk. If celibate men would only live apart from women, they would never be distracted or led astray; the same applies for married men as well.

Aphrahat opens his discussion on appropriate living arrangements for the celibate *bnay qyama* with a basic scare tactic. He warns couples who live together in "spiritual marriages" that through these domestic arrangements they still open themselves up to the Evil One. He looks for openings in all people—to get inside through their weaknesses and failings. He approaches the arrogant, vain, and gluttonous—and particularly the lustful. If one is at all tempted by the "lust of Eve" (and I presume he means that all men are temptable), then by all means men should not live with women! To prove his point, Aphrahat lists all of the biblical men who have been brought low by their womenfolk. He implies here that even the best of men, even legitimately married ones, through their lust (and sometimes just trust) for their wives, can be brought low by those very women. He writes:

> For it was through Eve that [the Evil One] came against Adam, and in his innocence Adam was enticed by him (Gen. 3:1–7). He also came against Joseph, through his master's wife, but Joseph was aware of his deceptiveness and did not wish to obey him (Gen. 39:7–20). Through a woman he fought with Samson, until he took away his naziriteship (Judg. 16:4). Reuben was the firstborn among all his brothers, but through his father's wife [the Adversary] cast a blemish upon him (Gen. 35:21–22; 49:3–4). Aaron was high priest of Israel, but because of Miriam his sister he envied Moses (Num. 12:1–2). Moses was sent to deliver the people from Egypt, but he took with him a wicked counselor; the Lord came upon Moses and wanted to kill him, until he sent back his wife to Midian (Exod. 4:24–26). David was victorious in all his battles, but by means of a daughter of Eve a blemish was found in him (2 Sam. 11:1–4). Amnon was attractive and handsome to look at, but [the Adversary] imprisoned him with a desire for his sister, and Absalom killed him because of the humiliation of Tamar (2 Sam. 13). Solomon was greater than all the kings of the earth, but in his old age his wives led his heart astray (1 Kings 11:1–13). Through Jezebel, daughter of Ethbaal, the wickedness of Ahab increased, and he became greatly defiled (1 Kings 21:25). [The Adversary] also tempted Job, through his children and his possessions, but when he found that he could not overpower him, he went out to get his [secret] weapon. He came back and brought with him a daughter of Eve, who caused Adam to sink, and through her mouth he said to Job, the righteous man, "Curse God!" But Job rejected her counsel (Job 1–2; 2:9). King Asa also conquered the Accursed of Life when he wanted to come against him through his mother. For Asa knew his deceit, and he removed his mother from her high position and cut the idol to pieces and threw it down (1 Kings 15:13; 1 Chron. 15:16). John was greater than all the prophets, but Herod killed him because of a dance of a daughter of Eve (Matt. 14:1–14; Mark 6:14–29). Haman was rich, and the third in command after the king, but his wife counseled him to destroy the Jews (Esther 5:9–14). Zimri was the chief of the tribe of Simeon, but Cozbi, daughter of the chiefs of Midian, overthrew him, and because of one woman twenty-four thousand [men] fell in one day (Num. 25:6–25).[104]

Aphrahat's list starts with the obvious—Adam (Eve)—but also includes Joseph (Potiphar's wife), Samson (Delila), Reuben (Bilha), Aaron (Miriam), Moses (Zipporah), David (Bat Sheva), Amnon (Tamar), Solomon (all of his wives), Ahab (Jezebel), Job (his wife), Asa (his mother), John the Baptist (Salome), Haman (his wife), and Zimri (Cozbi). While Reuben, David, Amnon, and Zimri arguably are brought down by sexual lust, Moses, Haman, Job, Solomon, and Ahab are brought low or tested because they trusted their wives—they merely listened to their bad counsel. Aaron likewise followed the poor counsel of his sister in criticizing Moses. Asa is tempted by his mother's idols—a point brought forward by Aphrahat to emphasize the dangers of all female company. With this list, Aphrahat emphasizes that it is not just sex that will ruin a man but also that association with all women damages a man's reputation. Returning to his opening strategy Aphrahat emphasizes that it is not that women are evil per se, but that they are the instruments of the Evil One—he plays on them as if on a musical instrument. It is through women that the Evil One gets to men.

Strict separation of the sexes is, therefore, yet another fence around *ihidayuta* properly practiced, in that it limits access to sexual and other domestic temptations. Professing a singleness of mind is not enough, argues Aphrahat; one must physically distance oneself from all dangers that would sully one's vocation. *Ihidayuta* is, in turn, a protection around *qaddishuta*, in that it emphasizes alienation from society and family—where sexuality takes place— and highlights the separation/alienation/otherness inherent in the *qaddishuta* that an *ihidaya* practices. *Qaddishuta* remains on one level a fence around Christian salvation, in that sexual renunciation safeguards the holy spirit. As noted, some of the earlier Syriac traditions from which Aphrahat draws promoted *qaddishuta* (whether as sexual purity or sexual renunciation) as a necessary protection around Christian salvation for all Christians. Aphrahat, however, in combining his discussion of *qaddishuta* with his discourse on *ihidayuta*, construes *qaddishuta* as an exclusive vocation of the spiritual elite. In Aphrahat's discourse, *qaddishuta* and *ihidayuta* merge into a self-sustaining Christian religious pursuit for the *bnay qyama* that transforms these fences into ladders of spiritual ascent. *Qaddishuta*, as part of *ihidayuta*, becomes an activity spiritually profitable in and of itself, but practiced only by a few capable paragons. For the *bnay qyama*, the practices of celibacy and alienation create an alternative reality in which the practitioners partake more fully in God's holiness on earth and distinguish themselves from other Christians. They are the "holy of holies" among the holy community of the Christian faithful. Moreover, they open themselves up to the possibility of mystical ascent to God's abode in heaven. While never denying the holiness of the common faithful yet married Christian, Aphrahat builds a hierarchy of holiness based on achievement.

In the next chapters, we turn to the more or less coterminous rabbinic literature. The classical rabbinic writings, composed over several centuries between two geographic locations, focus a great amount of energy on the issue of holiness. While much of this discourse focuses on the Temple and its cult, other discussions focus on holiness and sexuality, particularly within marriage. In direct opposition (and perhaps in reaction to) Christian notions of holiness and sexual renunciation, the Rabbis dwell on the holiness created through Jewish marriage practices. Yet, like Aphrahat, they build internal hierarchies of holiness. Refusing to forgo biblical notions of ascribed Israelite holiness, the Rabbis understand all Israelites/Jews to be holy, but suggest that some can achieve further holy heights, particularly through restrictive sexual practices in marriage. Moreover, Aphrahat's holy and celibate Moses, as well as his "holy yoke," find themselves in the pages of the rabbinic midrash as well, and it is to these shared exegetical motifs and hermeneutics of holiness that we now turn.

6

Zipporah's Complaint: Moses Is Not Conscientious in the Deed!

Exegetical Traditions of Moses' Celibacy

In the last chapter, we saw that Aphrahat argues that the Jews are mistaken when they think they have exclusive rights to chosenness and, hence, holiness because they fulfill God's divine commandments, especially the first biblical commandment to be fruitful and multiply. While Aphrahat agrees that fulfilling the divine law imbues a person or community with holiness, the truly divine and superior commandment is "to be celibate," not "to procreate." Moreover, a sexually restrained person prepares himself more fully to stand in God's presence, for a person who chooses celibacy as part of the practice attached to his Christian faith better obeys the divine law and thereby makes himself into a superior holy thing to God. Thus, the celibates are seen as better answering God's call to holiness. In Aphrahat's conceptionalization of this Jewish-Christian argument, the issue is not who can claim *ascribed* holiness—that is, who has God chosen to be the exclusive holy community, or even who better protects his ascribed holiness—but, rather, who *achieves* that status. Who, by his better interpretation of text and thereby his better obedience to God's word, acquires that status? According to Aphrahat, the celibate do. Holiness, here, is something one aspires to but is not always guaranteed. In the fourth-century context, holy achievement overshadows holy chosenness, though the latter never disappears entirely.

Aphrahat supports his argument exegetically with Exodus 19 and builds particularly from Moses' example there. I have emphasized that Aphrahat's exegesis is unusual among Christian authors.

Boyarin further notes that Aphrahat, in particular, clearly situates himself outside the larger Greco-Roman Christian milieu, as he never references Genesis 1–3 or any notion of an androgyne in his discussions of celibacy. Aphrahat proves himself a maverick in this regard. While clearly Christian in this theology, his exegetical influences more often reflect what we might assume to be exclusively Jewish or rabbinic methodologies or reading practices. Hence, he does not easily fit into the Christian and Jewish worldviews that Boyarin constructs concerning sexuality and marriage.[1]

In this chapter, we explore how both Aphrahat's exegesis and equation of *qaddishuta* with celibacy resonate throughout the rabbinic discourse on holy community, sexuality, and divine service. While never legislating celibacy as a rabbinic spiritual activity, the Rabbis acknowledge and highlight the tensions between divine service (in their case Torah study) and family obligations. In so doing, they further develop their own sense of religious identity and duty in the evolving "religious market" that was part and parcel of late-ancient religious life.

In the mid-fourth century, the biblical Moses emerges as a central figure in late-ancient Aramaic Jewish and Christian discussions of holiness, sexuality, and religious identity. Jews and Christians explain their divine chosenness to themselves and others through their constructs of holiness. Sexuality and appropriate sexual behavior become focal points of difference. Moses' own sexual choices become foundational to this "conversation." As we saw in the last chapter, Aphrahat claims that Moses provides the perfect example of holy celibacy. As we shall see in this chapter, the classical Rabbis of the same general historic period and geographic location look to Moses to model their marriage and procreative strategies. Ironically, all of these late-ancient exegetes focus their attention on the same biblical passages and share an extra-biblical tradition that Moses abandons wife and family to serve God.

The extra-biblical tradition that Moses renounces sexual relations with his wife appears sporadically throughout early Jewish, rabbinic, and early Christian literature. This tradition, I argue, can be subdivided into two strains. The first evolves out of a more general notion that prophecy (and divine service of any sort) and family are incompatible, and the second derives from a particular reading of Exodus 19:10–14 (Moses at Sinai). While this passage soon became a standard prooftext for celibate-minded Christian readers, only Aphrahat, the fourth-century Syriac Christian homilist, and the early Rabbis provide similarly full-blown exegetical discussions of Moses' celibacy in the context of Exodus 19. Furthermore, the Rabbis and Aphrahat analogously promote and manipulate this particular Mosaic tradition within their respective discourses on sexuality, marriage, and holiness. In this study, I pursue several interlinking exegetical traditions concerning Moses' sexual renunciation, and show how the various biblical commentators engage in this exegetical discussion for their own ideological ends. I first discuss the Hellenistic Jewish and later rabbinic traditions concerning Moses' celibacy, and then I bring them together with Aphrahat's in a more comprehensive comparative analysis.

Moses, Prophecy, and Sexual Restraint

Philo

We start with Philo, who discusses Moses' sexual practices in his work *On the Life of Moses*. This first-century Greek-speaking Alexandrian Jew, writing within a Hellenistic-philosophical framework, elaborates on all aspects of Moses' leadership. Moses is leader, friend of God, lawgiver, priest, and prophet. He is the ultimate Hellenistic philosopher-king. He embodies numerous Greco-Roman virtues: humility, love of justice, hatred of iniquity, love of virtue, self restraint, continence, temperance, shrewdness, good sense, knowledge, evidence of toil and hardship, contempt of pleasures, justice, and advocacy of excellence.[2] Philo incorporates the tradition of Moses' celibacy into the preparatory process Moses undergoes to become high priest and the prophet of God. Philo focuses on Moses' overall control of his human passions as the means by which he achieves a purely spiritual life. Having previously addressed Moses' role as royal leader and legislator, Philo turns his attention to Moses' spiritual office, or what he calls his "priestly duties." Moses fulfilled his sacerdotal role in a most pious manner:

> But, in the first place, before assuming that office of priest, it was
> necessary for him [Moses] to purify not only his soul but also his
> body, so that it should be connected with and defiled by no passion,
> but should be pure from everything which is of a mortal nature, from
> all meat and drink, and from any connection with women. And this
> last thing, indeed, he had despised for a long time, and almost from
> the first moment that he began to prophesy and to feel divine
> inspiration [Loeb: possessed by the spirit], thinking that it was proper
> that he should at all times be ready to give his whole attention to
> God's commands [Loeb: receive the oracular messages].[3]

Philo draws a line between the corporeal/passionate life and spiritual pursuits: the one is necessarily incompatible with the other. As a prophet-priest of God, Moses understands that wine, women, and good food limit his ability to fulfill his divine duties; hence, he must distance himself from all these "mortal" things. From the moment God speaks to him, Moses "despises" his conjugal duties, since they diminish his "attention to God's commands." Moses, as

God's servant, priest, and prophet, clearly has no time for family, sex, or procreation—distractions that would undermine his devotion to God. Philo emphasizes the distractive nature of physical passion and lust. In fact, he ignores Zipporah, Moses' biblical wife, almost entirely.[4] For Philo, the issue is not based solely on temporal constraint—there is only so much time in the day to support a family and to serve God—but also on the question of the soul's focus, whether its attention is on the body or things spiritual. One can better concentrate on God's needs if one's own physical needs have been disciplined away (purified, nullified). Moses apparently appreciates this fact early enough to avoid the pitfalls of marriage. As far as Philo is concerned, Moses is to be lauded for his self-control and mastery of all bodily passions.[5]

In Philo's description, Moses fits the paradigm of an ascetic Hellenistic philosopher who disciplines his body as well as his mind in order to better commune with the divine.[6] A true philosopher controls his desires and passions as a means to the fullest exercise of his mind. The Greco-Roman elite would have recognized in Philo's Moses a man who, like themselves, valued discipline and management of the body in the pursuit of wisdom and philosophy. They would have rated his manliness on his ability to master himself in this way.[7] Moses here exemplifies the Greco-Roman superman. As Clement of Alexandria would later note: "The human ideal of continence, I mean that which is set forth by the Greek philosophers, teaches one to resist passion, so as not to be made subservient to it, and to train the instincts to pursue rational goals."[8] Interestingly enough, Clement further claims that Christians exceed the philosophers in their espousal of permanent control over sexuality and partial control over gluttony and thirst. Ironically, but perhaps not surprisingly, Moses exemplifies for Clement the perfect continent. Clement continues to follow Philo when he posits that Moses could not have remained on Mount Sinai for forty days had God's presence not stilled Moses' physical needs.[9] Once again, close contact with God necessitates that—and in this case provides the means by which—one overcomes physical needs such as hunger, thirst, and sexual contact.

Philo presents Moses here as both a prophet and a priest. Yet Moses was not an Israelite priest, that office having been conferred exclusively on Aaron and his sons in the biblical narrative. Nevertheless, because Moses is the leader of the Israelite people (whom the biblical text describes as a nation of priests), Philo casts Moses as the chief priest of a priestly nation.[10] It is also likely that Philo had in mind a generic Greco-Roman priestly model. The Hellenistic priest ministered to the needs of the deity in the deity's temple, but he also served as oracle and interpreter of the deity's words. Hence, Philo aligned Moses' prophetic role with the Greco-Roman priestly role of "receiving oracular messages."

Philo provides the earliest extant example of the figure of Moses being used as a means for promoting a spiritual life in which celibacy plays a key role. Although Philo focuses on Moses' mastery of his passions, the result is the same as Aphrahat's: Moses forgoes his married life in order "to give his whole attention to God's commands." Moses, foreshadowing the Hellenistic philosophers, simply recognizes that succumbing to his physical needs or leading a family life distracts him from the higher pursuit of divine service to which God has called him. Better he should overcome those needs in order to perform God's demands more fully. In a sense, Philo's Moses takes Greco-Roman philosophical discipline to the extreme. Nevertheless, like Aphrahat, Philo holds up Moses' example as a model to be imitated.

Since Philo provides neither a biblical nor other prooftext, there is no telling where he came across this specific Moses tradition.[11] If the notion of the incompatibility of family life and prophethood originates in the Greco-Roman sphere, Philo gives it a particular spin in advocating total renunciation for Moses. If the tradition of Moses' celibacy predates Philo, he dresses it up in Hellenistic garb. Yet, the tradition might very well start with Philo or, rather, he may have been the first to articulate this notion of incompatibility through the narrative of Moses' prophethood. Hence, Philo could be the innovator of the celibate Moses paradigm. The tradition's appearance in Philo indicates its antiquity and perhaps speaks to its life outside the biblical text, but it does not give a clue to any earlier origin.[12] No matter where the tradition developed (or how it might have first been drawn exegetically from the biblical text, if at all), it shows remarkable popularity and versatility. Despite geographic, chronological, and linguistic distances, it surfaces repeatedly in later rabbinic and patristic literature.

Early Rabbinic Traditions: Mekhilta

Nowhere in the biblical text is it stated explicitly that Moses divorces or even abandons his wife. Nevertheless, this tradition is widespread in both Jewish and Christian literature, as Philo and Aphrahat clearly attest. Moreover, it appears several times within the rabbinic corpus. It may be founded on Exodus 18:2, which states that when Jethro came out to meet Moses and the Israelites after they left Egypt, Zipporah and her sons accompanied him. The text further states that Zipporah had been in her father's company "after he (Moses) sent her"—presumably back to her father. The textual reference seems to point to some event earlier in the narrative, but we do not know from the biblical text when, where, or why that might have been. The *Mekhilta*, a third-century rabbinic commentary on Exodus, provides a plausible scenario. When Moses descended to Egypt with his family (Exod. 4:20ff), and Aaron came out to greet him, Aaron suggested to Moses that it would be too burdensome on the already oppressed people to assimilate yet another family into their suffering midst. Better Zipporah and the boys should remain with Jethro. Hence, it is at this point in the narrative (chapter 4) that Moses sent Zipporah back.[13]

One could easily assume from the rest of the narrative in chapter 18 that Jethro expressly greets Moses with his (Moses') family in tow in order to reunite them. Although Zipporah now disappears from the narrative, the biblical text continues to refer to Jethro as Moses' father-in-law. Furthermore, at the end of this chapter, Moses sends his father-in-law home—alone: "And Moses sent away his father-in-law and he made his way back to his country" (Exod. 18:27). Zipporah presumably stays at her husband's side where she belongs. Nevertheless, the *Mekhilta* raises the issue of divorce in this context. In the same passage mentioned above, Rabbi Joshua suggests that this verse (Exod. 18:2) parallels Deuteronomy 24:1, in which a man who is displeased with his wife divorces her with a *get* (a written document of divorce) and sends her from his home.[14] There in Deuteronomy it says "sent away" with a *get*— so here in Exodus it must mean "sent away" with a *get* as well. The similarly deployed verb *shalah* (sent) prompts Rabbi Joshua to conclude that a divorce must have occurred in Exodus 18:27. Perhaps this reading appeals to Rabbi Joshua, since there is no explicit statement in the biblical text that Moses and Zipporah are happily reunited at Sinai (they do not, after all, produce any more children) and from that point forward, Zipporah disappears from the narrative. Whether or not this reading is acceptable to the other rabbis is not clear. It is certainly not refuted but rather followed—and perhaps opposed by—the aforementioned suggestion concerning Moses' encounter with Aaron upon returning to Egypt.

Early Rabbinic Traditions: Sifre

The tradition that Moses divorces his wife might very well have developed from this interpretation of Exodus 18:27. Yet this midrash does not provide a larger ideological context to explain the divorce. The question the *Mekhilta* seems to ask is not why Moses separated from his wife but whether he divorced her legally (with a document) or simply sent her back to her father's house for the duration of his trip to Egypt. The Rabbis here do not pursue the implications of, the motivations for, or the consequences of such a separation. Nevertheless, the tradition that Moses divorces his wife, or at least neglects his familial duties, is explored in other rabbinic exegetical contexts where the Rabbis theorize Moses' motivations and rationalize his actions.

In the *Sifre*, another third-century Tannaitic composition, Moses' marital difficulties arise from an inconsistency between the first two verses in Numbers 12. The biblical text states: "Miriam and Aaron spoke against Moses concerning the Cushite woman whom he had married; for he had married a Cushite woman. And they said: Does God speak only through/with Moses? Does God not also speak through/with us?" (Num. 12:1–2).[15] The biblical text presents two seemingly unrelated reasons for Miriam and Aaron's complaint. The first verse suggests that the complaint has something to do with Moses' wife, Zipporah, the Cushite woman he married.[16] One might assume from the continuation of the first verse that Miriam and Aaron's complaint concerns the fact that Moses had married a Cushite (Ethiopian) woman and not a Hebrew woman, or at least that something particular about Zipporah bothered them, that she was in some way a bad or inappropriate wife. Yet the second verse expressly states that the complaint centers on Moses' sense of superiority over his siblings. The Rabbis attempt to fuse the two complaints into one through the following midrash. Concerning Numbers 12:1 the *Sifre* expounds:

> "And Miriam and Aaron spoke against Moses [concerning his Cushite
> wife for he had married a Cushite woman]" (Num. 12:1): From where
> did Miriam know that Moses had abstained from procreation? She
> saw Zipporah, who was not dressed up in the ornaments of women.
> She said to [Zipporah], "What is wrong such that you are not dressed
> up in the ornaments of women?" [Zipporah] said to her, "Your
> brother is not conscientious in the deed." Thus Miriam knew and she
> spoke to her brother [Aaron] and the two of them spoke against him
> [Moses]. Rabbi Nathan says Miriam was beside Zipporah at the
> moment that it was said, "And the youth ran [and told to Moses and
> said that Eldad and Medad were prophesying in the camp]" (Num. 11:27)
> because she [Miriam] heard Zipporah say, "Oy for the wives of those
> men!" And thus Miriam knew.[17]

The language of the first verse allows for two contradictory readings; it can be understood to mean that Miriam and Aaron spoke *to* Moses *against* his wife, or as the Rabbis prefer, that they spoke *against* Moses *on behalf of* his wife. This reading allows the Rabbis to combine the two complaints into one, which they do through the two midrashim on Miriam and Zipporah. The first part of the complaint concerns Moses' neglect of his conjugal duties. The biblical text itself may have suggested this line of reasoning—namely, that the issue was Moses' marital behavior because of its repeated use of the word *lakaḥ* (take, as in marriage). The Rabbis here emphasize "married" over "Cushite."

The rabbinic authors then produce two scenarios in which Miriam discovers the problem. In the first, which is disconnected from the text and the narrative, Miriam comes upon a bedraggled Zipporah wandering around the camp and asks her why she has not taken care of herself. Zipporah's accusatory cry, "Your brother is not conscientious in the deed," lets Miriam know that Moses has been neglecting his conjugal duties, but it does not inform us as to why he does so. That answer can be found only in the second midrash of Rabbi Nathan. Here, Miriam happens to be standing with Zipporah when the spirit of prophecy lands on Medad and Eldad, and the "youth ran" to tell Moses that they were prophesying in the camp. Zipporah's sympathetic reaction, "Oy for the wives of those men," gives the reader deeper insight into the anguish of her own situation. Those men, because of their newly found prophetic calling, will now also neglect their wives. From this, the reader and Miriam together deduce that Moses neglects Zipporah precisely because of his prophetic role. The first midrash gives a reason for Miriam's complaint concerning Zipporah, and the second connects this complaint to the next verse, in which Miriam and Aaron grumble about Moses' leadership and prophethood. In both cases, Miriam learns of the situation by observing her sister-in-law. Wives and families suffer when a husband/father presumes that his divine calling supersedes his domestic obligations.

This gendered view of the effects of prophecy furthers the Rabbis' next contention that prophets (except for Moses) should not break with their families. Hence, the midrash continues with an explication of the real complaint against Moses:

> *"And they said, 'Did God speak only through/with Moses?'* (Num. 12:2): Did He not speak through/with the Patriarchs, and they did not withdraw from procreation? *'Did God not speak also through/with us'* (Num. 12:3), yet we did not withdraw from procreation?"[18]

From this text we see that it is not just Zipporah's neglect that worries them but also the presumptive logic behind Moses' behavior, specifically, that because God speaks through/with Moses he necessarily must renounce procreation. The older siblings, including themselves among others who have spoken with God (or through whom God has spoken), do not renounce marriage but do rather strongly censure Moses' behavior. Miriam and Aaron take issue with what they perceive to be Moses' overreaching self-righteousness. Following the biblical narration, the midrash suggests that this is how God answers their question:

> *"'If there will be for you a prophet I will make it known to him in a vision'* (Num. 12:6): Perhaps just as I speak with the prophets in dreams and visions, so I speak with Moses, therefore Scripture tells us, *'Not so is*

my servant Moses' (Num. 12:7). *'In all my house he is entrusted'* (Num.
12:7)—except for the ministering angels." Rabbi Yose says, "even more
than the ministering angels." *"'Mouth to mouth do I speak to him'*
(Num. 12:8): Mouth to mouth I told him to withdraw from his wife."[19]

God hears their complaint and answers: Yes, with other prophets I appear in
dreams and visions, but with Moses I speak directly. Moses is special—in fact,
he is equal to the ministering angels and hence, God commands him specifically to separate from his wife. God may call others to prophecy, but only Moses
is required to give up his family life. Yet, the Rabbis do not flesh out the rationale for this requirement. Instead, they bestow an abstract notion of specialness on Moses: he is close (but not quite equal) to the ministering angels. God
speaks "mouth to mouth" with Moses, whereas all other prophets hear or see
God indirectly through dreams or visions only and cannot talk back or respond
to what they have seen or heard from God.

Starting from a position similar to Aphrahat's, the *Sifre* claims that Moses
refuses his conjugal duties because of his service to God—that is, his prophetic
calling. While Zipporah bemoans his conjugal neglect, Miriam accuses him of
something more severe than neglect, for he has withdrawn from the act of
procreating completely. Most important, he presumes to do so because of the
demands of his prophetic role. Miriam is indignant not only on Zipporah's
behalf but also because Moses appears to be placing himself in a separate category from all other leaders of Israel who have had personal relationships with
God. Miriam appears (in the rabbinic eye) just in her criticism of Moses on this
account. Neither Miriam nor Aaron know of any other leaders of Israel who
have been required to renounce their family, so why should Moses? Yet, God
comes to Moses' defense: not all prophets are made alike. Moses is special.
Other prophets communicate with God through dreams and visions. Only
Moses speaks directly to God. Moses does not presume to take leave of his
family duties; rather, God has expressly commanded him to do so. Other
prophets need not (nor should they) abandon their conjugal duties. Nevertheless, the reason Moses' special prophethood requires such a condition is never
explored in depth. The Rabbis only state that his unique position warrants it.
The *Sifre* authors construe Moses' renunciation not as an ideal, but as an exception that requires little explanation.

A Comparison

The *Sifre* text does not seem to be familiar or concerned with the *Mekhilta* text
because the issue of divorce is not at stake here. If Moses had already divorced

Zipporah in Exodus 4 or 18, she would not have any right to complain about Moses in the desert. The *Sifre* text counters the notion (advocated by Philo and Aphrahat) that all prophets need abandon their family lives as part and parcel of their vocation, but it does not deny the notion's applicability to Moses.

The major difference between the *Sifre*, and Philo and Aphrahat is in the value placed on Moses' example. The *Sifre* severely limits its applicability to Moses and Moses alone. It emphatically holds that other prophets should not renounce their families or procreation, whereas Philo and Aphrahat find Moses' life choices admirable and even worthy of emulation. Moreover, the Rabbis' emphasis on Zipporah's suffering (absent from both Philo and Aphrahat) highlights what they find problematic even in Moses' case. As Daniel Boyarin aptly notes, while the Rabbis reconcile two contradictory biblical statements, they also take the opportunity to invest their response ideologically. That is, this midrash also addresses their own concerns about marriage and the spiritual life. The Rabbis recognize that their frequently long absences from home and lengthy days in the study house put enormous pressures on their families. Yet at the same time, they admire Moses' audacity, if only from a great distance.[20]

This Tannaitic text, as read against Aphrahat or Philo, certainly appears to be polemical. Yet it cannot be aimed at Aphrahat, since he wrote his treatise at least a century later. Boyarin has suggested that the *Sifre* passage refutes an early and widespread Jewish tradition—its unattributed status in Philo only highlights this point. In so doing, the *Sifre* neutralizes this tradition in limiting celibacy to Moses.[21] The *Sifre* clearly questions the notion of an inherent incompatibility between family life and all prophethood or spiritual leadership. If the particular tradition that the *Sifre* authors had in mind was Philo's, they do not seem to be concerned with its more Hellenistic elements—that is, the notion of discipline and the managing of one's passions. The *Sifre*'s Moses neglects Zipporah either because God directs him to (for unknown reasons), or because he has no time for Zipporah owing to the overwhelming attention needed by God, or because of some other unexplained nature of the job—but not out of a concern to discipline his body. As Boyarin notes, the *Sifre* focuses not on celibacy per se, but on celibacy in marriage. This could be a reflection on any number of practices by contemporaries of the *Sifre* authors, Christians and Jews alike.[22] Certainly some Christian groups advocated giving up procreation at baptism, as we witnessed in the *Acts of Judah Thomas*. In reality, this often happened late in life, after one had completed one's familial duties of procreation. Elderly celibate couples then continued to live together. As noted in the last chapter, Aphrahat manipulates the Mosaic tradition to support the post-marriage move to celibacy and to counter this practice of "spiritual marriage" by advocating that one must abandon one's domestic arrangements even if one's wife has also agreed to a celibate life.

In demonstration 6 ("Concerning the *Bnay Qyama*"), Aphrahat speaks to and for the already celibate. Moses here is more than an exemplar of celibacy; he is a model of the properly conducted continent life. The key is the separation of the sexes, which embodies a separation of the mundane from the spiritual. Celibate women should live with other women, and men with other men. Family of any sort is inappropriate and untenable for the truly committed renunciants. Moses provides an excellent role model precisely because he has a family to abandon. The call to *iḥidayuta*, the life of single-minded devotion to God, includes a physical as well as a mental element of separation.

While the Pauline and other New Testament texts promote leaving one's family in order to pursue spiritual goals, it would be limiting to suggest that this *Sifre* text argues specifically against Pauline or other early Christian claims. Rather, this rabbinic text demonstrates that Jews, too, were concerned with similar issues of balance in their lives. Boyarin suggests that the *Sifre* argues against a rabbinic practice of "married monks"—namely, married Rabbis abandoning their families for long stretches at a time in order to study. The *Sifre*, which disapproves of this sort of practice, focuses on the women's suffering.[23] These rabbis, Boyarin argues, would prefer that their students study before they marry. The *Sifre* authors manipulate this Moses tradition to suggest that given the realities of life (i.e., family), compromises must be made in one's "spiritual" life. A balance must be struck.

Yet these same rabbis never deny the tradition's associations to Moses—namely, that there remains an inherent incompatibility between family life and prophethood. While the *Sifre* text seems to polemicize against an unknown earlier text or tradition, Aphrahat deploys a tradition similar to the one the *Sifre* attempts to counter—namely, that Moses' celibacy provides an ideal model of religious behavior. What is his source, if he indeed has one? Except for the tradition itself, the textual associations do not seem to correspond. The Rabbis find sexual renunciation in Miriam's complaint against Moses and the prophesying of Eldad and Medad. Aphrahat, on the other hand, finds his proof in the "fact" that Joshua served Moses from his youth. However, textually and narratively, these prooftexts are quite close. Aphrahat's proof-text, Numbers 11:28 ("Joshua was a servant of Moses from his youth"), follows immediately upon the *Sifre*'s, verse 27 ("And the youth ran and told to Moses and said that Eldad and Medad were prophesying in the camp"). Coincidence? Perhaps. Yet it is more likely that these proof-texts surface from a common exegetical matrix of traditions surrounding Numbers 11–12.

It is, of course, difficult to speak of sources when we have so little information about the texts, their date of composition, and the breadth of their readership. The *Sifre* to Numbers, a Tannaitic commentary on the biblical book of Numbers, was most likely composed in mid-third-century Palestine. Similar to many of the rabbinic texts, this text is made up of earlier traditions that a later editor redacted into one volume. It is possible that some of these traditions had transmission histories, either written or oral, of their own and that they may also have come into nonrabbinic hands at one point or another. Some of these traditions may have emerged from nonrabbinic or pre-rabbinic circles, as the Philo text suggests. Aphrahat, who traveled the highways of fourth-century Persian Mesopotamia, may very well have come across any number of these sorts of texts and traditions without having a "*Sifre*" text, as we know it today, in his hands.

Aphrahat's training and background is even murkier than that of the Tannaitic rabbis. While he composed his twenty-three homilies in the mid-fourth century, we do not know with whom he studied, what sources he may have had at his disposal, or in what language(s) he pursued his scholarship. Though he has a Persian name, he writes in a Syriac minimally affected by Greek or Persian. One can only assume that his sources were limited to Syriac or other dialects of Aramaic. He may have learned and retained many of his sources orally from his teachers or from other itinerant preachers. There were probably former Jews and various "Jewish-Christians" among his teachers and audiences. Yet, his textual citation of this tradition is exegetically so close to the *Sifre* text, it is hard to dismiss the possibility of a relationship of some sort, even as its exact nature may be difficult to pinpoint. At the very least, I suggest, Aphrahat and the fourth-century Babylonian rabbis shared a common Aramaic "public" library; that is, they had access to similar compilations or collections of exegetical traditions.[24] As we shall see, the *Sifre* text resurfaces in later rabbinic texts.

Whether or not Aphrahat's source or inspiration is this *Sifre* text or something similar, he inverts the argument once again. If the *Sifre* counters an earlier notion that prophecy and family are incompatible, Aphrahat uses it to support that very notion. Furthermore, he applies this logic to his own life. Prophecy and divine service are indeed incompatible with family, and hence all *ihidaye*—those who, in imitation of Jesus and the prophets, dedicate themselves to divine service—should separate themselves from family and women, even other celibate women. This is not to say that Aphrahat polemicizes against the *Sifre* text specifically; rather, he seems to me simply to be making use of traditions at his disposal for his own purposes (as indeed the Rabbis do). In this case, he uses a known tradition to convince wayward celibates to live alone, while the Rabbis deploy it to discourage others from staying away from home for extended periods of time. For obvious reasons, Aphrahat is not concerned with the feelings of the abandoned wives; if anything, he feels they are better off without their menfolk so that they are free to pursue their own celibate lives. If Aphrahat were a direct participant in the rabbinic debate described by Boyarin, he might propose a third tactic: wholesale abandonment of the family by both men and women (after they had raised their children).

Nevertheless, Aphrahat's emphasis on the root QDS further differentiates him from the *Sifre* and Philo and may point to a different tradition entirely. Moses renounces sexuality (loves *qaddishuta*) because he is "sanctified" (*etqaddash*) by God. While not explicit in the *Sifre* text (it might be inferred from his angelic disposition and the fact that he talks "mouth to mouth" with God), the link between *qedushah/qaddishuta* and sexual abstinence is foundational to Aphrahat's claim. Yet, this connection is not exegetically supported by Philo or the *Sifre*; rather, their prooftexts speak more to the other tradition preserved in Aphrahat that Moses renounces his marriage because of his prophetic calling. Nevertheless, the notion that Moses is somehow "sanctified" through or because of his celibacy is reflected in other rabbinic midrash.

Moses at Sinai

Aphrahat's particular reading of Exodus 19, and specifically his understanding of the relationship between *qaddishuta*, readiness for divine audience, and sexual abstinence is not lost on the Rabbis, many of whose exegetical works were in the process of composition and redaction around the time that Aphrahat wrote and in the same geographic location in which he ministered. Perhaps it should not be too surprising, therefore, that a remarkably similar reading of Exodus 19 appears several times within the rabbinic corpus. In these texts—all variations of the same midrash—the rabbinic authors establish a direct link between necessary preparation before divine encounter and sexual renunciation. The midrash that most closely parallels Aphrahat's can be found in *Avot de Rabbi Natan A (ARN A)* 2:3, but it also appears in version *B*, as well in the *Babylonian Talmud* tractates *Shabbat* (87a) and *Yevamot* (62a) and in the midrash *Exodus Rabbah* 19:3 and 46:13.[25] Whereas the *Sifre* text is not as obviously exegetically similar to Aphrahat's Moses tradition, the thematic, linguistic, and terminological affinities, as well as the parallels in logical progression, between the *ARN A* text and Aphrahat's are hard to deny. The first question is what the relationship is among these various midrashim and particularly the place of Aphrahat's version in this literary matrix. The second question concerns the greater theme of Moses celibacy: how do these traditions relate to the traditions of Moses' prophecy discussed above? And finally, what do the Rabbis make of

Moses' celibacy? Why do they preserve such a tradition if they do not wish to emulate him?

The Midrash

The basic plot line of the core rabbinic midrash follows along the lines of Aphrahat's: Moses is on Mount Sinai receiving instruction from God concerning the Israelites' preparation for God's revelation. The biblical text relays instructions concerning two different actions that will prepare the Israelites for this revelation. The first comes from the mouth of God and concerns the laundering of the clothing. This is recorded in Exodus 19:10–11. God says to Moses: "Go to the people *veqiddashtam* today and tomorrow, and let them wash their clothes. And be ready by the third day; for on the third day the Lord will come down in the sight of all the people upon Mount Sinai." Moses takes these instructions to the people, but seemingly embellishes or interprets them by adding a second directive in verse 15: "Be ready by the third day, do not approach a woman." It is this last instruction—temporary sexual abstinence—that inspires our rabbinic midrashim. In these midrashic texts, then, after Moses either receives or creates this stipulation "do not go near a woman" (and the texts are vague concerning whether Moses or God gave the actual instruction) Moses has his own epiphany. He reasons thus: if the Israelites, for a one-time audience with God need to prepare themselves by abstaining from sex for three days, how much more so should he, Moses, abstain for all time, since he is called into God's presence on short notice. This is the *Babylonian Talmud Yevamot* 62a text, which is the most succinct of the versions:

> [Moses] separated himself from his wife; what interpretation did he
> make? He said, "And the Israelites, with whom the Shekhinah spoke
> but for one hour and for whom a fixed time was set, the Torah
> nevertheless said '*do not approach a woman*' (Exod. 19:15), how much
> more so must I [separate from my wife], I, who am liable to be
> spoken to at any hour and for whom no fixed time has been set," And
> his view agreed with that of God; for it is said, "*Go say to them: Return
> to your tents; but as for you, stand here by Me*" (Deut. 5:27–28).[26]

This particular reading of Exodus 19:15 appears six times in the rabbinic corpus and each time in a slightly different form. What remains the same in all six cases is the notion that Moses chooses to renounce his conjugal duties based on his understanding of the import of Exodus 19:15, and that that seemingly radical move is supposedly approved by God after the fact. But as I will try to demonstrate, some versions of the midrash are not so happy with Moses' decision. Nonetheless, all the midrashim are consistently found within a larger literary framework that starts with the sentiment that Moses' celibacy was one of several things Moses does on his own accord, which only after the fact God approves. In addition, all six texts bring in another biblical passage—Deuteronomy 5:27–8 ("Go say to them: Return to your tents; but as for you, stand here by Me")—as proof of God's consent. However, in two cases, I think it can be shown that this text is used to qualify Moses' move rather than to support it.

Despite these core similarities of theme and textual support, there are several outstanding differences among the midrashim that allow me to divide them into two categories. In the first category, one can find the two Babylonian talmudic texts (*Shabbat* 87a and *Yevamot* 62a), *Exodus Rabbah* 19:3 and the variation in *Avot de Rabbi Natan B*. Although *Exodus Rabbah* is reputedly a much later text, I include it here by way of comparison, since both versions, as I understand them, are found in that midrashic corpus. Two characteristics bring these four texts together. The first is that the rationale or need for preparation through sexual renunciation has something to do with God's speech or words. The two talmudic texts record similarly, and I quote this time Moses' rationale according to *Shabbat* 87a:

> "If the Israelites, with whom the Shekhinah spoke only for one hour and He set them a fixed time, yet the Torah says *'Be ready on the third day do not approach a woman*,' I, with whom the Shekhinah speaks at all times and does not set me a fixed time, how much more so [must I stay away from my wife]."

Here, Moses builds his *qal va-ḥomer* on the notion that if Israel needs sexual renunciation for the one time God, or the Shekhinah speaks to them directly, then all the more so does Moses need to refrain from sexual activity for all the many more times that God speaks to him directly. *Exodus Rabbah* 19:3 records a slightly different version: "At Sinai [Moses] interpreted and said: 'If Israel who is not appointed to the *dibbrot* he said to them *'do not approach a woman'* (Exod. 19:15), I who am appointed *la-dibbur* is it not just that I separate myself from my wife?'" The Rabbis play on the word *dibbrot* ("words" or "commandments"), as in the ten commandments and *dibbur* (speech). Israel heard those divine words (the ten commandments) for only a brief moment in time—while Moses speaks to God on a regular basis. Although there may be more layered into this wordplay, for my purposes here the fact that Moses' decision has something to do with divine words or speech places it safely in category I (sexual renunciation related to hearing divine speech). The *ARN B* 2:8 version records yet another variation, noting that Israel is not a special vessel (*kli meyuhad*)—a proper receptacle to receive God's words—but that Moses is and must therefore behave differently from Israel:

And he separated from his wife: [Moses rationalized] "If Israel—who is not a special vessel [*kli meyuḥad*] and to whom God does not speak except for the one hour—and yet the Holy Blessed One told them to be separated from their wives—and I who am a special vessel and to whom God speaks at all times and I do not know when He will speak to me—is it not just that I separate from my wife?"

Here, Moses' prophetic role—his special vesselhood—comes to the fore, reminiscent of our earlier *Sifre* text. Moses separates from his wife because of his prophetic classification; furthermore, this midrash connects this separation to Sinai.

The second characteristic of category I has to do with the subsidiary proof-text brought into the midrash to support Moses' move. In all four cases, this text is Deuteronomy 5:28: "But as for you stand here by me." In *Exodus Rabbah* 19:3, only these words from the passage are cited. But in the talmudic versions, the phrase found just before it, in verse 27, is added: "Return to your tents." The result of this combined citation is best displayed in *Shabbat* 87a: "And how do we know that the Holy Blessed One gave his approval? Because it is written, '*go say to them, "return to your tents"*' (Deut. 5:27) and it is followed by, '*"but as for you, stand here by me"*' (Deut. 5:28)." The midrash highlights Moses' separation from the people and his elevation to God's level. God's approval is further emphasized in the *ARN B* 2:8 version:

From where do we know that God consented? Because He said "*Go tell them: 'return to your tents'*" (Deut. 5:27); but was Moses with them in this permission? The Torah says "*And you stand here by me*" (Deut. 5:28). Meaning from that point on Israel returned [to their tents] with permission [to return to their wives] and Moses stood in his prohibition.

In these midrashim, Deuteronomy 5:27–28 lends support to the notion that God approved of Moses' sexual renunciation in retrospect, even though Moses came to that conclusion using his own reasoning skills. Nevertheless, *Shabbat* 87a stands out even within this category, for it concludes with yet another proof-text, Numbers 12:8, noting, "There are those that say, 'mouth to mouth I speak to him." Numbers 12:8 stands here in secondary support to Moses' sexual renunciation. It also seems to refer back to our *Sifre* text, in which the notion of God's speaking "mouth to mouth" with Moses separates him qualitatively from Miriam and Aaron. Moses' prophetic status is again cited in support of his self-induced decision to renounce his conjugal duties.

Such is not the case in the later two midrashim (*Exodus Rabbah* 41:3 and the *Avot de Rabbi Natan A* 2:3 = category II), where these same prooftexts are brought to *counter* Moses' move rather than to support it. Here, they suggest that Moses did not come to any radical decision about his sexuality by himself, but was directly instructed to do so by God. This is how *Exodus Rabbah* 41:3 presents its case:

> R. Akivah says: "[no!] It was God himself who told him [to separate himself from his wife], for it says '*with him do I speak mouth to mouth*'" (Num. 12:8). R. Judah also says that it was told to him directly by God. For Moses too was included in the injunction, "*do not approach a woman*," thus all were forbidden; and when He afterwards said: "*return to your tents*" (Deut. 5:27), he permitted them [the wives to their husbands]. Moses then asked: "Am I included in them?" And God replied, "*No, but as for you, stand here by me*" (Deut. 5:28).

This midrash's use of Deuteronomy 5:27–28, with support from Numbers 12:8, clearly shows this text's unease surrounding Moses' decision. While not denying that Moses becomes celibate, for all Israel is commanded to be celibate for the three days, the authors of the text wish to suggest that God, for some unknown or as yet unexplained reason, required Moses to remain celibate at this point in the Exodus narrative. The *Avot de Rabbi Natan A* 2:3 version is even stronger in its language of qualification: this is how it ends its version of the midrash:

> Rabbi Yehudah Ben Batira said he [Moses] did not separate from his wife until it was told to him by the mouth of God, as it says "*mouth to mouth I speak with him*" (Num. 12:8): "mouth to mouth I told him: separate from your wife" and he separated. There are others who say that he did not separate from his wife until it was told to him by the mouth of God as it says "*go tell them to return to their tents*" (Deut. 5:27) and afterwards [it says] "*and you stand here by me.*" He returned back and separated [from his wife].

The *ARN A* affirms that God commands Moses to abandon his wife (whether at the same time as the rest of the Israelites or not). At the very least, he must remain celibate while all the other Israelites may return to their families. This role reversal further suggests great rabbinic anxiety around the idea that a person, even as special as Moses, could choose to be celibate and God would approve of such a self-realized choice. Moreover, by using "mouth to mouth" as a prooftext for direct command, the *ARN* takes that text out of the category of special prophetic privilege. That is, if Aphrahat can look at "mouth to mouth" as a mystical goal for all of his celibates, the *ARN* on the one level simply reiterates that Moses happened to receive this command directly from God;

but it also points, in a backhanded sort of way, to his prophetic status as special, as in the *Sifre*. Yet, it remains God's prerogative to suggest different behavior for Moses because of his position.

In summary, so far, then, we have two related yet different midrashic traditions concerning Moses' celibacy exegeted from Exodus 19. The first supports the notion that Moses comes to this position on his own, and that God (and presumably the Rabbis) support this move in an unqualified manner. In the second tradition, the Rabbis clearly do not support Moses' move—as an individual choice on his part—but, rather, wish to suggest that God compels him. Thus, in distancing themselves from Moses' decision—but not his position— they further suggest, like the *Sifre*, that Moses' celibacy is a unique situation applicable to Moses alone. He is a special vessel, a prophet of God.

Nevertheless, these two latter midrashim share one more characteristic that also differentiates them from the others. This difference stems from the manner in which they understand the original rationale for Israel's temporary celibacy. Remember that in our first three midrashim, the reason Israel must prepare for three days via sexual renunciation has to do with receiving God's words or being able to withstand being spoken to by the Shekhinah. *Exodus Rabbah* 41:3, however, gives us a different rationale:

> "In connection with Mount Sinai, whose holiness [*qedushato*] was
> only for that hour [of revelation] it was said to them [Israel] '*do not
> approach a woman*' (Exod. 19:15). I [Moses] with whom God speaks at
> all hours, is it not just that I be separated from my wife?"

In this midrash, the motivating concern is the *qedushah* of the mountain. Owing to the mountain's *qedushah*, the people must refrain from sexual intercourse. One might presume, therefore, that the midrash would then continue to say that because Moses frequently goes up the same mountain, that it is due to that same *qedushah* that Moses should refrain from sex on a regular basis. Nevertheless, the midrash does not take that route, but suggests again that it is because Moses *speaks* to God on a regular basis, and at short notice, that he must renounce his sexuality. In any case, *qedushah* stands out as a variant rationale for this midrash.[27]

The *Avot de Rabbi Natan A* 2:3 version makes yet another claim about *qedushah*, which here concerns the people, not the mountain:

> This is one of the things that Moses did on his own and his opinion
> matched the opinion of God. . . . He separated from his wife, and his
> opinion agreed with the opinion of God. How so? [Moses] said,
> "Concerning Israel, that did not *nitqaddshu* except for the hour and

were not *nizdamnu* [prepared] except to receive upon themselves the
ten commandments from Mount Sinai [and yet] the Holy Blessed
One said to me: 'go to the people *veqiddashtam* today and tomorrow'
(Exod. 19:10); and I, who am *mezuman* [prepared/called] to this every
day at every hour and I do not know when He will speak to me either
in the day or in the night. How much more so should I separate from
my wife!" And his opinion agreed with the opinion of God.

Here the *ARN* makes a direct correlation between the Israelites' action
nitqaddshu and Moses' resulting reaction of permanent sexual renunciation.
Yet, the *Avot de Rabbi Natan*, unlike all the previously cited midrashim, actually
reads the original biblical text in a much more textually close fashion. For here
the issue of *qedushah* does not jump out of nowhere, but from the very verses
upon which the core of the midrash is based. If we return to Exodus 19:10–14
for a moment, we will remember that, indeed, God directs Moses to "*qiddesh*"
the people in verse 10, and that Moses goes ahead and does so in verses 14 and 15.
While the order to *qiddesh* is elaborated by the action of laundering in verse 10,
Moses amends or adds to that the requirement of sexual abstinence in verse 15.
Our midrash, however, assumes that God's instruction to Moses to *qiddesh* is
fulfilled directly and solely by sexual renunciation. This version of the midrash
dovetails with Aphrahat's the most closely. I will return to that comparison
shortly.

So where does this leave us? We have four midrashim that approve of
Moses' self-realization to become celibate based on the notion that speaking to
God necessitates such an action, and two midrashim that qualify Moses' decision—
by taking it away from him—and putting it in God's hands. At the same time,
the latter two midrashim that disapprove of Moses' decision also highlight the
notion of *qedushah* that is already apparent in the biblical equation—but is not
raised in the other midrashim. It seems to me, then, that there is a relationship
between the *qedushah* in the equation and the distancing from it that the Rabbis
perform in these latter midrashim that distinguishes this strain of the tradition
from the former ones cited above. That is not to argue that one strain must
necessarily be dated earlier than the other, but only to suggest that the midrash
appears in two (or more) variations. At the very least, there is a core theme, an
interpretation of Exodus 19:10–15 that gives rise to the tradition of Moses' celibacy, which is taken in different directions by later midrashists. However, it is
not insignificant that the midrashim that distance themselves from Moses'
decision and position are also the midrashim that include the rationale of *qedushah*.
The rabbinic anxiety highlighted above surely is connected to their understanding
of *qedushah* and a desire to distance *qedushah* from sexual renunciation. Somehow,

the link between *qedushah* and sexual renunciation—so apparent to Aphrahat—gives the Rabbis of these midrashim reason to pause. How the Rabbis understand *qedushah* is, of course, key to uncovering their anxieties. I will return to this question below.

Martin Jaffee, building on the work of earlier scholarship, has recently argued that the key to understanding relationships between parallel texts is not to search (sometimes fruitlessly) for the authentic original, but to start from the position that there were always several variations on any particular theme. He brings as an example the practice of the Greek rhetorical schools that would require—just for practice and pedagogic reasons—students to create variations on themes, passages, or texts as academic exercises.[28] His theory suggests, then, that my set of midrashim might reflect similar practices among the Rabbis. There may or may not have been an original text, though there may have been a theme—Moses' celibacy derived from Exodus 19—that was extrapolated in several different ways all at once within the pedagogic exercises of the rabbinic academies. What the rabbinic texts present us reflects a sample collection of some of the students' resulting exegesis. Our *Sifre* text might also fall within this paradigm, but form a category of its own, based on its differing underlying prooftexts. Yet, it must be noted that there is crossover between the *Sifre* text and some of these other midrashim (such as the *ARN A*, as we shall soon see) that also cite Numbers 12:8.

The rabbinic texts, then, like Aphrahat's, preserve an extra-biblical tradition supporting Moses' celibacy. Similar to Aphrahat, the Rabbis explain that tradition with several different exegetical strategies. Underlying many of them (but not all) is an appeal to the notion that prophethood—or at least Moses' specific prophethood—necessitates sexual renunciation. We have already seen how similar the *Sifre* text is to Aphrahat's hermeneutics in demonstration 6. Now let us take a closer look at Aphrahat's text in demonstration 18 in comparison to the *ARN A* text, which has the most in common with Aphrahat's. I discuss both texts next.

Another Comparison

AVOT DE RABBI NATAN A 2:3

> This is one of the things that Moses did on his own and his opinion matched the opinion of God. . . . He separated from his wife, and his opinion agreed with the opinion of God. How so? [Moses] said, "Concerning Israel, that did not *nitqaddshu* except for the hour [*le-fi sha'ah*)] and were not prepared [*nizdamnu*] except to receive upon themselves

the ten commandments from Mount Sinai [and yet] the Holy Blessed
One said to me: '*go to the people veqiddashtam today and tomorrow*' (Exod.
19:10); and I, who am prepared/called [*mezuman*] to this every day at
every hour and I do not know when He will speak to me either in the
day or in the night. How much more so should I separate from my
wife!" And his opinion agreed with the opinion of God.

[However] R. Yehudah ben Batira said . . . "as it is said (Num.
12:8): '*Mouth to mouth [peh el peh] I will speak to him,*' 'mouth to
mouth' I said to him separate from your wife and he separated" . . .
and his opinion agreed with the opinion of God.

Some say: Moses did not keep away from his wife until he
was told so by the mouth of the Almighty; for it is said, Go say to
them: "*Return ye to your tents*" (Deut. 5:27), and it is written, "*But as
for thee, stand thou here by Me*" (Deut. 5:28). He went back but kept
away from his wife. And his judgment coincided with God's.[29]

APHRAHAT *DEMONSTRATIONS* 18.4–5.

And concerning virginity and *qaddishuta* I will persuade you that
even in that nation [Israel] they [virginity and *qaddishuta*] were more
loved before God. And even among that earlier people it [*qaddishuta*]
was better than a great number of births that bring no success.
Moses, the man, the great prophet, leader of all Israel, from the time
that his Lord spoke to him he loved *qaddishuta* and he served the
Holy One. And he abstained from the world and from procreating
and he remained by himself in order to please his Lord . . . [for]
Israel was not able to receive the holy text and the living words that
the Holy One spoke to Moses on the mountain until he had *qaddsheh*
the people for three days. And only then the Holy One spoke to them.
For he said to Moses: "*Go down to the people and qaddesh them for three
days*" (Exod. 19:10). And this is how Moses explained it to them: "*do
not go near a woman*" (Exod. 19:15). And when they were *etqaddashu*
these three days, then on the third day God revealed himself. . . .

For Moses was speaking, and God answered him with a voice.
Israel stood on that day in terror, fear and trembling. They fell on their
faces, for they were unable to bear it. And they said to Moses "*Let not
God speak with us so, that we may not die*" (Exod. 20:19). O hard-hearted
one who is vexed by these things and stumbles! If the people of Israel,
with whom God spoke only one hour [*dahda sha'ah balhud*], was
unable to hear the voice of God until [Israel] had *etqaddash* itself three

days, even though [Israel] did not go up the mountain and did not go into the heavy cloud; how then could Moses, the man, the prophet, the enlightened eye of all the people, who stood all the time before God, and spoke with him mouth to mouth [*min pum l-pum*], How was it possible that he be living in the married state?!³⁰

Like Aphrahat, the *ARN A* reads the commandment to "be QDS" in verses 10 and 14 in conjunction with the commandment to "be ready" in verses 11 and 15. They conclude, like Aphrahat, that when God said "be QDS" he meant, as Moses claims, "Prepare yourselves through sexual restraint." Furthermore, they contend, as does Aphrahat, that Moses deduces from this that he must refrain from sexual relations permanently, since he would not necessarily have three days for proper preparation every time God called on him. In both texts, Moses speaks to God "mouth to mouth" and Israel stands but for an "hour" interview with God. The deductive analogies made by the exegetes are the same: Moses models his behavior on Israel—only more so.

Several parallels in narrative language arise in this comparison. The first statement, based on the biblical narrative in Exodus 19, stresses that the people would have only a "one hour" interview with God, while Moses was constantly "on call." Aphrahat asks, "If the people of Israel, with whom God spoke *only one hour* [*daḥda sha'ah balḥud*], were unable to hear the voice of God until they had sanctified themselves three days . . . [how] then could Moses, the man, the prophet, the enlightened eye of all the people, who stood all the time before God?" The Rabbis also compare Israel, "who are not QDS except *for the hour* [*le-fi sha'ah*]" to Moses who is called to this duty "every day at every hour and [does] not know when God will speak with [him]—in the morning or in the night." The biblical text does not say how long Israel's interview would be, but both the Rabbis and Aphrahat claim that God spoke to them for one hour or moment in time.

In the second parallel, the writers emphasize that God spoke to Moses *mouth to mouth*. This phrase is found in Numbers 12:8 and is quoted in part in our rabbinic passage: "mouth to mouth (*peh el peh*) I will speak to him." Aphrahat insists that because God spoke to Moses *mouth to mouth (min pum l-pum)*, up close and in person, Moses could not have continued to be actively married. In the *ARN A*, Rabbi Yehuda Ben Batira cites the verse to suggest that God commanded Moses to be celibate. Nevertheless, both Aphrahat and the Rabbis agree that one who speaks "mouth to mouth" with God cannot be concerned with earthly matters such as marriage and children.

The biggest difference between the texts is in the literary structure. Whereas in Aphrahat's rendering, it is Aphrahat who makes a deduction concerning Moses, in the *ARN A*'s telling Moses draws his own conclusions. This difference is not insignificant, for Aphrahat wants only to support his previous contention that celibacy is divinely desired, even commanded—that is, it is better than marriage and a key element in *qaddishuta*. The *ARN A*, like the *Exodus Rabbah* 19:3 text above, questions that very choice. The two closing addenda introduce a tension into the rabbinic discourse as the text backpedals and suggests that Moses did not decide on his own, but was commanded by God to leave his wife. Whereas Aphrahat eagerly imitates Moses' move, the Rabbis equivocate. They do not resoundingly conclude to follow Moses' example, nor do they equate celibacy with a universally desired behavior. Only those who are specifically instructed by God should be celibate. Finally, although the Rabbis and Aphrahat similarly fuse the meanings of QDS and "prepare," the Rabbis emphasize the latter while Aphrahat focuses on the former. Aphrahat's whole exegesis hinges on his understanding that *qaddishuta* does indeed equal celibacy and is "commanded" by God. The Rabbis, in perhaps allowing such a suggestion, limit its applicability to Moses. While the Rabbis, in the end, allow for Moses' celibacy because of his divine calling, Aphrahat expands God's call to all capable Christians.

This rabbinic midrash on Exodus 19 remains significantly different from the *Sifre*'s, even as it seemingly "cites" the *Sifre* text as support. The *ARN A* focuses on universal sexual restraint before a divine encounter. It shows no particular concern for prophecy and celibacy (except perhaps as support for its central claim concerning Moses, but not about sexual renunciation and a divine encounter for everyone else). Aphrahat's conclusion—that Moses' move is exemplary—is a logical conclusion drawn from this reading of the text and has little to do with Moses' prophethood per se. Nonetheless, Aphrahat suggests that one can and should emulate and aspire to be like Moses. That he was a prophet proves all the more reason to emulate him for Aphrahat. Yet, the Rabbis do not follow through on this idea and again limit its application to Moses alone. Nevertheless, Rabbi Yehudah's addendum seems to refer back to the *Sifre* text in its citation of Numbers 12:8: God spoke to Moses "mouth to mouth"; "mouth to mouth" God told Moses to separate from his wife. This citation reaffirms the conclusions drawn from the *Sifre*'s discussion that Moses is in a separate category of people altogether. In the *Sifre*, he is a super-prophet distinguishing himself from among other prophets; in the *ARN A*, he simply distinguishes himself from the rest of Israel. Furthermore, in the *ARN A*, the central issue is not specifically prophecy, but a more general encounter with God. The *Sifre* suggests an inherent incompatibility between Moses' role as a prophet and his obligations as a husband and father. The *ARN A* affirms only that sexual restraint is incumbent upon all Israel before an extraordinary encounter with God—such as the revelation of the Torah at Sinai—and that Moses' peculiar position within Israel necessitates total withdrawal from his sexual life for the rest of his career.

Most significantly for this discussion, in the *ARN A* this preparatory process (i.e., sexual restraint) is linked to *qedushah/qaddishuta,* as it is by Aphrahat. While Aphrahat builds his theological case from this apparent connection, the *ARN A* makes no such broad conclusions concerning *qedushah* and celibacy. In fact, it makes every effort to downplay it. Moses' celibacy is unique, and its connection to *qedushah* is contested as the addenda attest. For in reference back to the *Sifre,* Rabbi Yehudah suggests that it was a command of God, *not* a decision on Moses' part, that caused Moses to renounce his sexual activity. Moreover, after the revelation of the Torah, the people are "commanded back to their tents," whereas Moses is directed to stay where he is at God's side. The Rabbis acknowledge the link between *qedushah* and temporary celibacy for Israel before the revelation, but they hesitate to apply *qedushah* to Moses' *permanent* abstinence or to extend the possibility to the rest of Israel. These added references reaffirm Moses' extraordinary situation while at the same time they subvert the original exegesis.

Daniel Boyarin reads this midrash in its Babylonian talmudic incarnation (*Shabbat* 87a) as supporting a particular Babylonian rabbinic marriage pattern. He places this midrash in opposition to the earlier *Sifre* version within an internal, yet "global" rabbinic debate concerning marriage practices for rabbis. As noted above, Rabbis early and late, Palestinian and Babylonian, recognized the tensions between family duties and full-time study—that very activity which they considered to be analogous to the work of the prophets and priests of ancient Israel. In Babylonia the debate, which perhaps started with Philo, comes almost full circle. Unwilling to give up family life and procreation, the Rabbis construct two opposing models: either a scholar should marry young and then leave home to study for extended periods of time, or he should put off marriage until his education is well under way (the modern graduate student model!). Both solutions posed their own problems, which the Rabbis continuously critique. The *Sifre* midrash seems to censor the marry-early, study-late model in that these "married monks," as Boyarin labels them, because they do undue harm to and cause anxiety for their abandoned or neglected womenfolk; thus, the *Sifre* focuses on Zipporah. The later midrashim, devoid of any female voices (or complaints), do not clearly condemn the practice of married monks and so leave the door open to emulating Moses. While the *Sifre* differentiates between Moses and all other prophets (read: spiritual leaders of all sorts), the other midrashim differentiate Moses from the *hoi polloi* of Israel; nothing is said about the other leaders of Israel—that is, the Rabbis.[31]

Supporting Boyarin's theory of internal polemic, the version from *Shabbat* 87a that he quotes appears again in *Yevamot* 62a, within a discussion of procreation. To Aphrahat, Moses' actions here are clearly a positive precedent; the Rabbis, not able to make the exegetical leap of faith made by Aphrahat, resolve to emulate Moses in a different fashion. Their emulation contains an important element: they, like Moses, procreate before withdrawing from married life. Moses may have separated from his wife, but he at least had a wife, Zipporah, who produced two sons from their conjugal union. *Mishnah Yevamot* 7:6, in discussing the issues of procreation and children, states: "A man shall not do away with procreation, unless he already has children. Shammai adds that he should have two male children; Hillel says one male, one female." The Babylonian talmudic commentary to this passage (also found in *Tosefta Yevamot* 8:2–3), elaborating on Shammai's qualification, reasons that because Moses had two sons, Gershom and Eliezer, the same should be required of all Jewish men. Moses certainly is not the only biblical character with two sons, but it is Moses whom the Rabbis most wish to emulate. Having fulfilled his duties as a father, Moses is free to pursue his relationship with God. Similarly, the Rabbis allow themselves the luxury of spending most of their lives studying God's word, following the model of Moses, the "proto-rabbi," only after they have produced at least two children. Howard Eilberg-Schwartz argues that this mishnaic ruling should be seen as a maximum number, as opposed to a minimum. One need produce only two children, not two or more children.[32] Hence, these rabbis use Moses' procreative model, *followed* by his celibate one, to allow themselves extended study breaks from home, as Boyarin suggests.

So while Aphrahat builds a hermeneutic of celibacy from the supposed sanctification and divine commandment he believes to be present in Scripture, the Babylonian rabbis understand Moses' celibacy simply as a guideline for how to manage the conflicting demands of procreation and study. Nevertheless, their detailed discussion of Moses' celibacy reveals their deep ambivalence toward their own marriages and sexuality. One gets the feeling that if they were aware of Aphrahat's reading of Exodus 19—they might find it theoretically attractive while practically repulsive. I suggested earlier that Aphrahat probably had recourse to similar traditions and literary texts as the Rabbis—a shared public library, as it were. Demonstration 6 shares interpretive and extra-biblical traditions with *Sifre* even as it counters a *Sifre*-like argument. Likewise, demonstration 18 could be related in some way to the *ARN A* text, for they both build from a notion of *qedushah/qaddishuta* and sexual renunciation; they both assume Moses is or becomes celibate on similar grounds and use Numbers 12:8 as textual support. Even though the *ARN A* depends on Numbers 12:8 to qualify Moses' self-appointed decision, it does not deny his celibacy. But at the same time, I do not assume that Aphrahat depends on the *ARN A* as a source, for it could also be argued that he shares similarities with *Shabbat* 87a, which also brings Numbers 12:8 as positive support. While Aphrahat is notoriously silent on his sources, one would think that in this particular case, if he recognized this midrash as "Jewish," he would have gleefully announced that the Jews actually agree with him, yet stupidly persist in procreating and condemning celibacy. Recall that he writes demonstration 18 in an anti-Jewish polemical mode. He starts his "midrash" with the caveat: "And concerning virginity and *qaddishuta* I will persuade you that even in that nation [Israel] they [virginity and *qaddishuta*] were more loved before God." And he ends the exegetical essay on the following note.

> And if with Israel, that had *etqaddash* itself for only three days, God
> spoke, how much better and desirable are those who all their days are
> *mqaddshin*, alert, prepared and standing before God. Should not
> God all the more love them and his spirit dwell among them?[33]

While the *ARN A* twice qualifies and backs off from Moses' move toward permanent celibacy, Aphrahat lauds it. Wouldn't it be wonderful, he suggests, if we could all be like Moses for all time and Israel for that one glorious moment—standing, prepared and alert and celibate—before God? If Aphrahat had a recognizably (to him) Jewish source containing this midrash, I cannot imagine that he would not exploit that point in this homily. Whatever the relationship socially between Aphrahat and the Rabbis, the literary characteristics of Aphrahat's exegesis fits more neatly into my second midrashic category, without claiming originality with either the rabbinic texts or Aphrahat.

Returning for a moment to Jaffee's paradigm of multiple midrashic variations, I further suggest, then, that Aphrahat could easily fit this pattern as well. He was an Aramaic-speaking Christian living in close proximity to Aramaic-speaking Jewish communities of the Mesopotamian river valleys. The tradition of Moses' celibacy derivative of Exodus 19 could arise from the Aramaic literary milieu he shared with the Rabbis. Aphrahat's version presents us with yet another variation on a familiar theme to biblical exegetes in fourth-century Persian Mesopotamia, even as he takes it to very different practical ends.

Whichever solution these late-ancient scholars and spiritual leaders adopted—marrying early or late, or abandoning family life altogether—Moses remains central to their notions of sexual practice and spiritual pursuit. Moses serves as a focal point for contemplating the perceived conflicts between sex and marriage and the divine calling, for Philo, the Rabbis, and Aphrahat. While Philo prefers to see Moses as the embodiment of Hellenistic virtues such as self-discipline, the authors of the *Sifre* understand Moses' special prophethood (but no one else's) as necessitating his distancing himself from domestic life. Within this Jewish–Christian polemic, however, Moses' celibacy becomes the exegetical foundation for constructing religious identities based on sexual behavior. Through his exegetical construct of holiness as celibacy, Aphrahat both polemicizes against Jewish marriage practices and establishes a hierarchy of spirituality for his Christian readers. Celibacy is holiness and therefore remains the ultimate manifestation of true Christian living. Aphrahat practices his celibacy with pride, for it marks him as holy, divinely blessed, and chosen. While the Rabbis never specifically counter Aphrahat's conclusions, Moses' sexual history, both procreative and celibate, allows them to construct their own sexual and religious identities. Never forgoing marriage, they struggle to balance their domestic lives and their spiritual pursuits, basing their choices on Moses' example.

Scholars such as Isaiah Gafni, Daniel Boyarin, Eliezer Diamond, and Michael Satlow have helped us differentiate Palestinian and Babylonian rabbinic marriage and sexual practices, as well as their attitudes toward sexuality in general.[34] I will discuss these patterns in greater detail in the next chapter. It appears that the Palestinian rabbis were more comfortable with the ideal of celibacy, or at least sexual restraint, even in marriage, owing to their Roman and eventually Christian milieu, which also advocated self-control in marriage. Babylonian rabbis, in contrast, seem both more accepting of their sexuality and more welcoming of its presence and place in human nature. Thus, my two divisions of the midrashim might map onto this same division—those that support Moses' decision stem from Palestinian circles, while those that do not are more Babylonian—even as this division does not exactly map onto the texts as we have them (chronologically nor geographically) in which the passages are found.

Moreover, when Aphrahat is added to the mix, he proves himself a maverick once again. He takes from both sides, as it were, and moves the combined traditions in a completely new direction. For while he supports and advocates celibacy, it is not because of an ambivalence toward or need to control the body or its sexual urges. Rather, the loss of his sexuality is a by-product of the divine call. If one wants to be in God's presence, sexuality must go, but he does not dwell on its loss or challenges. He is not uncomfortable with his sexuality, yet at the same time he has greater reason to give it up: holiness. Ironically, holiness through sexual renunciation is a goal Aphrahat shares with other Christian exegetes, as we saw in the last chapter. Yet, as I hope I have demonstrated, Aphrahat shares an exegetical tradition in support of that goal that is quite different from his other co-religionists in the Greco-Roman world.

The Question of Purity

The rabbinic texts—when compared to Aphrahat's—still prompt me to ask the question: How do the Rabbis understand QDS in the context of Exodus 19? Do they recognize the biblical Hebrew distinction of sexual renunciation, quantified by QDS as physical purity in this case? For all of these rabbinic midrashim on Exodus 19 could be read with the understanding that QDS signifies physical purity (rather than sanctity) in conformity with the biblical text. Hence, all Israelites need to do at Sinai is "ritually" purify themselves of semen-related defilements. Moses, for his part, simply recognizes that in order to be "on call" to God, he must be perpetually "ritually" pure—that is, refrain from sexual relations so as not to be impure by means of semen pollution when God needs him. This question would be easily resolved if only the biblical author had utilized THR instead of QDS in this passage. The *ARN A* backs up this notion of "ritual" purity when it asks why the Israelites need three days of sexual abstinence rather than one. This is how it answers its own question:

> What hedge did Moses make to God's words? *"And God said to Moses, go to the people and purify them today and tomorrow"* (Exod. 19:10). Moses the righteous did not want to speak to Israel in the manner that God spoke to him rather thus he said to them: *"Be prepared for the third day—do not approach a woman"* (Exod. 19:15). And Moses added for them a third day by himself because Moses said to himself—a man will go to his wife and [semen/seed] will come out of her on the third day and they will be impure and in a situation in which Israel would receive the words of Torah in impurity at Mt. Sinai—rather he added a third day in order that a man would not go to his wife and that semen would not come out of *her* on the third day and they would be pure and in a situation to receive the words of Torah in purity from Mt. Sinai.[35]

First, this midrash addresses a supposed discrepancy in the biblical text. God directs Moses to purify Israel "today and tomorrow," yet Moses instructs the Israelites to prepare themselves for three days through sexual abstinence. Why was the extra day necessary? Because Moses, the wise, knew that if the people of Israel restrained themselves for only two days there remained potential for physical defilement on the third day (through the reflux of semen from the woman), when Israel was to receive the Torah. And Moses did not want Israel to receive the Torah in "ritual" impurity (*tumah*).[36] Second, the *ARN* clearly understands QDS in the context of purity rather than sanctity. QDS easily translates as "purify" here and could have been replaced by THR. Sex per se is not at issue, but the "ritually" defiling nature of semen produced during sexual intercourse.[37] Hence the Rabbis do indeed preserve here the different meanings of QDS.[38]

Nevertheless, the upshot remains the same: Moses must abstain from sexual relations permanently—but on different theological grounds. The issue at hand is not holiness or sanctity, nor some embodiment or verification of God's chosenness (as Aphrahat seems to indicate), but simply "ritual" purity. Yet, I continue to wonder if the Rabbis ever confuse or merge the two notions of purity and sanctity. B. J. Schwartz goes so far as to suggest that the Rabbis consistently preserve this distinction.[39] I am not so convinced. Another text from the *Mekhilta* implies at the very least that the purity gained through *qedushah* is qualitatively different from that gained through *taharah*.

The *Mekhilta*, exegeting on verse 15 states:

And [Moses] spoke to the people—"*be ready*," etc. (Exod. 19:15). But we did not hear that God said "*separate/abstain from the woman*."[40] Rather "*be ready*" (v. 15) and "*and be ready*" (v. 11). [They] are a *gezera shavah* [an analogy]. "*Be ready*" (v. 15) here signifies "*separate/abstain from the woman*" therefore "*and be ready*" (v. 11) there [also] signifies "*separate/abstain from the woman*." Rabbi says from its own context it can be proven. [God said] "*go to the people and [qiddashtam] today and tomorrow*" (v. 10). If [the command] concerned bathing only they should have bathed on the fifth [day] and they would have been pure [*tahor*] by the evening sun. But why does the text say "*Go to the people and qiddashtam today and tomorrow?*" (v. 10). To indicate that God said to Moses, "*separate/abstain from the woman*."[41]

In this passage, the Rabbis make a similar association between the verses of Exodus 19 as Aphrahat does. The "be ready" of God's commandment in verse 11 is translated in verse 15 to "separate/abstain from the woman." The Rabbis imagine that God actually explains to Moses on the mountain that "to be ready" means "to abstain from the woman." The connection is made by a *gezera shavah*, an analogy between the two verses—a methodological move similar to Aphrahat's. If God intended "be ready" to mean "refrain from sexual intercourse," as stated by Moses in verse 15, then obviously God meant the same in verse 11. The first part of this text focuses on the commandment "be ready," which God apparently explains to Moses—yet we do not hear the explanation there in verse 11, but only when Moses speaks to the people in verse 15. Hence, Moses relays what God told him earlier only when he says "be prepared" means "do not go near a woman." Yet, Aphrahat makes a move not directly reflected in the rabbinic text. His exegetical analogy is between "*qiddashtam*" and "abstain from women," rather than "be ready" and "abstain from women." Thus, Aphrahat can conclude that sexual abstinence equals *qedushah/qaddishuta*. The issue of *qedushah* only appears by implication in the second part of this Tannaitic midrash. Rabbi (Judah the Prince) notes that the first analogy is not necessary, but can be understood from verse 10, which reads "*qiddashtam* today and tomorrow." If the Israelites had only needed to be "ritually" purified for the revelatory event, then bathing (after sexual intercourse) should have been enough, but since the text commands bathing *and* *qedushah*, the implication must be for total sexual abstinence, as "don't go near a woman" indicates. Hence, for Rabbi Judah, *qedushah* does indeed equal sexual renunciation (albeit only for that occasion and only for three days). While Rabbi Judah reaffirms the original conclusion—that being prepared means sexual abstinence—he does not depend on a backward analogy; the answer, he claims, is right there in the text. For if simple purity—that is, *taharah*—were at stake, he claims, bathing on the fifth day (that is, Thursday, the day before Friday, the day upon which the revelation occurred) should have been ample preparation for that kind of *taharah*. Rather, the text states "*qiddashtam* today *and* tomorrow." Purity is a one-day affair—you bathe, wash your clothes, wait until the evening, and you are pure of most defilements. This certainly applies to semen defilement. *Qedushah*, by contrast, takes two days of preparation—three according to Moses—and includes sexual renunciation. It connotes something different from *taharah* here, though it is not clear from the text how Rabbi Judah would translate it. At the very least, *qedushah* refers to a super or extreme form of *taharah*—the best translation would probably be "prepare them." That is, after all the focus of this particular midrash, how are the Israelites to prepare for God's revelation? How are they to fulfill the divine directive in verses 11 and 15, "be prepared"? The answer, apparently, is: by sexual abstinence. And, indeed, this is how the Targum Onkelos translates QDS in this context: it replaces it completely with ZMN— "prepare"—thereby avoiding the whole problem; in the Onkelos version, God only says "prepare," not "be QDS." Nevertheless, the coupling of *qedushah* with sexual renunciation and differentiating it from *taharah* leaves open my original question of whether the Rabbis here understand *qedushah* to refer to purity or sanctity or something else (super-purity?).

In the end, I do think the Rabbis here maintain a difference between purity/preparation and holiness. For them this whole series of midrashim center on the issue of avoidance of semen pollution as a way to prepare oneself to enter God's presence. Another text, I think proves my point. In the *Babylonian Talmud*, tractate *Berachot* 21b,[42] the Rabbis discuss whether or not a man need purify himself from semen pollution before entering the study house. The association is made between the Sinai event when the Israelites received God's Torah and these men who study that same Torah in their academies. While the Rabbis eventually abrogate the requirement for reasons of efficiency, the issue of purity at Sinai, and its ramifications for everyday life, remains the same. Interestingly enough, the Rabbis in this passage refer to place of the event as "Horeb," using Deuteronomy 4:9–10 as prooftext, and not to "Sinai" as in Exodus 19, perhaps avoiding the holiness question all together. Boyarin understands the abrogation of this law to highlight the difference between the Palestinian and Babylonian views on sexuality. The Palestinians required immersion because of their discomfort with sexuality, whereas the Babylonians, in their ease of comfort, did away with the requirement. Yet, he also sees this as a psychological distinction rather than an issue of purity because the question revolves around semen impurities specifically and not all impurities.[43] Yet, I think that is precisely the point. All of these texts focus on one impurity and one alone: semen pollution. The question is how to deal with this particular (and perhaps pernicious) form of impurity, because it is the one impurity mentioned as detrimental to preparation before Sinai. The biblical link between QDS and the absence of semen pollution remains problematic for the Rabbis, thus they allow transformation for Moses alone. For the same reason, early Christians focus on semen pollution and advocate celibacy, rather than on menstruation or other forms of ritual impurity.

After Sinai for the Rabbis the expectation is that one will always leave God's presence (or God's words) and go back to one's normal everyday activities. The audience with God is special and needs special care, but the act of purification for that audience in and of itself is not transformative. In entering and leaving God's presence, the Israelites have not changed themselves; they have not moved from a profane state to a holy state. One could obviously argue that, through the act of accepting the Torah at Sinai, the Israelites have transformed themselves, but that is not the focus of these passages. These passages assume that Israel is already chosen, already holy. The act of sexual restraint in and of itself did not change them; rather, the act of receiving the Torah did—which they had already agreed to do beforehand. In contrast, for Aphrahat, all sense of purity and preparation has been subsumed into the transformative act. They *do* change themselves from something profane into something holy by crossing that sexual renunciation line and, hence, cannot go back because they have become something else—chosen, special, holy, and thereby reside exclusively in God's presence. Thus, they constitute a new and distinct holy community, marked by their sexual renunciation—one that has been called into existence by and for the Holy One, God.

Yokes of the Covenant

Before we turn to a deeper look at the Rabbis' discourse on marriage, sexuality, and rabbinic notions of holy community in the next chapter, it might be helpful to explore how other images of holy community are shared by Aphrahat and the Rabbis. In the last chapter, I discussed Aphrahat's notion of covenant through the image of the yoke—namely, that he construes his "contract" with God through his celibacy. Aphrahat's sexual renunciation is the yoke that he wears that perpetually links him to God. All the yoke-bearers together make up the community of divinely chosen people. Similarly, the Rabbis understand their covenant with God through the image of a yoke. Moreover, both communities understand their yoke to be an embodiment of the divine commandments they fulfill that confer holiness upon themselves.

In one of his yoke passages, Aphrahat describes the yoke as the "yoke of the Messiah" rather than the "yoke of the holy ones." He writes, "Thus it is proper, my beloved, for he who carries the yoke of the Messiah, that he guard His yoke in purity."[44] In contrast to the light and easy "yoke of the Messiah" in Matthew 11:30 ("For my yoke is easy and my burden is light"), Aphrahat's yoke, derived from Lamentations 3:27, is a heavy burden. It is an active vocation, guarding oneself in celibate purity. And as Aphrahat notes, it is not necessarily an easy one, especially under pressure.[45] Nevertheless, without direct allusion to Matthew, Aphrahat's last invocation of the yoke connects it again to messianic discipleship. He writes, "These things are proper for the *iḥidaye*, those that accept the heavenly yoke and become disciples of the Messiah, for it is proper for the Messiah's disciples to emulate the Messiah their Lord."[46] The *iḥidaye*, the virgins and the holy ones, imitate Jesus in receiving his yoke, but in contrast to Matthew's depiction, it is not a trivial load. Aphrahat combines the two yoke images and creates a new metaphor more suitable to his needs. From Matthew he invokes the authority of discipleship, but from Lamentations he extracts the behavioral directive. And it is to Lamentations that he returns repeatedly in this demonstration. Given the ready-at-hand messianic yoke in Matthew and the etymological and theological connections between the *iḥidaya* and the *Iḥidaya*, it is surprising to find stronger scriptural analogies for Aphrahat's yoke reflected in the rabbinic literature.

A look at the rabbinic "yoke of Torah" and its derivation from Lamentations 3:27 will better illuminate Aphrahat's imaging. In the *Mishnah* the Rabbis claim,

> He who accepts upon himself the yoke of Torah ['ol torah], the yoke of government and the yoke of labor ['ol derekh eretz], are removed from

him; and he who throws off the yoke of Torah, upon him is placed
the yoke of government and the yoke of labor.[47]

The yoke of the Torah—the study of Torah and the fulfillment of God's
commandments—saves a person from labor and obligations to governing
bodies, such as taxes. Similar to Aphrahat, the *Mishnah* seems to state that the
person who occupies himself with spiritual matters (studying Torah and fulfilling the commandments) necessarily distances himself from commerce, labor,
and civic obligations. The dichotomy between Torah and labor does not, however, lessen the weight of either yoke.[48]

Alternatively, one can understand the freedom from the "yoke of labor"
and from the "yoke of government" not so much as a release from certain
obligations but rather as the relief from the worry about these obligations.
Providing for a family and paying taxes can be a psychological burden.
But the divine commandments, the yoke of Torah, imbue everyday life and
action with holiness and meaning, relieving the commandee of mundane
anxieties. The very behaviors that Aphrahat condemns as unholy (marriage
and commerce) the Rabbis perceive as invested with holiness when under-
taken as divine commandments. For instance, in reference to Numbers
15:39–40 ("That shall be your fringe; look at it and recall all the commandments of the Lord and observe them. Thus, you shall be reminded to observe
all My commandments and to be holy to your God"), the Rabbis ask if only
the commandment to wear fringes is sanctified or if all the commandments
are sanctified. They conclude that they are all represented in the fringes,
hence they are all sanctified.[49] Hence, even procreation and business activities can be holy. Obedience to the divine law remains key; one must make
oneself into a holy thing to God, which one does when one obeys all the
commandments. No matter how burdensome, the yoke of Torah imbues its
wearer with holiness.

A much later edited text, albeit with Amoraic Palestinian roots, declares
that the yoke of Lamentations 3:27 is not only the yoke of Torah but the yoke
of family and work as well: "'*It is good for a man to carry his yoke in his youth*'
(Lam. 3:27a): the yoke of Torah, the yoke of a wife and the yoke of labor."[50] This
stands in contrast to Aphrahat and the *Mishnah* in content, but not in construct; the yoke is here defined in behavior: a man must support a wife, have a
job, and study Torah. All these activities are God-directed responsibilities; all
of them are biblically instructed commandments. Similarly, I think, Aphrahat
perceived of his celibate vocation as a divinely commanded obligation. If one
is to undertake the single-minded life, one has to bear the yoke of celibacy.
Deftly combining these two images, the yoke of the Messiah and the yoke of

Lamentations, Aphrahat forges a yoke of divinely commanded celibacy, whose echo resonates in several rabbinic discussions. Again, the key is obedience.

There appears to be a tension for the Rabbis concerning the onus and necessities of everyday life. The Rabbis continue to be full participants in their communities, but they perceive of this participation as a distraction from their true vocation: the study of Torah. They are not able to free themselves from the yoke of society in order to fully enjoy the yoke of Torah in the same way that Aphrahat dedicates himself to his holy yoke—while at the same time they understand its attractiveness. For instance, another midrash claims:

> Why was it [the Torah] given in the desert? Because the desert is not sown and is not worked, such that he who receives the yoke of the Torah removes from himself the yoke of worldly cares; and since the desert does not yield taxes—the sons of Torah [bnei torah] are sons of freedom [bnei horin] in this world. Another thing: in the desert, who upholds the Torah? He who makes himself as a desert and separates himself from everything.[51]

This passage, concerning the giving of the Torah in the desert and the acceptance of its commandments, echoes Aphrahat's terminology: the rabbinic yoke-bearer is a "son of Torah," as Aphrahat's is a "son of the covenant." He flourishes when he imitates the desolation of the desert by removing himself from society, as Aphrahat's single-minded ones do. The ideal locale for dedicating oneself to God and Torah is the unpeopled desert.

Yet, there is also another way to understand this passage. The Rabbis' commitment to the yoke of Torah exempts them from the "yoke" of societal obligations, or perhaps the anxieties connected with those obligations. The very act of studying Torah, a book filled with civil legislation, relieves the student of the psychological burden of those same responsibilities by emphasizing the holiness in the act of studying itself. The desert provides no distractions, hence the Torah discipline should be all-consuming and frees one from other disturbances. While Aphrahat's ihidaye create a desert in the midst of the mundane through their celibate lifestyle, the Rabbis can imitate the desert only in their houses of study.[52]

Conclusions

Can one further transform one's status into something more holy? While we have seen in this chapter that the Rabbis still describe themselves as "chosen" by God, they, like Aphrahat, concern themselves with ways of either protecting or promoting that holy status—in some ways, becoming "even more holy." Their holy yoke of commandments binds them to God and marks them as holy. While God chose to offer them this yoke, they also actively chose to wear it and follow the commandments. Aphrahat defines his holy yoke through celibacy—that is, his divine commandment. Yet, he comes to the conclusion that celibacy is his divine commandment through the example of Moses at Sinai. For the Rabbis, Moses' position at Sinai is unique, not translatable to others.

Nonetheless, Moses at Sinai provokes yet another issue: how to interact with the ultimate source of their holiness, the Holy One, God. Moses at Sinai exemplifies for these exegetes the problems innate to humans participating in moments of divine closeness—for example, that sexuality, which seems so "natural" to humans, appears "unnatural," even anathema, in the divine realm. The wording in Exodus 19 strongly suggests that there is no room for sexual activity in God's "space." Aphrahat resolves this problem by advocating that all who wish to enter that space must renounce sexual activity. Following Moses, Aphrahat abandons the home front for a purely spiritual space. In so doing, he claims celibacy as part and parcel of his spiritual vocation, his yoke, his commandment. Here, we witness a merging of paradigms of purity and holiness through Aphrahat's transformative rhetoric. What once was protecting holy space (purity) becomes status-promoting (holiness).

The Rabbis, however, never make that move, as much as they might admire it from a distance. The Rabbis, who wish to uphold their holy yokes of Torah study and family life, can only admire Moses' ability to enter that holy space. They persist, as Aphrahat points out, to claim that the divine yoke is their obligation to the commandments, starting with procreation. Yet, as these midrashim demonstrate, the Rabbis remain perfectly aware of the tensions between their spiritual pursuits and their obligations in the domestic sphere, as well as biblically based potentials for a hermeneutic of holiness and sexual renunciation that exacerbate those tensions. In the next chapter, we will focus on how the Rabbis resolve their spiritual-practical holy dilemma by (re)constructing marriage and sexual relations within marriage through other hermeneutics of holiness. In so doing, they, too, create internal hierarchies of holiness built on sexual practice.

7

Sanctify Yourself

Rabbinic Notions of Holiness and Sexuality

I started this book with a question about Aphrahat and his notion of
holiness and celibacy, which I have traced backwards and forwards from
its biblical roots. His hermeneutic grows out of biblical notions of
holiness achieved (Be holy for I am holy) mapped onto other biblical
notions of purity necessary for divine audience (Moses at Sinai). In the
last two chapters, I have also demonstrated how close exegetically, and
yet so far apart theologically, Aphrahat appears to be to his rabbinic
neighbors. Thus, I think it behooves us to take a closer look at other
rabbinic hermeneutics of holiness and sexuality that diverge from these
initial paradigms and comparisons, for sexuality remains a live issue for
those who refuse to follow in Aphrahat's footsteps. How do the Rabbis
conceive of their holiness? Is it ascribed? Achieved? How do they resolve
the issue of no sex in God's space? I would like to suggest here that,
while some rabbis adhere to an ascribed holiness construct, this dichotomy between sexuality and holiness provokes another hermeneutic
of holiness achieved through sexuality or sexual practices, particularly in
marriage, for other segments of the rabbinic population.

Ascribed Holiness

Notions of ascribed holiness can be found widely in the midrashic
literature, but less so in the halakhic.[1] While the Rabbis never
completely forgo the notion of ascribed holiness, that holiness is not

usually connected to sexual practices. The Rabbis discuss Israel's ascribed holiness in many contexts and support the notion with various biblical texts. Jeremiah 2:3 ("Israel is Holy to God") arises often, but equally frequently the Rabbis defer to the levitical statements that declare Israel to "be holy."[2] While I argue in chapter 1 that, in the biblical context, the language of "make yourselves holy for I am holy" (Lev. 11:44–45, 20:8) and "you shall be holy" (Lev. 19:2) embodies the notion of achieving holiness through certain actions (and/or refraining from others), the Rabbis often understand this call to holiness as a statement of fact: that Israel is already holy—by divine decree.[3] At times, we even witness a concern for a contested "Holy Israel," a tacit acknowledgment, perhaps, that others lay claim to that very title. In these cases, these texts strongly reaffirm their claim to Holy Israel, but not usually in connection to sexual practices in any way.

Moreover, rabbinic notions of holy community prove more flexible than those we saw in Ezra and Jubilees. While the Tannaitic rabbis maintain a notion of Israel as a holy community—Israelites are holy, non-Israelites are not—they allow a more porous border: a nonholy Israelite may convert and become a holy Israelite, something the Jubilean author found abhorrent and inherently impossible. Furthermore, it is possible for a person to be conceived in unholiness (while the mother is yet a Gentile) but born in holiness (after the mother has converted). This person (as with his mother) is considered by the Rabbis not to be fully equal to a native-born Israelite, particularly in matters of marriage and inheritance laws. Nevertheless, their children, conceived and born in holiness, are fully equal to native-born Israelites.[4] Michael Satlow has argued that Palestinian rabbinic society remained remarkably endogamous; hence, they would be particularly concerned with the ways in which an outsider might be incorporated into their community.[5] Yet, in contradistinction to Ezra and Jubilees, these rabbis do allow some outsiders in.

Holiness Protected

The Rabbis continue to be concerned with issues of unholy behavior. They often define their holy behavior as a marker of holy community against the unholy behavior of others that mark them as "other." Hence, they show interest particularly in the mechanisms that police those borders—and even tighten the borders somewhat. It is not surprising, then, that they also construct those borders through the "unholy" behaviors of Leviticus: improper sexual partnering. The Rabbis actually tighten those restrictions by expanding the laws of consanguineous relations. Thus, they continue the work of differentiating "us" from "them," while also creating stronger yet, ironically, more porous borders. For while creating more restrictions on marriage partners for native-born Israelites, they also allow the most "other," the Gentiles, to transform themselves and become Israel by creating new categories and hierarchies. These *sheniyot*, or supplementary rabbinic regulations in the area of consanguineous relations, will come into play again in my discussion of holiness achieved, below.

Nevertheless, for purposes of this discussion, I focus on rabbinic constructs of holy achievement—status gained particularly through certain sexual practices. As we shall see, the discussion begins with a model of priestly hierarchy and, hence, concerns itself with proper marriage partners; but this hierarchy is eventually converted to one of supporting rabbinic authority, and finally to personal rabbinic achievement in the realm of marriage and sexuality. The following rabbinic texts fully transform the notion of holy protection through restricted sexual partnering into a new paradigm of holy achievement through restricted sexual practices with legitimate sexual partners (i.e., wives). Rather than concern themselves only with whom they marry, they formulate ways to act sexually with their wives that conform to their emerging notions of holy achievement. That is to say, some rabbis see restrictions on their sexual practices as a means to improve their holy status.

Holiness Achieved

Holiness by achievement differs from ascribed holiness in that it does not always begin and end with the notion that Israel's holiness is inherent. Rather, it builds on the notion that Israel's holiness is dynamic and can fluctuate with Israel's behavior. Often, it takes the form of building on an already inherent Israelite holiness by creating a new level of holiness for those who are able. Hence, most of these rabbinic texts refer not to Israel as a whole but to individual Israelites (often rabbis) who "upgrade" their holiness through certain behaviors. So, in one sense, underlying much of this discourse is the notion that all Israel is inherently holy, but some Israelites (again, mostly rabbis) can elevate or enhance their individual level of holiness. Achieved holiness here refers, then, to the idea that a higher degree of holiness can be acquired through prescribed practice. In stark contrast to Qumran, the Rabbis create an inclusive (for Israelites) hierarchy of holiness rather than an exclusive "holy club" (only those Israelites who follow Qumran interpretation are admitted). In the end, the rabbinic construct more profoundly resembles early Christian hierarchies than Second Temple precedents because it allows for more fluid boundaries both within and outside the rabbinic community. Moreover, in distinction from the biblical priests, upon whose hierarchy the Rabbis build, the Rabbis ground their authority (and hence their placement within the hierarchy) in their achievements as interpreters of Scripture, rather than as divinely appointed ritual experts.

Many of the achievement-oriented rabbinic statements on holiness look to ways in which one can create or enhance one's holiness, as well as protect it. These texts exhibit a merger of these two notions whereby protection often doubles as enhancement. Moreover, more often than not, the Rabbis focus on sexuality as *the* means to that holy end. As we will see, sexual restraint—often in legitimate sexual unions—comes to the fore as the primary rabbinic way to "be holy." Namely, the Rabbis attempt to create a category of holiness that is achieved through rabbinically advised, or some-times even ordained, supererogatory (and usually ascetic) behaviors. That is to say that the Rabbis, while allowing that all Israel is holy already, suggest a means for some of Israel (mainly the Rabbis themselves) to achieve a higher degree of holiness. This goal is reached by following, on the one hand, cer-tain rabbinic regulations that go beyond the letter of the biblical law by refraining from activities (sex, eating, or further limited eligible marriage partners) that are otherwise biblically permitted or pursuing individualized ascetic behavior beyond what has been regulated even by the Rabbis. This latter category includes behavior that is often considered extreme by some rabbis and certainly not encouraged by or for everyone. All the while, the Rabbis struggle with their authority and ability (willingness?) to legislate ascetic behavior. In the end, they attempt to make obedience to rabbinic law more holy (or at least better protection) than obedience to biblical law alone, particularly in the area of sexual relations. Finally, it seems, rather than leg-islate for all Israel, they leave most holiness in the realm of sexual practice as a spiritual ideal to aspire to.

Holy Achievement through Ascetic Practice

Eliezer Diamond has argued that, contrary to popular belief, the early Rabbis widely practiced asceticism. A religious community that defines its practices in terms of difference from other communities' practices necessarily thinks in an ascetic/separatist mode. That is to say, by refraining from certain practices (particularly the dietary and sexual practices of the Canaanites) from the out-set, biblical Israelite religion provides a framework for rabbinic asceticism. Diamond, following Steven Fraade, defines asceticism as the voluntary with-drawal from permitted activities, particularly when that abstention distin-guishes the practitioner from the surrounding people(s).[6] That the Rabbis did not promote celibacy as a universal ideal, as many Christians did, does not mean they did not value it from a distance and/or follow other ascetic practices. Hence, asceticism is as natural and formative to Judaism as it was for other ancient religions.

Diamond focuses the lion's share of his work on the rabbinic practice of fasting, which he claims stems both from Nazirite food abstinence (wine) and priestly fasting practices (ma'amadot).[7] The Naziriteship was a biblically ordained means for allowing a lay person a temporary and quasi priest-like status. Diamond argues that the biblical *nazir*, labeled "holy to God," in reality was more like a sacrificial offering than an offerant. His hair becomes a substitute for himself in his offering to God. The Rabbis shift the locus of Naziriteship from the hair of the *nazir* (which could not be sacrificed without the Temple, or shrine) to the food restrictions. A *nazir* was forbidden all grape products, but especially wine. The Rabbis innovate this notion and declare:

> [One who fasts] is called holy, as Scripture states [concerning the Nazirite], "*He shall remain consecrated, the hair of his head being left to grow untrimmed*" (Num. 6:5). And if this one [i.e., the Nazirite], who denied himself only one thing [i.e., wine and other grape products], is called holy, how much more so one who denies himself everything.[8]

Through fasting, the Rabbis, too, perceive themselves as offering a part of themselves to God, as the *nazir* offered his hair.[9] Diamond argues here that fasting becomes the quintessential rabbinic ascetic practice because of the way it evolved into an essential practice for spiritual enlightenment from its original instrumental position. The model of the *nazir* is only one part of this transformation.

I focus here on sexual practices that also exemplify the rabbinic notion of asceticism, defined as *qedushah* achieved. The rabbinic literature evinces abundant cases where certain sexual practices, particularly ones of restraint, are equated with *qedushah*. While the Rabbis can base their fasting ethic in part on Nazirite food-abstention practices, the Nazirites were never restricted in their sexual practices. Moreover, as far as I can tell, this one passage in *Babylonian Talmud Ta'anit* is the only one that calls fasting *qadosh*. What interests me in these discussions is the intersection of the holy and the ascetic. While fasting clearly was practiced by the Rabbis, it is not rhetoricized within a hermeneutic of holiness in the same way that sexuality is. Our modern understanding of asceticism brings fasting and sexual restraint into one category; our ancient authors may not have constructed them in the same way. Fasting substitutes for the sacrifices of the *nazir* and the *ma'amadot* practices of the priests, but so does eating in ritual purity at the rabbinic dinner table, where the table becomes the altar.[10] In contrast, the sexual practices discussed here are consistently couched within a hermeneutic of holiness.[11] What interests me here is not so much whether or not the Rabbis were sexually ascetic but when and where they called their ascetic practices "holy." Moreover, I would be interested in places where other sexual practices are called holy, but they are not as apparent as the ascetic ones in the rabbinic texts. While observance of all the *mitzvot* imbue holiness to Israel, there remains a particular association between *qedushah* and restricted sexual practices, and that is the focus of this chapter.

Rabbinic *qedushah,* as ascetic behavior, stems from biblical notions of separation, but it focuses less explicitly on physical dedication to God (the priests are *qadosh* because they are separated out for God's service). Taking their clue from the holiness code of Leviticus, some rabbis conclude that any behavior that separates one from others is what constitutes holiness. In Leviticus, God calls on the people not to behave like the Canaanites, who came before them— and if they obey, God will dedicate/consecrate them as a people to God (or perhaps their very act of obedience will thereby consecrate themselves, as their distinguishing behaviors automatically separate them from others). So, too, the Rabbis claim that behaviors that distinguish rabbinic Jews from others (particularly Gentiles) mark them as holy. Sexual behavior becomes key to this notion of separation and distinguishing.

Diamond demonstrates that some rabbis perceive voluntary abstinence from activities otherwise permitted as a means to this spiritual elevation that they designate as *qedushah*. Distinguishing their practices from the practices of others is what defines *qedushah* for them. When all of Israel distinguishes itself from others, all of Israel is holy. When certain rabbinic figures distinguish themselves from other Jews, they are even more holy. Fasting and sexual abstinence come to the fore as ascetic practices that best exemplify voluntary withdrawal from things permitted and thereby constitute rabbinic *qedushah*.[12] Diamond further notes that those rabbis who are called holy by their disciples are so labeled because of their ascetic behaviors. In most cases, these behaviors are sexual, but in at least one it involves food. While Diamond argues that the rabbinic paradigm of fasting as ascetic and holy behavior is modeled primarily on the example of the biblical *nazir* (who separates himself from all of Israel by his ascetic behavior), I further argue that the rabbinic practice of sexual restraint in particular, and the general notion of withdrawal as holy behavior, is modeled on the marriage restrictions applied to the priesthood.[13] Furthermore, I suggest that the rabbinic notion of sexual practice as *qedushah* is further influenced by the Moses at Sinai tradition, discussed in the previous chapter, in which Israel's three days of celibacy and Moses' permanent sexual renunciation stand as exemplars of spiritual and physical purity, as well as devotion to God. While the

Rabbis never go so far as to declare celibacy a laudable goal, I think the idea that active sexuality somehow distracts from or is even anathema to devotion to God/spiritual pursuits ultimately influences their hermeneutics of holiness and sexuality within marriage. Although Exodus 19 is never cited in these cases, I think it lurks in the background, influencing how they understand holy separation, dedication, and the spiritual elements of their day-to-day lives.

In his book *Borderlines*, Daniel Boyarin suggests that both Jews and Christians constructed heresiologies in order to delineate religious borders and define religious community in the second to fourth centuries CE. In so doing, they determined who was "in" and who was "out." Boyarin further argues that the Rabbis, borrowing the idea of heresiology from their Christian counterparts, attempted to establish themselves as the arbiters of things "Jewish." Thus, for the earlier Rabbis (mostly Tannaitic and Palestinian), one could differentiate between "real" Jews (i.e., rabbinic Jews) and others who might also consider themselves Jewish or descendants of ancient Israel through differences in practice and faith. The later, Babylonian rabbis felt less compelled to distinguish among ethnic Jews in this manner.[14] The rabbinic hermeneutics of holiness I discuss here fit into these patterns of differentiation. On the one hand, the *Mishnah* and the *Palestinian Talmud* do try to delineate those among Israel who are truly holy (and "in") and those who are not. Along the way, they create internal hierarchies of holiness even within the "in" group. The *Babylonian Talmud*, on the other hand, builds on these internal hierarchies and perfects them, all the while allowing all Israelites by birth to remain in the holy group. In this way, these hermeneutics of holiness provide a practical application of Boyarin's theory of heresiology—namely, an early attempt to work within the dichotomy of "orthodoxy" and "heresy," and an eventual rejection of that construct. I will first discuss rabbinic manipulations of *qedushah* that attempt to support their role as communal leaders and then turn to rabbinic notions of asceticism as an alternative hermeneutic of holiness.

Constructing Rabbinic Authority and Holiness

We can follow the essential rabbinic logic by focusing on the apparent inherent hierarchy of holiness among Israelites as it is displayed in the discussions surrounding levirate marriage in the *Mishnah* and how it is transformed by the latter talmudic discussions. The underlying assumption in *Mishnah Yevamot* is that every Israelite male is born into and remains in a specific level of holiness, and this level of holiness will in the end determine whether a man must consummate a levirate marriage or not. Israelites are holy, priests are holier, and high priests are holiest. Yet the talmudic commentary on these mishnaic passages transform this hierarchy into a basis for establishing and maintaining rabbinic authority through increasingly restrictive rabbinic legislation of secondary forbidden sexual relations (*sheniyot*). Rather than maintaining the traditional hierarchy, the Rabbis create a system in which the degree of one's holiness is determined by whether one follows the rabbinic legislation. For instance, in *Mishnah Yevamot* 2:3–4, we see a categorization of Israelites according to their level of holiness.

Mishnah 2:4 states:

> *Issur mitzvah* [a prohibition on account of a divine commandment]: [is the same as] the *sheniyot* [secondarily derived prohibitions] made by the scribes. *Issur qedushah* [a prohibition due to one's sanctity]: [refers to the following prohibitions]: (1) a widow [is forbidden] to a high priest (Lev. 21:14); (2) a divorcée, or a woman who has executed the rite of *halitzah* [is forbidden] to an ordinary priest (Lev. 21:7); (3) a *mamzeret*, [or] a *netinah* to an Israelite; (4) a daughter of an Israelite to a *netin* or to a *mamzer*.[15]

In this mishnah, the Rabbis expand on their notion of *mitzvah*. For one might assume that a *mitzvah* is that which God commands and is recorded in the Torah. Yet, this mishnah claims that the category of *mitzvah* actually applies to the secondarily derived commandments (or prohibitions, in this case) made by the Rabbis themselves (the scribes).[16] This mishnah, then, differentiates between prohibitions established by the Rabbis/scribes (*sheniyot;* which they equate with *issur mitzvah*) concerning consanguineous relations for all Israel (see below) and prohibitions that apply according to the "holiness" of the levir (the brother-in-law). While these restrictions also follow the biblical restrictions for priests (who are holy among Israel), the Rabbis expand the category "holy of Israel" to include the lay Israelites and add two new categories: *netinim* and *mamzerim*.[17]

The rulings (*sheniyot*) of the scribes encompass the ordinances established by the postbiblical scribes (i.e., the Rabbis[18])—namely, consanguineous relationships that are not included in the biblical laws. For instance, Leviticus forbids a man from conducting sexual relations with his father's wife or sister, but the scribes prohibit a man from conducting sexual relations even with his father's mother or grandmother.[19] "By virtue of holiness" relates to the degree of holiness of the individual Israelite male. If he is a high priest, he cannot contract a levirate marriage with his sister-in-law under any circumstances because she, as a widow, is among the forbidden marriage partners for him (Lev. 21:14). If the brother-in-law is a common priest, he is forbidden to marry a divorcée or a woman who has previously performed *halitzah* (Lev. 21:7).[20] Lay Israelites, who are in a lesser status of holiness, have their own restrictions; they may not marry a *mamzeret* or a *netinah*.

What we discern, then, in this halakhic discussion is not only an urge to further regulate marriage partners in order to avoid the forbidden marriage partners but also a presumptive hierarchy of holiness. Every Israelite (male) fits somewhere along the continuum of "holy" to "very holy." Marriage partners are then influenced by one's place on that continuum. While the biblical books attest to the limitations placed on the priests because of their holiness (they cannot marry harlots or divorcées, and additionally the high priest cannot marry widows), the levitical texts at least say nothing about the lay Israelite (beyond the consanguineous relationships). Hence, the restrictions concerning *mamzerim* and *netinim* must be found elsewhere. *Mamzerim* (children of illicit unions) are forbidden to marry legitimate Israelites up until the tenth generation, according to Deuteronomy 23:2. The idea that the *netinim*—presumed descendants of the Gibeonites—are similarly excluded seems to be extra-biblical, if not rabbinic, in origin.[21] Whatever their origins, the *Mishnah* brings these restrictions on Israelite marriage as a parallel category to the restrictions on the priests. Nonetheless, all this mishnaic passage establishes is that there is a hierarchy and that certain restrictions apply due to one's place in the hierarchy. Each set of restrictions is constructed to protect the ascribed holiness of the men at each level. Yet, with this new level of legislation, with all its added restrictions, the question arises: what happens to the person who does not comply? Does one descend the ladder of holiness (and perhaps out the back door)? It is here, possibly, that we see Boyarin's theory at work: rabbinic attempts at internal heresiology. All those who do not comply with rabbinic law lose their holy status and hence are considered "out." Michael Satlow further suggests that for the Tannaitic rabbis in particular, incest and other improper marriage partnering were perceived as particularly endemic to the Gentiles. Thus, those Israelites who behaved more like the Gentiles in their marriage practices, as well as against rabbinic legislation, necessarily made themselves into Gentiles and were no longer of the holy community.[22] The *Palestinian Talmud's* commentary on this mishnah makes this transformation more explicit. Here, we see that holiness refers not to one's level of holiness on the priestly scale but whether or not one follows rabbinic law.

The *Palestinian Talmud*, in commenting on this mishnaic passage, adds the following additional remarks:

> *Issur mitzvah* refers to forbidden sexual relations ruled by the scribes.
> For it is a religious duty enjoined by the Torah to obey the teachings of
> the scribes. And *issur qedushah* refers to [the biblically ordained

forbidden unions]: a widow to a high priest, a divorcée or a woman who has performed *halitzah* to an ordinary priest: [this is as Scripture states:] "*These are the commandments [which the Lord commanded Moses for the people of Israel on Mount Sinai]*" (Lev. 27:34), all commandments are as one commandment, and "*You shall consecrate him for he offers the bread of your God*" (Lev. 21:8).

And there are those who reverse [the categories such that]: the [prohibition of the] widow to a high priest, [and that of] the divorcée and the woman who has performed *halitzah* to an ordinary priest [are *issur mitzvah*], as Scripture states: "*These are the commandments*" (Lev. 27:34), and all commandments are as one commandment.

And *issur qedushah* [refers to] secondarily derived forbidden relations from the words of scribes. Said R. Judah b. Pazzi: "And why has Scripture juxtaposed the passage dealing with the forbidden consanguineous relationships (Lev. 18) to the passage on sanctification (Lev. 19)? It is to teach you that whoever separates himself from forbidden sexual relations is called holy. For so does the Shunamit woman say to her husband: '*Behold now, I know that this man of God is holy*'" (2 Kings 4:9).

Said R. Yonah, "[this means that] he [Elisha] is holy, but his disciple [Gehazi] is not holy." R. Abin said: "because he never looked at her." And the Rabbis say: "for he never saw a drop of semen in his life." The maid of R. Samuel b. R. Isaac said: "All my days I have never seen any unseemly thing [i.e., semen] on my master's bed-clothes."[23]

The Palestinian Amoraic commentators start with a question: Does *issur mitzvah* refer to ordinances/decrees legislated by the scribes/Rabbis? The answer provided is that: "It is a religious duty enjoined by the Torah to obey the teachings of the scribes."[24] In other words, the biblical law provides means for later scribal or rabbinic rulings to be considered under the category of *mitzvah*. However, our text does not bring a prooftext for this dictum here. The Amoraic commentators move on to explain *issur qedushah* (a prohibition on account of sanctity). Here, they bring the levitical text (21:8), which establishes that an ordinary priest cannot marry a divorcée or a woman "defiled." The rationale provided by the biblical text for these restrictions is that the priests are consecrated to God in order to offer the divine sacrifices to God. The priestly designation as servants of God separates them from the ordinary Israelites and moves them into the category of holy because they belong to God. Their marital restrictions are an outgrowth of this status.

How these particular women (divorcées, etc.) would affect or damage their holy status is not made clear.[25] Nevertheless, the *issur qedushah* is explained by reference to the priests' special restrictions owing to their holy status. But in so doing the priests are bumped up the holiness ladder. If all Israel is holy—and hence has certain marriage restrictions—then the priests must be more holy. Hence, levirate marriage is determined by the level of *qedushah* possessed by the levir. Protection of ascribed holiness continues to operate as the determining factor here, allowing as well for the possibility of profanation and exclusion.

Yet this pericope goes on to explain that some rabbis reverse the categories and alter their meanings. These rabbis place the restrictions on the priests into the category of *issur mitzvah* rather than *issur qedushah*, rationalizing this move with reference to Leviticus 27:34: "These are the commandments [which the Lord commanded Moses for the people of Israel on Mount Sinai.]" All of these restrictions on the priests fall into the larger category of *mitzvot* that God gave to Israel at Sinai and that appear specifically in Leviticus. The commandment to obey God (which the Israelites accepted upon themselves at Sinai) is one meta-*mitzvah*, which encompasses all of the minutiae of the *mitzvot*, including those of the priests. *Issur qedushah*, therefore, refers to the prohibitions of the scribes/Rabbis. That is to say, the sanctity in question is not with reference to an established and immovable hierarchy, but to a holiness protected (or even enhanced) when Rabbis and their followers fulfill the *mitzvot* ordained by the Rabbis. In this case, observing the secondary degrees of consanguineous marriages as refined by the Rabbis constitutes holiness for the individual and community. In other words, just following the biblical laws is not enough to protect (and certainly not to enhance) one's holiness; one must also follow rabbinic law. In this way, the Rabbis attempt to solidify their authority. One cannot protect or improve one's ascribed holiness without rabbinic leadership. Moreover, this text assumes that he who does not follow the rabbinic interpretation of the law is not only "lesser" but also "other." He simply falls off of the holiness charts. Thus, on the one hand, the Rabbis establish a more general principle: one achieves holiness through full compliance with rabbinic law; yet on the other, this principle grows out of interpretive moves concerning marriage/sexual practices, which, I think, is not insignificant.

The *talmudic* passage continues, however, with a slightly different hermeneutic of holiness:

Said R. Judah b. Pazzi: "And why has Scripture juxtaposed the passage dealing with the forbidden consanguineous relationships

(Lev. 18) to the passage on sanctification (Lev. 19)? It is to teach you that whoever separates himself from forbidden sexual relations is called holy."

Here, the Rabbis, in the name of R. Judah b. Pazzi, declare that whoever keeps himself far from forbidden marriages (*poresh min ha-'ariyot*) is called holy. The Rabbis see more than just a simple correlation of chapters and themes—forbidden marriages (Lev. 18 and 20) and holiness (Lev. 19). It is not one who does not participate in forbidden marriages who is called holy but, rather, one who separates oneself (*poresh*) from all possibilities of forbidden marriages—namely, one who follows the secondary degrees of forbidden relations as determined by the Rabbis. This notion is supported by a midrash on the prophet Elisha:

> For so does the Shunamit say to her husband: *"Behold now, I perceive that this man of God is holy"* (2 Kings 4:9). Said R. Yonah: "He [Elisha] is holy, but his disciple [Gehazi] is not holy." R. Abin said: "It is because he never looked at her." And the Rabbis say: "For he never saw a drop of semen in his life."

In the biblical passage, this Shunamit woman proclaims Elisha to be *"ish elohim, qadosh hu"*—that is, "a holy man of God" or, rather, "a man of God who is holy." In this talmudic passage, the Rabbis wonder how it is that this Shunamit woman knows that Elisha is a holy man. What outward signs of holiness does he manifest? One rabbi suggests that she was merely distinguishing him from his disciple; hence, his *qedushah* is only in reference to his relative superiority. Another suggests that it was because he never looked at her. The Rabbis conclude that the Shunamit never found semen on his sheets when she came to change his bed in the morning. In other words, the Rabbis perceive Elisha as taking measures to protect himself from a forbidden relationship (namely, an adulterous one with the married Shunamit who provides him with a room). Either he avoids looking at her so that he will not be attracted to her or he goes so far as to restrain himself from fantasizing about her even when alone in his bed at night. Although Elisha's ascetic behavior is individualized here, the Rabbis bring it up as a model of one whose sexual restraint is called holy. It stands as an exemplary parallel to the rabbinically ordained secondary degrees of consanguineous relations discussed above. Both are modes of holy protection. Most important, Elisha demonstrates behavior that goes beyond the biblical law, which only states that he must not be involved in adulterous relations. It does not state how far he must go to protect himself. The Rabbis take on that challenge and claim their legislation as the only means toward true holiness protection/enhancement. But the last line of this text points in another direction, back to Moses at Sinai—namely, that Elisha never sullied himself with semen pollution. Like Moses, Elisha is presented as perpetually "ritually" pure and thus is able to stand in God's presence (as a prophet) or to be "like" God, as a holy man.

Finally, the Rabbis conclude this midrash on Elisha with a comparison to one of their own: "The maid of R. Samuel son of R. Isaac said: 'All my days I have never seen any unseemly thing [i.e., semen] on my master's bed-clothes.'" Elisha's extreme "ritual" purity and holiness is projected forward onto R. Samuel b. R. Isaac and is seemingly a commendable thing for this rabbi.[26] More significantly, this addendum suggests that the Rabbis' self-regulation is translated into holiness for themselves as well. Diamond points out that several other rabbis are also called holy by their disciples. He suggests that they gain that title because of their various ascetic practices—namely, their practice of withdrawing from what is permitted to them. Hence, the very act of separation or withdrawal—no matter the content of the act itself (fasting, sexual restraint, etc.)—is called "holy" because it resembles the Nazirites' practices. Diamond points out that the Rabbis make this very connection:

> The Nazir vowed in a manner of withdrawal [perishut] and purity [taharah] therefore he is called holy [qadosh]. A Nazir forswears grapes and grape products, thereby withdrawing from the permitted, and, by forbidding himself to come into contact with the dead, he maintains a level of ritual purity normally required only of the priests. The very act of accepting such restrictions, says the sages, marks him as holy-to-God.[27]

Likewise, Elisha and R. Samuel are described as voluntarily withdrawing from what is permitted to them—sexual activity. And like the nazir, they are both perush (separated/withdrawn) and tahor ("ritually" pure), but in this case through one and the same action: sexual abstinence. Though not stated explicitly in any of these cases, I think it is implied that Elisha, as a prophet, and these rabbis, as men of God in their own right, practice holiness—like Moses—because of their divine calling. Furthermore, their holiness has something to do with their celibacy (defined as avoidance of semen pollution). In this way, qedushah (holiness) and taharah ("ritual" purity) can be fused into one broader notion of holiness and becomes an ideal of spiritual achievement among the Rabbis. Finally, I suggest, that because qedushah (whether as purity or holiness) is linked both to sexual restraint and to Moses at Sinai, it is not insignificant to the Rabbis. As Moses is both the direct recipient of God's law (both written and oral according to rabbinic tradition) and Moshe Rabbeinu, "our teacher," the Rabbis draw connections between Moses' celibacy on Sinai, as part and parcel of his job as leader and prophet, and the example (self-restraint) that he set for his followers and disciples, the Rabbis, even when applied to active sexuality in marriage. And while they never go the Aphrahatic route of total sexual renunciation, I do not doubt that that primary equation of *qedushah* (sexual restraint) and Moses filters through and influences these rabbinic hermeneutics of holiness that I have been discussing here. If the Rabbis make a commandment out of procreation, Aphrahat attempts to do the same with celibacy. These (primarily Palestinian) rabbis, nonetheless, remain stuck between the two extremes and attempt to reach for one glory (celibacy) while maintaining the other (procreation).[28]

Nonetheless, the Babylonian context proves to be different. The Babylonian talmudic discussion of the original mishnah in *Yevamot* attempts to go yet another step further than the *Palestinian Talmud* and the midrash to solidify the Rabbis' sense of authority. However, that discussion is derailed by dissenting voices in the *Babylonian Talmud*, and in so doing the community of Holy Israel is "restored" to its ethnic whole. As Boyarin argues, the Babylonian rabbis appear queasy about excluding any native-born Israelite from what they construct as "Jewish," and hence they also back away from legislating ascetic behavior for all Israel, and they particularly distance themselves from a direct connection between ascetic behavior and holiness. The *Babylonian Talmud* expounds:

MISHNAH: *Issur mitzvah* [refers to the] secondarily derived prohibitions.
TALMUD: Why are these called, *issur mitzvah*? Abaye replied:
"Because it is a commandment to obey the words of the Sages."
Issur qedushah [refers to] a widow to a high priest; a divorced
woman, or one who had performed *ḥalitzah*, to a common priest.
Why are these called *issur qedushah*? Because it is written in the
Scriptures, "*They shall be holy onto their God*" (Lev. 21:6). It was
taught: R. Judah reverses the order: *Issur mitzvah* [refers to following the biblically prohibited categories:] a widow to a high priest;
a divorced woman or one that had performed *ḥalitzah*, to a common
priest. And why are these called *issur mitzvah*? Because it is written
in the Scriptures, "*These are the commandments*" (Lev. 27:34). *Issur
qedushah* [refers to] the secondarily derived prohibitions from the
words of the scribes. And why are these called *issur qedushah*? Abaye
replied: "Because whosoever upholds the words of the Rabbis is
called holy". Said Rava to him: "Then anyone who does not uphold
the words of the Rabbis is not called holy? He should neither be
called holy nor evil." Rather, said Rava: "Sanctify yourself by that
which is permitted to you."[29]

The Babylonian discussion of *Mishnah Yevamot* 2:3–4 follows the basic argument presented in the *Palestinian Talmud*, including the reversal of the categories "holy" and "commandments." Here, the text claims that R. Judah reverses the categories, but the argumentation is the same: all the restrictions on the priests can be filed under "These are the commandments" (Lev. 27:34), which makes them restrictions by commandment/*mitzvot*, not by holiness. "Prohibited by virtue of holiness," then, refers to the secondary degrees of consanguineous relationships established by the sages (Rabbis). The Babylonian text, however, gives a different rationale for this claim. Here, Abaye posits that, "whosoever acts in accordance with the rulings of the Rabbis is called a holy man." He does not refer back to Elisha and the Shunamit. This statement takes the *Palestinian Talmud's* earlier position ("it is a religious duty enjoined by the Torah to obey the teachings of the scribes") one step further. Not only is it a religious obligation, but also the very act imbues in the actor a new level of holiness. The *Babylonian Talmud* states explicitly what the *Palestinian Talmud* makes only implicit—that real holiness comes from rabbinic law, not biblical law.

Nevertheless, this pericope ends with an alternative hermeneutic suggested. Rava counters Abaye by arguing that the Israelite who does not follow rabbinic law, though not called holy, is not called evil, either (note that he does not suggest that if not holy, they might be impure; rather, he uses a less laden term "evil"). This sort of supererogatory holiness is gained or not according to one's ability and inclination, and it has nothing to do with one's ascribed holiness. Thus, he concludes: "Sanctify yourself by that which is permitted to you." Hence, Rava allows for a different category to carry the day: individual holy achievement. A hierarchy of holiness among Israelites—as long as everyone is included—is not so bad (and matches the priestly hierarchy in any case). Through personal choices of supererogatory behavior, the individual Israelite ascends to a higher level of holiness, but nobody loses by not following through. Thus, the Babylonian rabbis, despite Abaye, prove themselves more inclusive of all Israelites. Boyarin argues that the Palestinian heresiological advances do not carry over into Babylonia. There, the Rabbis hesitate to exclude any ethnically born Jew, however poorly he behaves. Following Boyarin, I suggest that this passage reflects a willingness to include all Israelites by shifting the hierarchy to favor the behavior of the Rabbis without having to "other" anyone out of his diasporic Jewish community.[30] Nonetheless, Satlow suggests that, rather than associating bad sexual behavior only with Gentiles, the Babylonian rabbis imply that sectarian Jews *do* similarly exhibit bad behavior. The bad behavior of the sectarians (incest, adultery, etc) reflects a lack of self-control. The Rabbis, if they can prove their own excellence in self-control, evince their right to exegetical authority and communal power over and above any competition.[31]

Yet, it is Rava's notion of sanctifying oneself by withdrawing/separating from what is permitted that most likely influences the ascetic practices we will turn to now. In their "birthplace," these ascetic practices remain firmly attached to an ideal of rabbinic fence building, which is the rabbinic means to creating authority for themselves—at least in the area of suitable sexual partners. Finally, this mode of supererogatory behavior takes shape more strongly in the Babylonian halakhic material than in the *Palestinian Talmud*, which up until the end seems to be advocating for a hegemonic hermeneutic of rabbinic holiness at least in the realm of sexual relations. The Babylonian material evinces a willingness to create an alternative hermeneutic, one in which each individual achieves his own level of holiness. Here, *qedushah* is defined as the ascetic means one undertakes to distinguish oneself from other Israelites. Since all Israelites are holy, these supererogatory behaviors can only enhance one's native holiness, rather than merely protect it. And while the Elisha tradition "drops out" of the exegetical basis for the Babylonian talmudic hermeneutic of holiness and sexuality, I think it lurks in the background as the basis for restrained sexual behavior in marriage that I discuss below, for the early midrashic imagination links the sexually restrained behavior of both Moses and Elisha, established men of God, to holiness. Hence, supererogatory behavior of all sort (withdrawing from what is permitted) translates as holy achievement because it distinguishes the practitioner from the commoner, and supererogatory sexual practices become holy through an evolution of the midrashic understanding of Moses' and Elisha's sexual behavior. And while Moses and Elisha are holy, in part, because they avoid semen pollution (really they are super-pure, though the act is called *qedushah*), I think this tradition has evolved into a more general notion of sexual restraint and holiness, for as we shall see it is restrained (yet consummated) sex in marriage that is called holy. Hence, the purity of avoiding semen pollution, combined with holiness protection through restrictive marriage partners, morphs into supererogatory acetic behavior in sexual relations in marriage and is called holy.

Supererogatory Ascetic Behavior and Holiness

Supererogatory behavior comes in several forms in the rabbinic texts. In some places, all of Israel claims holy credit because they have taken on some ascetic practice that is not specifically legislated in the biblical texts. In other cases, certain individuals can claim the title "holy," or at least to have behaved "in holiness," because of some individualized ascetic practice. As a result of this holy behavior, the individual is somehow rewarded by God. In most cases, the practices have to do with sexual restraint, but in others they have to do with limiting certain food consumption. For instance, several times in the Babylonian talmudic texts the Rabbis declare "Israel is holy" (*yisrael qedoshim hem*); hence, they act in such and such a way. In these cases, it seems that Israel's ascribed holiness determines their behavior. In the five cases in which this phrase is connected with prescribed behavior, the practice encouraged is supererogatory—that is, above and beyond the call of duty—or, in this case, halakhah or even minhag. Three out of the five cases have to do with sex, two with the eating of the fat around the sciatic nerve.[32] In the latter cases, the Rabbis tell us that, technically, the eating of the fat from which the sciatic nerve has been extracted is kosher, yet Israelites nonetheless refrain from eating it because "Israel is holy."[33] The Rabbis describe a fence that has grown up organically around a perfectly acceptable halakhah.[34] The fat of the sciatic nerve is acceptable kosher meat if the nerve is extracted. Nonetheless, Israelites (not the Rabbis!) have determined that it would be better if they forgo that fat altogether. Their rational is that all "Israel is holy." Perhaps this move is seen as a protection against the possibility of eating the fat with the nerve still intact and hence transgressing a divine law, which would damage Israel's holy status. Yet, it also seems to be promoting a voluntary community-wide withdrawal from eating this perfectly kosher meat. Israelites have chosen to go beyond the letter of the law, either to better preserve their holy status or, perhaps, to improve on it. Here, the two notions again merge. Although the notion of upgrading is not explicit in these passages, I think it lurks in the background.[35] For Israelites would still be holy whether or not they partook of properly prepared meat. Refusing to do so must have some other greater value, and this is called holiness.

The other three dicta (or references to the same statement) claim, in the name of Mar Huna, "Israel is holy: they do not use their beds (have conjugal relations) in the daylight."[36] It is not clear to me why this sexually modest behavior should necessarily follow logically from the statement that Israel is holy, or cause Israel to call itself holy. But to the rabbinic mind it made sense. Clearly, there is either something in Israel's holy status that seems to dictate a necessity to behave discreetly in sexual matters or there is a notion that behaving discreetly in sexual behavior causes Israel to be holy.[37] Is it to protect Israel's image or enhance its reputation? Is it simply to distinguish Israelite behavior from that of others? A related statement in *Babylonian Talmud Niddah* clarifies somewhat why the Rabbis prefer to have sex at night, but it does not illuminate how this is connected to Israel's holy status:

Rabbi Yohanan says "It is forbidden for a man to serve his bed [have sexual relations] during the day." What is the reason? As it is written

(Job 3:1), "*Let the day on which I was born be lost; and the night too*
which said, 'a man is conceived.'" Night is given for conception but the
day is not given for conception.[38]

According to this text, nighttime is preferable for procreative activities, as this
rabbinic reading of Job determines babies are conceived at night and not in the
day—hence, the Rabbis rule that it is permissible to attempt procreation only at
night. Is this a polemic against other peoples' practices? Or, as others have
argued, is this an attempt at limiting sexual activity in general among rabbis
and their wives?[39] Is it perhaps a not so subtle way to keep the rabbinic students
at their studies all day? The texts do not clarify this. Another reason for this
behavior is offered at a later point in this discussion: for fear that the husband
will find his wife physically repulsive, he should have sex only in the nighttime.
Moreover, the discussion of sex in the daylight is contextualized within a
broader discussion of behaviors one should not do for fear of the evil eye and
other superstitions. At the very least, this dictum reveals rabbinic anxieties concerning too much sexual activity.

Yet, another way to read the statement "Israel is holy" is to understand it as
an objective: Israel is holy when it does such and such; or Israel becomes holy
because it does such and such. In this case, modest behavior in legitimate sexual
relations somehow adds to Israel's holy status in the same way that avoiding the
fat of the sciatic nerve does. Going above and beyond the call of duty (as delin-
eated in the biblical texts) enhances one's holiness. This is the emerging rabbinic
notion of achieved holiness. It does not stand necessarily in opposition to ascribed
holiness, but often is in addition to it. If all Israel is holy, how are rabbinic Jews,
let alone rabbis, to distinguish themselves from the others? Holiness achieved
through supererogatory behavior, but especially sexual restraint, comes to the
fore in rabbinic discourse on holy advancement, as it does in Aphrahat and other
early Christian writings. Nevertheless, the Rabbis proceed cautiously. There are
behaviors that all Israel is capable of taking on itself (avoiding the fat of the sciatic
nerve); but other more extreme or difficult behaviors, exemplified by Moses and
Elisha, should be limited to those who are capable. Full or partial sexual abstinence comes to the fore as one of these behaviors.[40]

Sexual Restraint and Individual Holiness

Sexual restraint can take several forms in the Babylonian rabbinic discussions.[41]
One such restraint we have seen already—not having sex in the daylight.
Another, as we saw above, builds on the regulations of *gilui 'arayot* (prohibited
sexual partners), in that the Rabbis add to the lists of prohibited relations.

Finally, yet connected to the first, the Rabbis advocate restraint in sexual intercourse itself. In several different rabbinic discussions we see the dictum "all who sanctify themselves in the act of sexual intercourse will have male children." But what does it mean to sanctify oneself in sex? *Babylonian Talmud Shevuot* 18b gives us a clue: "R. Benjamin b. Japhet said that R Eleazar said: 'He who sanctifies himself during sexual intercourse will have male children, even as it is said: "*Sanctify yourselves, and be holy*" (Lev. 11:44), and next to it: "*If a woman conceives [and bears a male child]*" (Lev. 12:2).'" In this passage, the Rabbis make an exegetical connection between two levitical passages: "Be holy" and "If a woman conceives and bears a male child." The proximity of these two verses alerts the Rabbis to the possibility that there is a direct link between sanctity and a male child. This statement, however, does not tell us at all how one is supposed to "be holy" in order to obtain male children. The statements preceding this one in this pericope seem to make a connection between good (rabbinic) behavior and the reward of male children. That is, when a rabbi obeys God's commandments, God will reward him with male children. Earlier in this passage, the Rabbis state that all who separate from their wives in advance of the women's menstrual periods will have male children. Moreover, they claim that all who distinguish the holy (Sabbath) from the profane (week) in the Havdalah service also will gain male progeny. While both of these practices suggest something holy in the act of separating (clean from unclean; holy from profane), and they are biblically ordained *mitzvot* (*niddah, havdalah*), they do not directly address the question of sanctifying oneself in sexual intercourse. The answer, I think, lies in the exegetical link—there must be something one does in sexual intercourse that is here called "holiness," such that in that moment of sexual connection the wife will conceive a male child.

Further clues can be found in *Babylonian Talmud Niddah* 70b-71a:

> What must a man do that he may have male children? He replied: "He shall marry a wife that is worthy of him and sanctify himself in sexual intercourse." They said to him: "Did not many act in this manner but it did not avail them? Rather, let him pray for mercy from Him to whom are the children, for it is said, '*Lo, children are a heritage of the Lord; the fruit of the womb is a reward*' (Ps. 77:3)." What then does he teach us? That one without the other does not suffice. What is exactly meant by "*the fruit of the womb is a reward*"? R. Hama b. R. Hanina replied: "As a reward for containing oneself during intercourse in the womb, in order that one's wife may emit the seed first, the Holy Blessed One, gives one the reward of the fruit of the womb."[42]

This passage begins where the other left off—repeating the statement that a man must sanctify himself in sexual intercourse in order to produce male children. However, this passage gives us an explanation of how to do so. First, a counterargument is presented: should not a person simply pray to God for male children, since God is the ultimate provider of children? This argument is supported with a verse from Psalms: "Children are the heritage of the Lord; the fruit of the womb is a reward," meaning that God ultimately decides who deserves male progeny. Presumably, the faithful and the righteous will be so rewarded. Nevertheless, a compromise is struck: both sanctity in intercourse and prayer should be practiced. Yet, R. Hama argues that "fruit of the womb is a reward" does not just refer to the product—the child—but to the act of sex itself. That is, if during intercourse a man can "produce" the "fruit" (i.e., "seed") of the womb, his child will be male—namely, if the man allows the woman to reach orgasm first (i.e., produce her seed first), the child conceived of that union will be male. The only way to do so, according to the Rabbis, is for the male to restrain himself. This act of restraint is the act of sanctification described here. Furthermore, it exemplifies Rava's statement above: "sanctify yourself with what is permitted to you." Of course, a man is permitted to conduct sexual relations with his wife in a manner suitable to him. Furthermore, he is required to reproduce. But if he can control his sexual urge—just a bit—he will be rewarded with male children. One might argue that this is medical advice, as can be found in Greco-Roman handbooks on family life; and indeed, Michael Satlow argues that all of these discussions on eugenics in child conceiving reflect Greco-Roman cultural mores.[43] Yet, the Rabbis insist on couching it in the language of holiness. Why?

Another way of phrasing this question would be to ask: why is sanctity in the marriage bed equated with sexual restraint rather than, say, sexual abundance? What is it about restraint that is more appealing? One could argue that the Hellenistic philosophical notion of control (not indulging in desire) infiltrates this discourse. As we noted above, certain rabbinic discussions evince a distaste for too much sex (limiting sex to the nighttime). Boyarin has argued that while this may have been the case among Palestinian rabbis, the Babylonian rabbis prove themselves to have a healthier (by modern estimations) attitude toward sex.[44] Yet, these dicta appear only in the *Babylonian Talmud*.[45] I suggest, therefore, that the connection between sexual restraint and holiness, according to the Rabbis, goes back to Moses at Sinai and Elisha with the Shunamit. While the Babylonian commentators have lost or subverted any notion of semen pollution and *qedushah* here, they retain the link between sexual restraint and holiness, and integrate it into their growing hermeneutic of achieved holiness based on distinction by supererogatory behavior. They thus further build on and merge their notions with earlier notions of separating themselves from unholy sexual behavior, such as incest.

It is interesting to note that even within the last passage, the practice itself is questioned, for the text suggests praying to God for male children instead of "sanctifying" oneself in sexual intercourse. This counterargument claims that "sanctification" in sexual intercourse in order to produce male children does not always work. Rather, the only holy thing involved in procreation is God. This notion of divine intervention in the production of children is a literary motif that can be found throughout the biblical narratives and later midrash.[46]

These several passages that discuss how one should act in *qedushah* in sexual intercourse give us several demonstrations (restraint in quality or quantity, depending on God), but do not necessarily explain why such behavior is called holy. The Rabbis advocate that men can either pray to God and/or constrain themselves if they are able. The issue of male restraint in sexual intercourse is less clearly understood. What is holy about sexual restraint? The answer is found in part in Rava's dictum: sanctify yourself by what is permitted to you—that is, by going beyond the restrictions of the law you sanctify yourself. They are not required by biblical law to restrain themselves, but if they do, they will produce sons. As we shall see more clearly below, it is not just the sexual restraint per se that is holy, but the general notion of holding oneself back, withdrawing. Rabbinic asceticism, this holding back, then helps distinguish and separate the practice and the practitioners from others. Yet, it is all the more significant for this study that the examples of withdrawing from what is permitted, which appear again and again, are examples of restraint in sexual intercourse. Asceticism within legitimate sexual relations becomes one mode of rabbinic spiritual achievement that they call holiness. Moreover, this sanctification through sexual restraint parallels Satlow's discussion of sexual restraint as a manifestation of sexual control. While Satlow discusses self-control in the context of avoiding improper sexual partners (incest, adultery, etc), I think it equally applies here. In proving their ability to restrain themselves even in the act of legitimate sex, they demonstrate their incredible self-control.[47]

Celibacy and Rabbinic Holiness

In the last chapter, we saw how the Rabbis lauded Moses for giving up sexual relations with his wife. While they do not label *him* "holy" for his choice, they surely admire his choice and its supposed consequences (the ability to be totally devoted to God's service). Nevertheless, the Rabbis do not shy away from calling his *behavior* "holy," even as they do not advocate emulating him. Here, we witnessed some semantic slippage between QDS as physical purity and QDS as holiness. Similarly, the Rabbis define Elisha's holiness by recourse to his practice of extreme "ritual" purity. Aphrahat, of course, has completely erased the difference between purity and holiness. He blissfully concludes that Moses is called to celibacy (a mode of extreme "ritual" purity) because it is holy (obedience), and all who want to be holy (obedient) should follow in Moses' footsteps. The Rabbis, for their part, equivocate, giving credit to Moses for choosing "ritually" pure behavior (celibacy) as part of his unique position vis-à-vis God, but they do not allow themselves to emulate him, nor do they completely merge the different meanings of *qedushah*, though they come very close. Yet, Moses is not the only biblical character who exhibits holy or pure sexual behavior in the rabbinic literature. Noah and Elisha (as we have seen) fall into this category as well.

Noah, like Moses is noted for refraining from sex even after the flood, in this midrashic passage:

> And God spoke to Noah and his sons: "*Now I establish [my covenant],
> etc.*" (Gen. 9:8–9). R. Judah said: "Because he transgressed [God's]
> command he was put to shame." R. Nehemiah said: "He went
> beyond [God's] command and acted with *qedushah*. Therefore, he and
> his sons were favored with [God's] word [i.e., covenant], as it is
> written, '*And God spoke to Noah and his sons, etc.*'"[48]

In this passage, there is a dispute as to whether Noah acted properly or not in planting a vineyard upon first exiting the ark. R. Judah suggests that he should rather have resumed sexual relations with his wife (following the divine directive to be fruitful and multiply that immediately precedes the verse in question about the covenant). And for this disregard of God's commandment he was subsequently shamed (by being found drunk and naked in his tent by his son, Ham). Rabbi Judah follows the reasoning established in an earlier midrash, which states that as soon as Noah entered the ark, sexual relations were forbidden to him.[49] Assuming R. Judah is right—that Noah neglected his conjugal duties after exiting the ark—R. Nehemiah responds that this sexual restraint on Noah's part is actually a good thing. For, according to this midrash, God commanded Noah, and his family, to refrain from sexual activity while aboard the ark. The Rabbis deduce this information from the fact that Genesis 6:18 reports that the men and women of Noah's family entered the ark separately and, hence, the Rabbis assume this means that they remained quartered separately throughout the flood.[50] Hence, there was no human sexual activity on the ark. Noah, by remaining celibate after the flood, only continues the status quo of ark life. What Noah did was act in *qedushah*— that is, he went beyond God's command in not procreating further after the flood. God permitted him, but Noah declined. For this holy behavior God rewarded him with the covenant.[51] While here *qedushah* refers to Noah's ascetic act of withdrawing from what is permitted, and not specifically or exclusively to celibacy, the two are easily fused. Rabbi Nehemiah's opinion highlights one formation of rabbinic notions of self-sanctification that we encountered above: "sanctify yourself in what is permitted to you." Rabbinic holiness can come from going beyond the law's requirements. It is all the more significant for our discussion that Noah's celibacy—withdrawing from what is permitted him (procreation)—is that action that is labeled "holy behavior," for he could simply be referring to this act of *qedushah* as "ritual" purity (i.e., temporary celibacy), but the text makes no such indication. And, furthermore, because he chose not to procreate, he is rewarded with a divine covenant. Nevertheless, like Moses, Noah at least has procreated in the past. He does not neglect his duties to reproduce entirely. Elisha, on the other hand, finds himself in a different situation: the Bible reports no progeny or even a marriage partner for Elisha. The rabbinic texts report several times that Rabbi Judah the Prince, who was also known as *Rabbeinu Ha-qadosh* (our holy teacher), was called "holy" because of his own sexual restraint.[52] And, as I demonstrated above, Elisha the Prophet's holiness is also tied to his sexual practices, particularly his sexual restraint. The Rabbis define Elisha's title *ish qadosh*, in part by reference to his purity. His act of fence building (avoiding illicit sexual relations) and his extreme purity (celibacy) come together here to define his holiness. While celibacy could be limited to a "ritually" pure act for either Moses or Elisha, I believe the Rabbis combine the two definitions in order to claim celibacy as a holy act for both prophets. It is an act that elevates the prophets spiritually above their compatriots. Certainly, celibacy becomes an act of holiness for Noah, for whom there is no claim to purity.

Nevertheless, the more explicit midrashic connections between celibacy and holiness (Moses, Noah, Elisha) come from within the Palestinian literature, but fall out of the Babylonian. The Babylonian talmudic versions of the Moses at Sinai texts discussed in the last chapter do not allude to holiness. Elisha disappears completely from the Babylonian texts above and this passage on Noah appears in a Palestinian midrashic collection. Yet, it is in the Babylonian texts that we see this development of individual supererogatory behavior that is sexual in nature and is labeled "holy" by the Rabbis. I suggest, therefore, that the link between sexual renunciation and holiness is an ancient one, and is upheld in theory by the earlier Rabbis. By the time of the Babylonian rabbis, however, even the idea of full-blown celibacy, or total sexual renunciation (as practiced by the Christians, for example), was frowned upon. Yet the holiness–sexual practice nexus remained and was transformed into sexual restraint within marriage.

Many scholars before me have noted the differences in attitude or approach to ascetic practice in general and sexually ascetic practice in particular between

Palestinian and Babylonian rabbis. Diamond, for instance, argues that the Palestinian rabbis viewed voluntary fasting more positively than did their Babylonian counterparts.[53] Following Satlow, Diamond suggests that the Palestinian understanding of sexuality as meant for procreation only further suggests a stronger ascetic impulse within the Palestinian rabbinic community. This trend can be explained in two ways.

On the one hand, the Palestinian rabbis lived within a Greco-Roman culture that also had its own version of *ascesis*, which translated into disciplined living within a household. A head of household was expected to set the example for his householders, and he would not be able to manage and control his household if he were not already in control of his own impulses and desires. Daniel Boyarin argues that under this influence Palestinian rabbinic Judaism comes closest to its Hellenistic Jewish forebears in its approach to sexual asceticism. That is, the Palestinian rabbis are more willing to make a place for ascetic sexual practice by relegating sexuality for procreation only. Boyarin makes the point, however, to differentiate between the essentially dualistic and negative attitude that the Greco-Roman culture held toward the human body and the rabbinic monistic, and more positive one.[54]

On the other hand, Diamond suggests that the more immediate nature of Israel's tragedy—the destruction of the Temple and the loss of hegemony over the land—caused a stronger strain of mourning and despair among Palestinian Jews, that led them to extreme forms of mourning and penitence such as fasting and sexual abstinence. The Babylonians, in contrast, were more secure and settled in their lives and geography, and were less prone to bouts of ascetic mourning.[55] Satlow further notes that the Babylonians had a more relaxed view of sexuality, even within marriage, that manifested itself in an appreciation for the joys of sex and the benefits of intimacy within marriage. This attitude most likely was influenced by the surrounding Persian culture's more positive understanding of human sexuality.[56]

As I discussed in chapter 6, Boyarin argues for an overall tension between Torah study and marriage that manifests itself in different ways within the Palestinian and Babylonian rabbinic literature. The image of the celibate Moses at Sinai becomes the place where that tension is played out. True Torah study necessitates, at times, total dedication. But what is one to do about one's obligation to procreate? Fulfill it early or put it off?[57] Yet, what I have tried to trace here is not so much sexual attitudes but how some of these attitudes or practices are couched within a rhetoric of *qedushah*. The early Rabbis seem to place their understanding of sexual activity not just within a dichotomy between marriage and Torah study (the former getting in the way of the latter) but also within a discourse of purity and holiness. The best example of this perhaps is the discussion around the *ba'al qeri* (a man who has produced semen during the night) in *Babylonian Talmud Berakhot* 21b:

> Rabbi Yehoshua b. Levi said: "How do we know that those who have had a seminal emission may not study Torah, for it says, '*And you shall make them known to your children*' (Deut. 4:9), and He appended to it: '*The day on which you stood before the Lord, your God at Horev*' (Deut. 4:10): Just as there, those who have had seminal emissions were forbidden, so here, those who have had seminal emissions are forbidden."[58]

The text makes a connection between Torah study and God's revelation at Sinai: both require purity from semen pollution. The presumption here is that, in the absence of the Temple (lurking in the background behind the Sinaitic scene), God's house, the study house, and particularly the activity of studying Torah, God's word, assumes the Temple's original sanctity and the need for "ritual" purity. This presumption highlights the very essence of the tension between marriage and Torah study. Hence, the text almost immediately questions this need for immersion before Torah study. If a man is required to bathe after every sexual act, will he stop studying Torah? Or would he choose not to be sexually active? Which would be worse? While the later Amoraic rabbis eventually decide the requirement to immerse would be too burdensome, the argument in the discourse of our earlier Rabbis is couched in the language of purity and is exegetically tied to Moses at Sinai.

Boyarin argues that this discussion and its exegetical support point to a "moral/psychological" understanding of the giving of the Torah at Sinai rather than to cultic purity. Since ritual purity was never a Torah requirement for study, it would be better to understand the sexual restraint at Sinai (and, hence, in the study house) to be a further indication that "sexual activity was somehow incompatible with holy activity." Thus, for the Rabbis who upheld the requirement, the ritual immersion symbolically created a temporal division between one's sexual and spiritual lives.[59] While not disagreeing with Boyarin's reading, I would not so quickly dismiss the ritual purity issue here. As we have seen in other Tannaitic midrashim, the language of *qedushah*, as linked to sexual restraint in Exodus 19, provokes great concern for purity, which is no doubt wound up in Moses' closeness both physically and spiritually to God. The ritual and the spiritual go hand in hand. The fear, perhaps, of the slippery slope that this association can make (toward full sexual renunciation, as advocated by some Christian fathers) provoked the Babylonian rabbis to resist such a position and perhaps even this exegetical move. Hence, any notion of *qedushah* falls out of the Babylonian discussion of Moses at Sinai.

So if one can tie the two together, those who associate Moses at Sinai with purity, holiness, and celibacy or some sort of sexual restraint tend to be earlier, Palestinian, if not Tannaitic sources. Here, the *qedushah* is more closely tied to purity than to any sense of obedience or supererogatory behavior and achieved holiness. The Babylonian texts, while eschewing any notion of *qedushah* in Moses' specific behavior of celibacy, create a notion of sanctifying their own ascetic behavior, which manifests itself in restraint, going beyond the letter of the law, denying themselves that which is permitted (within limits), and calling it holy. It is significant that this restraint, nonetheless, takes place within marriage and is limited to a subset of rabbis. This is a self-elevating, circularly reasoned spiritual exercise for the elite, which also proves that the elite deserve to be elite because of their spiritually athletic achievements. The holy act of restraint in married sex was not limited to procreation, but was an act in and of itself that proved the worthiness of the practitioners' authority.

Returning for a moment to a notion of ascribed holiness, it seems that the Palestinian and Babylonian rabbis approached this issue from different angles. Most of the texts that put forward an exegetical proof that Israel is indeed holy are Palestinian. The Babylonian texts, on the other, tend to assume that holiness without a need to prove it. Perhaps the Palestinian rabbis' Greco-Roman milieu prompted more self-reflection on this issue. Indeed, had some of Israel's special relationship with God been lost after the two wars and several centuries of Roman hegemony? Thus, the Tannaitic and Palestinian Amoraic legal discourse on holiness achieved through rabbinic interpretative processes suggests a means for the Palestinian rabbinic community, and particularly its rabbinic leaders, to reestablish their pre-eminent and superior holiness as a community. The Babylonian community, on the other hand, perhaps felt these tensions less and thus pursued more individual spiritual routes, while assuming their communal holiness as a given, for they had survived several generations without the Temple and without hegemony over the land of Israel.

Conclusions

The early rabbinic hermeneutic of holiness seems to have been not so distantly removed from earlier Jewish attempts to answer "Who is a Jew?" by recourse to holiness. The early layers of Tannaitic rabbinism seem to suggest that these rabbis also attempted to distinguish "real" (that is, rabbinic) Jews from other Jews—particularly in the way they legislated eligible marriage partners. Those who follow the baseline biblical law are not as holy—or perhaps not even holy at all—as those who follow the emended and expanded rabbinic laws of marriage.

One's ascribed holiness must be further protected by rabbinic legislation. Thus, not all Israel will remain a part of Israel if they do not follow rabbinic authority. This position manifested itself most often in Palestinian contexts. Babylonians seem less willing to let go of any Israelites, even if they flouted rabbinic authority.

Rather than focus on protecting ascribed holiness, later, and mostly Amoraic, rabbis create yet another hermeneutic of holiness, one in which a hierarchy of achieved holiness dominates. In a sense, these rabbis create for themselves a category of spiritual advancement that they call *qedushah*. That is to say, they mark their association with God by building on the biblical notion of separation and attempt to distinguish themselves (separate themselves) from the rest of Israel (even rabbinic Israel) through supererogatory and ascetic behavior. Here, "withdrawing from what is permitted," going beyond the letter of the law (biblical or rabbinic), provides means for individualized spiritual advancement. The holiest among the Rabbis are ones who succeed in these spiritual challenges of self-distinction. These rabbis appeal both to the *nazir* and the priest as inspirational models, thereby theorizing and expanding the notion of separation as a spiritual ideal in and of itself. While the priests' dedicated, separated, and ascribed holy status necessitates a limiting of their eligible marriage partners, and the *nazir* temporarily chooses an ascetic lifestyle as a vow of devotion to God, the Rabbis go one step further. This rabbinic notion of separation/dedication/holiness goes beyond these models in that it takes from each and creates something new: a hierarchy of achieved holiness. This transformation, in part, is provoked by an incorporation of notions of "ritual" purity that surround Moses' divine vocation at Sinai, notions that are associated with *qedushah* in the biblical texts.

In either case, I argue that the ascetic agenda of the Rabbis (limited marriage partners or limited sexual activity in marriage) resonates within or alongside their need to establish themselves as legislative authorities for all of Israel, particularly in sexual practices. Hence, their argumentation concerning holiness takes two directions. The first attempts to use notions of holiness as obedience to the law, and in particular rabbinic law, as a means to bolster rabbinic authority. The second supports the rabbinic agenda that equates ascetic behavior (particularly sexual restraint) with holiness and elevates such practice to a spiritually elitist category. While the former is a general principle, the Rabbis turn to the same texts that support their sexually ascetic agenda, as well as bolster their more general legislative authority. I think it not insignificant that sexuality becomes central to rabbinic discourse on authority and holiness, and that it provides a means both to actualize their own elitist ascetic agenda and a tool for achieving hegemony over the Jewish community. Aphrahat, too, looks to sexuality, and particularly to sexually related behavior that he defines as holy (celibacy), to help him create borders between competing religious communities in Mesopotamia. For these religious leaders, sexual restraint plays a pivotal role in formulating their sense of self, both individually and communally. Consequently, these exegetes turn to the biblical texts that link holiness with sexual continence to bolster their social and religious positions.

Conclusions

This book set out to demonstrate how sexuality became central to Jewish and Christian notions of holiness and holy community in the post-biblical period. In particular, this study was motivated to determine why sexuality, especially sexual restraint, became a primary demarcation of sacred community boundaries among Jews and Christians in fourth-century Persian Mesopotamia. To accomplish this task, I focused on the exegetical underpinnings that link holiness to sexuality in these communities' emerging hermeneutics of holiness and sexuality. I traced three primary patterns of holiness: holiness ascribed, holiness achieved, and holiness acquired through avoidance of semen pollution. These three holiness trails, which begin within the biblical texts themselves, were followed through the Second Temple literature (both Jewish and Christian) and into the Syriac Christian and rabbinic literature of the fourth century.

The Aphrahatic and rabbinic positions on sexuality and sacred community evolved slowly, over centuries, out of a complex matrix of inherited biblical exegesis, interpretive strategies, and localized cultural influences—many of which they shared in common. Notions of covenant, holy community, images of Moses, and sexuality are multivalenced and conflicting even within the Hebrew biblical texts; yet, several distinct patterns come to the fore in the Second Temple literature that attempt to harmonize or regulate ideals of holiness. Eventually they come to an uneasy rest in the early rabbinic and Christian literature of the fourth century. Aphrahat and the Rabbis' sometimes similar yet often competing hermeneutics of holiness and sexuality emerge from parallel and overlapping internal and external discussions concerning boundary building and religious self-identification based on sexual practices. Their discourse also does not arise as something new in their age, but from deep within an ongoing discourse on holiness, community identity, and sexuality that begins in the Hebrew biblical literature.

Aphrahat flourished in mid-fourth century Persian Mesopotamia at the same time as the Babylonian rabbinic academies were at their height. I place Aphrahat in the same literary matrix as the Rabbis not only to compare and contrast fourth-century Jewish and Christian sexual practices but also to highlight where they come together, theologically and exegetically. So what do the Rabbis think about sexuality? Aphrahat's suggestion that Jews equate holiness with procreation, does not begin to uncover the many opinions on the subject voiced throughout the rabbinic literature. It is not my purpose here to catalogue all of those voices—that job has been ably accomplished by other scholars.[1] I am most interested in those moments when the Rabbis also link their sexuality, and particularly their sexual practices, with holiness and then build on the already demonstrated pervasive theological and exegetic assumption of that essential link.

Very early on in the development of the Syriac tradition, celibacy became linked to holiness. Aphrahat reinvigorates this received tradition by explicating and supporting it in new and innovative ways. One of the ways in which he formulates his argument is to place it within his anti-Jewish debate. Aphrahat is not unusual among early Christian polemicists to define his religion in terms of its distinctions from Judaism, for Christianity evolved out of the crucible of prolonged attempts to distance Christianity from Judaism. Aphrahat's discourse on holiness is part and parcel of this larger debate. Yet, his emphasis on sexuality's main role in achieving holiness, its significance as the distinguishing physical marker of faith, but especially his exegetical strategies of support, I believe, are Aphrahat's unique contribution.[2] Holiness and sexuality serve as the fulcrums of both internal Syriac Christian and external anti-Jewish discussions, for it is in the context of his anti-Jewish polemic that Aphrahat best delineates his own sense of Christian self.

Yet, at the same time, Aphrahat's anti-Jewish, self-promoting Christian rhetoric reveals many biblical traditions, interpretive methods, and exegetical strategies in common with his supposed Jewish rivals, the Babylonian rabbis. Aphrahat's *Demonstrations* point to neighboring biblical scholars in common exegetical endeavour rather than sworn enemies at cross-purposes and engaged in empty debate. Even if Aphrahat never colloqued in person with a Babylonian rabbi, his essays illustrate the larger intellectual pursuits in which both he and the Rabbis engaged. In turn, the rabbinic discourse on sexuality reflects, in part, a recognition that others—such as Aphrahat—also focus their discussions of holiness and base their sense of religious identity on sexual practice.

Recognizing the centrality of Aphrahat's hermeneutic of holiness within his larger program of delineating Christian identity and practice allows one to study the question of sexuality and religious identity in the ancient world from a new angle. Aphrahat's perspective from mid-fourth-century Persian Mesopotamia challenges the established paradigms of sexual behavior and their supporting biblical traditions for both Jews and Christians in the late-ancient Near East. Aphrahat's celibate Christians identify themselves through their sexual renunciation, call themselves "the holy ones," and juxtapose themselves against the procreating Jews. As accused, the Rabbis also express their (married) sexuality in similar terms of holiness and purity. Yet, despite this stark dichotomy, the rabbinic writings likewise express appreciation for the link between (temporary) celibacy and holiness, thus complicating the supporting arguments for the practices Aphrahat utilizes as identifying markers between Jews and Christians in this era.

Sexuality provides an appropriate prism for studying both the *Demonstrations* and the rabbinic literature, for it illuminates these cultures' interrelated discourses on holiness and spiritual fulfillment. It is the locus of these interrelations—where Aphrahat claims differences from the Jews, but manifests sameness—that drove this inquiry. These strikingly similar Hebrew biblical traditions, theological claims, and interpretive stratagems highlight the literary and cultural heritage that Aphrahat shares with the Babylonian rabbis. I am equally interested in determining where a tradition might have originated, as well as in comparing how these authors deploy these traditions, claims, and stratagems in their respective discourses. These sorts of comparisons help contextualize both the Rabbis and Aphrahat in the larger Aramaic-Mesopotamian milieu in which they flourished.

Finally, scholars have argued that celibacy is a non-Jewish, or at least non-biblical, practice imported into Christianity from elsewhere and completely absent from rabbinic Judaism. In *Reading Renunciation*, Elizabeth Clark, for instance, argues persuasively that the fourth-century Greek Christian writers expend much of their exegetical energy trying to read asceticism back into biblical texts that do not support such a suggestion.[3] While the Hebrew Bible in particular provides many an example of divinely blessed procreating individuals, it also manifests a notion of holiness and sexual restraint. We find in the Hebraic/Aramaic context a visible continuum from the biblical texts to Aphrahat, on the one hand, and the Rabbis, on the other, concerning this nexus of sexual restraint and holiness. Celibacy is only one exegetical variation among many on holiness. The Rabbis, for their part, pick up on some of the same variables (celibacy) but emphasize others in practice (procreation). Eliezer Diamond has also argued for an ascetic strain in rabbinic Judaism with strong biblical roots, which manifests itself both in sexuality and in fasting and other dietary practices.[4] In the fourth-century Mesopotamian context, ascetic practitioners accept biblical textual support as compelling as any other outside cultural norm. Sexual asceticism finds its rightful place in the formative periods of both religious traditions, viewed through the lens of comparative biblical exegesis, social constructs, and study of the theological developments of the biblical notions of holiness.

Notes

INTRODUCTION

1. *Demonstrations* (hereafter, *Dem.*) 18.12/841.3–9. All citations to Aphrahat's *Demonstrations* are according to Parisot's text [demonstration. chapter/column.line]. All translations are my own unless otherwise noted. John Parisot, "Aphraatis Sapientis Persae Demonstrationes," in *Patriologia Syriaca*, ed. R. Graffin (Paris: Firmin-Didot), 1: 1–2.

2. Sexuality in this context refers primarily to sexual practice. Whether one is sexually active or sexually restrained, that "act" expresses one's sexuality.

3. Aramaic here refers to the languages that Jews and Christians spoke in Mesopotamia and the Levant. It was not always an exclusive language (Jews spoke Hebrew or Greek at times; some Christians there also spoke Greek). Aramaic also refers to the larger cultural milieu in which these languages existed. I use it primarily to distinguish these communities from other Jewish and Christian communities that spoke Greek, lived during the Roman Empire, and were surrounded primarily by Hellenistic culture rather than Persian. I use it also to distinguish these minority communities from the larger Persian culture that dominated Mesopotamia in these centuries. I admit that in so doing I may over-isolate my communities from the Persian milieu in which they often lived, but this is mostly due to lack of scholarship in this field. Much work has been advanced by Yaakov Elman, but, of course, much more needs to be done.

4. Phyllis Trible, *God and the Rhetoric of Sexuality* (Philadelphia: Fortress Press, 1978), 23.

5. Rudolf Otto, *The Idea of the Holy: An Inquiry into the Non-Rational Factor in the Idea of the Divine and Its Relation to the Rational*, trans. John W. Harvey (London, New York: H. Milford and Oxford University Press, 1923).

6. Mircea Eliade, *The Sacred and The Profane: The Nature of Religion* (San Diego and New York: Harcourt, 1959).

7. Williard G. Oxtoby, "The Idea of the Holy," in the *Encyclopedia of Religion*, ed. M. Eliade (New York: Macmillan, 1987), 6: 434–36.

8. David P. Wright labels these two classifications "inherent" holiness and holiness "achieved through ritual means," David P. Wright, "Holiness," *Anchor Bible Dictionary* 3: 237.

9. Commonly dated from the return from exile, c. 538 BCE to the fall of Jerusalem to the Romans in 70 CE.

10. A process starting before the Babylonian exile (c. 586 BCE) and only coming to completion in the Hellenistic period (c. 332–63 BCE), if not later.

11. Jonathan Klawans, *Impurity and Sin in Ancient Judaism* (New York: Oxford University Press, 2000). See also Christine E. Hayes, *Gentile Impurities and Jewish Identities* (New York: Oxford University Press, 2002).

12. While I uphold this distinction, I am uncomfortable with the nomenclature. Hence, I will leave the terms in quotations throughout my text.

13. I am certainly not the first to argue this, but depend heavily on the work of Israel Knohl, Baruch Schwartz, and Jacob Milgrom. See next chapter. I differentiate myself in that I focus on the nexus of holiness with sexuality.

14. Martha Himmelfarb, *A Kingdom of Priests: Ancestry and Merit in Ancient Judaism* (Philadelphia: University of Pennsylvania, 2006), 10. This phrase comes from Exodus 19:6.

15. This is not to argue that Aphrahat does not give equal or more time to Jesus, but only that he gives more space and credit to Moses than many another Christian theologian.

16. W. Kornfeld argues that *qds* cognates in all the Semitic languages never includes an ethical or moral element; *Theological Dictionary of the Old Testament* (Grand Rapids, Mich., and Cambridge: Eerdmans, 2003), 12: 526.

17. Hannah Harrington, for instance, makes this blanket claim for all of biblical as well as rabbinic holiness. See her book *Holiness: Rabbinic Judaism and the Graeco-Roman World* (London and New York: Routledge, 2001).

18. It is not my intention here to rehearse a full history of Christian asceticism. On the subject, a good place to start is Wimbush and Valantasis's edited volume *Asceticism* (New York: Oxford University Press, 1995). See also Peter Brown, *The Body and Society: Men, Women, and Sexual Renunciation in Early Christianity* (New York: Columbia University Press, 1988).

19. Elizabeth Clark, *Reading Renunciation: Asceticism and Scripture in Early Christianity* (Princeton, N.J.: Princeton University Press, 1999), 18, 22.

20. Clark, *Reading Renunciation*, 18–27.

21. Clark, *Reading Renunciation*, 26–27. In this argument Clark is particularly persuaded by the writing of Dennis R. MacDonald, *The Legend and the Apostle: The Battle for Paul in Story and Canon* (Philadelphia: Westminster, 1983).

22. For Gaca's argument, see the introduction to her book, *The Making of Fornication: Eros, Ethics, and Political Reform in Greek Philosophy and Early Christianity*

(Berkeley and Los Angeles: University of California Press, 2003), 1–20, esp. 4–10 and 17–20. For my critique of Gaca, see chapter 3 and my article on "Re-Imaging Tatian," in the *Journal of Early Christian Studies* 16, no. 1 (2008): 1–30.

23. I differentiate between Syriac Christians and Syrian Christians on linguistic and geographical grounds. Syrian Christians come from Syria; Syriac Christians speak Syriac, an Aramaic dialect. Obviously, many Syriac-speaking Christians lived in Syria, but many also lived in Mesopotamia. Many Syrian Christians also spoke Greek, such as Theodoret of Mopsuestia.

24. Concerning the history of Syriac Christian asceticism see A. Vööbus, *History of Asceticism in the Syrian Orient: A Contribution to the History of Culture in the Near East*, 3 vols. (Louvain: Secrétariat du CSCO, 1958–88); R. Murray, "The Exhortation to Candidates for Ascetical Vows at Baptism in the Ancient Syriac Church," *New Testament Studies* 21 (1974–75), 58–79; S. Brock, "Early Syrian Asceticism," *Numen* 20, no.1 (April 1973): 1–19; S. Griffith, "Asceticism in the Church of Syria: The Hermeneutics of Early Syrian Monasticism," in *Asceticism*, ed. Wimbush and Valantasis, 220–45; and S. A. Harvey, *Asceticism and Society in Crisis: John of Ephesus and the Lives of Eastern Saints* (Berkeley: University of California Press, 1990).

25. Brown, *Body and Society*, 88. Following a similar line of argument, Susan Ashbrook Harvey contends that the Syrian East was less Hellenized (but no less urban) than other areas of early Christian development, at least before the fifth century. Syriac Christianity evolved unhindered by the forces of Greek and Hellenistic philosophy and in a relatively autonomous social and political atmospheres; *Asceticism and Society*, 2.

26. Note how Brown sees Greco-Roman culture as "moderating," while Clark and Gaca see it only as a possible outside influence on Christian asceticism's extreme nature. Nevertheless, the question of the extent and nature of Hellenization in the territories under Persian control is still debated. See, for instance, the work of Christine Shephardson.

27. With this argument Fraade counters and corrects earlier scholarship that dismissed rabbinic asceticism (if its existence was recognized at all) as an aberration and foreign import. See his important article "Ascetical Aspects of Ancient Judaism" in *Jewish Spirituality: From the Bible through the Middle Ages*, ed. Arthur Green (New York: Crossroads, 1986), 253–88.

28. See his book, *Borderlines: The Partition of Judaeo-Christianity* (Philadelphia: University of Pennsylvania Press, 2004), 1–33.

29. Boyarin uses the metaphor of a wheelbarrow utilized to smuggle things across state borders as a symbol for the practice of heresiology, which he suggests the Rabbis learned from the Christians. See introduction to *Borderlines*.

30. While I approach rabbinic sexuality from a very different direction than does Michael Satlow, I agree with him that sexuality, and in his case marriage, forms essential social constructs within growing rabbinic discourses on Jewish community and rabbinic authority over those communities. See his two works, *Tasting the Dish: Rabbinic Rhetorics of Sexuality* (Atlanta: Scholars Press, 1995), and *Jewish Marriage in Antiquity* (Princeton, N.J.: Princeton University Press, 2001).

31. Ephrem, too, has suffered from negligence. But see new work by Christine Shepardson, *Anti-Judaism and Christian Orthodoxy: Ephrem's Hymns in Fourth-Century Syria* (Washington, D.C.: The Catholic University of America Press, 2008).

32. At the end of the fifth century a Western Church father, Gennadius, cites the *Demonstrations*, but he also misattributes them to Jacob and misnumbers them as well; John Gwynn, "Aphrahat," in *Nicene and Post Nicene Fathers*, second series, vol.13, part 2 (Oxford and London: Christian Literature, 1898), 154.

33. Gwynn, "Aphrahat," 156; Marie-Joseph Pierre, *Aphraates, "Les Exposes"* (Paris: Editions du Cerf, 1988), 1: 35; Parisot, "Aphraatis," 1: xii. Parisot references Manuscript C, British Museum, Oriental collection, no. 1017—"On the Grapecluster."

34. Parisot, "Aphraatis," 1: xv.

35. Pierre, "*Les Exposes*," 1: 36, and n.15; William Wright, *The Homilies of Aphrahates: The Persian Sage* (London: Williams and Norgate, 1869), 8; Gwynn, "Aphrahat," 157.

36. For example, Wright, *The Homilies of Aphrahates*, 8–9.

37. Gwynn, "Aphrahat," 158.

38. Both Gwynn (p.157) and Pierre (1: 33, 39–40) believe that he was a convert of pagan parents.

39. The manuscripts contain the letter of the cleric who asked Aphrahat concerning Christian faith. It is in answer to this letter that Aphrahat wrote the first set of sermons in the *Demonstrations*. He often addresses the questioner as "beloved" a term used between members of the clergy indicating that the letter writer was a fellow cleric. Perhaps it also implies that Aphrahat's *Demonstrations* were addressed primarily to other clerics. The letter, of course, could also be a literary ruse on Aphrahat's part.

40. *Dem.* 22.25/1044.9–20.

41. It is interesting to note that Aphrahat does not argue against Zoroastrianism—the religion of the Persians. Either it was not a threat to his flock or he felt that he could not argue against the state religion publicly. Nevertheless, in the martyrologies, like that of Shimon bar Sabba'e, the Christian martyrs polemicize vigorously against the Magian priests.

42. Compare to E. Clark's book, *Reading Renunciation* discussed above. In some ways I am only continuing her work of showing how some Syriac Christians (and rabbinic Jews) related their sexual choices to the biblical texts. But in another way I also counter her general argument that fourth-century ascetic Christians only eisegeted rather than exegeted.

43. See the many examples in Robert Murray's *Symbols of Church and Kingdom: A Study of Early Syriac Tradition* (Cambridge: Cambridge University Press, 1975).

44. S. Funk, *Die Haggadischen Element in den Homilien des Aphraates, des persischen Weisen, inaugural-Dissertation* (Vienna: M. Knöpflmacher, 1891); Louis Ginzberg, "Aphraates, the Persian Sage," in *Jewish Encyclopedia* (New York: Funk and Wagnalls, 1901–6), 1: 663–65; Frank Gavin, "Aphraates and the Jews," *Journal of the Society of Oriental Research* 7 (1923): 95–166.

45. Jacob Neusner, *Aphrahat and Judaism: The Christian-Jewish Argument in Fourth-Century Iran* (Leiden: Brill, 1971).

46. Ibid., 189

47. Ibid., 124.

48. Ibid., 148, 150; Neusner labels the Jews "Yahwistic," implying Jews who followed the laws of the Bible untampered by rabbinic interpretation.

49. Ibid. 148. The ten tribes of Israel were exiled from their land by Sennacherib in 721/2 BCE. The royalty of Adiabene converted to Judaism in the first century CE before the destruction of the Second Temple. That some of the Jews of northern Mesopotamia could be descendants of the Adiabenes is quite plausible, however that there could be descendants of the lost ten tribes ten centuries after their exile seems speculative.

50. See the fold-out maps at the end of A. Oppenheimer, B. Isaac, and M. Lecker, *Babylonia Judaica in the Talmudic Period* (Wiesbaden: L. Reichart, 1983).

51. Dr. David Golinkin pointed out these sources to me in personal correspondences. Ya'akov of Adiabene is mentioned in *BT Baba Batra* 26a, and Zuga is mentioned in *BT Niddah* 21b and *Moed Katan* 28a. Golinkin notes that "Zuga" could be a formal name, or it could mean "a pair of scholars"; either way there was at least one rabbinic Jew in Adiabene. Furthermore, where there was one Jew there probably were more since Jews rarely lived alone.

52. J. B. Segal, "The Jews of North Mesopotamia before the Rise of Islam," in *Studies in the Bible presented to Prof. M. H. Segal* [Sefer Segal] (Jerusalem: Kiryat Sefer, 1964), 38–39.

53. Segal, "The Jews," 42. Segal claims the reason Christianity spread quickly in northern Mesopotamia was that Jewish populations were already established there.

54. See discussion above and his book, *Borderlines*.

55. Aphrahat's fourteenth demonstration is addressed to the clerics and rulers of the Christian community concerning a wayward bishop of high standing. "Catholicos" is the term used for the metropolitan or patriarch in the later centuries. In Aphrahat's day the bishop of Seleucia-Ctesiphon was not yet at the top of the Mesopotamian hierarchy, but fighting for his supremacy.

56. The Syriac is *ḥakima d-yehudaye*. *Dem.* 21.1/932.9.

57. From the rabbinic discussions of these meetings it is not at all clear that they weren't more debates than dialogues. See Elman's discussions in "A Tale of Two Cities: Mahoza and Pumpeditta as Representatives of Two Legal Cultures" (Hebrew), in *Torah Lishmah a Festschrift for Shamma Friedman*, ed. D. Golinkin, et al. [Machon Shechter] (Ramat Gan: Bar Ilan University Press, 2007), 3–38; and "Middle Persian Culture and Babylonian Sages: Accommodation and Resistance in the Shaping of Rabbinic Legal Tradition, in *The Cambridge Companion to the Talmud*, ed. C. E. Fonrobert and M. S. Jaffee (Cambridge: Cambridge University Press, 2007), 165–97.

58. Pierre, "*Les Exposes*," I: 122, 129. Contra Pierre, Adam Lehto argues that Aphrahat is of Jewish descent. Adam Lehto, *Divine Law, Asceticism and Gender in Aphrahat's "Demonstrations."* Ph.D. dissertation, University of Toronto, 2003. The term "Jewish-Christian" has been problematized to the point of being rendered useless. The term itself is really an invention of nineteenth-century scholarship. Neither Aphrahat nor his parishioners would have referred to themselves as "Jewish-Christians" even if they had been Jews at some point. For a lengthier discussion of the subject, see Matt

Jackson-McCabe, *Jewish-Christianity Reconsidered: Rethinking Ancient Groups and Texts* (Minneapolis: Fortress Press, 2007). I will use the term as sparingly as possible.

59. Pierre, *"Les Exposes"*, 1: 115.

60. See, for instance, *Dem.* 11.1, 17.12, and 18.12.

61. See most recently Christine Shepardson, "Defining the Boundaries of Orthodoxy: Eunomius in the Anti-Jewish Polemic of his Cappadocian Opponents," *Church History* 76, no. 4 (December 2007): 699–723; and her book, *Anti-Judaism and Christian Orthodoxy*, esp. chaps. 4–5; and Averil Cameron, "Jews and Heretics—A Category Error?" in *The Ways That Never Parted: Jews and Christians in Late Antiquity and the Early Middle Ages*, ed. Adam Becker and Annette Yoshiko Reed (Tübingen: Mohr Siebeck, 2003), 345–60. See also Paula Fredriksen, *Augustine and the Jews: A Christian Defense of Jews and Judaism* (New York: Doubleday, 2008), esp. the epilogue.

62. Neusner, *Aphrahat*, 155.

63. Michael P. Weitzman, *The Syriac Version of the Old Testament: An Introduction* (Cambridge: Cambridge University Press, 1999), 86–91, 129–30.

64. Murray, *Symbols of Church and Kingdom*, Introduction.

CHAPTER 1

1. Martha Himmelfarb, *A Kingdom of Priests: Ancestry and Merit in Ancient Judaism* (Philadelphia: University of Pennsylvania Press, 2006), 10.

2. Baruch J. Schwartz, "Israel's Holiness: The Torah Traditions," in *Purity and Holiness: The Heritage of Leviticus,* ed. M. Poorthuis and J. Schwartz (Leiden: Brill, 2000), 48. See also the Hebrew text upon which the English article is based, *The Holiness Legislation: Studies in the Priestly Code* (Jerusalem: Magnes Press, 1999), 250–66.

3. Schwartz, "Israel's Holiness," 53. Schwartz notes as well that QDS is used by nonpriestly writers also to signify "separate" and "designate" without "consecrate." See, for instance, Jer. 1:5; Schwartz, *Holiness Legislation*, 253. For more biblical textual examples consult Schwartz's work.

4. This argument sums up and follows on Schwartz, "Israel's Holiness," 49–50.

5. Michael Fishbane differentiates between unconditional ascribed holiness in D and conditional in E—namely, that Israel's ascribed holiness in E is dependent on Israel's following the law. See his *Biblical Interpretation in Ancient Israel* (Oxford: Clarendon Press, 1985), 121.

6. Schwartz, "Israel's Holiness," 52.

7. Israel Knohl, *The Sanctuary of Silence: The Priestly Torah and the Holiness School* (Minneapolis, Minn.: Fortress Press, 1995), 3, 6–7, 44, 101.

8. Israel Knohl labels the schools PT and HS to differentiate from the larger textual strata P. I will stick here to the more standard P and H. Israel Knohl also argues, against the mainstream scholarship, that H follows P chronologically and functions as a corrective to it. But he further emphasizes that both emanate from the priestly ranks; Knohl, *Sanctuary*, 2, 6–7, 197. On the dating of these texts, see his first chapter in *Sanctuary*, where he takes on Wellhausen and the like. See also Jacob Milgrom, *The Anchor Bible: Leviticus* (New York: Doubleday, 1991–2001), 1:3–34, who

agrees with the larger parts of Knohl's argument, but contests him on a few of the minor issues.

9. Knohl, *Sanctuary*, 6–7, and esp. conclusions of chap. 5. Knohl posits a long period of composition for H stretching from the eighth century to the Persian period. Milgrom, although agreeing that H postdates P, believes all of H (give or take a few late redactional phrases) is pre-exilic; *Anchor Bible: Leviticus* 2:1361–64. In contrast, Robert A. Kugler, in "Holiness, Purity, the Body and Society: The Evidence for Theological Conflict in Leviticus," *Journal for the Study of the Old Testament* 76 (1997): 3–27, has argued that H should be seen as nonpriestly. I do not find his argument convincing.

10. Schwartz, "Israel's Holiness," 54.

11. In the same way that impurity is contagious (see discussion below) so, too, is holiness. Milgrom suggests that contagious holiness caused great concern among the priestly writers, who attempted to "contain" its contagiousness in several ways. *Anchor Bible: Leviticus* 1:45, 443.

12. Schwartz, "Israel's Holiness," 53; Knohl, *Sanctuary*, 182.

13. This is Schwartz's metaphor; "Israel's Holiness," 57.

14. Schwartz, "Israel's Holiness," 57.

15. The one exception to this rule is 2 Samuel 11:4, the story of Bat Sheva bathing on her roof-top "after she had purified herself." This exception proves the rule, I think, that menstrual impurities were not of great concern to either the biblical or the Second Temple writers. Among the authors discussed here, the Rabbis are the only ones who discuss menstrual impurities at any great length.

16. See, for example, 2 Chronicles 29:1–36.

17. The semantic relationship between *purify* and *sanctify* or *pure* and *holy* is not unique to Hebrew but can be found in other Semitic languages, as well as in Latin. See, for example, Kornfeld, "קדש", *Theological Dictionary of the Old Testament* (Grand Rapids, Mich., and Cambridge: Eerdmans, 2003), 12: 521–45.

18. This is my translation. Note that while the NJPS and the NJB both translate QDS here as "purify," the NRSV translates it as "sanctify." I will use my own translations in this section, unless noted otherwise.

19. The Hebrew is difficult here and especially complicated because of the crossover of singular adjectives for plural nouns and the double use of QDS. Note that the NJPS translates all QDS words as "consecrated," and the NRSV as "holy," yet the NJB differentiates between the "consecrated" bread and the men's "clean" vessels, as I do.

20. J. Licht also suggests that the *kelim* in 1 Samuel 21 are the men's clothing that can be defiled by semen, as noted in Leviticus 15. See J. Licht's article on QDS in the *Encyclopedia Mikrait* (Jerusalem: Mosad Bialik, 1950): 7:48–49. Rashi reads QDS as THR. The RaDaK understand the *kelim* to be clothing, too.

21. Furthermore, one could understand Deuteronomy 23:11–15 as stipulating the cultic purity (rather than holiness) of the military camp because God walks about in it as their military adviser and benefactor.

22. Again, a difficult passage to translate. The NRSV here translates QDS as "consecrate," the NJB uses "sanctify." The NJPS has "warned the people to stay pure." The difficulty of the passage can already be discerned from the LXX's translation, in

which the QDS in v. 10 is rendered: *hagnison autous* from *hagnvizô* ("purify them") and in v. 14 it is *hegiasev autous* from *hagiaz* ("sanctify them").

23. The priestly texts acknowledge this danger as well, as can be seen in the story of Nadav and Abihu, Leviticus 10.

24. It should be noted here that the Qumran texts are also dependent on Deuteronomy 23:9–14, in which semen pollution is prohibited in the war camp. Here, however, the semen is prohibited because of the holy presence of God, and hence the camp must be QDS. But the act of purifying oneself of semen pollution is not called QDS, as it is in the texts discussed above.

25. James Kugel also notes that, in this metaphor, Jeremiah compares Israel to a first-born son who is dedicated or consecrated to God; "The Holiness of Israel and the Land in Second Temple Times," in *Texts, Temples and Traditions: A Tribute to Menahem Haran*, ed. Michael V. Fox, et al. (Winona Lake, Ind.: Eisenbraun, 1996), 22. Michael Fishbane proposes another connection between Ezra 9 and holy seed or remnant of Israel in Isaiah 6; *Biblical Interpretation in Ancient Israel*, 123.

26. Milgrom, *Anchor Bible: Leviticus* 1:360–61. Ezra refers to the returning Judeans as "Israel" in order to distinguish the Judeans who remained behind from those who went into exile. In this way Ezra also redefines the notion of Israelite holy ascription. Only those who went into exile and returned to Judea are truly Israelite and hence holy. Thus the non-exilic Judeans become muddled with the other "peoples of the land."

27. See note 31 below.

28. NJPS translation. All biblical citations in the rest of the chapter are from the NJPS translation unless otherwise noted. Much of the recent discussion concerning Ezra's exegetical derivations for his ban on intermarriage focuses on this list of the peoples of the land. Many have noted that this list is a composite of several different biblical lists that each partially ban certain relations (sometimes marriage) with these people. But as S. J. D. Cohen notes, no one biblical text, nor all of them together, promote a universal ban against intermarriage as Ezra does. See his article, "From the Bible to the Talmud: The Prohibition of Intermarriage," *Hebrew Annual Review* 7 (1983), 23–39.

29. Christine Hayes, "Intermarriage and Impurity in Ancient Jewish Sources," *Harvard Theological Review* 92, no.1 (1999): 6–14. See also her larger study in *Gentile Impurities and Jewish Identities* (New York: Oxford University Press, 2002), 28–34.

30. H. G. M. Williamson, *Ezra and Nehemiah* (Sheffield, England: Sheffield Academic Press, 1987), 96. Kugel similarly notes that *kilayim*, the mixing of the unmixable, is a cultic sacrilege; "Holiness of Israel," 24.

31. Hayes, "Intermarriage," 10–11; *Gentile Impurities*, 29. See also Milgrom's discussion of sancta contamination, *Anchor Bible: Leviticus* 1:345–61.

32. Milgrom, *Anchor Bible: Leviticus* 1:319–28. According to Milgrom's readings of the texts, a sacred item once profaned cannot be reconsecrated, it can only be re-placed—hence the need for reparation, which can be given in cash rather than as a sacrifice.

33. Compare to Leviticus 5:14, in which the penalty for a *ma'al* is a ram from the flock.

34. Milgrom, *Anchor Bible: Leviticus* 1:325–26.

35. Christine Hayes argues similarly; *Gentile Impurities*, 28.

36. Hayes, *Gentile Impurities*, 28–34.

37. B. J. Schwartz, in his commentary on Leviticus 21 in the *OJSB* (p. 259), suggests that these restrictions have to do with preventing illegitimate priests. That is to say, only a virgin can provably not be carrying anyone else's seed at the time she marries a priest. In Ezekiel's case, in chap. 44, he has extended the restrictions on the high priest to all priests.

38. Scholars have noted that this passage, while not witnessed in the biblical corpus, is probably dependent on Leviticus 18:21, 24–27 and Ezra 36:17–21. See Jonathan Klawans, *Impurity and Sin in Ancient Judaism* (New York: Oxford University Press, 2000), 44, esp. n. 4.

39. Klawans, *Impurity*, 44.

40. For murder as a polluting behavior, see Numbers 35:33–34, an H text. See handy chart on pp. 104–6 in Knohl, *Sanctuary*.

41. Ezra may also be alluding to Deuteronomy 7:26, in which an idol is called a *to'evah*, an abomination. This could be construed as an idolater in this context, such that bringing an idolater (most likely an idolatress) into one's house is also an abomination—an ethically impure act. See Hayes, who makes the same claim for a direct reference to this passage in 4QMMT; "Intermarriage," 31, and *Gentile Impurities*, 87–89; and my discussion in the next chapter.

42. Contra Klawans, who states quite clearly that they are: "Thus in the passages quoted above [Ezra 9:1, 11 and Neh. 13:26], it is the foreign wives' idolatry that is defiling the land of Israel and threatening the moral purity of the community of Judah. It is precisely because of this source of moral impurity that the marriages were opposed by Ezra and Nehemiah. . . . What is new in Ezra and Nehemiah is the view that the moral impurity of Gentiles is inherent. . . . The books of Ezra and Nehemiah, however, consider local Gentiles to be inherently morally impure"; *Impurity and Sin*, 45. Hayes likewise disagrees with Klawans on this point; *Gentile Impurities*, 64–65.

43. And indeed, the author of Jubilees leans further in this direction; see discussion in the next chapter.

44. Nevertheless, Ezra's hermeneutic leaves him with an unresolved issue: if the present-day Gentiles, by habit, behave impurely, what effect does their pollution have on the land? If the Judeans live among them, will they be spewed out together? Whatever the consequence of the Gentiles' behavior to themselves, Ezra proves himself more concerned with the Judeans' own behavior.

45. The term "religious *zenut*" was coined by Christine Hayes. I will discuss this notion in greater detail below.

46. While one presumes that the overarching theme of H is directed at all of Israel, male and female, the language of these particular passages (Lev. 18 and 20) is aimed at a strictly male audience—most likely the heads of households who had control over the lives of the men and women in those households. Milgrom argues that the incest laws reflect a situation in which unmarried (often widowed or divorced) women live under the roof and protection of a male householder/patriarch who is related to them in some way. In order to prevent the man from taking advantage of

these women's proximity and "easy access," all such relationships are deemed "morally" impure; *Anchor Bible: Leviticus* 2:1523–51. It is interesting to note that many of the marriages outlawed by these priestly legislators are standard practice in the biblical narratives. Abraham marries his half sister, Jacob marries two sisters, Judah has intercourse with his daughter-in-law, and Amram marries his aunt, to name just a few. This priestly legislative reform may have appeared radical (if not "unconstitutional") to the people. In order to emphasize the importance of these innovations these directives are directly linked to impurity. These behaviors are cultically destroying the community from within, for they taint the community members themselves. Impure (i.e., "unethical") people cannot be holy to God.

47. Other socially unjust behaviors such as theft, exploitation of the poor and the alien, prejudiced misjudgments in court, etc. are forbidden, but neither defile nor profane.

48. *BDB*: 275.

49. See note 46 above.

50. A reference to Molekh worship no doubt; Ezra 16.

51. In chapters 16 and 23, Ezekiel warns Israel that God will judge her as an adulterous woman who also has the blood of murder on her hands (for her sacrificed children). Hence, on top of prostitution and adultery, Israel has created "moral" impurity by blood.

52. In common English usage, *fornication* most often refers to illicit sexual relations and means extra- or pre-marital sex. However, here it refers specifically to the forbidden consanguineous relations that do not preclude pre- or extra-marital sex if one's partner is not consanguineously related to you. The Bible is rather vague on the mechanisms of marriage (i.e., how one goes about getting married), but the assumption of these biblical laws is that a man can have as many wives as he likes as long as they are not related to each other or married to someone else (Lev. 18 and 20). And an unmarried women can have sex with whom she chooses—though by losing her virginity she limits her choices in future spouses, especially if she is a priestly daughter (Lev. 21:7). Once married, she is limited to her husband. Nevertheless the forbidden consanguineous relations also forbid a man from having sexual relations with a menstruant woman, including his wife. See discussion in Rachel Biale, *Women and Jewish Law: An Exploration of Women's Issues in Halakhic Sources* (New York: Schocken Books, 1984), 44–45.

53. This is not to say that Leviticus supports free sex but, rather, it argues that a man is not limited to one wife. Sexual relations usually presume marriage (see also Deut. 22:13).

CHAPTER 2

1. In the LXX, *porneia* is the usual Greek translation of *zenut*.

2. The book of Tobit, a late third- or early second-century BCE text, most likely written originally in Hebrew or Aramaic, is part of the standard Greek apocrypha. Although Hebrew and Aramaic fragments were discovered among the documents of the Dead Sea, none of the fragments contains verse 4:12.

3. According to Hayes, the Aramaic *zeniyan* is the equivalent of the Hebrew *zenut*. See her discussion, *Gentile Impurities and Jewish Identities: Intermarriage and Conversion from the Bible to the Talmud* (Oxford: Oxford University Press, 2002), 72. For a full text and translation of Aramaic Levi, see F. Garcia Martinez and E. J. C. Tigchelaar, *The Dead Sea Scrolls: Study Edition* (Leiden: Brill, 1997), 1: 52–53.

4. Damascus Document, CD IV 15–V 11. See discussion below.

5. See discussion of 4QMMT below. The gendered language (*zonah* is feminine) simply represents a patriarchal principle in legislation that "speaks" primarily to a male audience. Presumably an Israelite woman who marries a forbidden partner is equally at fault as her forbidden spouse.

6. There is much scholarly debate concerning the dating of Jubilees, but most scholars place it just before or after the Maccabean revolt. J. VanderKam, "Origins and Purposes of the Book of Jubilees," in *Studies in the Book of Jubilees*, ed. Matthais Albani, Jörge Frey, and Armin Lange (Tübingen: Mohr Siebeck, 1997), 20, goes with 160–150 BCE, in the aftermath of the revolt; Martha Himmelfarb, *A Kingdom of Priests: Ancestry and Merit in Ancient Judaism* (Philadelphia: University of Pennsylvania Press, 2006), 55, places it a little later, in the last third of the second century, because she sees it as a broader reaction to Maccabean Hellenizing policies; and Betsy Halpern Amaru, *The Empowerment of Women in the Book of Jubilees* (Leiden: Brill, 1999), 1, more vaguely dates it to somewhere before the first century BCE.

7. Although Ezra speaks from the biblical canon, Jubilees, who builds from Ezra's hermeneutic represents an extreme minority opinion. Other Second Temple literatures (e.g. Josephus, Aram. T. Levi) concern themselves with the holiness of the priests, but are not aware or concerned with the holiness of all Israel that affects their marriageability with foreigners. And while Tobit also supports endogamy, he does not refer specifically to Israel's holiness as rationale. See Hayes' discussion and argument in *Gentile Impurities*, 70–73.

8. Jubilees 16:18 and 26; 22:27; and 25:12. All translations are taken from the translation of James C. VanderKam, *The Book of Jubilees* (Louvain: Peeters, 1989), I.

9. My argumentation follows and is dependent on Christine Hayes. I really only differ in my emphasis on the nature and effects of miscegenation on the land and on Israelite partners. See *Gentile Impurities*, 74. In contrast, Himmelfarb, *Kingdom*, 68–69, argues that while the Jubilean author considers incest (such as the relations between Reuben and Bilha) to defile the people involved, he "makes up" that intermarriage defiles the sanctuary. While I may be glossing Jubilees, I'm not sure he wouldn't claim that intermarriage also defiles the individuals. Certainly it is more serious than incest as it also defiles the sanctuary. Reading all the passages that concern *zenut* together, the Jubilean author clearly was not happy about any illicit sexual partner, be it incest, Jewish-Gentile intermarriage, or human-angelic intercourse.

10. Himmelfarb, *A Kingdom of Priests*, 81.

11. Cana Werman, "Jubilees 30: Building a Paradigm for the Ban on Intermarriage," *Harvard Theological Review* 90 (1997), 6.

12. There is a problem of translation and transmission here. Though the original text was written in Hebrew, the fullest text we have in hand is in Ethiopic. Along with

Hayes I presume the language behind the Ethiopic "adultery" is really "fornication"—
that is, *zenut*. See VanderKam, *Jubilees*, 2:193, and Christine Hayes, "Intermarriage and
Impurity in Ancient Jewish Sources," *Harvard Theological Review* 92, no. 1 (1999): 19,
n. 55, and *Gentile Impurities*, 75 n. 33. Hayes makes the same assumption and it is
reflected in her translation as opposed to VanderKam's.

13. See Jubilees 30 and the discussions thereof in Werman, "Jubilees 30," 11–14,
and Amaru, *Empowerment*, 127–32. Amaru adds that the father is most to blame and
compared to an adulterer. Shaye J. D. Cohen sees Leviticus 18:21 as the only Levitical
verse lying behind Jubilees 30. He is more interested in how Jubilees appears more
concerned with the marriage of an Israelite daughter to a foreigner, while rabbinic texts
appear focused on Israelite men marrying foreign women. See "From the Bible to the
Talmud: The Prohibition of Intermarriage," *Hebrew Annual Review* 7 (1983): 34–35. I
might add that Leviticus 19:29 plays in the background too, in that the author wants to
portray exogamy, like harlotry as lewdness, which in turn defiles the people and the land.

14. In both the cases of Reuben and Bilha (chap. 33) and Dinah (chap. 30) the
sexual act (incest for the one, sexual relations with a non-Israelite for the other), create
defilement. Chapter 33 states that the defilement affects the land, while chapter 30
notes that it also affects the sanctuary. Either way the defilement threatens the security
of Israel in its land.

15. The Watchers married human wives, leading to corruption and chaos, which
influenced the other humans of Noah's generation and eventually caused the flood.
See Jub. 7:21; 16:5; and 20.

16. Hayes, "Intermarriage," 21; *Gentile Impurities*, 77. Werman, "Jubilees 30," 14.
Himmelfarb comments that in the passage concerning Dinah, the Jubilean author
invents more than exegetes, *Kingdom*, 71 n. 43.

17. Hayes, "Intermarriage," 18; *Gentile Impurities*, 74.

18. Jubilees 20. Though it must be noted here that presumably the Jubilean
author does not accuse the Sodomites of intermarriage but, rather, of general sexual
immorality. Yet this catchall use for the term *zenut*/fornication all the more emphasizes the impurity generated by intermarriage, since it falls into the same category of
forbidden sexual unions as the sins of Sodom and Gomorrah. And most important,
these two cities suffer eternal destruction because of their behavior.

19. QMMT Col iv = 4Q397 6–13; 4QMMT B72–82, as reconstructed and
translated by Elisha Qimron and John Strugnell, *Discoveries in the Judean Desert X:
Qumran Cave 4 V: Miqsat Ma'ase Ha-Torah* (Oxford: Clarendon Press, 1994), 54–57.
Qimron and Strugnell note on page 171, comment 5.7.17, that *zonot* here is a variation
on *zenut*. And indeed in a later section of the text *zenut* is used in the same way (see
text C4–9, p. 58). Interestingly enough, the translators of the passage cited above
translate the first *zonot* as "illegal marriages" and the second as "illegal wives"—
women whom they are forbidden to marry,—and the *zenut* of the later passage as
"fornications." I have added transliterations of the Hebrew terminology in brackets to
highlight these problematics.

20. Leviticus differentiates between objects (sacrifices mostly) that are holy and
most holy, but not among people; the Qumran texts seem to add this distinction. See
Hayes, *Gentile Impurities*, 83.

21. See, for instance, Cohen, "From the Bible to the Talmud," 23–39. Martha Himmelfarb argues here that the Jubilean author is perfectly aware that he is forcing the issue by emphasizing that the law is not in the Torah but on the heavenly tablets he has the angel present to Moses while on Sinai; *Kingdom*, 70.

22. Hayes, *Gentile Impurities*, 87.

23. Most likely the Jerusalem priesthood but the text is not specific.

24. CD IV 15–V 11; Garcia Martinez and Tigchelaar, *Dead Sea Scrolls* 1:554–59. According to Leviticus 18:13, a man is forbidden to marry his maternal niece only; the sectarians amend that law to include paternal nieces as well. I presume that the *niddah* issue has to do with how long a woman remains a *niddah*. Lev. 18:19 stipulates that a man may not ever sleep with a menstruating woman, yet Lev. 15:24 suggests only that if a man should lie with a women during her menstrual period, that he acquires her impurity and must wait out the same number of days with no other ramifications—he contracts an impurity just like hers that can be remedied through appropriate purification processes. Nevertheless, Lev. 18:19 implies that the act of sleeping with a *niddah* creates impurity on the land and irredeemably defiles the man. The Rabbis will later solve this problem by adding the "white days" of a *zavah* (a woman with an abnormal uterine bleeding) to the *niddah*'s cycle, making each healthy woman wait an extra seven days of separation from her husband as a precaution against accidental sexual congress with a *niddah*. This practice probably was not universal in the Second Temple period. The Yahad may even have innovated it, and here polemicizes against those who do not add precautionary days to a woman's cycle.

25. Lev. 18:18 stipulates that one cannot marry one's wife's sister while one's wife is still alive, implying that one could after the first wife dies.

26. This classification, used by Milgrom, Klawans, and others, refers to the most sectarian of the Qumran literature. It includes the Community Rule (1QS), the Damascus Document (CD), the Messianic Rule (1QSa), and many of the peshers and *hodayot* literature. I focus on the first three texts because of their usage of holy terminology.

27. Although it appears that much of Israel has disqualified itself from the covenantal agreement, the Yahad does not seem to open up any doors to non-Israelites. Their polemic is an internal Israelite one.

28. QS V 20–23; Garcia Martinez and Tigchelaar, *Dead Sea Scrolls* 1:83. This and all subsequent citations are adapted from and referenced to this translation. I have paid particular attention to the language of holiness and purity, and adapted the translations accordingly.

29. Himmelfarb, *Kingdom*, 85ff.

30. Concerning the priestly nature of the Qumran community, see Robert A. Kugler, "Priesthood at Qumran," in *Dead Sea Scrolls after Fifty Years*, ed. Peter Flint and James C. VanderKam (Leiden: Brill, 1999), 2.93–94, n.1.

31. CD III 2–4; Garcia Martinez and Tigchelaar, *Dead Sea Scrolls* 1:555.

32. See Steven D. Fraade for a similar argument; "Ascetical Aspects of Ancient Judaism," in *Jewish Spirituality: From the Bible through the Middle Ages*, ed. Arthur Green (New York: Crossroads, 1986–87), 253–88.

33. Jonathan Klawans, *Impurity and Sin in Ancient Judaism* (New York: Oxford University Press, 2000), 75–89.

34. QS V 18–20; Garcia Martinez and Tigchelaar, *Dead Sea Scrolls* 1:80–81. The Qumran literature, like the late biblical literature, uses *niddah* and *tameh* interchangeably.

35. Whether one considers the war camp (Deut. 23:10–15) or Sinai (Ex. 19) to be pure or holy depends on your understanding of QDS in these passages. For a discussion on the matter see Devorah Dimant, *"4QFlorilegium* and the Idea of the Community as a Temple," in *Hellenica et Judaica: Hommages à Valentin Nikiprovetzky [z"l]*, ed. André Caquot, Mireille Hadas-Lebel, and Jean Riaud (Leuven: Peeters, 1986), 174–89.

36. Nevertheless, other impurities, such as bribe-taking, must also be avoided in order to preserve the integrity of the Temple. Klawans notes that, in terms of purity legislation, the Temple Scroll's only innovation is to add that bribe-taking defiles the Temple; *Impurity and Sin*, 50.

37. Himmelfarb discusses these purity laws in detail in *Kingdom*, chaps. 3 and 4. It is a curiosity of the Temple Scroll that it does not describe a shelter outside the city for menstruants, as it does for those who incur other sorts of impurities. As Himmelfarb notes (pp. 94–97), although not explicit, the Temple Scroll assumes sexual activity takes place only outside the city. Hence, I suggest that women were kept out of the city as well, as they were considered "unessential personnel." They did not need shelters outside the city because they lived in their own homes, which were already outside the city.

38. See further discussion in Himmelfarb, *Kingdom*, 95–98.

39. War Scroll I 16; VII 6; X 11; XII 1, 4, 7–8; Garcia Martinez and Tigchelaar, *Dead Sea Scrolls* 1:114–15; 124–25; 128–29; 132–33.

40. 4QMMT, it should be noted, also concerns itself with preserving the purity of Jerusalem and the sanctuary. More forcefully than either the Temple Scroll or the War Scroll, 4QMMT states, "Jerusalem is the camp of the holy [*mahaneh haqodesh*], and is the place which He has chosen from among all the tribes of Israel. For Jerusalem is the capital of the camps of Israel." The statement comes in the middle of a laundry list of "ritual" purity issues, the import of which is that Jerusalem is in great danger of pollution if these listed instructions are not followed to the letter. Yet only thirteen lines later, 4QMMT launches into a polemic against *zenut* and mixed marriages. These obviously affect the sanctuary as well as the people because, following Jubilees' construct, *zenut* is a more detrimental kind of impurity. Several lines earlier 4QMMT notes that "[For all the sons of Israel should beware] of any mixed [*ta'arovet*] unions and be full of reverence for the sanctuary," 4QMMT B 48–9, Qimron and Strugnell, *Discoveries in the Judean* Desert, 50–51. On one level, *zenut* or any other forbidden union is just another of many impurities that affect the Temple. Nevertheless, 4QMMT emphasizes *zenut*'s detrimental effect on the holy people as well. Furthermore, in its list of impurity issues, nether semen nor menstrual blood are mentioned. In 4QMMT, there is no correlation between sexual restraint/no women and holy space/Jerusalem. In contrast, the Temple Scroll and War Scroll remain oblivious to issues of *zenut* and its effects on the holiness of Israel. All three, however, focus on the purity required for Jerusalem—however categorized. In Klawan's categorization, 4QMMT has homogenized this "moral" impurity into its list of "ritual" impurities, most likely because of its reputed effect on the sanctuary. The Temple Scroll and War

Scroll remain concerned with impurities that affect the sanctuary more than those that affect the people.

41. QSa (1Q28a) I 25–27; II 3–9; Garcia Martinez and Tigchelaar, *Dead Sea Scrolls* 1:102–103.

42. QS III 4–6; Garcia Martinez and Tigchelaar, *Dead Sea Scrolls* 1:74–75.

43. Klawans argues that baths were needed after repentance—even of behavioral impurity; *Impurity and Sin*, 75–89.

44. QS III 6–9; Garcia Martinez and Tigchelaar, *Dead Sea Scrolls* 1:74–75.

45. Josephus does refer to some of their practices as "pure," but it is not clear at all that he has levitical purity in mind; see, for instance, *The Wars of the Jews* 2.129. Concerning Josephus' depiction of the Essenes, Martin Goodman argues that one should not necessary conclude that he was describing the Qumranites. Concerning first-century Jewish practice, Goodman further argues that one should not assume that all the religious practices of first-century Jews were biblically derived. See Goodman's collected articles in *Judaism in the Roman World: Collected Essays* (Leiden and Boston: Brill, 2007); see especially chs. 11 ("A Note on the Qumran Sectarians, the Essenes and Josephus") and 16 ("Kosher Olive Oil in Antiquity"). See also Hayes, *Gentile Impurities*, 91, who argues similarly that Josephus and Philo are not as concerned about the holiness of the people Israel as Ezra, the author of Jubilees, nor the Qumranites seem to be.

CHAPTER 3

1. The language of holiness pervades the New Testament literature where it oscillates between the divine and human worlds. In the synoptic Gospels, for instance, holiness resides firmly in the divine realm. God, God's spirit and name, the angels, the sanctuary and its furniture, the covenant, and Jesus are holy. By and large, people are not so described. Only Paul's letter to the Galatians and 2 and 3 John do not use "holy" terminology of any sort. I use the term "Christian" conventionally, but Paul refers to his audience most often as *hagioi*, "saints."

2. Concerning *porneia* as a direct translation of *zenut* into Greek idiom, see David Frankfurter, "Jews or Not? Reconstructing the 'Other' in Rev. 2:9 and 3:9," *Harvard Theological Review* 94, no. 4 (2001): 415–16. See especially his footnotes 52–55 for other resources. A small note on Rev. 14:4 (discussed by Frankfurter on page 416) concerning "those who have defiled themselves with women" most likely refers to the men who have defiled themselves by their own semen emissions in the act of coitus with women—not, as some have suggested, by contact with menstruating women, nor I think as Frankfurter argues as a direct reference to sexual activity as *porneia*. *Porneia* I think still refers to forbidden sexual relations, be they construed levitically or more generally as sex with outsiders. Sexual activity in and of itself is also an impurity creator (through the semen), but I do not think that John is calling it here *porneia* (have no fear, others certainly will!). John's reference here to chaste men is more similar to the Temple Scroll's advocating of priestly chastity while on duty in the holy city for fear of producing semen impurities. See also the work of Ernst Haenchen, *The Acts of the Apostles: A Commentary*, trans. B. Noble and G. Shinn (Philadelphia: Westminster Press, 1971), 448, n.4.

3. It is not my intention to define Pauline "faith"; it is only important to understand that it is this faith, however defined, that brings one into Paul's holy community. In speaking to a primarily Gentile community, Paul wants only to emphasize that faith trumps birth lineage in his community.

4. Admittedly, Paul remains ambiguous (in Romans, at least) as to how he understands the ascribed holiness of unconverted native Israelites. Have they lost their God-given holy status? I think he skirts this issue by claiming that holiness achieved through faith supersedes, or is at least more valuable than, historically ascribed holiness. Nor does he here address the issue of creating a new ascribed holiness through the children *produced* in this community. Are they holy through birth or must they achieve it, too? See discussion of 1 Corinthians 7 below. Martha Himmelfarb argues, using the work of Denise Kimber Buell, who bases her argument on her reading of the *Shepherd of Hermas*, that the early Christians began to consider themselves a new race, but a race one joined through merit (faith) rather than birth. And despite the fact that after several generations Christians were born into Christianity through their families, this self-understanding did not lose relevance as "an identity that transcended birth and was enshrined in the New Testament and other works from the early period"; *A Kingdom of Priests: Ancestry and Merit in Ancient Judaism* (Philadelphia: University of Pennsylvania Press, 2006), 175–76, esp. nn. 82–85.

5. All New Testament translations are based on the NRSV with slight adjustments for my argument.

6. An image conjured by Kathy Gaca, *The Making of Fornication: Eros, Ethics and Political Reform in Greek Philosophy and Early Christianity* (Berkeley: University of California Press, 2003), 164, but in reference to "screwing" with the law.

7. *Akathartos* is the LXX's standard translation for *tameh; akatharsias* translates *tumah*. I am translating *porneia* as "prohibited sexual relations or partners," rather than as "fornication," to keep it in line with my understand of *zenut*, which I think it translates.

8. Also noted by Philip Carrington, *The Primitive Christian Catechism: A Study in the Epistles* (Cambridge: Cambridge University Press, 1940) and Edward G. Selwyn, *The First Epistle of St. Peter* (London: Macmillan, 1946), 369–75, as cited in Larry O. Yarbrough, *Not Like the Gentiles: Marriage Rules in the Letters of Paul* (Atlanta: Scholars Press, 1985), 79.

9. Here I argue contra Gaca (*Fornication*, 154), who claims that this *porneia* best translates as "other-theistic copulation," whereas I see it more in line with the levitical "customs of the peoples of the land" such as incest, adultery, etc. Similarly, Christine Hayes argues, in *Gentile Impurities and Jewish Identities: Intermarriage and Conversion from the Bible to the Talmud* (Oxford: Oxford University Press, 2002), 92–98, that Paul equates *porneia* with mixed Christian–non-Christian marriages. See discussion below. While there is no knowing if Paul really thought Gentiles committed bestiality and the like, sexual invective was a known and useful polemical tool. See work of Jennifer Knust, *Abandoned to Lust: Sexual Slander and Ancient Christianity* (New York: Columbia University Press, 2006).

10. See also 5:32 and Luke 16:18. It is probably from these Gospel texts that adultery comes to dominate the early Christian notion of sexual impurity. Yet, *porneia*

probably best translates here as "prostitution," "promiscuity," or some form of forbidden consanguineous relations, if not specifically adultery. Perhaps it comes to the fore here due to a growing distaste for Roman and/or Jewish marriage practices such as concubinage among the former, polygyny among the latter, and divorce among them both. See Aline Rousselle on Roman marriage practices, *Porneia: On Desire and the Body in Antiquity* (Oxford and New York: Basil Blackwell, 1988).

11. Damascus Document, CD IV 15–V 11.

12. Yarbrough, *Not Like the Gentiles*, 67–78. He gives Tobit 4:12 and T. Levi 9:9–10 as examples of Hellenistic Jewish moral literature. Thus, Yarbrough distinguishes Paul from his Jewish Hellenistic forbears. But I think one could similarly argue that these Hellenistic Jewish writers similarly understand endogamy to be a commandment from God. What is most important for this discussion is that they also couple the "commandment" to endogamy with the commandment to avoid *porneia*. Yarbrough also notes, on page 79, how central the notion of holiness is to Paul's discussion, but Yarbrough does not extend his discussion beyond this one paragraph. As I noted in the last chapter, Tobit implicitly and Aramaic T. Levi explicitly link endogamy to holiness.

13. Jonathan Klawans, *Impurity and Sin in Ancient Judaism* (New York: Oxford University Press, 2000), 143–50.

14. In contra distinction to the other Second Temple authors discussed in the last chapter, the Gospel writers (whether of the Second Temple period or later) never directly oppose *porneia* to holiness nor equate *porneia* with exogamy.

15. Some other manuscripts read *hagneia* rather than *enkrateia*. See apparatus to Gal. 5:23, in Nestle-Aland *Novum Testamentum Graece* (Stuttgart: Deutsche Bibelgesellschaft, 1979), 502.

16. Yarbrough, *Not Like the Gentiles*, 92, 115, 124.

17. See discussion below of Kathy Gaca's work.

18. According to Dale Martin, *malakoi* can also refer to the sexually indulgent in the sense that one who has too much sex is weak in character (has no self-control) and also weakens his physic by too much sex—draining of his "life essence" and virility; *The Corinthian Body* (New Haven and London: Yale University Press, 1995), 226.

19. That Paul's *hagiasthete* may be a translation or reflection of the biblical *hitqaddash*, which purifies rather than sanctifies, is an intriguing possibility.

20. Yarbrough, *Not Like the Gentiles*, 115.

21. Contra Hayes (*Gentile Impurities*, 92–98), who argues that Paul creates his own paradigm of Christian endogamy, which forbids holy believers from sexual contact with "morally" impure unbelievers for fear they will contract their impurity. See discussion below.

22. See Lev. 18:8; 20:11. If one presumes that the man in question has taken up with his father's wife (but who is not the man's mother) only after the father has died, he commits incest. If he takes up with her while the father is still alive (and still married to the woman), that would be adultery. But since Paul complains that the man does something that "is not found even among pagans" makes the case for incest stronger. Presumably a general notion of adultery as criminal was shared around the Mediterranean basin, but considering one's father's widow off limits might not have

been. Hence the Corinthians' disregard this problematic relationship. Dale Martin argues that it is because the "Strong" at Corinth do not share Paul's concern about pollution that they ignore the incestuous man's position in the community, but I would argue that it is equally possible that they are not familiar with the levitical laws upon which Paul bases his notions of pollution. See Martin, *Corinthian Body*, especially chap. 6. See also Rousselle, *Porneia*, esp. chap. 6 on divorce laws in Greco-Roman culture.

23. Martin, *Corinthian Body*, 163.

24. Ibid., 146–48.

25. Hayes, *Gentile Impurities*, 92–93. She cites Martin, *Corinthian Body*, 174–78.

26. Martin, *Corinthian Body*, 209. See also Will Deming, *Paul on Marriage and Celibacy: The Hellenistic Background of 1 Corinthians 7* (Cambridge: Cambridge University Press, 1995), 222, who sees *porneia* as reason to marry rather than as a reason not to marry—namely, because of the fear of *porneia*, one should marry. Nevertheless Deming, like Martin, understands *porneia* to refer to any extra-marital sex and not to specific forbidden sexual partners.

27. Some rabbis, such as Rava, similarly argue that legislating too much sexual restraint (particularly if it goes beyond the biblical restrictions) would be burdensome to most people. See discussion in chap. 7.

28. Yarbrough, *Not Like the Gentiles*, 115, 125. See also Martin, who argues that 1 Corinthians can be read within Greco-Roman literary/rhetorical genre as a call to *concordia*—unity and harmony within the community; *Corinthian Body*, chap. 2.

29. Gaca, *Fornication*, 165–83, argues that the LXX, more than the Hebrew biblical text, emphasizes the dangers of foreign spouses as well as foreign worship, hence Paul's "ready at hand" association of prostitutes with non-Christian idol worshipers. Yet, it seems to me that this is exactly the conclusion that the Jubilean author, who read the Bible in Hebrew, comes to—that foreigners (because of their idolatry) can be called "*zonot*." Paul, who reads his Bible in Greek, nevertheless, I argue, does not associate all foreigners with *porneia*.

30. Gaca, *Fornication*, 124–31, 137–46, argues that Paul is led to this conclusion by the nature and priorities of the Greek Bible he would have read. She argues specifically that Paul is motivated by the narratives of Israel's "spiritual fornication" rather than by the prohibited sexual relations legislation. There are two problems with this argument. First, in order to make her argument that Paul understands *porneia* to be "sex with foreigners," she reads the LXX as if it makes the same claim. While there is no doubt that several parts of the LXX (but not all) do not approve of sex with (certain) foreigners, to claim that that is the main agenda of the book is to overlook most of the text. Hence, Gaca gives short shrift to the LXX as a complex and composite text on its own by reading it rather homogeneously and particularly narrowly through the eyes of Paul, who happens to pick up on this particular notion of endogamy. Second, she dismisses the purity language that I find so obvious and central to Paul's hermeneutic as unimportant and beside the point because she wants to argue that *porneia* is specifically heterosexual and anti-foreigner. In the end, Gaca reads not only the LXX through a (limited) Pauline lens but also Paul through his later interpreters.

31. Gaca, *Fornication*, 143, 167, claims that Paul receives this translation of *porneia* as "sex with foreigners" and *pornê* as "foreigner" directly from the LXX, yet

this is not the whole picture. In the LXX, particularly in the prophetic works, *pornê* can refer to a foreign woman, but it can also be simply a prostitute. Equally as often, the *pornê* in question is Israel, who prostitutes herself with foreign gods. *Porneia* often refers to illicit sexual relations, but it does not necessarily in all places refer to sex with foreigners. Often as not, it is used metaphorically to refer to foreign worship. Even for Paul, *porneia* carries more meaning than just "sex with foreigners," as I demonstrate above.

32. Likewise, Hayes argues that Paul's hermeneutic fits within a trajectory of Second Temple paradigms that align exogamy with *porneia*, and as she argues, influences later patristic constructs of the same. My reading of Paul demonstrates, I think, that he proves to be an exception to the rule as far as his hermeneutic of holiness and *porneia* goes. Later readers surely read a construct of exogamy and *porneia* into Paul, but I do not think it is even implicitly there in his thought processes. Gentiles practice *porneia*, but marriage to one does not necessarily constitute *porneia* for the Christian partner nor does he contract an impurity from his nonbelieving spouse. For Paul, no Gentile can be completely off-limits if there is a possibility that that Gentile might convert.

33. Gaca, *Fornication*, 124, 143; again, I see Gaca reading the LXX texts primarily through a Pauline lens, and a limited one at that.

34. There is some question about the authenticity of this passage. See Gaca, *Fornication*, 149, n. 80; and Yarbrough, *Not Like the Gentiles*, 2, n.7.

35. Hayes, *Gentile Impurities*, 97. See also Gaca, *Fornication*, 149–51, who makes a similar connection to the levitical law on mixing, but ignores the context of holy behavior in which it is situated.

36. See Matt. 5:31; Mark 10:11; Luke 16:18. Note that Jesus too gives one exception, in the case of *porneia*, which here most likely means adultery. Since Matthew does not deal directly with Gentiles, by and large, it is better to understand *porneia* to be strictly relating to internal Christian issues rather than between Christians and non-Christians.

37. See discussion in Hayes, *Gentile Impurities*, 94.

38. Y. M. Gillihan, "Jewish Laws of Illicit Marriage, the Defilement of Offspring and the Holiness of the Temple: A New Halakhic Interpretation of 1 Corinthians 7:14," *Journal of Biblical Literature* 121, no. 4 (2002): 711–30. I think Gillihan goes too far in calling this a halakhic ruling. Surely legal decisions were rendered from the day the biblical legal code was canonized—but these decisions and legal interpretations need not be labeled by the much later rabbinic terminology nor explained by their methodology.

39. Gillihan, "Jewish Laws," 719–21. Gillihan understands the children to be impure, but they are simply profane—not fully Israelite. By bringing in Qumranic and rabbinic discussions on illicit marriages and their illegitimate offspring, Gillihan demonstrates that there was a broad spectrum of views concerning this very subject. It is interesting to note that the LXX to Deut. 23.3 translates *mamzer* as *ekpornê*.

40. Gillihan, "Jewish Laws," 731. One could also argue that Paul, in redefining holy community, hesitates to exclude anyone who might convert and hence refuses to use *porneia* in these cases.

41. Hayes, *Gentile Impurities*, 95.

42. See Deming, *Paul on Marriage*, 133, who also argues that it is not clear why the children are holy, just that Paul and the Corinthians understand that they are.

43. That Ephesians here also labels the old nature "corrupt" will play into later Christian understandings of *porneia* as general sexuality and therefore part of their old nature and corrupt. 1 Peter 1:14 also upholds this notion that Gentiles behave in defiling ways.

CHAPTER 4

1. Contrary to other scholars, I do not see a strong ascetic trend in nor trace great influence from Tatian. See my article, "Re-Imagining Tatian: The Damaging Effects of Polemical Rhetoric," *Journal of Early Christian Studies* 16, no. 1 (Spring, 2008): 1–30.

2. While the *Acts* is by no means the earliest Syriac Christian document, for it is predated by the *Odes of Solomon* and the writings of Tatian, among others, these texts provide us with no further or older information regarding the use of *qaddishuta* and sexuality. And while Tatian in particular is held up as primarily (if not single-handedly) responsible for the ascetic tendencies of the Churches of the East, he exhibits no hermeneutic of holiness and sexuality. See note above. Two texts I do not consider here, mostly for lack of space and questions of applicability, are the *Didascalia Apostolorum* and the *Pseudo-Clementines on Virginity*. Further study of these interesting texts would no doubt prove useful to this discussion.

3. See Han J. W. Drijvers, "The Acts of Thomas," in *New Testament Apocrypha*, ed. W. Schneemelcher, Eng. trans. A. J. B. Higgins (Philadelphia: Westminster Press, 1963–66), 2:323; and A. F. J. Klijn's introduction to his English translation of the Syriac, in *The Acts of Thomas: Introduction, Text, and Commentary* (Leiden: Brill, 1962), 16.

4. The only exception to this division is the story of the bride and groom of Andropolis in the first act. This is most likely a well-placed interpolation that provides an encratic framework to the whole piece, thus subsuming the miracle stories into the larger martyrdom narrative. In so doing, the redactor simply adds the miracle stories to his encratic narrative without actually ironing out the striking sexual behavioral differences between the two.

5. Andrew Jacobs argues that, in its Greek version at least, the *AJT* fits the subversive class-driven themes apparent in the other apocryphal Acts of the Apostles—namely, in attacking and subverting the harmony of upper-class marriage, these narratives suggest the moral vacuousness of those unions in comparison to the new "families" forming around the apostles that attracted followers from all strata of society; "A Family Affair: Marriage, Class and Ethics in the Apocryphal Acts of the Apostles," *Journal of Early Christian Studies* 7, no.1 (1999): 105–38.

6. Harold W. Attridge, "Intertextuality in the Acts of Thomas," *Semeia* 80 (1997 [1999]), 88; Yves Tissot, "Les acts apocryphes de Thomas, example de receuil composite," in *Les actes apocryphes des apotres, Christianisme de monde païen*, ed. Françoise Bovon, et al. (Geneva: Labor et Fides, 1981), 223.

7. Drijvers, "The Acts of Thomas," 2: 327.

8. Ibid., 2: 324–25.

9. See his article summarizing the state of scholarship on the subject: "The Writings Ascribed to Thomas and the Thomas Tradition," *Nag Hammadi Library after 50 Years: Proceedings of the 1995 Society of Biblical Literature*, ed. Anne McGuire and John D. Turner (Leiden: Brill, 1997), 295–307.

10. This theme is well developed by Elaine Pagels in her classic book, *The Gnostic Gospels* (New York: Vintage Books, 1979), esp. 131. But there she depends on the *Gospel* more than the *Acts*.

11. Poirier, "Writings," 302.

12. Drijvers, "The Acts of Thomas," 2:329, 334.

13. Yves Tissot, "L'encratisme des Acts de Thomas," *Aufseig und Niedergang der römischen Welt* II.25.6 (1988): 4419.

14. Attridge, "Intertextuality," 88; see also Drijvers, "The Acts of Thomas," 2: 326.

15. On this developing ideology, see Susanna Elm, *Virgins of God: The Making of Asceticism in Late Antiquity* (Oxford: Oxford University Press, 1994), 47–51.

16. In some sense, the term *enkrateia*, meaning "controlled," could equally apply to the monogamous marriages in that they are purposefully limiting their sexuality to one life-time marriage partner.

17. Drijvers, "Acts of Thomas," 2: 334. I have downplayed Drijver's argument in that he believes that the whole of the *Acts* is a direct transposition of Tatian's soteriology into narrative form.

18. *Acts of Judah Thomas (AJT)* 15; Drijvers, "The Acts of Thomas," 2: 345. See note 26 below.

19. On other soteriologies of knowledge, see the wide range between the writings of Valentinus, Gospel of Philip, and Justin Martyr—all of which share some similarities with and many differences from Tatian. See the work of Emily J. Hunt, *Christianity in the Second Century: The Case of Tatian* (London and New York: Routledge, 2003).

20. I also wonder if there is a gender difference at play here. Tatian and the author of the "Hymn of the Pearl" could certainly see themselves as twins or at one with Jesus if they were thinking in a male-gendered mode (they share the male gender with Jesus and could see him as a twin or brother). Yet, Judah converts mostly women who cannot claim to be identical twins to Jesus if they are female. Hence, the marriage metaphor perhaps works better for the author of the *Acts*.

21. Drijvers, "The Acts of Thomas," 2: 327. See also Klijn's introduction, *The Acts of Thomas*, 14.

22. See notes 1 and 2 above.

23. The one time in the *Oration* where Tatian mentions marriage and adultery in the same breath he refers to the Greek gods, not to humans (*Oration* 8.1).

24. James H. Charlesworth has written about the *Odes* in several places. See his introduction to *Odes of Solomon: The Syriac Texts* (Missoula, Mont.: Scholars Press, 1977); *Critical Reflections on the Odes of Solomon* (Sheffield: Sheffield Academic Press, 1998), esp. vol. 1: chap. 1; and his introduction to the *Odes* in the *Old Testament Pseudepigrapha* (Garden City, N.Y.: Doubleday, 1983–85), 2: 725–34. All translations

come from Charlesworth's text and translation found in his critical edition of the *Odes of Solomon*. I use the term "Jewish-Christian" rather broadly to refer to the greater shared literary milieu rather than to any one group of people.

25. The QDS words used by the odist most often are manipulated in their biblical mode and refer to God and his property, such as his holy spirit (6:7, 11:2, 14:8), holy abode (4:1), holy power (32:3), holy thought (9:3), and holy day (15:3). The poet alludes to God once as the Holy Father (31:5). Holiness belongs to God, emanates from God, and marks God's things. Furthermore, the poet hallows God through the words of his ode (27:1). The odist also alludes to his composition as a holy ode—namely, an ode dedicated to God. God's "holy ones" appear to be the community of believers as constructed by the poet. The poet's notion of holy community resembles that of other Jewish communities we explored in earlier chapters. While borrowing the biblical language traditionally reserved for the nation of Israel (holy, elect), the poet designates as holy only those among Israel who have accepted Jesus as their Messiah. This community's boundaries are defined by faith. The holy ones will dwell in God's kingdom (22:12)—that is, only those who gain salvation through faith in the Messiah will achieve immortality. The joy (of the Messiah) is for the holy ones (23:1) while his grace and love are for the elect (23:2–3). Only the holy and elect (those who accept God's Messiah) will benefit from his love. The elect ones walk with God (33:13), and God, the Most High One, will be known by his holy ones (7:16). Holiness seems here only to be defined by faith. Those who believe in the Messiah are holy/elect. There is no allusion to purity, defilement, or profanation.

The term *qaddishuta* appears only once in the *Odes* 13:1–4:

¹Behold the Lord is our mirror/ open your eyes and see them in Him.
²And learn the manner of your face/ then declare praises to his Spirit.
³And wipe the paint from your face/ *love his qaddishuta and put it on.*
⁴Then you will be unblemished at all times with him.
Halleluyah.

Qaddishuta clearly belongs to God—it is God's *qaddishuta* that should be worn. It most likely refers to the spirit in line 2. When the lover puts on God's holiness—that is, God's holy spirit—the lover will see his reflection in God. The lover will recognize how the spirit connects him to God and makes him resemble God—that is, resemble the human form that the Messiah took on earth. The holy spirit will similarly perfect the humanity of the lover by rendering him unblemished—sinless. Although the poet "puts on" *qaddishuta*, it remains here in God's realm unconnected to sexuality.

26. I cite from Drijvers' translation of the Greek with his emendations from the Syriac in the <>. I have only emended his translation of *porneia* to read "improper sexual behavior" rather than "fornication." I note according to the chapter divisions of the Greek text and to the page numbers in Drijvers' translation.

27. Burton Visotsky notes how similar this story is to several other versions in the rabbinic literature; see his "Three Syriac Cruxes," *Journal of Jewish Studies* 42, no.4 (1991): 171–73.

28. *AJT* 28; Drijvers, "The Acts of Thomas," 2: 350. Emphasis added as this is a central theme that is repeated several times in the *Acts*.

29. Mark 7:21–23; Jubilees 7:20. Note also that Aphrahat lists idolatry, prostitution, adultery, and theft as the worst of sins. *Dem.* 11.6/484.6–7.

30. *AJT* 51; Drijvers, "The Acts of Thomas," 2: 361. The Syriac reads: "because I could not bear to see her while she was having intercourse with other men."

31. *AJT* 51; Drijvers, "The Acts of Thomas," 2: 361.

32. The Syriac has *shawtaputa ṣata*, "foul intercourse."

33. I am assuming that *hagiôsunê* is the Greek translation of the Syriac *qaddishuta*. And while *qaddishuta* appears elsewhere in the Syriac, where it is not backed up by a *hagiôsunê* I presume those locations may have suffered some later editing. I also note that Thessalonians uses *hagiasmos* rather than *hagiôsunê*. Both terms are standard NT usages. *Hagiasmos* seems to connote "consecration" or "sanctification," the result of an action taken, whereas *hagiôsunê* takes on the more abstract notion of absolute "holiness."

34. *AJT* 58; Drijvers, "The Acts of Thomas," 2: 363. Emphasis added.

35. This language is echoed in the *Testament of Simeon*, who claims: "And beware of committing sexual immorality, for sexual immorality is the mother of all evils; it separates from God and drives those who indulge in it to Beliar" (*Test. of Simeon* V: 3–4).

36. *AJT* 12; Drijvers, "The Acts of Thomas," 2: 344.

37. *AJT* 12; "The Acts of Thomas," 2: 344.

38. One might argue at the same time that the mere act of bringing children into the world necessarily is cause for more pollution to spread throughout the land through *their* bad behavior. Hence, it is wise not to participate in this folly of human sexuality because it brings more sinners to the world.

39. *AJT* 12; Drijvers, "The Acts of Thomas," 2: 344.

40. *AJT* 13; Drijvers, "The Acts of Thomas," 2: 344.

41. *AJT* 84–5; Drijvers, "The Acts of Thomas," 2: 372–73. Drijvers has "impurity" where I have "disgraceful deeds of the body."

42. *AJT* 85; Drijvers, "The Acts of Thomas," 2: 373.

43. *AJT* 86; Drijvers, "The Acts of Thomas," 2: 373.

44. *AJT* 83; Drijvers, "The Acts of Thomas," 2: 372.

45. *BT Shabbat* 31a.

46. *AJT* 88; Drijvers, "The Acts of Thomas," 2: 373–74.

47. *AJT* 117; Drijvers, "The Acts of Thomas," 2: 386.

48. *AJT* 124; Drijvers, "The Acts of Thomas," 2: 389. I have added the "earthly" and "heavenly" in brackets to make it easier to distinguish between "that" marriage (earthly) and "this" marriage (heavenly), but they are not so spelled out in the text.

49. *AJT* 100; Drijvers, "The Acts of Thomas," 2: 377.

50. *AJT* 101; Drijvers, "The Acts of Thomas," 2: 378.

51. *AJT* 104; Drijvers, "The Acts of Thomas," 2: 379.

52. Although this phrase is missing from the Greek, Thomas' response does not make sense without it.

53. *AJT* 126; Drijvers, "The Acts of Thomas," 2: 389–90.

54. *AJT* 127; Drijvers, "The Acts of Thomas," 2: 390.

55. *AJT* 85; Drijvers, "The Acts of Thomas," 2: 373.

56. *AJT* 97; Drijvers, "The Acts of Thomas," 2: 376.

57. *AJT* 104; Drijvers, "The Acts of Thomas," 2: 379.

CHAPTER 5

1. It is possible that the letter of inquiry that opens Aphrahat's *Demonstrations* is simply a foil to his expositions. Yet, even so, it most likely represents questions and issues that Aphrahat confronted in his position and wished to settle once and for all with his *Demonstrations*.

2. Aphrahat composes one final demonstration (23), "On the Grape Cluster," which outlines a history of Christian salvation, sometime later.

3. I examine several of these polemical treatises in my Ph.D. dissertation, *Jewish-Christian Polemics in Fourth-Century Persian Mesopotamia: A Reconstructed Conversation*, Stanford, 1993; and in several articles: "A Jewish-Christian Conversation in Fourth-Century Persian Mesopotamia," *Journal of Jewish Studies* 47, no. 1 (1996): 45–63; "Aphrahat on Noah's Righteousness in Light of the Jewish-Christian Polemic," in *The Book of Genesis in Jewish and Oriental Christian Interpretation*, ed. Judith Frishman and Lucas Van Rompay (Louvain: Peeters, 1997), 57–71; and "Psalm 22's Christological Interpretive Tradition in Light of Christian Anti-Jewish Polemic," *Journal of Early Christian Studies* 6, no. 1 (1998): 37–57.

4. Sebastian Brock, "Early Syrian Asceticism," *Numen* 20, no. 1 (April 1973): 7; Susan Ashbrook Harvey: *Asceticism and Society in Crisis: John of Ephesus and the Lives of the Eastern Saints* (Berkeley: University of California Press, 1990), 4–8; Robert Murray, *Symbols of Church and Kingdom: A Study in Early Syriac Tradition* (London and New York: Cambridge University Press, 1975), 15; and Murray's earlier article, "The Exhortation to Candidates for Ascetical Vows at Baptism in the Ancient Syriac Church," *New Testament Studies* 21 (1974–75): 58–79; Arthur Vööbus, *Celibacy, a Requirement for Admission to Baptism in the Early Syrian Church* (Stockholm: Estonian Theological Society in Exile, 1951), vol. 1; and his *History of Asceticism in the Syrian Orient* (Louvain: Secretariat du Corpus SCO, 1958–88), 1:10–14, 69–76.

5. It is less clear with angels as to whether they simply do not need sex or are genderless. Given that most named angels bear masculine names, I assume the former: they are gendered male, but remain celibate. To further clarify the Syriac terminology, *ihidaye* is the plural of *ihidaya* as *qaddishe* is the plural of *qaddisha*.

6. See John 1:14, 1:18, 3:16, 3:18 for scriptural prooftexts and Aphrahat's use of them in *Dem.* 6.6/268.26–269.6; see also Sidney Griffith, "Asceticism in the Church of Syria: The Hermeneutics of Early Syrian Monasticism," in *Asceticism*, ed. Vincent L. Wimbush and Richard Valantaisis (New York: Oxford University Press, 1995), 224–25; and also Murray, "The Exhortation," 67.

7. Griffith, "Asceticism," 224–25.

8. See Susanna Elm, *Virgins of God: The Making of Asceticism in Late Antiquity* (Oxford: Oxford University Press, 1994), 47–51.

9. Peter Brown, *The Body and Society: Men, Women and Sexual Renunciation in Early Christianity* (New York: Columbia University Press, 1988), 100.

10. I discuss this diatribe in more detail in the last section of this chapter.

11. As we shall see in the following chapters, the Rabbis are similarly obsessed with protecting their spiritual work and arena from intrusion and defilement by women.

12. Adam Lehto, *Divine Law, Asceticism, and Gender in Aphrahat's "Demonstrations,"* Ph.D. dissertation, University of Toronto, 2003, 68–70. Lehto also argues that one cannot necessarily make a direct link between male virgins and the holy ones, either. He sticks to the more conventional and rigid differentiation between virgins and nonvirginal celibates. Only the latter are called *qaddishe*. While I am sure this is true in origin, it seems to me that Aphrahat tends to lump his categories.

13. In essence, Aphrahat's position on female spiritual lives reflects more accurately the concurrent rabbinic attitude toward female spiritual lives—it does not interest them as long as it does not take away from their own. Yet, taking all of the demonstrations into consideration, Aphrahat is inconsistent on the issue of women. On the one hand, like his rabbinic neighbors he claims that Adam was better than Eve (*Dem.* 18.8/837.7–9) and on the other, Aphrahat argues that there were plenty of biblical women who equaled the men in their greatness (*Dem.* 14.11/596.1–597.22).

14. See note 4 above.

15. One could argue similarly concerning the classical Rabbis' discussion of women. While still "members of the tribe," women are somehow not "real" Jews—a category reserved for the covenantally circumcised men who exclusively are commanded (according to these Rabbis) to worship God through study and fulfillment of God's word, the Torah. Likewise, Aphrahat presents married parishioners, though certainly blessed, as inferior to the celibates. See, for instance, the work of Judith Baskin, *Midrashic Women: Formations of the Feminine in Rabbinic Literature* (London and Hanover, N.H.: Brandeis University Press, 2002).

16. Note that the Peshitta and Vetus Syriaca Sinai add "and bride" to "bridegroom" in v.1. So, too, do some of the Greek Gospel manuscripts.

17. *Dem.* 6.1/240.6–12. Citations according to Parisot's text; all translations are my own, unless otherwise noted. The motif of wedding garments here is mostly borrowed from Matt. 22:12, but the Gospel texts say nothing of "uncleanness" in relation to the garments. This is a development of the early Syriac tradition as manifested by Aphrahat. Concerning the pervasiveness of the wedding motif in early Syriac writings, see Murray, *Symbols of Church and Kingdom*.

18. *Dem.* 6.1/253.4–9. Aphrahat never cites his sources. I have added the biblical references as understood by the scholarly community in brackets within his text. Nonetheless, many scholars have noted that Aphrahat seems to depend at least in part on a harmonized version of the Gospels. This passage, which interweaves verses from Luke and Matthew, might be an example of such a passage. However, is it also possible that Aphrahat, who seems to have had a masterful handle on the biblical texts, brought these passages together himself for more effective argumentation. See Tjitze Baarda, *The Gospel Quotations of Aphrahat, the Persian Sage: Aphrahat's Text of the Fourth Gospel* (Amsterdam: Vrije Universiteit, 1975) and, more recently, William L. Petersen, *Tatian's Diatessaron: Its Creation, Dissemination, Significance, and History in Scholarship* (Leiden: Brill, 1994).

19. The image of the female virgin as bride of Christ may indeed have originated in the Syriac Church. The earliest mention of brides of Christ in the East appears in the "Peri Parthenon," which A. Vööbus argues was originally a Syriac document. Nonetheless, the concept is crystallized in Basil of Ancyra's theological treatise, *De Virginitate.* S. Elm argues that the notion of brides of Christ as religious vocation for Christian female virgins triumphs at the same time as the Church attempts to legislate against "spiritual" marriages. See Vööbus, *History of Asceticism* 1:67–69; and Elm, *Virgins of God,* 34–38, 50–51.

20. *Dem.* 6.7/272.4–8.

21. The Parisot text leaves *meshtuta* in the singular, but it does not make sense grammatically—at least in English.

22. *Dem.* 6.6/269.6–14. Compare *AJT* 12.

23. See also Elizabeth Clark on Jerome, Gregory of Nyssa, and Basil, who differentiate between virgins and matrons in that the matron's life is burdensome, that a woman cannot please two husbands at once (conflict-of-interest theory), and that a virgin avoids the curse of Eve (death); *Reading Renunciation: Asceticism and Scripture in Early Christianity* (Princeton: Princeton University Press, 1999), 314ff.

24. The Peshitta and Vetus Syriaca gospels use *meshtuta, beit meshtuta,* or *beit ḥlula,* but never *gnona* in their discussions of weddings either earthly or celestial.

25. *Dem.* 6.1/248.5.

26. On the history of this term, see Gary Anderson, "The Garments of Skin in Apocryphal Narrative and Biblical Commentary," in *Studies in Ancient Midrash,* ed. James L. Kugel (Cambridge, Mass.: Harvard University Press, 2001), 101–43. The notion of "garments of glory" descends from the discussions surrounding what type of garments God made for Adam and Eve when they left the Garden. The Massoretic Text of Gen. 2:31 states that God made them "garments of skin." But very early on in its exegetical history the "leather" was transformed into "light" because of the mixup between the *ayin* and *aleph* in the word *'or.* In the Syriac tradition, then, the garments of light are perceived as something made by God—as the original garments of leather were—but they are left behind in Eden rather than worn outside of Eden.

27. Sebastian Brock, "Clothing Metaphors as a Means of Theological Expression in Syriac Tradition," in *Typus, Symbol, Allegorie bei den östlichen Vätern und ihren Parallelen im Mittelalter,* ed. M. Schmidt (Regensburg: Pustet, 1982), 11–38. The "Hymn of the Pearl," as found in the *AJT,* suggests that the garment of glory is the person's "image of God"—that which is left behind in the Garden of Eden and which can only be repossessed through a return to God through faith in the Messiah. Tatian likewise states, "It is possible for everyone who is naked to get this adornment [the heavenly garment] and race back to his ancient kinship [God]; *Oration to the Greeks and Fragments,* ed. and trans. Molly Whittaker (Oxford: Clarendon Press, 1982), 20.3.

28. *Dem.* 6.14/292.24–293.5.

29. *Dem.* 6.14/296.1–3.

30. *Dem.* 6.1/240.11–12.

31. *Dem.* 6.1/248.4–7.

32. *Dem.* 6.6/268.7–8.

33. *Dem.* 6.1/240.11–12.

34. *Dem.* 6.1 /252.10–12. Aphrahat also invokes temple/body imagery at 6.14/292.19–20.

35. *Dem.* 6.14/293.24–296.7.

36. *Dem.* 1.4/12.16; 3.1/97.4. Although here *qaddishuta* is invoked within the same passage as *btulata/btule*.

37. *Dem.* 6.4/260.22–261.1.

38. Dem. 6.5/261.16–18.

39. *Dem.* 6.5/261.18–20, based on Num. 11:28. See discussion below.

40. Given the inclusion of King Asa and his mother on the list of bad female-male relationships, I would assume that living at home with one's widowed mother was not acceptable, either. This might also be related to Paul in 1 Cor. 5, who criticizes a man for living with his step-mother.

41. *Dem.* 6.5/261.20–26.

42. According to Pierre, Exod. 38.8: "He made the laver of copper and its stand of copper, from the mirrors of the women who performed tasks at the entrance of the Tent of Meeting" (JPS trans.) is one possibility; Marie-Joseph Pierre, "Les Exposés" (Paris: Editions du Cerf, 1988–89). Adam Lehto, "Women in Aphrahat: Some Observations," *Hugoye*, July 2001, offers another: 1 Sam. 2:22: "Now Eli was very old, and he heard all that his sons were doing to all Israel, and how they lay with the women who served at the entrance to the tent of meeting" (RSV trans.).

43. *Dem.* 6.5/261.26–264.1.

44. Lev. 21:6–8.

45. Lev. 8:33. *Mishnah Yoma* 1:1 similarly stipulates that the high priest (but not all priests) be separated from his house seven days before Yom Kippur, lest he incur some defilement that would disqualify him from service.

46. *Dem.* 6.5/264.1–12.

47. *Dem.* 6.1/253.9–10; 18.7/833.1–5.

48. Aphrahat and the Peshitta call her the Shulamite, rather than the Shunamite. This may just be a scribal error—a merging with the female character in Song of Songs.

49. *Dem.* 6.5/264.13–22.

50. Is this also a description of the proper *ihidaya*'s sparse quarters?

51. Since we do not know for sure on which sources, texts, or teachers Aphrahat depended, it is difficult to trace such variations. It is always possible that the variations are unique to Aphrahat. See J. R. Owens, *The Genesis and Exodus Citations of Aphrahat the Persian Sage* (Leiden: Brill, 1983).

52. Nevertheless, the fact that Elisha is labeled *qadosh*/ Syr: *qaddisha* may have influenced the variant reading. Elisha is the only prophet who is anointed—though the biblical text is not clear as to how that anointing transpires. See 1 Kings 19:16. He is also the only prophet called a holy man.

53. *Dem.* 6.5/264.22–265.2. An example of Aphrahat's paraphrasing of biblical text to suit his needs.

54. Although Aphrahat does not cite it here, Mark 6:20 notes that John is a righteous and holy man.

55. The notion that prophecy, priesthood, or service to God somehow requires undivided attention to God is not unique to Aphrahat. See Clark, *Reading Renunciation*, 118–27, in which she discusses the celibate models of Elijah, Elisha, and Jeremiah, as well as the pre-lapsarian Adam and Eve. Aphrahat, however, brings in many more prophetic and priestly models—though he does not refer to Adam and Eve in this context.

56. I have argued elsewhere that I believe Aphrahat's community faced severe competition and pressure from the local Jewish community to convert to Judaism and avoid the pitfalls of the anti-Christian persecution. Aphrahat composes his anti-Jewish polemic not so much to answer back directly to the Jews as to give support to the faith and practice of his own community. See note 3 above.

57. Lehto, *Divine Law*, 55.

58. Adam Becker pointed out to me in personal correspondence that the very use of "prepare" probably resonated and attracted Aphrahat to this Moses passage because it echoes the parable of the virgins in Matt. 25. Aphrahat refers repeatedly to this parable and the need to be prepared for the Bridegroom throughout *Dem.* 6.

59. *Dem.* 18.4/824.25–27; 825.15–23.

60. Indeed, George Nendugatt argues that Aphrahat's notion of *qaddishuta* as celibacy is based on this biblical notion of what he calls ritual purity. However, he never posits the possibility that *qaddishuta,* in this context, could mean just purity and not sanctity; rather, he assumes they are one and the same; "Covenanters of the Early Syriac Speaking Church," *Orientalia Christiana Periodica* 39 (1973), 213.

61. *Dem.* 18.12/841.3–9.

62. *Dem.* 18.5/828.19–829.8.

63. *Dem.* 18.5/829.8–14.

64. Aphrahat, like many other early Church fathers, creates a spiritual hierarchy in which marriage is acceptable, but inferior to celibacy. See Clark, *Reading Renunciation*, 154. See also discussion below. Moreover, Stephanie Skoyles Jarkins argues that Aphrahat opens a mystical opportunity for ascent to God through the *bnay qyama's* ascetic practices. If Moses stood face to face with God, maybe others can, too, by following his celibate example. See her book, *Aphrahat the Persian Sage and the Temple of God: A Study of Early Syriac Theological Anthropology* (Piscataway, N.J.: Gorgias Press, 2008), esp. chap. 5.

65. Jeremy Cohen, *"Be Fertile and Increase, Fill the Earth and Master It": The Ancient and Medieval Career of a Biblical Text* (Ithaca and London: Cornell University Press, 1989), chap. 3, esp. 158–65.

66. *Dem.* 18.1/819.10–18.

67. Cohen, *"Be Fertile,"* 115.

68. Aphrahat, as a celibate Christian, is not the first to encounter these types of accusations. He certainly would agree with other Christian critiques of this position that God's commandment to procreate had a time and a place, but was no longer applicable. He even goes so far as to show that the blessing of fertility in and of itself was a curse, as the products (the children) often turned out for the worse; see Cohen, *"Be Fertile,"* 231, 234, and *Dem.* 18.2/820.19–824.6.

69. Clark, *Reading Renunciation*, 215–24.

70. Tertullian, *De exhortatione castitatis*, ed. Turnhout (Typographi Brepols, 1953), 10.4 (*CCL2* 1029–30); trans. from *ANF* 4:112. See also discussion in Clark, *Reading Renunciation*, 219ff.

71. Clement of Alexandria, *Stromateis*, ed. Otto Staehlin and Ludwig Freihtel (Berlin: Academic-Verlag, 1960), 3.73. Trans. from *FOTC* 86: 301.

72. Brown, *Body and Society*, 136.

73. Ibid., 171.

74. Origen, Exodus Homily 11.7, *Homilies on Genesis and Exodus*, trans. from *FOTC* 71:365 by Ronald E. Heine (Washington, D.C.: Catholic University Press, 1982). This translation is based on the Latin text, since the original Greek was lost.

75. Ibid.

76. Egyptian-style monasticism does not develop in Syrian Mesopotamia until well into the fifth century; See Harvey's introduction to *Asceticism and Society*.

77. *Dem.* 6.1/241.16–18.

78. *Dem.* 6.9/276.23–27.

79. This section appeared in slightly different form in a previously published article, "Yokes of the Holy-Ones: The Embodiment of a Christian Vocation," *Harvard Theological Review* 94, no. 2 (2002): 205–18. Permission to reproduce granted from publisher.

80. *Dem.* 6.1/248.26–249.2.

81. *Dem.* 6.1/253.12–13.

82. *Dem.* 6.1/252.23–253.4.

83. A few examples are, Parisot: "iugum sanctorum," (*Patrologia Syriaca*, 250); John Gwynn: "Yoke of the Saints," (*NPNF* 13.364); Marie-Joseph Pierre: "joug des saints," (*Les Exposés*, 1.366).

84. Sebastian Brock, "Early Syrian Asceticism," comes to a similar position. Likewise, in Syriac Christian wedding ceremonies, a bride is marked as designated for her man and as such she is given in marriage to only that man. In the same way, these holy-yoked ones are separated out for their spiritual master, Jesus.

85. These images are mentioned earlier; *Dem.* 6.6/269.1–6; 6.1/248.1–8.

86. *Dem.* 6.4/261. 2–14.

87. Many ancient biblical exegetes held that Jeremiah wrote Lamentations.

88. *Dem.* 6.8/276.18–22.

89. See discussions in Nendugatt, "Covenanters," 437–38; Vööbus, *History of Asceticism*, 1:93.

90. Lehto argues similarly, *Divine Law*, 55.

91. Griffith, "Asceticism," 230–32.

92. Ibid., 232.

93. See discussion on *"qeiama"* in Vööbus, *History of Asceticism*, 1:98–103. Brock, "Early Syrian Asceticism," 7–8, also comes to the conclusion that *qyama* most likely connotes "covenant," though he is intrigued by the possibility of "resurrection." He, too, feels the connections to Qumran, despite the parallels, are tenuous. Yet Murray, *Symbols*, 17, is willing to state, "With all due caution, however, I find more probable the hypothesis that behind the phenomena we have been reviewing lies a Jewish sectarian ideology of a kind like that now known to us from Qumran." Steven Fraade, "Ascetical

Aspects of Ancient Judaism," in *Jewish Spirituality*, ed. Arthur Green (New York: Crossroads, 1986–87), 256, notes that the sanctity of the Qumran community is in the actions of the community as a group, not in the individual piety, perhaps implying a stronger and differently nuanced sense of community-as-covenant than Aphrahat intends. See also this book, chap. 3, on the Qumran texts and holiness.

94. *Dem.* 6.1/248.25–26.

95. The idea that angels do not marry is not new or unique to the New Testament texts, but finds expression in other Second Temple and pseudepigraphic work such as 1 Enoch and Jubilees. There, the fallen angels find themselves accused of sexually defiling behavior; see Jub. 4:22–23. See note 5 above.

96. *Dem.* 6.1/248.26–249.2.

97. *Dem.* 6.6/268.26–269.1.

98. *Dem.* 6.6/269.1–6.

99. While his celibacy is noted in *Dem.* 6, Aphrahat calls him a virgin in *Dem.* 18.

100. *Dem.* 6.1/253.9–10.

101. *Dem.* 6.1/253.10–13.

102. *Dem.* 6.1/249.5–6.

103. This Jarkins argues in her book; see note 64 above.

104. Dem. 6.3/256.25–260.12 (full text translation from Lehto, "Women in Aphrahat.")

CHAPTER 6

Some material in this chapter is adapted from my article of the same name, which appeared in *The Ways That Never Parted*, edited by Adam H. Becker and Annette Yoshiko Reed; copyright © 2007 Fortress Press. Reproduced by permission of Augsburg Fortress Publishers. Some other material was adapted from my article "Yokes of the Holy-Ones: The Embodiment of a Christian Vocation," *Harvard Theological Review* 94, no. 2 (2001): 205–18. Permission to reproduce granted from publisher. An earlier and less developed version of some of these ideas also appeared in my article "Sexuality and Holiness: Semitic Christian and Jewish Conceptualizations of Sexual Behavior," *Vigiliae Christianae* 54 (2000): 375–95.

1. Daniel Boyarin, *Carnal Israel: Reading Sex in Talmudic Culture* (Berkeley: University of California Press, 1993), 40. Yet, on this point Aphrahat also differentiates himself from rabbinic discourse.

2. David Dawson, *Allegorical Readers and Cultural Revision in Ancient Alexandria* (Berkeley: University of California Press, 1992), 108–20.

3. Philo, *Life of Moses* 2.68–69. This translation is by C. D. Young, *The Works of Philo* (Peabody, Mass.: Hendrickson Publishers, 1993), 487, and amended as noted from the Loeb translation, F. H. Colson, *Philo* (Cambridge, Mass.: Harvard University Press, 1929), 6:483.

4. Whereas Philo acknowledges Zipporah's existence elsewhere, he is quick to allegorize her into a nonphysical reality; see *On the Cherubim* 5.41, 47; *On the Posterity and Exile of Cain* 77; *On the Change of Names* 120. In *Life of Moses* 1.59, Philo acknowledges Zipporah's existence, but there she remains nameless.

5. Philo scholars continually discuss the extent to which Philo was a true Middle Platonist. A consensus seems to point to the more general notion that Philo, while

sympathetic to many of the Hellenistic philosophical schools, never aligned himself wholeheartedly with one or the other. See Ellen Birnbaum's work, *The Place of Judaism in Philo's Thought: Israel, Jews, and Proselytes* (Atlanta: Scholars Press, 1996), especially the introduction. See also Robert M. Berchman, "Arcana Mundi: Prophecy and Divination in the Vita Mosis of Philo of Alexandria," *SBL Seminar Papers* 27 (1988): 385–423; John Pinsent, "Ascetic Moods in Greek and Latin Literature," in *Asceticism*, ed. Vincent L. Wimbush and Richard Valantasis (New York: Oxford University Press, 1995), 211–19; and Jaap Mansfeld, "Philosophy in the Service of Scripture: Philo's Exegetical Strategies," in *The Question of "Eclecticism": Studies in Later Greek Philosophy*, ed. John M. Dillon and A. A. Long (Berkeley: University of California Press, 1988), 70–107. Nevertheless, one can trace Platonic influence throughout Philo's work. For instance, the quote above in which Philo lauds Moses' self-control over lust and gluttony is reflected in Plato's *Phaedo* (64D), where Socrates makes similar claims.

6. Steven D. Fraade, "Ascetical Aspects of Ancient Judaism," in *Jewish Spirituality: From the Bible through the Middle Ages*, ed. Arthur Green (New York: Crossroads, 1986), 256–57.

7. Peter Brown, *The Body and Society: Men, Women and Sexual Renunciation in Early Christianity* (New York: Columbia University Press, 1988), 19.

8. Clement of Alexandria, *Stromateis* 3.7.57, ed. Otto Staehlin and Ludwid Freihtel (Berlin: Academic-Verlag, 1960).

9. This midrash is also found in Philo, *Life of Moses* 2.69, immediately following the above quote. Clement, here, I think, makes a distinction between what is right for Moses and what is right for others.

10. See Philo, *Life of Moses* 1.149. Burton L. Mack, "Imitatio Mosis: Patterns of Cosmology and Soteriology in the Hellenistic Synagogue," *Studia Philonica* 1 (1972): 27–55; and Peder Borgen, "Moses, Jesus and the Roman Emperor: Observations in Philo's Writings and the Revelation of John," *Novum Testamentum* 38, no. 2 (1996): 149.

11. While most Philo scholars tend to think of Philo as a biblical exegete first, the *Life of Moses* can be seen also as an encomium or biographic exposition that, while generally following the biblical narrative, sets out to explain Moses to the world in the terms most comprehensible to that world—in this case, first-century Alexandria. See Birnbaum, *Place of Judaism in Philo's Thought*, 16; and Philip Shuler, "Philo's Moses and Matthew's Jesus: A Comparative Study in Ancient Literature," *The Studia Philonica Annual* 2 (1990): 88.

12. Boyarin, *Carnal Israel*, 163.

13. *Mekhilta*, Masekhet de-Amalek Yitro 1.26–29.

14. *Get* is the rabbinic term for the document of divorce, which the biblical text refers to as a *sefer kritut*.

15. I prefer to leave in the various options of translations to help underscore the problematics of the Hebrew.

16. The Rabbis note in this *Sifre* passage that Moses married a Midianite woman according to Exod. 3:21. They then attempt to understand what "Cushite" really says about Zipporah—namely, that she was dark-skinned and beautiful. A different tradition, that Moses had two wives, one Ethiopian (Cushite) and one Midianite (Zipporah), can be found in (and perhaps created by?) Josephus (*Antiquities of the Jews* 2:252). Rashbam also cites this tradition, as does Orson Wells in his epic film *The Ten*

Commandments, though presumably their lines of transmission and reception were not the same. The Rabbis, however, assume here that the Cushite woman in question is the one and same Zipporah.

17. *Sifre Numbers* 99. All midrashic textual translations are my own unless otherwise noted. The italicized texts are the biblical texts cited within the rabbinic text.

18. *Sifre Numbers* 100.

19. Ibid., 103.

20. Boyarin, *Carnal Israel*, 161.

21. Ibid., 163.

22. Ibid., 164, see especially note 47.

23. Ibid., 164.

24. Even the exact nature of the biblical texts Aphrahat had at his disposal is far from clear. See J. R. Owens, *The Genesis and Exodus Citations of Aphrahat the Persian Sage* (Leiden: Brill, 1983). For a more in-depth discussion of Aphrahat's background, see my Ph. D. dissertation, *Jewish–Christian Polemics in Fourth-Century Persian Mesopotamia: A Reconstructed Conversation*, Stanford, 1993); or my article of similar name, "A Jewish–Christian Conversation in Fourth-Century Persian Mesopotamia," *Journal of Jewish Studies* 47, no. 1 (1996): 45–63; and the introduction to this book.

25. Rabbinic literature in general is difficult to date. These texts in particular pose rather thorny examples. Scholars agree that the *Babylonian Talmud* was "closed," or finished, by the end of the fifth century. Yet, scholars have pinpointed various strata within the finished text. Likewise, scholars consider the *Midrash Exodus Rabbah* a compiled text with earlier and later pieces. The *Avot de Rabbi Natan*, moreover, remains all but undatable. While its historic "present" appears to be Tannaitic Roman-Palestinian, it evolves under later Amoraic and even Geonic heavy editorial hands. At the very least it, too, is a composite text that existed in several variations. The most widely known are the variations *A* and *B* as reconstructed by Solomon Schechter. See the recent discussions by Jonathan Schofer, *The Making of a Sage: A Study in Rabbinic Ethics* (Madison, Wisc.: University of Wisconsin Press, 2005), 25–30. While I attempt to keep my examples to texts that fall between the second and fourth centuries and that might have existed in some form in fourth-century Persian Mesopotamia, my comparative aim is to establish patterns and possibilities of exegesis rather than linear trajectories or relationships. For a more in-depth discussion of the dating of rabbinic texts, see Lawrence Shiffman, *From Text to Tradition: A History of the Second Temple and Rabbinic Judaism* (Hoboken, N.J.: Ktav Publishing, 1991), chaps. 10–12; Shmuel Safrai, ed., *Literature of the Sages* (Philadelphia: Fortress Press, 1987); and H. L Strack and G. Stemberger, *Introduction to the Talmud and Midrash* (Edinburgh: T&T Clark, 1991).

26. All talmudic translations are my own unless otherwise noted.

27. God's presence on the mountain confers holiness to the mountain. My point is that though our text references the holiness of the mountain, that is not the rationale for why Moses must be celibate. Rather, they refer back to the face-to-face quality of Moses relationship with God (whether on the mountain or elsewhere).

28. Martin S. Jaffe, *Torah in the Mouth: Writing and Oral Tradition in Palestinian Judaism 200 BCE–400 CE* (New York: Oxford University Press, 2001), 135–40. See also the extensive textual work of Saul Lieberman, such as his *Tosefta Ki-fshuta: A Comprehensive*

Commentary on the Tosefta (New York: Jewish Theological Seminary of America, 1955–88) and various writings by Shamma Friedman on the Tosefta, such as "The Primacy of Tosefta to Mishnah in Synoptic Parallels," in *Introducing Tosefta: Textual, Intratextual and Intertextual Studies,* ed. H. Fox and T. Meacham (Hoboken, N.J.: KTAV, 1999), 99–121.

29. This last paragraph follows the translation by Judah Goldin, *The Fathers According to Rabbi Nathan* (New Haven: Yale University Press, 1955), 19.

30. *Dem.* 18.4/824.25–27; 825.15–23, 18.5/828.19–829.8.

31. Boyarin, *Carnal Israel,* 165. Isaiah Gafni also notes these differences in his article, "The Institution of Marriage in Rabbinic Times," in *The Jewish Family: Metaphor and Memory,* ed. D. Kraemer (New York and Oxford: Oxford University Press, 1989), 13–30. There, he further suggests that the Palestinian rabbis, due to their more Roman and Christian milieu, were less generous toward the institution of marriage than their Babylonian counterparts.

32. Howard Eilberg-Schwartz, *God's Phallus and Other Problems for Men and Monotheism* (Boston: Beacon Press, 1994), 216.

33. *Dem.* 18.5/829.8–14.

34. Boyarin, *Carnal Israel;* Gafni, "Institutions of Marriage"; Eliezer Diamond, *Holy Men and Hunger Artist: Fasting and Asceticism in Rabbinic Culture* (Oxford: Oxford University Press, 2004); Michael Satlow, *Tasting the Dish: Rabbinic Rhetorics of Sexuality* (Atlanta: Scholars Press, 1995).

35. *ARN A* 2:25–27.

36. Semen, according to Lev. 15:16–17, defiles both the man and the woman in sexual intercourse. Hence, they are both required to bathe and wait until evening before they can be purified and participate in sacred ritual. If they should not immediately purify themselves, their impurity can be passed on to others who come into contact with them. But the *ARN A* notes—due to the physiological nature of sexual intercourse, semen, and a woman's body—she is vulnerable for three days after sexual intercourse to re/produce the semen. Hence, Moses adds the third day so that, if for three days the Israelites are celibate, there is no chance of semen from a sexual contact four days prior refluxing from the woman. Note that this is a more strict understanding of semen pollution than the levitical text, which allows that it will defile the man or the woman only until evening of the day it was produced.

37. The Rabbis focus here on the defiling nature of semen pollution—no matter from whom it originates. They are not here concerned with impurities associated with female menstruation.

38. Note also this distinction in *Tanhuma Naso* 13 (*Varsha*), in which the midrash recaps most of the midrashim I have been discussing here. Yet, it adds in, at the moment that God calls to Miriam and Aaron (after they have complained about Moses' wife, Zipporah [Num. 12]) that they yell out "Water, water" because they are suddenly aware that they are impure by semen pollution, as they have not separated from their spouses, and in approaching God (who begs an audience with them) they court danger through their impurity in the face of God's holiness.

39. B. J. Schwartz, "Israel's Holiness: The Torah Traditions," in *Purity and Holiness: The Heritage of Leviticus,* ed. Marcel Poorthuis and Joshua Schwartz (Leiden: Brill, 2000), 49. And surely in some cases they do. See Schwartz's examples.

40. It is important to note that the Rabbis, in describing the text, do not quote the biblical text exactly, but translate the biblical Hebrew phrase "do not approach the woman" [*al tigshu el ha-isha*] as "to separate/abstain" [*lifrosh*] from the woman. The root word *parash* takes on the connotation of separation, as well as sexual abstinence in the rabbinic texts. See Fraade, "Ascetical Aspects," 269–71.

41. *Mekhilta* Yitro Bahodesh 3.

42. Can be found also in *PT Megilah* 4.1 75a; *BT Baba Qama* 82a; *PT Berakhot* 3.4 6c. See Diamond, *Holy Men*, 45.

43. Boyarin, *Carnal Israel*, 49–50.

44. *Dem.* 6.4/261.12–14.

45. "And those who love *qaddishuta* (holiness) it is right, just and proper that even under pressure a man remains by himself" (*Dem.* 6.4/261.5–8).

46. *Dem.* 6.8/276.18–22. The only place where Aphrahat quotes Matt 11:29–30 is in *Dem.* 15: "On the dietary laws," a polemic against the Jews' insistence on dietary restrictions. This use here has everything to do with a comparison of Jesus' law/yoke which is light and the Jewish law/yoke which is heavy. Nevertheless, here, in *Dem.* 6, the images of the yokes (despite the light/heavy contrast) have merged.

47. *Mishnah Avot* 3.5. Shmuel Safrai has noted that *derekh eretz* can be understood in several ways: (1) politeness, accepted customs, appropriate behavior; (2) business, labor, and craftsmanship; (3) polite language for sexual intercourse and cohabitation; and (4) good deeds and moral instruction. In his article, "The Meaning of the Term: *Derekh Erets*," *Tarbiz* 60 (1991): 147–62 (in Hebrew), Safrai outlines in which rabbinic texts the term takes on the different meanings. He notes on page 151 that in this particular passage *derekh eretz* connotes labor and livelihood. I wonder, however, if it is possible to understand the term to have multiple levels of meaning at any one time.

48. Diamond, *Holy Men*, 27–28, also notes that through this analogy the rabbis elevate Torah study over physical labor.

49. See *Sifre Numbers* 115 (p. 127 in Horowitz's edition). See also the *Mekhilta of Rabbi Shimon bar Yohai* 19:6. See further Eliezer Diamond's discussion of *qedushah* in *Holy Men*, 76–78.

50. *Midrash Lamentations* 3:9. Note that the Buber edition 3.33 (*Midr. Zuta*) reads *malkhut* (kingdom) in place of *melakhah* (labor).

51. *Numbers Rabbah* 19:26. It should be noted that this work is a medieval construct that nonetheless probably contains earlier pieces.

52. Boyarin suggests that the rabbis often construe their study of Torah as the "other" woman in their lives; *Carnal Israel*, chap. 5.

CHAPTER 7

1. By "midrashic literature" I refer primarily to nonlegal material, no matter in what corpus it is found. Likewise, "halakhic" refers to legal discourse, no matter where it appears.

2. See, for instance, *Genesis Rabbah* 81:1, *Exodus Rabbah* 49:2, *Numbers Rabbah* 2:15, and *Midrash Tehilim* (Shohar Tov) 104:3.

3. See, for instance, *Leviticus Rabbah* 24:2 and *Exodus Rabbah* 16:24.

4. See *Mishnah Yevamot* 11:2.

5. Michael Satlow, *Tasting the Dish: Rabbinic Rhetorics of Sexuality* (Atlanta: Scholars Press, 1995), 80.

6. Eliezer Diamond, *Holy Men and Hunger Artists: Fasting and Asceticism in Rabbinic Culture* (Oxford: Oxford University Press, 2004), 8; Steven Fraade, "Ascetical Aspects of Ancient Judaism," in *Jewish Spirituality: From the Bible through the Middle Ages*, ed. Arthur Green (New York: Crossroads, 1986–87), 253–88.

7. Diamond, *Holy Men*, 101–15.

8. *BT Ta'anit* 11a. Text as cited in Diamond, *Holy Men*, 114.

9. Diamond, *Holy Men*, 114.

10. Ibid., 118.

11. Ironically, Aphrahat, while retaining *qaddishuta* for celibacy alone, subsumes sexual abstinence under the rubric of fasting; *Dem.* 3.1/97:13–14: "There is the one who fasts through holiness."

12. Diamond, *Holy Men*, 75–76, 82.

13. Eliezer Diamond's discussion of rabbinic *qedushah* can be found in *Holy Men*, 81–85. Through copious e-mail exchange, Diamond has further explicated and nuanced his argument for me and I have attempted to reflect those nuances here. There is much overlap in our discourse on rabbinic *qedushah* and sexuality, and I thank Professor Diamond for being so willing to discuss his material with me further. Diamond also outlines the connection between sexual restraint and holiness in this section.

14. Daniel Boyarin, *Borderlines: The Partition of Judaeo-Christianity* (Philadelphia: University of Pennsylvania Press, 2004), introduction. This is not to argue that the Rabbis as a class were fully tolerant or ecumenical or even nice, as Jeffrey Rubenstein argues in *The Culture of the Babylonian Talmud* (Baltimore: John Hopkins University Press, 2003). The *am ha-aretz*, whoever they were, prove to be an interesting case. While Rubenstein argues, in chapter 7, that the Stammaitic layer of the *Babylonian Talmud* proves itself to abhor the *am ha-aretz*, they still remain part of the "*amha*." Nowhere in that discourse do the Babylonians cut off the *am ha-aretz* completely from the people of Israel, nor is any of the discourse couched in holiness language, though further study on this issue would be useful for a fuller understanding of the *Babylonian Talmud's* construct of "real" Jews.

15. *Mishnah Yevamot* 2:4; my translation with explanatory interpolations. All translations of the rabbinic texts are my own unless otherwise indicated. This section of the *Mishnah* considers levirate marriage, a biblical law which stipulates that a man must provide a child for his brother's childless widow by taking the widow on as a wife. See Deut. 25:5–10.

16. The Rabbis here see themselves either as the same as the earlier scribes or as their direct descendents.

17. According to the notes in the Albeck *Mishnah* (vol 3: Nashim; p. 21), a *natin* is a descendant of the Gibeonites, who converted surreptitiously under Joshua and were subsequently forced to be water carriers and wood hewers in service of Israel and the

Temple. Elsewhere, *natin* translates as a servant of the Temple (Ezra, Nehemiah, Chronicles), but it is not clear when the word *natin* is first applied to the descendants of the Gibeonites. It appears several times in the *Mishnah* and *Talmud* besides this text (*Mishnah Makkot* 3.1; *Tosefta Qiddushin* 5:4; *BT Yevamot* 78b).

18. It should be noted that some of these prohibited relationships are attested to earlier in the sectarian literature of the Dead Sea Scrolls.

19. See, for instance, *Tosefta Yevamot* 3. Michael Satlow discusses the slipperiness of these terms in *Tasting the Dish*, 26–27, 56–62.

20. Lev. 21:7 says nothing about *halitzah*—was it considered shameful by the Rabbis? Somehow defiling? According to Shammai in *Mishnah Yevamot* 1:4, it is a cause for ineligibility to marrying a priest. Presumably the Rabbis understand *halitzah* to come under the category of "defiled." Perhaps they understand a women rejected or scorned to be defiled even though the deuteronomical text that legislates levirate marriage clearly places the shame of *halitzah* on the rejecting brother-in-law. Alternatively, they considered *halitzah* to be a form of divorce.

21. See note 17 above.

22. Satlow, *Tasting the Dish*, 64–66.

23. *PT Yevamot* 2:4.The last statement of this midrash concerning a particular rabbi will be discussed below. Michael Satlow notes, in reference to these passages, that the categories of *issur mitzvah* and *issur qedushah* are Tannaitically derived. The Amoraic commentators prefer the term *sheniyot* when referencing rabbinically ordained marriage restrictions. He further notes that the Amoraic rabbis do not attempt to find scriptural proof for *sheniyot*; Satlow, *Tasting the Dish*, 44–47. Yet, I think the *Palestinian Talmud* here is trying very hard to establish its authority and legal rectitude through exegetical means, however convoluted.

24. A quick database search finds the phrase *mitzvah lishmo'a divre hakhamim* three times: *BT Yevamot* 20a (discussed below); *BT Sanhedrin* 53b; *BT Hullin* 106a. The Sanhedrin passage repeats the Yevamot passage, but the Hullin passage has to do with purity and washing the hands. The phrase *mitzvah min hatorah lishmo'a et divre sofrim* is unique in this Palestinian talmudic passage.

25. Yet, I believe an anxiety surfaces here that focuses on the fear that a woman who has already experienced sexual relations with another man may still be carrying his seed within her, and that the descendants produced by the new relationship with the priest might not be truly priestly. Hence, this priestly writer closely follows (or probably precedes) Ezra's holy-seed paradigm, even within Israelite marriages, in order to preserve the genealogy of the priesthood.

26. The *Leviticus Rabbah* (26:4) version of this passage has Rabbi Ishmael rather than Samuel. According to Aaron Hyman's *Toldoth Tannaim Ve'Amoraim* (Jerusalem, 1987 reprint), R. Yishmael bar R. Yitzhak was a Tanna. He has a very short and undistinguished bibliography. R. Samuel bar R. Yitzhak warrants almost four full columns. He was a Babylonian Amora contemporary of Rav Huna who later moved to Israel. Hyman notes that his father was a great hasid—because he fasted two days for Yom Kippur (another form of supererogatory self-restraint); and that R. Samuel was "holy" because of what his maid said about his bed! (Vol. 3: 838, 1139–40.)

27. Diamond, *Holy Men*, 82 citing *Sifra Zuta*, Num. 6:8 (242).

28. The Elisha paradigm is taken even further in support of rabbinic authority in *Leviticus Rabbah* 24:6.

29. *BT Yevamot* 20a.

30. Boyarin, *Borderlines*, Introduction.

31. Satlow, *Tasting the Dish*, 146–53.

32. All of these citations are Babylonian talmudic. I could not find the phrase *yisrael qedoshim hem* by database search anywhere else. In a sixth case, the phrase refers to Israelite ascribed holiness, but not to a specific behavior that is derived from it; *BT Hullin* 7b.

33. *BT Pesahim* 83b; *BT Hullin* 91a.

34. Similarly, the Rabbis will declare that the daughters of Israel have "naturally" taken upon themselves a stricter reading of the *niddah* laws, though I do not believe they are called holy there for doing so! See *BT Niddah* 66a.

35. Diamond, *Holy Men*, 82, I think sides more with the notion of enhancement here.

36. *BT Niddah* 17a, *BT Shabbat* 86a, *BT Ketubot* 65b.

37. Satlow notes how important modesty is for the Rabbis without actually exploring the rabbinic rationale. I presume it is in part a cultural norm; *Tasting the Dish*, 298–302. Other scholars assume that *qedushah* in this case refers to or is an equivalent of modesty; see Burton Visotsky's "Three Syriac Cruxes," *Journal of Jewish Studies* 42, no. 4 (1991). David Brodsky goes furthest in trying to fathom a reason. He argues that these passages continue a tradition that starts in the *Masekhet Kallah* (which he dates to the second or third generation of Babylonian Amoraim), in which a wife is considered *heqdesh*— that is, through rabbinic marriage, *qiddushin*, she becomes a sacred/consecrated object, likened to any sacred object in the Temple, and her husband becomes a sacred subject, likened to the Temple or God, Godself. Yet, the husband is still human, and though he has control of his sacred object, his wife, he must interact with her appropriately (in modesty) and not "misuse" or abuse her—or his rights to her (as sexual outlet). If he behaves accordingly, he will enhance or advance his position, allowing him better access to the divine. In my terminology, he moves up the holiness hierarchy. Brodsky goes so far as to suggest that modesty is provoked by a sense of the woman's sexual organs as creators of life (like God), and hence should not be viewed because they are "holy" and dangerous in the same way that God's holiness can be dangerous; *A Bride without a Blessing: A Study in the Redaction and Content of Massekhet Kallah and Its Gemara* (Tübingen: Mohr Siebeck, 2006), chaps. 3 and 4. While this may be true to *Masekhet Kallah*, it seems to me that the Rabbis here grapple with an accepted tradition that has lost its exegetical underpinnings (if indeed it had any) and to them appears to have no obvious exegetical hook. Hence, they experiment with several different exegetical approaches.

38. *BT Niddah* 16b.

39. Diamond, *Holy Men*, 35–40, 44; See also Daniel Boyarin, *Carnal Israel: Reading Sex in Talmudic Culture* (Berkeley: University of California Press, 1993), chap. 5.

40. Nonetheless, there remains a difference in approach to sexual practices in marriage particularly between Palestinian and Babylonian rabbis. Palestinians, informed by their surrounding Greco-Roman culture, understand sex in marriage to be for procreative purposes only. Hence, they frown on sex with a pregnant wife, for

instance. The Babylonians, perhaps equally influenced by their surrounding Persian milieu, understand sex to have value in and of itself beyond procreation, for it can be pleasurable and enhance a couples' relationship as well. For a fuller discussion, see Satlow's *Tasting the Dish*, especially chaps. 6–7.

41. Sexual restraint within marriage seems to be a particularly Babylonian issue. In this regard, see especially Brodsky, *A Bride without a Blessing*.

42. This passage is situated within a larger discussion of "matters of conduct," which bring good ends: wisdom, wealth, and male children.

43. Satlow, *Tasting the Dish*, 311–13.

44. Boyarin, *Carnal Israel*, 57.

45. Though Satlow points out that they are all in the names of Palestinian rabbis. Something clearly happened between their "creation" in Palestine, perhaps elimination by the *Palestinian Talmud's* redactors, and their emergence in the Babylonian (Satlow, *Tasting the Dish*, 310). Following Brodsky's theory for the *Massekhet Kallah*, these could be Palestinian by origin but redacted in Babylonia; Brodsky, *A Bride without a Blessing*, 40.

46. See midrash on Hannah in the *Tanhuma Buber* Naso Perek 13. What is interesting here is that Greco-Roman medical textbooks tend to focus on the woman's actions in bed as opposed to the man's. Thus, this midrash, which incorporates a known Greco-Roman folktale on the Arabian king, centers on the woman's focus of attention during intercourse. All of the Babylonian talmudic discussions focus on the male activities—sexual restraint. The Tanhuma text is a late-Palestinian midrash. It may very well carry forward a more solidly Palestinian and Greco-Roman approach to eugenics that in the *Babylonian Talmud* has been subverted to focus on male sexual self-control.

47. Satlow, *Tasting the Dish*, 80.

48. *Genesis Rabbah* 35:1.

49. Ibid. 34:7.

50. Ibid.

51. It is interesting to note that in Aphrahat's interpretation of the Noah story, Noah is also celibate and is thus saved during the flood. Ironically, Noah, in order to fulfill God's command, must first give up his celibacy in order to produce the sons who will continue human life on earth after the flood. Nevertheless, it is because Noah refrained from procreating until God called him that he is rewarded by God. See my article, "Aphrahat on Noah's Righteousness in Light of the Jewish-Christian Polemic," in *The Book of Genesis in Jewish and Oriental Christian Interpretation*, ed. Judith Frishman and Lucas Van Rompay (Louvain: Peeters, 1997): 57–71.

52. In this case, not looking at or holding his penis. See Visotzky, "Three Syriac Cruxes," 175. Note that all references to Rabbi Judah as holy are Palestinian.

53. Diamond, *Holy Men*, 124–27.

54. Boyarin, *Carnal Israel*, 33–35, 46–47.

55. Diamond, *Holy Men*, 128–29.

56. Satlow, *Tasting the Dish*, 319.

57. Such is the debate that Boyarin outlines in *Carnal Israel*, 134–66.

58. As translated by Boyarin, *Carnal Israel*, 49.

59. Ibid., 49–50.

CONCLUSIONS

1. See for instance, Michael Satlow, *Jewish Marriage in Late Antiquity* (Princeton, N.J.: Princeton University Press, 2001); Daniel Boyarin, *Carnal Israel: Reading Sex in Talmudic Culture* (Berkeley: University of California Press, 1993).

2. In the Greco-Roman context, the discourse on virginity is usually found within the polemics against Greco-Roman religion.

3. Elizabeth Clark, *Reading Renunciation: Asceticism and Scripture in Early Christianity* (Princeton, N.J.: Princeton University Press, 1999).

4. Eliezer Diamond, *Holy Men and Hunger Artists: Fasting and Asceticism in Rabbinic Culture* (New York: Oxford University Press, 2004).

Bibliography

Amaru, Betsy Halpern. *The Empowerment of Women in the Book of Jubilees.*
  Leiden: Brill, 1999.
Anderson, Gary M. "Celibacy or Consummation in the Garden: Reflections
  on Early Jewish and Christian Interpretations of the Garden of Eden."
  Harvard Theological Review 82, no. 2 (1989): 121–48.
———. "The Garments of Skin in Apocryphal Narrative and Biblical
  Commentary." In *Studies in Ancient Midrash*, ed. James L. Kugel, 101–45.
  Cambridge, Mass: Harvard University Press, 2001.
Attridge, Harrold W. "Intertextuality in the Acts of Thomas." *Semeia* 80
  (1997 [1999]): 87–135.
Avot de Rabbi-Natan. Edited by Solomon Schechter. Vienna: Knöpflmacher,
  1887.
Baarda, Tjitze. *The Gospel Quotations of Aphrahat, the Persian Sage:
  Aphrahat's Text of the Fourth Gospel.* Amsterdam: Vrije Universiteit,
  1975.
Babylonian Talmud. Vilna Edition, 1982. Reprint, Jerusalem: Tal-Man, 1990.
Babylonian Talmud in English. Edited by I. Epstein. London: Soncino Press,
  1935–52.
Baskin, Judith. *Midrashic Women: Formations of the Feminine in Rabbinic
  Literature.* London and Hanover, N.H.: Brandeis University Press,
  2002.
Becker, Adam H., and Annette Yoshiko Reed. *The Ways That Never Parted:
  Jews and Christians in Late Antiquity and the Early Middle Ages.* Tübingen:
  Mohr Siebeck, 2003.
Berchman, Robert M. "Arcana Mundi: Prophecy and Divination in the Vita
  Mosis of Philo of Alexandria." *SBL Seminar Papers* 27 (1988): 385–423.

Biale, Rachel. *Women and Jewish Law.* New York: Schocken, 1995.

Birnbaum, Ellen. *The Place of Judaism in Philo's Thought: Israel, Jews, and Proselytes.* Atlanta: Scholars Press, 1996.

Boismard, M. E. *Le Diatessaron: de Tatien à Justin.* Paris: J. Gabalda, 1992.

Borgen, Peder. "Moses, Jesus and the Roman Empire: Observations in Philo's Writings and the Revelation of John." *Novum Testamentum* 38, no. 2 (1996): 145–59.

Boyarin, Daniel. *Borderlines: The Partition of Judaeo-Christianity.* Philadelphia: University of Pennsylvania Press, 2004.

———. *Carnal Israel: Reading Sex in Talmudic Culture.* Berkeley: University of California Press, 1993.

Brock, Sebastian. "Clothing Metaphors as a Means of Theological Expression in Syriac Tradition." In *Typus, Symbol, Allegorie be den Östlichen Vätern und Ihren Parallelen im Mittelalter,* ed. M. Schmidt, 11–40. Regensburg: Pustet, 1982.

———. "Early Syrian Asceticism." *Numen* 20, no. 1 (April 1973): 1–19.

Brodsky, David. *A Bride without a Blessing: A Study in the Redaction and Content of Massekhet Kallah and Its Gemara.* Tübingen: Mohr Siebeck, 2006.

Brown, Peter. *The Body and Society: Men, Women and Sexual Renunciation in Early Christianity.* New York: Columbia University Press, 1988.

Buell, Denise Kimber. *Why This New Race: Ethnic Reasoning in Early Christianity.* New York: Columbia University Press, 2005.

Burkitt, F. Crawford. *Early Christianity Outside the Roman Empire: Two Lectures Delivered at Trinity College, Dublin.* Cambridge: University Press, 1899.

Cameron, Averil. "Jews and Heretics—A Category Error?" In *The Ways That Never Parted: Jews and Christians in Late Antiquity and the Early Middle Ages,* ed. Adam Becker and Annette Yoshiko Reed, 345–60. Tübingen: Mohr Siebeck, 2003.

Charlesworth, James H. *Critical Reflections on the Odes of Solomon.* Sheffield, England: Sheffield Academic Press, 1998.

———. *Odes of Solomon: The Syriac Text.* Missoula, Mont.: Scholars Press, 1977.

———. *The Old Testament Pseudepigrapha.* Garden City, N.Y.: Doubleday, 1983–85.

Clark, Elizabeth. *Reading Renunciation: Asceticism and Scripture in Early Christianity.* Princeton: Princeton University Press, 1999.

Clement of Alexandria. *Stromateis,* books 1–6. Edited by Otto Staehlin and Ludwig Freihtel. Berlin: Academie-Verlag, 1960.

Cohen, Jeremy. *"Be Fertile and Increase, Fill the Earth and Master It": The Ancient and Medieval Career of a Biblical Text.* Ithaca and London: Cornell University Press, 1989.

Cohen, Shaye J. D. "From the Bible to the Talmud: The Prohibition of Intermarriage." *Hebrew Union Annual Review* 7 (1983): 23–39.

Colson, F. H. *Philo.* Cambridge, Mass.: Harvard University Press, 1929.

Cross, F. L., and Elizabeth A. Livingstone. *The Oxford Dictionary of the Christian Church.* Oxford: Oxford University Press, 1983.

Dawson, J. David. *Allegorical Readers and Cultural Revision in Ancient Alexandria.* Berkeley: University of California Press, 1992.

Deming, Will. *Paul on Marriage and Celibacy: The Hellenistic Background of 1 Corinthians 7*. Cambridge: Cambridge University Press, 1995.

Deuteronomy Rabbah. Edited by Saul Lieberman. Jerusalem: Bamberger and Wahrman, 1940.

Diamond, Eliezer. "'And Jacob Remained Alone': The Jewish Struggle with Celibacy." In *Celibacy and Religious Tradition*, ed. Carol Olson, 41–64. New York: Oxford University Press, 2008.

———. *Holy Men and Hunger Artists: Fasting and Asceticism in Rabbinic Culture*. New York: Oxford University Press, 2004.

Dimant, Devorah. "4QFlorilegium and the Idea of the Community as a Temple." In *Hellenica et Judaica: Hommages à Valentin Nikiprovetzky [z"l]*, ed. Andre Caquot, Mireille Hadas-Lebel, and Jean Riaud, 165–89. Leuven: Peeters, 1986.

Drijvers, Han J. W. "The Acts of Thomas." In *New Testament Apocrypha*, vol. 2, ed. W. Schneemelcher, Eng. Trans. A. J. B. Higgins, 322–411. Philadelphia: Westminster Press, 1963–66.

Duncan, Edward Joseph. *Baptism in the Demonstrations of Aphraates, the Persian Sage*. Washington, D.C.: The Catholic University of America Press, 1945.

Eilberg-Schwartz, Howard. *God's Phallus and Other Problems for Men and Monotheism*. Boston: Beacon Press, 1994.

Eliade, Mircea. *The Sacred and the Profane: The Nature of Religion*. San Diego and New York: Harcourt, 1959.

Elm, Susanna. *Virgins of God: The Making of Asceticism in Late Antiquity*. Oxford: Oxford University Press, 1994.

Elman, Yaakov. "A Tale of Two Cities: Mahoza and Pumpeditta as Representative of Two Legal Cultures" [Hebrew]. In *Torah Lishmah: A Festschrift for Shamma Friedman*, ed. D. Golinkin, et al., 3–38. Ramat Gan: Bar Ilan University Press, 2007.

———. "'He in His Cloak and She in Her Cloak': Conflicting Images of Sexuality in Sasanian Mesopotamia." In *Discussing Cultural Influences: Text, Context and Non-Text in Rabbinic Judaism*, ed. Rivka Olmer, 129–63. New York: University Press of America, Inc., 2007.

———. "Middle Persian Culture and Babylonian Sages: Accommodation and Resistance in the Shaping of Rabbinic Legal Tradition." In *The Cambridge Companion to the Talmud*, ed. C. E. Fonrobert and M. S. Jaffee, 165–97. Cambridge: University of Cambridge Press, 2007.

Exodus Rabbah. Edited by Avigdor Shinan. Jerusalem: Devir, 1984.

Fishbane, Michael. *Biblical Interpretation in Ancient Israel*. Oxford: Clarendon Press, 1985.

Fraade, Steven D. "Ascetical Aspects of Ancient Judaism." In *Jewish Spirituality: From the Bible through the Middle Ages*, ed. Arthur Green, 253–88. New York: Crossroads, 1986–87.

Frankfurter, David. "Jews or Not? Reconstructing the 'Other' in Rev. 2:9 and 3:9." *Harvard Theological Review* 94, no. 4 (2001): 403–25.

Fredriksen, Paula. *Augustine and the Jews: A Christian Defense of Jews and Judaism*. New York: Doubleday, 2008.

Freedman, David Noel. *The Anchor Bible Dictionary*. New York: Doubleday, 1992.

Friedman, Richard Elliot. *Who Wrote the Bible?* San Francisco: HarperSanFrancisco, 1997.

Friedman, Shama. "Literary Development and Historicity in the Aggadic Narrative of the Babylonian Talmud: A Study Based Upon B.M. 83b-86a." In *Community and Culture: Essays in Jewish Studies in Honor of the Ninetieth Anniversary of the Founding of Gratz College, 1895–1985*, ed. Nahum Waldman, 67–80. Philadelphia: Gratz College; Seth Press, 1987.

———. "The Primacy of Tosefta to Mishnah in Synoptic Parallels." In *Introducing Tosefta: Textual, Intratextual and Intertextual Studies*, ed. H. Fox and T. Meacham, 99–121. Hoboken, N.J.: KTAV Publishers, 1999.

Fonrobert, Charlotte E. *Menstrual Purity: Rabbinic and Christian Reconstructions of Biblical Gender*. Stanford: Stanford University Press, 2000.

Funk, Salomon. *Die Haggadischen Elemente in den Homilien des Aphraates, des persischen Weisen*. Vienna: M. Knöpflmacher, 1891.

Gaca, Kathy. *The Making of Fornication: Eros, Ethics, and Political Reform in Greek Philosophy and Early Christianity*. Berkeley: University of California Press, 2003.

Gafni, Isaiah. "The Babylonian Academy according to Baba Kama 117a." [Hebrew] *Tarbiz* 49 (April-Sept. 1980): 292-301.

———. "The Institution of Marriage in Rabbinic Times." In *The Jewish Family: Metaphor and Memory*, ed. D. Kraemer, 13–30. New York and Oxford: Oxford University Press, 1989.

———. *The Jews of Babylonia in the Talmudic Era: A Social and Cultural History* [Hebrew]. Jerusalem: Zalman Shazar Center for Jewish History, 1990.

García Martínez, Florentino, and Eibert J. C. Tigchelaar. *The Dead Sea Scrolls: Study Edition*. Leiden: Brill, 1997–98.

Gavin, Frank. "Aphraates and the Jews." *Journal of the Society of Oriental Research* 7 (1923): 95-166.

Genesis Rabbah. Second edition. Edited by J. Theodor and Hanokh Albeck. Jerusalem: Shalem Books, 1996.

Gillihan, Y. M. "Jewish Laws of Illicit Marriage, the Defilement of Offspring and the Holiness of the Temple: A New Halakhic Interpretation of 1 Corinthians 7:14." *Journal of Biblical Literature* 121, no. 4 (2002): 711-30.

Ginzberg, Louis. "Aphraates, the Persian Sage." In *The Jewish Encyclopedia*, I: 663-65. New York: Funk and Wagnalls Company, 1901-6.

———. *Die Haggada bei den Kirchenvätern*. Amsterdam, 1899.

———. *Die Haggada bei den Kirchenvätern un in der Apokryphischen Litteratur*. Berlin: S. Calvary, 1900.

Goldin, Judah. *The Fathers According to Rabbi Nathan*. New Haven: Yale University Press, 1955.

Goodman, Martin. *Judaism in the Roman World: Collected Essays*. Leiden and Boston: Brill, 2007.

Green, Arthur, ed. *Jewish Spirituality: From the Bible through the Middle Ages*. New York: Crossroads, 1986.

Griffith, Sidney. "Asceticism in the Church of Syria: The Hermeneutics of Early Syrian Monasticism." In *Asceticism*, ed. Vincent L. Wimbush and Richard Valantasis, 220–45. New York: Oxford University Press, 1995.

Gwynn, John. "Aphrahat: Select Demonstrations." In *Nicene and Post Nicene Fathers*, second series, vol. 13, part 2, ed. P. Schaff and H. Wace. New York: Christian Literature. 1898.

Haenchen, Ernst. *The Acts of the Apostles: A Commentary*. Translation by B. Noble and G. Shinn. Philadelphia: Westminster Press, 1971.

Harrington, Hannah. *Holiness: Rabbinic Judaism and the Graeco-Roman World*. London and New York: Routledge, 2001.

Harvey, Susan Ashbrook. *Asceticism and Society in Crisis: John of Ephesus and the Lives of the Eastern Saints*. Berkeley: University of California Press, 1990.

Hayes, Christine Elizabeth. *Gentile Impurities and Jewish Identities: Intermarriage and Conversion from the Bible to the Talmud*. New York: Oxford University Press, 2002.

———. "Intermarriage and Impurity in Ancient Jewish Sources." *Harvard Theological Review* 92, no.1 (1999): 6–14.

Himmelfarb, Martha. *A Kingdom of Priests: Ancestry and Merit in Ancient Judaism*. Philadelphia: University of Pennsylvania Press, 2006.

Hirshman, Marc. *A Rivalry of Genius: Jewish and Christian Biblical Interpretation in Late Antiquity*. Translated by Batya Stein. Albany, N.Y.: State University of New York Press, 1996.

Hunt, Emily J. *Christianity in the Second Century: The Case of Tatian*. London and New York: Routledge, 2003.

Hyman, Aaron. *Toldoth Tannaim Ve'Amoraim*. Reprint, Jerusalem: Pri Ha'aretz, 1987.

Irenaeus. *Against Heresies*. Edited by A. Roberts and W. H. Rambaut. In *The Ante-Nicene Library*, vol. 2. Edinburgh: T. and T. Clark, 1869.

Jackson-McCabe, Matt, ed. *Jewish-Christianity Reconsidered: Rethinking Ancient Groups and Texts*. Minneapolis: Fortress Press, 2007.

Jacobs, Andrew. "A Family Affair: Marriage, Class and Ethics in the Apocryphal Acts of the Apostles." *Journal of Early Christian Studies* 7, no. 1 (1999): 105–38.

———. *Remains of the Jews: The Holy Land and Christian Empire in Late Antiquity*. Stanford: Stanford University Press, 2004.

Jaffee, Martin S. *Torah in the Mouth: Writing and Oral Tradition in Palestinian Judaism, 200 BCE-400 CE*. New York: Oxford University Press, 2001.

Jarkins, Stephanie Skoyles. *Aphrahat the Persian Sage and the Temple of God: A Study of Early Syriac Theological Anthropology*. Piscataway, N.J.: Gorgias Press, 2008.

Kalman, Richard. *Jewish Babylonia between Persia and Roman Palestine*. New York: Oxford University Press, 2006.

Kasher, Rimon. "The Aramaic Targumim and their Sitz im Leben." In *Proceedings of the Ninth World Congress of Jewish Studies: Panel Sessions on Bible Studies and Ancient Near East*, ed. Moshe H. Goshen-Gottstein and David Assaf, 75–78. Jerusalem: World Union of Jewish Scholars and Magnes Press, 1988.

Kessler, Gwynn. *Conceiving Israel: The Fetus in Rabbinic Narratives*. Philadelphia: University of Pennsylvania Press, 2009.

Klawans, Jonathan. *Impurity and Sin in Ancient Judaism*. New York: Oxford University Press, 2000.

Klijn, Albertus Frederik Johannes. *The Acts of Thomas: Introduction, Text, and Commentary*. Leiden: Brill, 1962.

Knust, Jennifer. *Abandoned to Lust: Sexual Slander and Ancient Christianity*. New York: Columbia University Press, 2006.

Koltun-Fromm, Naomi. "Aphrahat on Noah's Righteousness in Light of the Jewish-Christian Polemic." In *The Book of Genesis in Jewish and Oriental Christian Interpretation*, ed. Judith Frishman and Lucas Van Rompay, 57–71. Lovain: Peeters, 1997.

———. "A Jewish-Christian Conversation in Fourth-Century Persian Mesopotamia." *Journal of Jewish Studies* 47, no.1 (1996): 45–64.

———. *Jewish-Christian Polemics in Fourth-Century Persian Mesopotamia: A Reconstructed Conversation*. Ph.D. dissertation, Stanford University, 1993.

———. "Psalm 22's Christological Interpretive Tradition in Light of Christian Anti-Jewish Polemic." *Journal of Early Christian Studies* 6, no.1 (1998): 37–57.

———. "Re-Imagining Tatian: The Damaging Effects of Polemical Rhetoric." *Journal of Early Christian Studies* 16, no. 1 (2008): 1–30.

———. "Sexuality and Holiness: Semitic Christian and Jewish Conceptualizations of Sexual Behavior." *Vigiliae Christianae* 54 (2000): 375–95.

———. "Yokes of the Holy-Ones: The Embodiment of a Christian Vocation." *Harvard Theological Review* 94, no. 2 (2001): 205–18.

———. "Zipporah's Complaint: Moses is not Conscientious in the Deed! Exegetical Traditions of Moses' Celibacy." In *The Ways That Never Parted: Jews and Christians in Late Antiquity and the Early Middle Ages*, ed. A. Becker and A. Yoshiko Reed, 283–306. Tübingen: Mohr Siebeck, 2003.

Kornfeld. W. "קדשׁ." *The Theological Dictionary of the Old Testament*, 12: 521–45. Grand Rapids, Mich.: Eerdmans, 2003.

Knohl, Israel. *The Sanctuary of Silence: The Priestly Torah and the Holiness School*. Minneapolis: Fortress Press, 1995.

Krauss, S. "The Jews in the Works of the Church Fathers." *Jewish Quarterly Review* 5 (1893): 122–57; 6 (1894): 82–99; and 225–61.

Kugel, James. "The Holiness of Israel and the Land in Second Temple Times." In *Texts, Temples, and Traditions: A Tribute to Menahem Haran*, ed. Michael V. Fox, et al., 21–32. Winona Lake, Ind.: Eisenbraun, 1996.

Kugler, Robert A. "Holiness, Purity, the Body and Society: The Evidence for Theological Conflict in Leviticus." *Journal for the Study of the Old Testament* 76 (1997): 3–27.

———. "Priesthood at Qumran." In *Dead Sea Scrolls after Fifty Years*, ed. Peter Flint and James C. VanderKam, 93–116. Leiden: Brill, 1999.

Lehto, Adam. *Divine Law: Asceticism and Gender in Aphrahat's "Demonstrations."* Ph.D. dissertation, University of Toronto, 2003.

———. "Women in Aphrahat: Some Observations." *Hugoye* 4, no. 1 (July) 2001.

Leviticus Rabbah. Edited by Mordechai Margaliot. New York and Jerusalem: The Jewish Theological Seminary of America, 1953–60.

Licht, J. "QDS." In *Encyclopedia Mikrait* 7: 48–49. Jerusalem: Mosad Bialik, 1950.

Lieberman, Saul. *Tosefta Ki-fshuta: A Comprehensive Commentary on the Tosefta*. New York: Jewish Theological Seminary of America, 1955–88.

MacDonald, Dennis R. *The Legend and the Apostle: The Battle for Paul in Story and Canon*. Philadelphia: Westminster, 1983.

Mack, Burton L. "Imitatio Mosis: Patterns of Cosmology and Soteriology in the Hellenistic Synagogue," *Studia Philonica* 1 (1972): 27–55.

Mansfeld, Jaap. "Philosophy in the Service of Scripture: Philo's Exegetical Strategies." In *The Question of "Eclecticism": Studies in Later Greek Philosophy*, ed. John M. Dillon and A. A. Long, 70–107. Berkeley: University of California, 1988.

Martin, Dale. *The Corinthian Body*. New Haven and London: Yale University Press, 1995.

McNamara, Martin. *Targum Neofiti 1: Genesis*. Collegeville, Minn.: Liturgical Press, 1992.

Mekhilta of Rabbi Yishmael. Edited by Haim Horovitz and I. A. Rabin. Reprint. Jerusalem: Wahrmann, 1970.

Mekhilta of Rabbi Shimon bar Yohai. Edited by J. N. Epstein and E. Z. Melamed. Jerusalem: Sumptibus Hillel Press, 1979.

Midrash Rabbah. Edited by M. A. Mirkin. Tel Aviv: Yavneh Publishing House, 1992.

Midrash Rabbah. Edited by H. Freedman and M. Simon. London and New York: Soncino Press, 1983

Midrash Tanhuma. Edited by Solomon Buber. Reprint. Jerusalem: Ortsel, 1964.

Milgrom, Jacob. *The Anchor Bible: Leviticus*. New York: Doubleday, 1991–2001.

———. "The Concept of Impurity in Jubilees and the Temple Scroll." *Revue de Qumran* 16, no. 2 (1993): 277–84.

———. "Studies in the Temple Scroll." *Journal of Bible Literature* 97, no. 4 (1978): 501–23.

Mishnah. Edited by Hanoch Albeck. Tel Aviv: Devir, 1952.

Murray, Robert. "The Exhortation to Candidates for Ascetical Vows at Baptism in the Ancient Syriac Church." *New Testament Studies* 21 (1974–75): 58–79.

———. *Symbols of Church and Kingdom: A Study in Early Syriac Tradition*. London and New York: Cambridge University Press, 1975.

Nendugatt, George. "Covenanters of the Early Syriac Speaking Church." *Orientalia Christiana Periodica* 39 (1973): 191–215; 419–44.

Nestle, Eberhard, Erwin Nestle, Kurt Aland, et al. *Novum Testamentum Graece*. Stuttgart: Deutsche Bibelgesellschaft, 1979.

Neusner, Jacob. *Aphrahat and Judaism: The Christian-Jewish Argument in Fourth-Century Iran*. Leiden: Brill, 1971.

———. *The Talmud of the Land of Israel: Yebamot*. Chicago and London: University of Chicago Press, 1987.

Numbers Rabbah. Edited by M. A. Mirkin. Tel Aviv: Yavneh, 1964–65.

Oppenheimer, Aharon, Benjamin H. Isaac, and Michael Lecker. *Babylonia Judaica in the Talmudic Period*. Wiesbaden: L. Reicher, 1983.

Origen. *Homiles on Genesis and Exodus*. Translated by Ronald E. Heine. Washington, D.C.: Catholic University Press, 1982.

Oritz de Urbina, Ignacio. *Die Gottheit Christi bei Afrahat*. Roma, Pont: Institutum Orientalium Studiorum, 1933.

———. "La contraversia di Afraate coi Guidei." *Studia Missionalia* 3 (1947): 85–106.

Otto, Rudolph. *The Idea of the Holy: An Inquiry into the non-Rational Factor in the Idea of the Divine and Its Relation to the Rational*. Translated by John W. Harvey. London and New York: H. Milford and Oxford University Press, 1923.

Owens, Robert J. *The Genesis and Exodus Citations of Aphrahat the Persian Sage*. Leiden: Brill, 1983.

Oxtoby, Williard G. "The Idea of the Holy." In *Encyclopedia of Religion*, vol. 6, ed. M. Eliade, 434–36. New York: Macmillan, 1987.

Pagels, Elaine. *The Gnostic Gospels*. New York: Vintage Books, 1979.

Parisot, John. "Aphraatis Sapientis Persae Demonstrationes." In *Patrologia Syriaca*, part 1, vols. 1–2, ed. R. Graffin. Paris: Firmin-Didot, 1894 and 1907.

Petersen, William Lawrence. *Tatian's Diatessaron: Its Creation, Dissemination, Significance, and History in Scholarship*. Leiden: Brill, 1994.

Pierre, Marie-Joseph. *Aphraates, "Les Exposés."* 2 vols. Paris: Editions du Cerf, 1988, 1989.

Pinsent, John. "Ascetic Moods in Greek and Latin Literature." In *Asceticism*, ed. Vincent L. Wimbush and Richard Valantasis, 211–19. New York: Oxford University Press, 1995.

Poirier, P. H. "The Writings Ascribed to Thomas and the Thomas Tradition." In *The Nag Hammadi Library after 50 Years: Proceedings of the 1995 Society of Biblical Literature*, ed. Anne McGuire and John D. Turner, 295–307. Leiden: Brill, 1997.

Poorthuis, Marcel, and Joshua Schwartz, eds. *Purity and Holiness: The Heritage of Leviticus*. Leiden: Brill, 2000.

Qimron, Elisha, and John Strugnell. *Discoveries in the Judean Desert X: Qumran Cave 4 V: Miqsat Ma'ase ha-Torah*. Oxford: Clarendon Press, 1994.

Rouselle, Aline. *Porneia: On Desire and the Body in Antiquity*. Oxford and New York: Basil Blackwell, 1988.

Rubenstein, Jeffrey L. *The Culture of the Babylonian Talmud*. Baltimore: John Hopkins University Press, 2003.

Safrai, Shmuel, ed. *The Literature of the Sages*. Philadelphia: Fortress Press, 1987.

———. "The Meaning of the Term: *Derekh Erets*." *Tarbiz* 60 (1991): 147–62 [Hebrew].

Sandmel, Samuel. "Parallelomania." *Journal of Biblical Literature* 81 (1962): 1–13.

Satlow, Michael. *Jewish Marriage in Antiquity*. Princeton, N.J.: Princeton University Press, 2001.

———. *Tasting the Dish: Rabbinic Rhetorics of Sexuality*. Atlanta: Scholars Press, 1995.

Schofer, Jonathan. *The Making of a Sage: A Study in Rabbinic Ethics*. Madison, Wisc.: University of Wisconsin Press, 2005.

Schwartz, Baruch J. *The Holiness Legislation: Studies in the Priestly Code*. Jerusalem: Magnes Press, 1999 [Hebrew].

———. "Israel's Holiness: The Torah Traditions." In *Purity and Holiness: The Heritage of Leviticus*, ed. Marcel Poorthuis and Joshua Schwartz, 47–59. Leiden: Brill, 2000.

Schwen, Paul. *Afrahat, Seine Person und seine Verständniss des Christentums*. Berlin: Trowitzsch und Sohn, 1907.

Segal, J. B. "The Jews of North Mesopotamia before the Rise of Islam." In *Studies in the Bible presented to M.H. Segal*, ed. J. M. Grintz and J. Liver, 32–63. Jerusalem: Kiryat Sefer, 1964.

Shepardson, Christine. *Anti-Judaism and Christian Orthodoxy: Ephrem's Hymns in Fourth-Century Syria*. Washington, D.C.: Catholic University of America Press, 2008.

———. "Defining the Boundaries of Orthodoxy: Eunomious in the Anti-Jewish Polemic of his Cappadocian Opponents." *Church History* 76, no. 4 (December 2007): 699–723.

Shiffman, Lawrence. *From Text to Tradition: A History of the Second Temple and Rabbinic Judaism*. Hoboken, N.J.: Ktav Publishing, 1991.

Shuler, Philip. "Philo's Moses and Matthew's Jesus: A Comparative Study in Ancient Literature." *Studia Philonica Annual* 2 (1990): 86–103.

Sifre Numbers. Edited by Haim Horovitz. Reprint. Jerusalem: Shalem Books, 1992.

Singer, Isodore, ed. *Jewish Encyclopedia*. New York: Funk and Wagnalls, 1901.

Smith, Jonathan Z. *Drudgery Divine: On the Comparison of Early Christianities and the Religions of Late Antiquity*. Chicago: University of Chicago Press, 1990.

Smith, Morton. *Tannaitic Parallels to the Gospels*. Philadelphia: Society of Biblical Literature, 1951.

Snaith, J. G. "Aphrahat and the Jews." In *Interpreting the Hebrew Bible: Essays in Honour of E. I. J. Rosenthal*, ed. John Adney Emerton, 235–50. Cambridge: Cambridge University Press, 1982.

Strack, H. L., and G. Stemberger. *Introduction to the Talmud and Midrash*. Edinburgh: T&T Clark, 1991.

Sussman, Jacob. "Returning again to Yerushalmi Nezikin." In *Mehqere Talmud* 1 [Talmudic Research 1], ed. J. Sussman and D. Rosenthal, 55–134. Jerusalem: Magnes Press, 1990 [Hebrew].

Tatian. *Oration to the Greeks and Fragments*. Edited and translated by Molly Whittaker. Oxford: Claredon Press, 1982.

Tertullian. *De exhortatione castitatis*. Corpus Christianorum Latina, vol 2. Turnholti: Typographi Brepols Editores Pontifici, 1953.

Tertullian. *Treatises on Marriage and Remarriage: To his wife, An Exhortation to Chastity, Monogamy*. Translated by William P. Le Saint. Westminster, Md.: Newman Press, 1951.

Tissot, Yves. "Les acts apocryphes de Thomas, example de receuil composite." In *Les Actes apocryphes des apotres, Christianisme de monde païen*, ed. François Bovon, et al., 223–32. Geneva: Labor et Fides, 1981.

———. "L'encratisme des Acts de Thomas." *Aufseig und Niedergang der römischen Welt* II.25.6 (1988): 4415–30.

Trible, Phyllis. *God and the Rhetoric of Sexuality*. Philadelphia: Fortress Press, 1978.

VanderKam, James C. *The Book of Jubilees*. Louvain: Peeters, 1989.

———. "Origins and Purposes of the Book of Jubilees." In *Studies in the Book of Jubilees*, ed. M. Albani, Jorge Frey, and Armkin Lange, 3–24. Tübingen: Mohr Siebeck, 1997.

Van Rompay, Lucas. "Antiochene Biblical Interpretation: Greek and Syriac." In *The Book of Genesis in Jewish and Oriental Christian Interpretation*, ed. Judith Frishman and Lucas Van Rompay, 103–23. Louvain: Peeters, 1997.

———. "The Christian Syriac Tradition of Interpretation." In *Hebrew Bible/Old Testament: The History of Interpretation*, vol. 1, pt. 1, ed. Magne Saebo, 612–41. Göttingen: Vandenhoeck and Ruprecht, 1996.

Vasiliev, Alexander Alexandrovich. *Kitab al-'Unvan, Histoire Universelle*. Paris: Firmin-Didot, 1910.

Visotsky, Burton. "Midrash, Christian Exegesis, and Hellenistic Hermeneutic." In *Current Trends in the Study of Midrash*, ed. Carol Bakhos, 111–32. Leiden: Brill, 2006.

———. "Mortal Sins." *Union Theological Quarterly Review* 44 (1990): 31–53.

———. "Three Syriac Cruxes." *Journal of Jewish Studies* 42, no. 4 (1991): 167–75.

Vööbus, Arthur. *Celibacy, A Requirement for Admission to Baptism in the Early Syrian Church*. Stockholm: Estonian Theological Society in Exile, 1951.

———. *History of Asceticism in the Syrian Orient: A Contribution to the History of Culture in the Near East*. Louvain: Secrétariat du CSCO, 1958–88.

Weitzman, Michael P. *The Syriac Version of the Old Testament: An Introduction*. Cambridge: Cambridge University Press, 1999.

Werman, Cana. "Jubilees 30: Building a Paradigm for the Ban on Intermarriage." *Harvard Theological Review* 90 (1997): 1–22.

Williamson, H. G. M. *Ezra and Nehemiah*. Sheffield, England: Sheffield Academic Press, 1987.

Wimbush, Vincent L., and Richard Valantasis, eds. *Asceticism*. New York and Oxford: Oxford University Press, 1995.

Wright, David P. "Holiness." In *Anchor Bible Dictionary*, vol. 3, ed. David Noel Freedman, 237. New York: Doubleday, 1992.

Wright, William. *The Homilies of Aphraates: The Persian Sage*. London: Williams and Norgate, 1869.

Yarbrough, Larry O. *Not Like the Gentiles: Marriage Rules in the Letters of Paul*. Atlanta: Scholars Press, 1985.

Young, C. D. *The Works of Philo*. Peabody, Mass.: Hendrickson Publishers, 1993.

Index of Citations

General Index